Peer rejection in childhood

Peer rejection in childhood

Edited by

STEVEN R. ASHER
University of Illinois, Urbana–Champaign

JOHN D. COIE
Duke University

CAMBRIDGE
UNIVERSITY PRESS

Published by the Press Syndicate of the University of Cambridge
The Pitt Building, Trumpington Street, Cambridge CB2 1RP
40 West 20th Street, New York, NY 10011-4211, USA
10 Stamford Road, Oakleigh, Melbourne 3166, Australia

© Cambridge University Press 1990

First published 1990
Reprinted 1992, 1995

Printed in the United States of America

Library of Congress Cataloging-in-Publication Data is available.

A catalogue record for this book is available from the British Library.

ISBN 0-521-39183-0 hardback
ISBN 0-521-39836-3 paperback

To our families
Gladys, Matt, and David
Lynne, David, and Susanne

Contents

Preface

The contributors to this volume are part of a growing community of scholars interested in understanding the dynamics of peer rejection in childhood. Research on children who have peer relationship problems has a long history; landmark studies have appeared in each decade since the 1930s. However, it is only since the mid-1970s that programmatic research on this topic has emerged. This is an exciting time to be doing research on children's peer relations, with investigators making long-term commitments to understanding why certain children come to be poorly accepted by their peers, what the consequences are of peer rejection, and how rejected children can be helped. The field is characterized by diversity and richness of perspective. There is also a shared view that the study of peer rejection is a productive context for exploring fundamental behavioral, social-cognitive, and affective processes, and that achieving deeper understandings will provide the basis for helping children at risk.

This book is designed to integrate existing knowledge, to communicate the kinds of substantive and methodological advances being made, and to offer models and theoretical perspectives that could serve as springboards for further inquiry in the decade that lies ahead. We hope our book will prove useful to experienced and beginning researchers, and to educators, clinicians, and other professionals who see at first hand both the positive significance of friendship in children's lives and the costs of peer rejection.

Work on this book began with a two-day conference at Duke University. The conference provided an opportunity to report findings and exchange ideas. After the meeting, participants circulated preliminary drafts of chapters to one another. The conference and the distribution of chapter drafts alike were designed to ensure that each chapter would be maximally informed by the work of others and that a cohesive and integrated volume would result.

We wish to thank the contributors for participating in the conference, for their careful reading of one another's work, and most of all for their outstanding contributions. We also want to thank the Department of Psychology at Duke University for hosting the conference and the Bureau of Educational Research at the University of Illinois, Urbana-Champaign, for its invaluable support throughout the process of manuscript preparation. We are also indebted to Phil Costanzo, Jeff Parker, and several contributors to this volume for making helpful comments and suggestions on our own chapters. Carma Diel and Marge Williams provided secretarial and technical assistance throughout, and Cynthia Erdley prepared the indexes. We are most appreciative of their excellent work. Preparation of this volume was supported in part by research grants from the National Institute of Child Health and Human Development and the National Institute of Mental Health.

STEVEN R. ASHER

JOHN D. COIE

December 1989

Contributors

Steven R. Asher
Bureau of Educational Research
University of Illinois at Urbana–
Champaign

Lynda J. Butler
Kitchener–Waterloo Hospital
Kitchener, Ontario

John D. Coie
Department of Psychology
Duke University

Kenneth A. Dodge
Department of Psychology and
Human Development
Vanderbilt University

Esther Feldman
Department of Neurology
University of Miami

Craig H. Hart
Department of Family, Child, and
Consumer Sciences
Louisiana State University

Anne Hope Heflin
Department of Psychology
University of North Carolina at
Chapel Hill

Shelley Hymel
Department of Psychology
University of Waterloo

Gina Krehbiel Koeppl
Psychological Associates
Rhinelander, WI

Janis B. Kupersmidt
Department of Psychology
University of North Carolina at
Chapel Hill

Gary W. Ladd
Department of Educational
Psychology
University of Illinois at Urbana–
Champaign

Lucy J. LeMare
Department of Psychology
University of Waterloo

Susan Lollis
Department of Family Studies
University of Guelph

Jacquelyn Mize
Department of Family and Child
Development
Auburn University

Jennifer T. Parkhurst
Department of Educational
Psychology
University of Nebraska

Joseph M. Price
Department of Psychology
San Diego State University

Martha Putallaz
Department of Psychology
Duke University

Kenneth H. Rubin
Department of Psychology
University of Waterloo

Esther Wagner
North York General Hospital
Willowdale, Ontario

Aviva Wasserman
Department of Psychology
University of North Carolina at
Chapel Hill

Gladys A. Williams
Department of Psychology
University of Illinois at Urbana–
Champaign

Introduction

1 Recent advances in the study of peer rejection

Steven R. Asher

This volume is focused on children who are having difficulty gaining acceptance and friendship among their peers. A substantial amount of research has been devoted to this topic during the past decade, and considerable progress is being made in understanding the phenomenon of peer rejection. Researchers are beginning to understand how certain children come to be disliked by their peers, the factors that maintain their rejection, the consequences of poor peer relations, and the results of intervention with various subgroups of rejected children. It is our hope that this volume will serve its readers by synthesizing and evaluating current knowledge and by providing models that organize the literature and point to avenues for future inquiry.

The contributors to this volume are developmental and clinical psychologists, most of whom have been doing research on peer rejection for over a decade. They share a view that progress in this area will be made by giving careful attention to the psychological processes that create and maintain peer rejection in childhood. A corollary assumption is that intervention efforts will be most effective when directed toward processes previously found to be associated with the origin and maintenance of status in the peer group.

Importance of peer relationships

Children's social contacts extend beyond the family to include a world of peers. Peer relationships are of significance even to the young child (Gottman & Parkhurst, 1980; Howes, 1988), and they assume increasing importance as children grow older (Ellis, Rogoff, & Cromer, 1981). Contacts with peers, especially with friends, serve many significant functions in children's lives and development (see Asher & Parker, 1989; Furman & Robbins, 1985; Hartup & Sancilio, 1986). Friends are important sources of companionship and recreation, share advice and valued possessions, serve as trusted confidants and critics, act as loyal allies, and provide stability in times of stress or transition.

Peer relationships may play an even more important role today than they did in earlier times. The increasing number of working mothers and single-parent fami-

3

lies has resulted in earlier entry of young children into organized peer group settings such as day-care homes, nursery schools, or day-care centers. Furthermore, children stay in school for more years than they did in earlier times. In addition, children today participate frequently in various afterschool and summer peer group activities (e.g., clubs, sports, church groups, and camps). These experiences guarantee that children will spend considerable time with similar-age peers throughout childhood and adolescence. Although most children have opportunities to participate in the rewarding world that comes with good peer relationships, there are others whose relationships with peers are much less satisfying. For these children, peer relations can be stresful and a source of anguish for themselves, their families, and their teachers. Indeed, the degree of peer contact children experience today only accentuates the plight of children who lack acceptance and friendship.

Reasons for studying rejected children

What is it that attracts researchers to the study of children who have serious peer relationship problems? Partly it is the opportunity to learn about the development of social competence by focusing on a group of children who are failing in their peer relationships. By comparing rejected children with children who are better accepted, not only do we learn how inappropriate behavior (e.g., aggression and disruptiveness) can lead to peer relationship difficulties, we also learn what kinds of positive skills children need to acquire in order to initiate and maintain relationships with peers. The social world is a complex and demanding place that requires children to coordinate potentially competing goals (Dodge, Asher, & Parkhurst, 1989; Taylor & Asher, 1984), process complex social information (Dodge, 1986), and respond effectively to diverse situations (Asher & Renshaw, 1981; Ladd & Oden, 1979). Consider for a moment the tasks a child might face while at recess on the playground. These include entering a group (Corsaro, 1981; Putallaz & Gottman, 1981), maintaining conversation and coordinated play (Gottman & Parker, 1986), dealing with teasing and other forms of ambiguous provocation (Dodge, 1986), and resolving overt interpersonal conflicts (Shantz, 1987). By studying how accepted and rejected children respond to tasks such as these, researchers can learn about adaptive and maladaptive ways of coping with the social world.

Researchers are also attracted to the study of peer-rejected children because these children are at risk and need help. Several studies published in the 1960s and 1970s suggested that unpopular children were at risk for later life problems (Cowen, Pederson, Babigian, Izzo, & Trost, 1973; Roff, 1961; Roff, Sells, & Golden, 1972). These papers caught the attention of developmental and clinical psychologists and fueled much of the interest in the topic of peer rejection. Evidence that unpopular children may be at risk has motivated researchers to help children improve their peer relationships in order to prevent later mental health problems and other negative outcomes.

As noted earlier, researchers in this area assume that achieving a better understanding of the development of social competence will provide the foundation for developing effective intervention programs. Indeed, within the past decade a distinctive social skills training paradigm has emerged (see Asher, 1985) in which unpopular children are selected for intervention and are taught skills that have been found in previous research to differentiate popular and unpopular children. The goal of these intervention efforts is not to facilitate high levels of popularity (i.e., to make children social "stars") but to ensure that children will have the sorts of competencies needed to achieve and enjoy group acceptance and close personal friendships. Additionally, these intervention studies are designed to further theory development by providing experimental tests of hypothesized connections between specific psychological processes and peer relationship outcomes.

How extensive are peer relationship problems?

The number of children found to have serious peer relationship problems varies with the particular assessment procedure. For example, when elementary school children are asked to nominate their three best friends in their class, about 10% of the children are not named by anyone (e.g., Hymel & Asher, 1977). If the criterion of reciprocal sociometric nominations is used (Bukowski & Hoza, 1989), the percentage is even higher. In addition, the percentage of children having peer relationship problems may be higher in some subgroups of children than others. For example, children who are mildly retarded (Gottlieb & Leyser, 1981; Guralnick & Groom, 1987; Taylor, Asher, & Williams, 1987), hyperactive (Henker & Whalen, 1989; Milich & Landau, 1982; Pelham & Bender, 1982; Whalen, in press), or in other ways learning handicapped (Bryan, 1976; Gresham, 1988; Siperstein, Bopp, & Bak, 1978) are especially likely to experience serious social relationship difficulties. Nonetheless, even among populations of average or high-achieving students there are many children who lack friends.

Types of unpopularity

It has long been recognized that there are different types of unpopular children (Gronlund, 1959; Northway, 1944), but it is only in recent years that systematic attention has been given to this issue. Two subtypes, in particular, are being intensively studied. Children in the group referred to as rejected are overtly disliked by their peers. Children in the other group, referred to as neglected, are reasonably well liked even though they lack friends in their class. For example, when children are asked to rate how much they like to play with each of their classmates, the ratings neglected children receive do not differ from those received by average children, whereas rejected children receive extremely low ratings (Asher & Wheeler, 1985; French & Waas, 1985).

Several recent lines of research indicate the importance of distinguishing between sociometrically rejected and neglected peer status. First, there is evidence that rejected status is more stable than neglected status over time or situations (e.g., Coie & Dodge, 1983; Coie & Kupersmidt, 1983; Newcomb & Bukowski, 1984). For example, data from Coie and Dodge (1983) indicate that approximately 30% to 50% of rejected children remain rejected over a 5-year period. Even when rejected children do move into another status group, it is rare for them to become extremely well accepted.

The data on stability suggest that many rejected children have enduring personal characteristics that lead to difficulties in their peer relations. Indeed, rejected children are found to differ from neglected children in their patterns of behavior and thought. During the last decade there has been an explosion of research on the behavioral and social-cognitive correlates of status in the peer group. Stimulated by studies by Hartup, Glazer, and Charlesworth (1967) and by Gottman and his colleagues (Gottman, 1977; Gottman, Gonso, & Rasmussen, 1975), scholars have used a variety of methods to assess how children think about various social situations and what they do in those situations. As several chapters in this volume demonstrate, it is rejected children, rather than neglected children, who exhibit seriously maladaptive modes of thought and action.

Finally, information about children's emotional experiences in school reinforces the distinction between neglected and rejected status. Rejected children are more likely than neglected children to report loneliness (Asher & Wheeler, 1985) and feelings of depression (Vosk, Forehand, Parker, & Rickard, 1982). Rejected children are also more likely to directly express an interest in getting help with social relationship problems. Asher (1988) recently asked third-through sixth-grade children whether they would like help in learning how to get along better with other children. Of the rejected children, 48% responded affirmatively, whereas only 16% of the neglected children did so.

Identifying rejected children

Sociometric measures offer researchers reliable methods for identifying rejected children (see Asher & Hymel, 1981; Hymel & Rubin, 1985, for reviews). One widely used technique involves collecting positive and negative sociometric nominations. Here, children are asked, for example, to indicate the names of their three most liked and three least liked classmates, or to name their three best friends and three children they would not want to have as friends. These types of nominations can be elicited by having children circle the names on a class or grade-level roster. With preschool and early elementary school children, photographs are typically employed and individual interviews are conducted.

Within the past decade, several types of classification systems have emerged using positive and negative nomination measures (Coie, Dodge, & Coppotelli, 1982; Newcomb & Bukowski, 1983; Peery, 1979). The specific way that nomination scores are transformed and combined to classify children into status groups varies among the systems. However, these systems have in common the central notion that rejected children are those who receive very few positive nominations and many negative nominations.

A somewhat different approach to sociometric identification involves using a rating-scale measure in which children rate each of their classmates on a Likert scale in terms of how much they like to play with, work with, or be in activities with each of their classmates. Here, children are given a roster of their classmates or grade-level peers and are asked to indicate by a rating how much they like each classmate. Typically a 1–5 scale is used for elementary school children (see Putallaz, 1987; Singleton & Asher, 1977) and a 1–3 scale is used for preschoolers (Asher, Singleton, Tinsley, & Hymel, 1979). Often, too, cartoon illustrations of frowning to smiling faces are used to help communicate the meaning of points on the scale. Again, photographs and individual interviews are commonly employed with young children. Using this type of measure, children can be defined as unpopular or rejected if the average rating they receive from peers is substantially below the class average.

There is incomplete overlap between the children who are identified as rejected using positive and negative nomination data and the children who receive low average ratings on the rating-scale measure (Hymel & Asher, 1977). However, recent research suggests the way in which positive nomination and rating-scale data can be productively combined to identify children who would be classified as rejected using positive and negative nomination data. Asher and Dodge (1986) found that using the number of "1" ratings children receive on the rating-scale measure serves as a useful substitute for negative nomination data.

The choice of which sociometric methods to use to identify rejected children depends in part on pragmatic considerations. For example, it is not always possible to use negative nomination measures in school settings. They sometimes elicit concern from parents or teachers, even though available data suggest that children are not adversely affected by the measure (Bell-Dolan, Foster, & Sikora, 1989; Hayvren & Hymel, 1984; Rattiner, Weissberg, & Caplan, 1986).

Overview of this volume

This volume is composed of five parts. The first part is concerned with the behavioral characteristics that are associated with acceptance versus rejection by the peer group. In Chapter 2 Coie, Dodge, and Kupersmidt discuss the behavioral correlates of sociometric status among preschool, elementary school, and secondary school students. One major conclusion is that aggression and disruptiveness are major causes of peer rejection throughout childhood and adolescence. The chapter also highlights the insights to be gained from a methodology in which previously unfamiliar peers are brought together in new play groups. This innovative and ambitious methodology makes it possible to learn the extent to which rejected children's social behavior in the peer group is indeed the cause of their low status rather than simply being the consequence. Previously, researchers have studied children in intact groups of familiar peers, making it impossible to determine whether the maladaptive behavior displayed by rejected children was the cause or the consequence of low status in the peer group. By placing children in entirely new groups it becomes possible to study the emergence of status and to learn whether children who are rejected in their everyday school contexts become rejected once again when faced with the opportunity to interact with an entirely new group of peers.

In Chapter 3 Putallaz and Wasserman focus on behavioral processes in the context of children's attempts to enter into ongoing interaction. Research on children's entry behavior highlights the role of positive interactional skills in peer acceptance, especially children's ability to take the frame of reference of those they seek to join. This research also demonstrates the value of using analogue settings in studying social interaction. Analogue settings are useful for amplifying particular events of interest and for facilitating videotaping, which, in turn, allows for detailed coding of behavior, including attention to sequences of interaction. As a result of methodological innovations such as this, observations are becoming more detailed, textured, and informative.

Historically, most observational research in schools has been conducted in the classroom. Yet the classroom may not always be the ideal location for studying group dynamics among children. Given the highly structured and task-oriented character of classroom life, much of the action in the peer group occurs elsewhere. One of the innovations reflected in this volume is the willingness to observe children's behavior in various nonclassroom contexts. In Chapter 4 Ladd, Price, and Hart show the benefits of focusing on the playground setting and also show the benefits of studying children longitudinally within the school year. Their research indicates that popular and unpopular children differ not only in the content of their social behavior but in how they distribute their interaction among different group members across the school year.

The second part of the volume considers the problem of peer rejection in terms of the social-cognitive processes that contribute to children's social behavior and their acceptance or rejection by peers. In Chapter 5 Dodge and Feldman organize a diverse literature on social-cognitive functioning and describe a study that focuses on gender and age differences in the relationship of social cognition to peer status. The authors use an information-processing framework to examine how children's interpretation of social events, ability to generate and execute strategies, and ability to evaluate social outcomes relate to children's behavior and acceptance by peers. The research Dodge and Feldman review indicates that social-cognitive functioning in specific contexts (e.g., entry and ambiguous provocation) is predictive of behavior in these contexts. This level of prediction between social cognition and social behavior contrasts with the results of earlier research in which constructs such as egocentricity were assessed without reference to specific social tasks. Dodge and Feldman's theme of situational specificity is an extremely important one. Most of the time, rejected children behave adaptively and constructively. It is in certain key situations that their behavior becomes incompetent and often aversive.

In Chapter 6 Hymel, Wagner, and Butler consider the link between social cognition and sociometric status from the viewpoint of the peer group rather than from the point of view of the rejected child. The authors make an important contribution by reviewing research, including their own studies with children, on ways in which interpersonal attraction influences judgments about others' behavior. The authors point out that biased information processing about a rejected child's behavior could make it difficult for that child to gain acceptance even when behavior change actually occurs. This perspective serves to balance the field's typical emphasis on the role of a child's own skill deficits in maintaining his or her peer rejection. The chapter also offers an innovative paradigm for studying information-processing biases in children.

The third part of this volume contains two chapters that review research on parental contributions to the development of children's social competence and that propose future research directions. When research on peer-rejected children began to accelerate in the 1970s, the peer system was studied independently of family influences. This emphasis was highly productive and led to many of the advances detailed in this volume. At the same time, little attention was given to the familial origins of peer rejection. The picture differs today as investigators have begun to consider how early parent–child relationships influence the development of children's social competence and children's adjustment in the peer domain.

In Chapter 7 Putallaz and Heflin consider research from various lines of inquiry, including literature on interpersonal characteristics of parents, parenting styles, parental disciplinary practices, and infant–parent attachment. Putallaz's groundbreaking research is also highlighted. There are clear and provocative links between the ways in which parents interact with their children and how the offspring, in turn, interact with their peers.

Chapter 8, by Rubin, LeMare, and Lollis, speculates about two possible pathways leading to peer rejection. The authors consider how various home background factors, the child's temperament, and the child's attachment history can lead to externalizing or internalizing modes of maladaptive functioning in the peer group. The former is characterized by high levels of aggressive and disruptive activity, whereas the latter is characterized by apprehension, insecurity, and withdrawal. Indeed, one of the contributions of this chapter is its attention to subgroups of rejected children, including the possibility of a withdrawn–rejected subgroup. Rubin, LeMare, and Lollis suggest that there has been a tendency in previous literature to equate sociometric neglect with behavioral withdrawal and in the process to ignore the real possibility that a behaviorally withdrawn pattern can, in fact, lead to rejection by peers.

The fourth part of the volume is focused on concurrent and long-term consequences of poor peer relationships in childhood. In Chapter 9 Asher, Parkhurst, Hymel, and Williams focus attention on the emotional reactions that accompany peer rejection, particularly children's feelings of loneliness and social dissatisfaction. Using a recently developed self-report methodology, the authors examine how rejected children feel about their social lives in school. The authors summarize evidence concerning differences in loneliness between submissive–rejected and aggressive–rejected children, evidence that reinforces Rubin, LeMare, and Lollis's call for attention to internalizing and externalizing subgroups of rejected children.

The consequences of peer rejection in childhood can be measured not only concurrently but in the later years as well. Indeed, as noted earlier, much of the impetus for research on peer rejection stems from several provocative studies concerning the successful prediction of later life adjustment from early peer status. These studies are widely cited but rarely analyzed or considered within the context of other literature on prediction. In Chapter 10 Kupersmidt, Coie, and Dodge discuss several important methodological considerations in risk research and carefully inspect research on various outcomes, including mental health disturbances, criminality, and early school withdrawal. The authors also discuss their own longitudinal research project. This work is unusual in its examination of behavioral and sociometric predictors of multiple types of outcomes, including both internalizing and externalizing adjustment difficulties.

As discussed earlier, the study of peer rejection has been motivated in large part by an interest in helping children at risk acquire social relationship competencies. The chapters in the fifth part of this volume focus on intervention. Chapter 11, by Coie and Koeppl, offers an insightful analysis of previous social skills training studies with unpopular children. Although several studies have demonstrated success, there is considerable variability in children's responsiveness to intervention. Coie and Koeppl focus on this variability. They suggest that aggressive– or disruptive–rejected children have been the least responsive to intervention and that efforts to modify the acceptance of these children will need to focus explicitly on their aggressive or disruptive behavior. In this context, Coie and Koeppl discuss literature on methods for reducing aggressive and disruptive behavior.

Researchers concerned with intervention also face the challenge of how to adapt the cognitively based social skills interventions that have been developed for middle elementary school children to younger children and to children with special learning problems (e.g., retarded or learning-disabled youngsters). In Chapter 12 Mize and Ladd take an important step in that direction. They use a previously developed model of social skills training (Ladd & Mize, 1983) to design an intervention for preschoolers. Readers familiar with earlier work by Chittenden (1942) will appreciate the way Mize and Ladd's intervention is informed by early social development research as well as current literature on social competence.

In sum, this volume describes the many advances being made in research on peer rejection. Advances in our knowledge, and in our methods for acquiring new knowledge, are helping to make this an exciting time for conducting research on children's peer relationships. Coie's concluding chapter considers what we have learned about the origins of peer rejection, its maintenance, its consequences, and its precursors. As Coie indicates, the expanding knowledge base in this field is providing the foundation for theory development and for improved methods of helping children whose need is great.

References

Asher, S. R. (1985). An evolving paradigm in social skill training research with children. In B. H. Schneider, K. H. Rubin, & J. E. Ledingham (Eds.), *Peer relations: Issues in assessment and intervention* (pp. 157–171). New York: Springer-Verlag.

Asher, S. R. (1988, April). *Peer rejection and loneliness in childhood.* Paper presented at the annual meeting of the American Psychological Association, New Orleans.

Asher, S. R., & Dodge, K. A. (1986). Identifying children who are rejected by their peers. *Developmental Psychology, 22,* 444–449.

Asher, S. R., & Hymel, S. (1981). Children's social competence in peer relations: Sociometric and behavioral assessment. In J. D. Wine & M. D. Smye (Eds.), *Social competence* (pp. 125–157). New York: Guilford.

Asher, S. R., & Parker, J. G. (1989). The significance of peer relationship problems in childhood. In B. H. Schneider, G. Attili, J. Nadel, & R. P. Weissberg (Eds.), *Social competence in developmental perspective* (pp. 5–23). Amsterdam: Kluwer Academic Publishing.

Asher, S. R., & Renshaw, P. D. (1981). Children without friends: Social knowledge and social skill training. In S. R. Asher & J. M. Gottman (Eds.), *The development of children's friendships* (pp. 273–296). New York: Cambridge University Press.

Asher, S. R., Singleton, L. C., Tinsley, B. R., & Hymel, S. (1979). A reliable sociometric measure for preschool children. *Developmental Psychology, 15,* 443–444.

Asher, S. R., & Wheeler, V. A. (1985). Children's loneliness: A comparison of rejected and neglected peer status. *Journal of Consulting and Clinical Psychology, 53,* 500–505.

Bell-Dolan, D. J., Foster, S. L., & Sikora, D. M. (1989). Effects of sociometric testing on children's behavior and loneliness in school. *Developmental Psychology, 25,* 306–311.

Bryan, T. H. (1976). Peer popularity of learning disabled children: A replication. *Journal of Learning Disabilities, 9,* 307–311.

Bukowski, W. M., & Hoza, B. (1989). Popularity and friendship: Issues in theory, measurement, and outcome. In T. J. Berndt & G. W. Ladd (Eds.), *Peer relationships in child development* (pp. 15–45). New York: Wiley.

Chittenden, G. F. (1942). An experimental study in measuring and modifying assertive behavior in young children. *Monographs of the Society for Research in Child Development, 7*(1, Serial No. 31).

Coie, J. D., & Dodge, K. A. (1983). Continuities and changes in children's social status: A five-year longitudinal study. *Merrill-Palmer Quarterly, 29,* 261–281.

Coie, J. D., Dodge, K. A., & Coppotelli, H. (1982). Dimensions and types of social status: A cross-age perspective. *Developmental Psychology, 18,* 557–570.

Coie, J. D., & Kupersmidt, J. B. (1983). A behavioral analysis of emerging social status in boys' groups. *Child Development, 54,* 1400–1416.

Corsaro, W. A. (1981). Friendship in the nursery school: Social organization in a peer environment. In S. R. Asher & J. M. Gottman (Eds.), *The development of children's friendships* (pp. 207–241). New York: Cambridge University Press.

Cowen, E. L., Pederson, A., Babigian, H., Izzo, L. D., & Trost, M. A. (1973). Long-term follow-up of early detected vulnerable children. *Journal of Consulting and Clinical Psychology, 41,* 438–446.

Dodge, K. A. (1986). A social information processing model of social competence in children. In M. Perlmutter (Ed.), *Minnesota symposia on child psychology* (Vol. 18, pp. 77–126). Hillsdale, NJ: Lawrence Erlbaum.

Dodge, K. A., Asher, S. R., & Parkhurst, J. T. (1989). Social life as a goal coordination task. In C. Ames & R. Ames (Eds.), *Research on motivation in education* (Vol. 3, pp. 107–135). New York: Academic Press.

Ellis, S., Rogoff, B., & Cromer, C. C. (1981). Age segregation in children's social interactions. *Developmental Psychology, 17,* 399–407.

French, D. C., & Waas, G. A. (1985). Behavior problems of peer-neglected and peer-rejected elementary-age children: Parent and teacher perspectives. *Child Development, 56,* 246–252.

Furman, W., & Robbins, P. (1985). What's the point? Issues in the selection of treatment objectives. In B. H. Schneider, K. H. Rubin, & J. E. Ledingham (Eds.), *Children's peer relations: Issues in assessment and intervention* (pp. 41–56). New York: Springer-Verlag.

Gottlieb, J., & Leyser, Y. (1981). Friendships between mentally retarded and non-retarded children. In S. R. Asher & J. M. Gottman (Eds.), *The development of children's friendships* (pp. 150–181). New York: Cambridge University Press.

Gottman, J. M. (1977). Toward a definition of social isolation in children. *Child Development, 48,* 513–517.

Gottman, J. M., Gonso, J., & Rasmussen, B. (1975). Social interaction, social competence, and friendship in children. *Child Development, 46,* 709–718.

Gottman, J. M., & Parker, J. G. (1986). *Conversations of friends.* New York: Cambridge University Press.

Gottman, J. M., & Parkhurst, J. (1980). A developmental theory of friendship and acquaintanceship processes. In W. A. Collins (Ed.), *Minnesota symposia on child psychology* (Vol. 13, pp. 197–253). Hillsdale, NJ: Lawrence Erlbaum.

Gresham, F. M. (1988). Social competence and motivational characteristics of learning disabled students. In M. C. Wang, M. C. Reynolds, & H. J. Walberg (Eds.), *Handbook of special education: Research and practice* (Vol. 2, pp. 283–302). Oxford: Pergamon.

Gronlund, N. E. (1959). *Sociometry in the classroom.* New York: Harper.

Guralnick, M. J., & Groom, J. M. (1987). The peer relations of mildly delayed and nonhandicapped preschool children in mainstream playgroups. *Child Development, 58,* 1556–1572.

Hartup, W. W., Glazer, J. A., & Charlesworth, R. (1967). Peer reinforcement and sociometric status. *Child Development, 38,* 1017–1024.

Hartup, W. W., & Sancilio, M. F. (1986). Children's friendships. In E. Schopler & G. B. Mesibov (Eds.), *Social behavior in autism* (pp. 61–80). New York: Plenum.

Hayvren, M., & Hymel, S. (1984). Ethical issues in sociometric testing: The impact of sociometric measures on interactive behavior. *Developmental Psychology, 20,* 844–849.

Henker, B., & Whalen, C. K. (1989). Hyperactivity and attention deficits. *American Psychologist, 44,* 216–223.

Howes, C. (1988). Peer interaction of young children. *Monographs of the Society for Research in Child Development, 53*(1, Serial No. 217).

Hymel, S., & Asher, S. R. (1977, April). *Assessment and training of isolated children's social skills.* Paper presented at the biennial meeting of the Society for Research in Child Development, New Orleans (ERIC Document Reproduction Service No. ED 136 930).

Hymel, S., & Rubin, K. H. (1985). Children with peer relationships and social skills problems: Conceptual, methodological, and developmental issues. In G. J. Whitehurst (Ed.), *Annals of child development* (Vol. 2, pp. 251–297). Greenwich, CT: JAI Press.

Ladd, G. W., & Mize, J. (1983). A cognitive–social learning model of social skill training. *Psychological Review, 90,* 127–157.

Ladd, G. W., & Oden, S. L. (1979). The relationship between peer acceptance and children's ideas about helpfulness. *Child Development, 50,* 402–408.

Milich, R., & Landau, S. (1982). Socialization and peer relations in hyperactive children. In K. D. Gadow & I. Bailer (Eds.), *Advances in learning and behavioral disabilities: A research annual* (Vol. 1, pp. 283–339). Greenwich, CT: JAI Press.

Newcomb, A. F., & Bukowski, W. M. (1983). Social impact and social preference as determinants of children's peer group status. *Developmental Psychology, 19,* 856–867.

Newcomb, A. F., & Bukowski, W. M. (1984). A longitudinal study of the utility of social preference and social impact sociometric classification schemes. *Child Development, 55,* 1434–1447.

Northway, M. L. (1944). Outsiders: A study of the personality patterns of children least acceptable to their agemates. *Sociometry, 7,* 10–25.

Peery, J. C. (1979). Popular, amiable, isolated, rejected: A reconceptualization of sociometric status in preschool children. *Child Development, 50,* 1231–1234.

Pelham, W. E., & Bender, M. E. (1982). Peer relationships in hyperactive children: Description and treatment. In K. D. Gadow & I. Bialer (Eds.), *Advances in learning and behavioral disabilities: A research annual* (Vol. 1, pp. 365–436). Greenwich, CT: JAI Press.

Putallaz, M. (1987). Maternal behavior and children's sociometric status. *Child Development, 58,* 324–340.

Putallaz, M., & Gottman, J. M. (1981). Social skills and group acceptance. In S. R. Asher & J. M. Gottman (Eds.), *The development of children's friendships* (pp. 116–149). New York: Cambridge University Press.

Ratiner, C., Weissberg, R., & Caplan, M. (1986, August). *Ethical considerations in sociometric testing: The reactions of preadolescent subjects.* Paper presented at the annual meeting of the American Psychological Association, Washington, DC.

Roff, M. (1961). Childhood social interactions and young adult bad conduct. *Journal of Abnormal and Social Psychology, 63,* 333–337.

Roff, M., Sells, S. B., & Golden, M. M. (1972). *Social adjustment and personality development in children.* Minneapolis: University of Minnesota Press.

Shantz, C. U. (1987). Conflicts between children. *Child Development, 58,* 283–305.

Singleton, L. C., & Asher, S. R. (1977). Peer preferences and social interaction among third-grade children in an integrated school district. *Journal of Educational Psychology, 69,* 330–336.

Siperstein, G. N., Bopp, M. J., & Bak, J. J. (1978). Social status of learning disabled children. *Journal of Learning Disabilities, 11,* 98–102.

Taylor, A. R., & Asher, S. R. (1984). Children's goals and social competence: Individual differences in a game-playing context. In T. Field, J. L. Roopnarine, & M. Segal (Eds.), *Friendships in normal and handicapped children* (pp. 53–78). Norwood, NJ: Ablex.

Taylor, A. R., Asher, S. R., & Williams, G. A. (1987). The social adaptation of mainstreamed mildly retarded children. *Child Development, 58,* 1321–1334.

Vosk, B., Forehand, R., Parker, J. B., and Rickard, K. (1982). A multimethod comparison of popular and unpopular children. *Developmental Psychology, 18,* 571–575.

Whalen, C. K. (in press). Attention deficit and hyperactivity disorders. In T. H. Ollendick & M. Hersen (Eds.), *The handbook of child psychopathology* (2nd ed.). New York: Plenum.

Part I

Behavioral characteristics of peer-rejected children

2   Peer group behavior and social status

John D. Coie, Kenneth A. Dodge, and Janis B. Kupersmidt

The goal of this chapter is to provide a comprehensive review of the behavioral correlates and antecedents of peer sociometric status. Because there has been a rapid increase in the quality as well as the quantity of research in the area, this review is timely and will be important to researchers of social development and preventive intervention. Several excellent reviews have been written recently (e.g., Asher & Hymel, 1981; Hartup, 1983; Hymel & Rubin, 1985). Whereas these reviews consider the general relationship between behavior and sociometric status, the current review focuses specifically on the *acquisition* of sociometric status. Furthermore, the focus of this chapter is explicitly developmental.

To what degree do the behavioral correlates of status vary across age? This review will reveal a remarkable consistency in these correlates across all ages studied but will also indicate subtle developmental differences that may actually be quite important. Cooperativeness and prosocial behavior emerge as major correlates of positive status at each age, but the processes involved in behaving cooperatively and prosocially seem to become increasingly complex as children get older. At the negative extreme of status, aggression is the primary correlate of status at all ages. Yet the nature of aggressiveness changes with age, and the strength of this relation seems to decline with age. At the younger ages, hitting and name-calling constitute aggressiveness, whereas at the older ages, aggressiveness becomes more differentiated and less overt. Indirect aggression and hypersensitivity to teasing or criticism come to be important features of negative status in adolescence. Finally, the role of social withdrawal in status seems to change with age. Withdrawal is not strongly correlated with status at young ages but comes to be a consequence of low status as children get older and become aware of their own negative position among peers. In order to attend to these developmental findings, we will discuss separately three age-groups: the preschool and primary grade years (ages 4 to 7), the later elementary school grades (ages 8 to 12), and the junior high and high school grades (ages 13 and older).

The preparation of this chapter and the collection of data reported herein were supported, in part, by grants from the National Institute of Mental Health.

Another key point of this chapter is that our understanding of the behavioral determinants of status is based on several different sources of information, including peers, relevant adults, and trained observers. These sources have different perspectives and can provide unique contributions. Peers, of course, are the judges of status, so their perspective is crucial. They have access to social interactions that often are outside the scrutiny of adults. They also have an implicit understanding of the norms for behavior within the child peer group and are apt to be sensitive to the implications of violating these norms. Their ability to describe reasons for their choices can be suspect, however, because of sometimes limited cognitive and verbal skills. Also, their perspective may be skewed if their reasons for liking a peer are solicited *after* status has been acquired; by that time, postdecision justifications may deviate from actual predecision events. Relevant adults, including teachers and camp counselors, may be more equipped to provide detailed observations, but their perspective may be biased by their role in maintaining order. They may place more emphasis on a child's interactions with adults than with peers. Also, they may not have access to relevant peer situations outside the classroom or the supervised playground activity. Much of the serious aggression among children seems to take place in such unsupervised places as the school restrooms or on the way to and from school. Trained observers who are unaware of status may be in the best position to provide objective behavioral information, but their intrusive role as outsiders may keep them from being able to observe private but important events. This point is especially true for observations of adolescents. In order to remain aware of the source of information, we have organized this review into three sections based on the type of data source. Each of these three sections is further subdivided according to developmental period.

A third key point of this chapter is that the conclusions of a study are a function of the observational methods and coding procedures employed. Studies employing molecular coding systems in real time enable a researcher to make conclusions concerning the short-term sequential nature of interactive behavior. By contrast, procedures in which children are rated on social traits lack the detailed clarity of ethological studies but provide a more global picture and may have more predictive validity (Cairns & Green, 1979). Studies also have varied in their methodological rigor and attention to important matters such as observer reliability and sampling procedures. These variations often affect the conclusions. For these reasons, we have taken care to describe studies in great detail.

Recent advances in sociometric classification (Coie, Dodge, & Coppotelli, 1982; Newcomb & Bukowski, 1983) have suggested the need to distinguish between groups at the low-status extreme (neglected vs. rejected) and between groups at the higher status extreme (popular vs. controversial). The distinctions are necessary because the dimensions of liking and disliking have been found to be fairly independent. Not so long ago, investigators used a single positive index of status and reported data on "isolated" children or "unpopular" children, treating all of these children as though they were the same. The importance of making distinctions among these groups will be made evident in this chapter. Indeed, behavioral distinctions among these groups constitute a fourth key point of this chapter. The present review is organized so that the single-dimension studies are discussed first, followed by the more sophisticated, two-dimensional studies.

This chapter also will devote a good deal of attention to the distinctions among antecedents, correlates, and consequences of status. A major problem with most studies is that status is identified first, followed by the observation of behavior. These studies have limited value in understanding the initial acquisition of status. Several recent studies have attended to the development of status by focusing observations on children's initial encounters with peers in quasi-naturalistic settings (Coie & Kupersmidt, 1983; Dodge, 1983). These studies, and the merits of this procedure, will be described in detail because they alter our understanding of status acquisition and may provide methods of choice in future research.

In the review that follows, some observational studies of peer status have been omitted intentionally. In some cases this is because the peer status information on the sample came from adult estimates rather than the child peer group. Furthermore, dyadic interaction studies and role-play observations have been omitted in favor of studies that describe actual interactions among peers who evaluate each other in sociometric terms. Chapter 3 contains a review of the research on children's behavior when entering dyads at play.

Finally, the findings of the many studies reviewed here will be treated as threads with which to weave a coherent theory of the behavioral development of sociometric status in children's peer groups.

Peer reports and sociometric status

Because peers are the judges of status, an obvious first source of information concerning the behavioral bases of those judgments is the perspective of the peer group. In many studies, peers have been asked why they like or dislike a child. A related procedure has been to ask peers to nominate children as most exemplifying certain types of social behavior (such as starting fights, being shy, and being cooperative) and to relate nomination scores on these behavioral dimensions to sociometric status scores. Three common instruments for assessing social roles are the Class Play (Bower, 1960), its revision (Masten, Morison, & Pellegrini, 1985), and the Pupil Evaluation Inventory (PEI) (Pekarik, Prinz, Liebert, Weintraub, & Neale, 1976).

Interestingly, most of the published studies utilizing the peer assessment approach have been descriptive of children aged 8 or older, presumably because younger children have a difficult time describing differentiated perceptions of peers. In fact, there is solid evidence that younger children are less differentiated in their perceptions of peers' behavior than are older children (Coie & Pennington, 1976; Livesley & Bromley, 1973; Yarrow & Campbell, 1963; and Younger, Schwartzman, & Ledingham, 1985, 1986). Younger's data suggest that this lack of differentiation is not due to a lack of differentiation in the behavior of young children; rather, it is clearly a function of a lack of differentiation in the social perceptions made by young children. Younger tested his notions by asking first-, fourth-, and seventh-graders, as well as teachers, to evaluate peers who were first-, fourth-, or seventh-graders. He found that first-graders tend to see other first-graders in undifferentiated terms, whereas seventh-graders see other seventh-graders in highly differentiated terms. More germane to the point, he also found that first-graders are undifferentiated in their views of seventh-graders, but seventh-graders are much more differentiated in their views of first-graders. Likewise, teachers of first-graders are as differentiated in their ratings of their pupils as are teachers of fourth- and seventh-graders. Thus, young children are generally less differentiating in their perceptions than are older children and adults. These findings suggest caution in the use of peer reports as a measure of young children's social behavior. They also suggest that the appearance of the social reality of peer relations is more unidimensional among younger children than older children. It also means that the bases for negative status among young children are likely to be highly visible negative behaviors (undifferentiated), whereas for older children, more subtle and differentiated negative behaviors are likely to be the bases for negative status.

As will be seen in the review that follows, the peer report studies suggest that social acceptance (positive status) is related, at all ages, to helpfulness, rule conformity, friendliness, and prosocial interaction. Social rejection (negative status) is related to disruptiveness and aggression at all ages, but the form of aggression becomes more differentiated and subtle as children get older. With increasing age, rejection becomes associated with more indirect forms of aggression, self-isolating behaviors, and hypersensitivity. Interesting gender differences have been found that suggest that cooperativeness is a relevant dimension that distinguishes among accepted and rejected girls more than it does among boys, whereas aggression is a more relevant dimension among boys than girls.

Studies of preschool and primary school children

Clifford (1963) employed a positive item sociometric measure with preschool children and found that high scores were positively related to the total number of positive "guess-who" behaviors ($r = .51$), whereas there was no significant relation between positive nominations and the cumulative negative behavior score. In contrast, Moore (1967) combined positive and negative nominations into a single dimension of peer status by subtracting negative scores from positive scores. This social preference score was found to be correlated with friendly approach behavior in six different preschool groups ($r = .24$ to .48). Aggressive behavior was negatively related to social preference ($r = -.29$ to $-.78$). Rule-violating behavior also was negatively related to social preference ($r = -.21$ to $-.67$). Peer reports of behavior thus indicate that high status is associated with helpful and friendly interactive behavior, and negative status is associated with aggressive and disruptive behavior and a disinclination to follow social routines.

Wasik (1987) administered seven peer assessment items to 52 kindergarten children (26 black boys and girls and 26 white), at midyear and at the end of the school year. These variables were then related to both social preference and rating-scale sociometric scores, with very similar results. Being cooperative was positively related to both social preference and peer ratings at both points in time ($r = .35$ to .58). Conversely, starting fights and being disruptive were negatively related to social preference and sociometric ratings at both assessments ($r = -.36$ to $-.62$). Being a loner was negatively related to both peer status measures at midyear ($-.67$ to $-.48$) but not at the end of the year. However, the opposite was true for being identified as a leader: At midyear the correlations were .32 (social preference) and $-.05$ (ratings), but by the end of the year these correlations were .48 and .54, respectively. Crying was negatively related to end-of-year peer status ($-.31$ and $-.28$) but not to midyear status.

The contrasting results of these three studies illustrate some of the confusion created by a research design employing only a positive nomination index of social status. In the Clifford study there was no relation between negative behavior and social status. The Moore and Wasik data suggest that there is a relation, but that negative peer judgments are required in order for it to be seen. Both social preference scores (positive minus negative nominations) and rating-scale sociometric measure provide children with the opportunity to indicate negative affect toward other children.

Studies of elementary school children

The data base for peer assessments of the behavioral correlates of status is more extensive for elementary school children. These studies provide even more support for the relations between prosocial behavior and peer acceptance and between antisocial behavior and peer rejection. For example, Smith (1950) had her fourth-grade class give both positive and negative sociometric choices and then asked them open-ended questions about the reasons for their choices. Helpfulness and consideration for others were positively related to positive nominations, and verbal abusiveness, rule violations, and bullying were associated with negative nominations. In a study of third- and fifth-graders, Ladd and Oden (1979) also found a positive relationship ($r = .62$) between peer ratings of helpfulness and peer ratings of social acceptance.

The relation between peer status and negative or deviant forms of social behavior among elementary school boys has been explored in several studies. Winder and Rau (1962) surveyed 710 boys from the fourth, fifth, and sixth grades with the Peer Nomination Inventory (Wiggins & Winder, 1961). Their Likeability factor (a measure of status) had its strongest negative correlation with the Withdrawal factor ($r = -.54$), followed by Depression ($r = -.41$), Dependency ($r = -.33$), and, finally, Aggression ($r = -.23$). It is important to note that the Wiggins and Winder dependency scale is composed of items that describe both attention-seeking and immature behavior and that the withdrawal scale consists of descriptions of both solitary behavior and active social rejection by peers. Thus, there is some confounding of types of behavior and social evaluation in several of these scales. The results suggest that likability was found to be negatively associated with both internalizing and externalizing behaviors.

Lesser (1959) attempted to examine the relation between different forms of aggressive behavior and peer status. Among fifth- and sixth-grade white males, social preference was negatively correlated with peer nominations for indirect ($r = -.69$), verbal ($r = -.45$), and unprovoked physical aggression ($r = -.36$). Popularity was positively related, however, to *provoked* physical aggression ($r = .31$). Apparently, peers dislike children who display unprovoked aggression and have an opposite reaction to children who appropriately stand up for themselves and do not allow themselves to be abused or dominated by others.

In two related papers (Hymel et al., 1983; Rubin, 1984) peer sociometric ratings were correlated with the three subscale scores for the Revised Class Play (Masten et al., 1985) in samples of second- through sixth-grade children. The correlations of status with the Sociable–Leadership factor were strongly positive, ranging from .56 to .75. The correlations of status with the Aggressive–Disruptive factor were negative, but the strength of the relation varied with age. The correlations were modest for the second-, third-, and fourth-graders, ranging from $-.32$ to $-.49$, and nonsignificant for the older two groups. Peer status had increasingly negative correlations with the Sensitive–Isolated factor with increasing age ($-.30$, $-.37$, $-.71$, $-.69$, and $-.43$ for second through sixth grades, respectively). The relationship between status and isolated behavior, although significant in second and third grades, increased dramatically in the fourth and fifth grades, suggesting greater attention by peers to asocial and overemotional behavior.

The pattern revealed in each of the preceding studies is for peer status, assessed unidimensionally, to have moderate negative correlations with direct aggression and stronger negative correlations with social withdrawal, indirect aggression, and hypersensitive types of behavior. Because linear correlations of status and behavior can mask contrasting patterns of behavior among different types of social status, a number of investigators have used both positive and negative nominations to form distinct status groups of children. Coie et al. (1982), for example, used positive and negative nomination scores to define five different social status groups: popular, socially rejected, socially neglected, controversial, and average. A total of 848 children from the third, fifth, and eighth grades were surveyed with a six-item peer assessment instrument. The popular group received high scores for cooperative and leadership behavior and low scores for starting fights, being disruptive, and asking others for help. Rejected children had the opposite profile: They were high on starting fights, being disruptive, and asking for help in school and low on cooperativeness and leadership. The controversial group were equally as high on leadership scores as the popular group but were also described by peers as being as disruptive and aggressive as the rejected group. Their cooperativeness ratings were midway between those of popular and rejected children and significantly different from both of these groups. Neglected children had scores below the mean for all but the shy and withdrawn item but were not significantly different from average children in this regard. The average subjects were, in fact, at the mean for all six items, in keeping with their sociometric status.

The status group profiles described above were found to hold for both boys and girls and at all three age levels, suggesting some ubiquity to these patterns. Still, there were important gender interactions with status, which reflected the fact that different behaviors were important discriminators of status for boys and girls. Among boys, aggressiveness and help seeking were powerful discriminators between rejected and popular groups. Although these behaviors also discriminated among girls' groups, the magnitude of these relations was less. On the other hand, cooperativeness discriminated among girls' status groups to a greater degree than it did among boys' groups. Apparently, aggressiveness and help seeking are particularly salient and relevant negatively viewed behaviors among boys, whereas cooperativeness is a relevant positive behavior among girls.

A status by race interaction effect was also found in this study, which reflected the fact that popular black children were not viewed as leaders, whereas controversial black children were. This curious finding for race is confounded by the fact that black children in this study were in the minority (about 25%). In a later study, Coie, Finn, and Krehbiel (1984) examined the correlates of status in an exclusively black sample. In this case, black popular children were clearly viewed by their peers as leaders. The two studies suggest that leadership and popularity are very much affected by one's majority or minority status. One hypothesis to account for these facts is that minority leaders may be viewed by majority children as acting presumptuously, with the result that they are categorized in sociometric terms as controversial. An alternative explanation is that children who have the social sensitivity to be well liked by peers and the social skill to be leaders will suppress some of their leadership tendencies in social circumstances where it would be controversial to be assertive. A third interpretation is that there may be cultural differences in the way children prefer to see leadership expressed.

In their study of a predominantly black fourth-grade population, Coie et al. (1984) used an eight-item modification of the original six-item peer assessment instrument to include items that might clarify the nature of controversial children's interactive style. Newcomb and Bukowski (1983) had challenged the validity of the controversial group, contending that it was merely a composite of marginally popular, rejected, and average children. In support of this contention, Newcomb and Bukowski reported the results of a discriminant function analysis in which factor scores from a 14-item peer assessment battery were used to distinguish among the five status groups of the Coie et al. typology. When these scores failed to classify correctly children from the neglected and controversial groups, they argued that the groups must lack identifiable behavioral characteristics. Coie et al. argued that this failure may have resulted either from an item pool that contained too few items that were descriptive of the controversial group or from the use of factor scores that combined items on which controversial subjects would have a very mixed performance, such as "smart," "good at sports," and "liked by everyone." Using item scores from their eight-item questionnaire to discriminate among the same five social status groups, Coie et al. found that 83% of the controversial boys and 63% of the controversial girls could be correctly reclassified, as well as 100% of the neglected boys and 83% of the neglected girls.

The status group comparisons in this same study revealed similar behavioral differences for the black sample as for the predominantly white sample in the earlier Coie et al. study. Popular children were seen as good at sports, leaders, and cooperative. Rejected children were described as aggressive, disruptive, easily angered, and unhappy. Neglected children were perceived only as being unhappy. The controversial children, like the rejected group, were viewed by peers as aggressive, disruptive, and easily angered, but like the popular children, they were also seen as the best athletes. Their unique characteristic, particularly among the boys, was that they were funny and made peers laugh. Once again they were intermediate to popular and rejected children on cooperativeness.

Bukowski and Newcomb (1984) reported correlations between four peer assessment factor scores and social preference among fifth-grade children. Aggression was negatively correlated with social preference ($r = -.38$) as was Immaturity ($r = -.49$), and Leadership and School Competence were positively related to social preference ($r = .59$ and $.54$). Tests of structural models based on correlations between peer assessment factors and social preference scores obtained at three successive 6-month intervals supported the idea that the social preference scores were determined by the social behavior scores.

Carlson, Lahey, and Neeper (1984) used positive and negative nominations with 358 second- and fifth-grade children to select popular, rejected, and neglected groups in a manner similar to that of Coie et al. (1982). They contrasted these three groups on a 32-item peer assessment instrument. Their findings for the rejected group were similar to those of the two preceding studies. Rejected children at both grade levels were perceived as more aggressive, disruptive, more likely to violate rules, and more likely to be inconsiderate of other children. Neglected children differed from the other two groups in that peers described them as less likely to say they could beat everybody up. At the fifth-grade level, rejected children were also different from the other groups in more subtle aspects of social behavior, such as not giving and receiving help easily, not sharing or waiting their turn, not knowing how to join a group, and being dishonest. At the second-grade level, these subtle aspects of behavior were not related to status. As found in other peer assessment studies, it is clear that among young children status is strongly related to overt and single-behavior patterns only.

Studies in which the behavior of status groups is contrasted on peer assessment items suggest a different picture of the character of deviance among rejected children than do studies in which unidimensional measures of peer status are employed. Both types of studies give the same picture of well-accepted, or popular, children. However, the unidimensional studies tend to emphasize the importance of the relationship between hypersensitive and isolated, withdrawn behaviors to social rejection more than aggression and disruptiveness, whereas the opposite is true in studies in which neglected- and rejected-status groups are contrasted with average-status children.

How can these differences be resolved? Two problems in resolving these differences are that the two types of studies have used different sociometric groupings as independent variables and different peer assessment items as dependent variables. The unidimensional studies confound two distinct status groups at the low end (rejected and neglected), and this heterogeneity may yield weaker findings than studies that separate children into more homogeneous groups. Concerning the dependent variables, Winder and Rau (1962), Rubin (1984), and Hymel et al. (1983) all analyzed their data in terms of factor scores rather than individual items. The factor scores were made up of quite distinct items and thus combined different types of behavior. The Withdrawn factor, for example, included items about withdrawal and also items about active rejection by peers. Two outcomes are likely when such factors are used. First, misinterpretations are likely when a positive finding that applies primarily to only one item is mistakenly applied to other items within the same factor. Second, the magnitude of all findings is often reduced, because divergent items are grouped together.

The two studies by Coie and his colleagues used a small set of items, only one of which described isolated behavior, and they analyzed their data in terms of item scores. Aggression items most strongly discriminated their rejected groups from others. Carlson et al. (1984) used a 32-item questionnaire that contained many of the Aggression factor items from the PEI; however, none of the Withdrawal factor items from the PEI were included in the Carlson et al. measure. The latter investigators did include some low-visibility items (e.g., "those who stand back and just watch others who are playing," "those who speak softly and are difficult to understand," and "those who give in to others too much"); however, these items lack the sense of emotional lability and social inadequacy that is reflected in the PEI Withdrawal cluster items (e.g., "feelings easily hurt," "unhappy and sad," or "not noticed much"). Carlson et al. (1984) also analyzed their data in terms of item scores. Thus, the two studies in which individual items were analyzed emphasized the importance of aggression for social rejection but did not include items that represented the aspects of social withdrawal having to do with inadequacy.

A study by Cantrell and Prinz (1985) provides data that may resolve some of these problems. They compared groups of rejected, neglected, and average children on the PEI, but they analyzed differences at the item level. The children were from the third through the sixth grade. The authors found significant main effects for social status and sex of subject only when multivariate analyses were conducted across the total set of 33 items. When the univariate results are examined in terms of the content of the items, this pattern holds up better for the Aggression and Likeability items than for the Withdrawal items, especially when just the items dealing with actual social withdrawal are considered. For all of the Aggression cluster items – items describing attention seeking, disruptiveness, and aggression – the rejected children (both boys and girls) had significantly more nominations than both average and neglected children. The average children had higher scores than rejected and neglected children on all five Likeability items, items describing popularity, helpfulness, and competence. Neglected girls had higher scores than rejected girls on two items, being nice and understanding things.

The results were less clear-cut for the Withdrawal items. Rejected boys had more nominations than neglected or average boys on five of the nine Withdrawal items. However, only two of these five items have anything to do with social withdrawal on the child's part. Two of the five items described rejection by peers and a third reflected distress at being called on in class. There were no group differences on three of the Withdrawal items, and on the last item ("unhappy or sad") rejected and neglected groups did not differ but had higher scores than the average group. The picture was much more straightforward for the girls, however. Rejected girls had higher scores than neglected and average girls on eight of the nine Withdrawal items. There were no status differences for one item, one of the three for which the boys showed no status differences ("too shy to make friends easily"). This study suggests that withdrawal per se is not strongly related to status among boys but is among girls. Withdrawal factor scores may be related to status among boys if they contain items concerning active rejection by peers.

Some conclusions about behavior and peer status in the age-group of 8 to 12 may be drawn from the peer assessment literature. First, popular or well-liked children seem to be those who are helpful to peers, follow the rules, cooperate in group situations, and are generally competent. There is no real disagreement on this point. Rejected children are always described as aggressive and disruptive; however, the strength of this relationship varies with the sociometric methodology employed. This relationship is only moderate for studies employing a unidimensional measure but is quite strong for studies using a two-dimensional approach. This difference may reflect two facts about status groups as they are defined in a two-dimensional system. One is that sociometrically neglected children will be confounded with rejected children at the low end of a single popularity index, at least to some extent (Hymel & Rubin, 1985). These neglected children are always low in peer nominations as aggressive or disruptive, whereas rejected children are quite high. Second, some controversial children have high popularity scores and are liked by peers even though they are also aggressive and disruptive (Coie et al., 1984). Both of these phenomena tend to weaken the correlation between aggression and a single index of peer status.

A last conclusion concerns behavioral withdrawal and social status. Here the conclusion must be more tentative. There is some evidence that withdrawal is related to social rejection; however, there is evidence that it is a form of social withdrawal other than shyness and lack of social assertiveness that is important to rejection. Rejected children are consistently found not to differ from average-status children on these types of peer assessment items. Instead, rejected children seem to be described as pulling back from peers and being shunned or ignored by their peers. Once again, the confounding of rejected and neglected children may account for the stronger relationship of social withdrawal with unidimensional indices of status. However, it must be stated that there is no evidence from the peer assessment literature that neglected children are withdrawn in their behavior, merely that they are very nonaggressive. Furthermore, it must be acknowledged that the dimension of social withdrawal has not been adequately represented in the peer assessment instruments of Coie and his colleagues or by Carlson, Lahey, and Neeper, so that only the mixed findings of Cantrell and Prinz properly speak to this issue.

A further point about withdrawal can be made by emphasizing that the described relations between status and behavioral patterns are correlational and open to multiple interpretations. It may be that children who are rejected withdraw from the peer group in response to their rejection, rather than being rejected because they are withdrawn. This withdrawal pattern may be a different form of isolating behavior than shyness but may not be discerned as such by young peers.

Studies of adolescents

There are far fewer investigations of social status among adolescents than among elementary school children. Kuhlen and Lee (1943) surveyed sixth-, ninth-, and twelfth-graders with a positive sociometric choice measure and contrasted the 25% most popular subjects with the 25% least popular subjects on 19 behavior traits. Being friendly, initiating social activity, having a sense of humor, being cheerful, and being enthusiastic were characteristics associated with high status for boys and girls at all three ages. Only at the sixth-grade level (the youngest age surveyed) were low-status boys rated as more restless than high-status boys. In general, there were few traits on which low-status subjects had higher scores than high-status subjects. This is probably because a negative sociometric item was not used to assess peer status among subjects, even though negative peer assessment items were included.

Feinberg, Smith, and Schmidt (1958) surveyed a sample of over 2,400 adolescent boys between the ages of 13 and 15. They asked them to describe four boys in their class whom they liked and four with whom they were uncomfortable or annoyed. The characteristics associated with positive status were athletic, intelligent, plays fair and is honest, good company and can take a joke, and quiet. The traits associated with negative status were disruptive, conceited, and silly. Always fighting was a negative status trait listed by middle and lower socioeconomic status (SES) boys but not upper SES boys. In a very similar study, Elkins (1958) asked 90 eighth-graders positive and negative sociometric questions and then interviewed them about the basis for their choices. Her analysis of these open-ended data yielded results consistent with those of Feinberg et al. High-status adolescents were viewed as helpful, good-natured, obeying the rules, having a sense of humor, and supportive. Low-status peers were described as disruptive, mean, rule violators, too sensitive, and unattractive in that they were dirty or smelled bad. No mention was made of withdrawn behavior in either study. This fact suggests that adolescents do not spontaneously think of withdrawal in connection with peers they dislike and that it is not a salient "cause" of rejection from the peers' perspective; this is consistent with the hypothesis that withdrawal is a consequence of rejection rather than a cause of rejection.

The earliest research in which popular, rejected, and neglected groups were compared was conducted by Gronlund and Anderson (1957) with 158 seventh-and eighth-graders. Socially accepted, or popular, boys and girls were described as good-looking, tidy, friendly, enthusiastic, cheerful, and having a sense of humor. The boys were active in games and the girls were quiet (not restless). Rejected boys and girls were described as unattractive, untidy, restless, and talkative. Very little was said about neglected boys and girls except that they were not talkative and tended not to be restless. In all of the preceding studies of adolescents, data analyses lack tests of statistical significance; however, the results were quite strong and consistent.

The relation between different forms of aggression and peer status was examined by Olweus (1977). A subset of sixth-grade boys was selected to rate all their male classmates on three aggressiveness items and to give a sociometric rating. The categories for the latter rating ranged from *liked by all of the boys* to *liked by a few of the boys*. The ratings were repeated at the end of the seventh grade. Sociometric status was uncorrelated with "starts fights" with peers ($r = .00$) in the sixth grade and in the seventh grade ($r = .01$). The same finding held for the correlations between status and verbal protest to teachers ($r = .01$ and $.17$). However, "being the target of other boys' aggression" was negatively correlated with peer popularity ($r = -.36$ and $-.48$). In a second study conducted with boys at the end of the sixth grade and then 3 years later, similar results were obtained. Olweus concluded that aggression is not related to popularity, but again it must be noted that his failure to include a negative sociometric item in his assessment of popularity may account for these findings.

The one other set of data is from the Coie et al. (1982) study discussed in the preceding section. In this study, eighth-graders were included in the sample along with third- and fifth-graders. A significant multivariate interaction effect for grade level by status reflected the fact that there was a decrease in the magnitude of status group differences from third to fifth to eighth grade. Slight differences in the correlates of status were also found. For the eighth-graders, rejected status was more highly correlated with not being included in peer group activities than with the acting-out items such as fighting and being disruptive. These latter items had lower correlations with peer status at older grade levels, possibly because the overall frequency of aggression decreases with age. The results of these analyses, along with the Olweus data, suggest that in adolescence one emerging dimension of social behavior related to peer status is being a target of abuse or ridicule. This may be interpreted in either of two ways. It may reflect a greater awareness by adolescents of the experience of rejection and rejecting others. Alternatively, it may mean that adolescents are describing a behavioral tendency of rejected peers that involves handling oneself inadequately in response to teasing and verbal bantering.

Conclusions

Across all age groups, social acceptance is related to the same general set of behaviors. According to the reports of peers, children who are helpful, who follow the rules, and who are friendly and interactive are accepted at all ages. The behavioral basis for social rejection is more complicated to describe. Aggression is the primary correlate of rejection, but the form of this behavior changes with age. Thus, the correlates of rejection change. With increasing age the behaviors associated with rejected status shift from overt aggression toward more indirect forms of aggression and toward hypersensitivity and being a target of peer ridicule and exclusion. Neglected status is associated with a lack of social involvement but not with any overtly deviant behavior. When gender differences have been examined, they indicate that aggression is less central to status among girls than boys and that fulfilling certain social obligations is more central to status among girls than boys.

One methodological issue that has gone unmentioned in the preceding review is the frequent use of large numbers of dependent variables in a peer assessment battery. This was often the case with early research, but it is also true of some more recent studies (e.g., Cantrell & Prinz, 1984; Carlson et al., 1984). In these studies, the number of dependent variables closely approximates the cell size of groups being compared. Spurious or chance findings may occur. One solution to this problem has been to use factor scores, yet as was noted above, the labels attached to these scores are sometimes misleading. A more important problem is that factor scores do not give a very differentiated picture of behavior. Another solution has been to move from general omnibus inventories to more focused studies of status and behavior in a single domain, such as those by Ladd and Oden (1979), who focused on helpfulness, and Lesser (1959) and Olweus (1977), who focused on aggression. This direction may be the more promising route for the future.

Adult reports and sociometric status

Adult caretakers, such as teachers, can provide a unique perspective on the behaviors associated with peer sociometric status. Their frequent contact with the children enables them to observe recurring behavior patterns, and their mature, differentiated perception of behavior (Younger, Schwartzman, & Ledingham, 1986) gives them an edge over children's perceptions. Their role, however, is that of an outsider to children's peer relationships, so their perspective is likely to be skewed. In addition, because they act as authority figures with responsibility for maintaining order, it is not surprising that they typically report that low-status children fail to conform to rules and are inattentive. In general, teachers also report that rejected children are highly aggressive, hyperactive, disruptive, and insensitive. As with peers' perceptions, teachers perceive that aggression is more central to status among boys than girls, whereas social participation and withdrawal are more central to status among girls than boys. Peer status has been studied in relation to adult reports of behavior for only the two youngest age-groups in this review.

Studies of preschool and primary school children

Teachers have been the primary group to provide data concerning the behavioral bases of social status of children. In one case (Hunt & Solomon, 1942), however, camp counselors provided trait behavior ratings across an 8-week summer camp for boys aged 5 to 8. Counselors rated the boys on four behavior traits at the end of the first and at the end of the eighth week of camp, and these ratings were correlated with positive sociometric nomination totals for each of those weeks. In the first week, only "lack of egocentricity" was correlated ($r = .45$) with positive peer status. This correlation also held up at the eighth week ($r = .50$), by which time generosity ($r = .34$) and ordered activity ($r = .47$) were also correlated with positive status. Translated into terms used in the previously reviewed peer assessment literature, counselors saw considerateness of others and rule-following behavior as being related to positive peer status.

Koch (1933), in one of the first studies of the basis of peer status, used a paired-comparison sociometric technique that yielded a rank ordering of peer status. In addition, teachers completed the Merrill-Palmer School Personality Scale on the same group of seventeen 4-year-olds. Compliance with routine was extremely highly correlated with positive social rank ($r = .92$). Lippitt (1941) conducted a similar study with 45 preschool children using identical status and teacher measures. She obtained similar but much weaker relations than did Koch.

Teacher ratings of emotional and antisocial aspects of preschoolers' behavior have been related to sociometric status in two studies. McMichael (1980) related positive and negative nomination scores for 198 five- and six-year-old Scottish boys to three types of personal adjustment (stable, antisocial, and neurotic) as assessed by Rutter's Children's Behavioral Questionnaire. Stable personality types were more popular than antisocial or neurotic types, and the last two types did not differ in rated popularity. Likewise, these two groups were both more rejected than the stable group. In the second study, Rubin and Clark (1983) related the three factors of the Behar and Stringfield Preschool Behavior Questionnaire to three levels of peer status among 123 preschool children. Peer status measures consisted of nomination totals for "like a lot" (positive), "kind of like" (neutral), and "don't like" (negative) items. The pattern of relationships between the three behavioral indices and status was consistent in that Anxious–Fearful, Hostile–Aggressive, and Hyperactive–Distractible behaviors were positively correlated with negative status and negatively correlated with positive and neutral status. Although the strength of the relation between status and each type of behavior was moderate at best, negative status scores were more strongly related to behavior (particularly aggressive and hyperactive behaviors) than were the other two status items. This conclusion is congruent with peer descriptions of status among preschoolers.

Studies of elementary school children

A number of studies have related sociometric status among 8- to 12-year-olds to teachers' ratings on various checklists. La Greca (1981), for example, examined correlations of sociometric ratings with the PEI factor scores obtained from teachers of 92 third-, fourth-, and fifth-grade children. There was a $-.51$ correlation with peer status for the Withdrawn factor, a correlation of $-.33$ for the Aggression factor, and a correlation of .42 for the Likeability factor. These correlations differed for boys and girls, however. Withdrawn behavior had a stronger negative correlation with peer status for the girls ($r = -.61$) than for the boys ($r = -.43$), whereas the opposite was true for aggressive behavior (girls $r = -.16$; boys $r = -.45$). Likeability scores were more positively related to boys' status ($r = .57$) than to girls' status ($r = .23$).

The Conners Teacher Rating Scale (CTRS) has been related to measures of peer status in four related papers. Lahey, Green, and Forehand (1980) correlated the CTRS subscales with peer ratings and with positive and negative nomination totals for 109 third-graders. Inattentive–passive behavior, hyperactivity, and conduct problems were negatively correlated with peer ratings; they were also correlated, but less strongly, with the two nomination scores. The Sociability score was positively related to peer ratings ($r = .38$). In a later paper (Green, Vosk, Forehand, & Beck, 1981), status groups were contrasted on these same variables for third-graders. Rejected children had higher Hyperactivity scores than neglected children, who, in turn, had higher scores than popular children. The only other significant group difference was that the rejected group was rated as more inattentive and passive than the popular group. In the third study (Vosk, Forehand, Parker, & Rickard, 1982), third- and fourth-graders were sorted into highly popular and unpopular groups on the basis of peer ratings and positive nomination scores. These extreme groups were significantly different on all five CTRS subscales. The fourth study (Green, Forehand, Beck, & Vosk, 1980) involved third-graders who completed both peer ratings and positive and negative nominations. In addition to the CTRS, for which only a total score was reported, teachers were asked to rate each of their children on 5-point scales for conduct disorder and withdrawal problems. The conduct problem ratings were unrelated to each of the three sociometric scores. Withdrawal problem ratings had low negative correlations with peer ratings ($r = -.26$) and positive nominations ($r = -.27$) and a low positive correlation with negative nominations ($r = .27$). The total CTRS scores had slightly higher correlations with status (ratings $r = -.46$; positive nominations $r = .39$; and negative nominations $r = -.37$). Although there is some inconsistency to the pattern of results from these four papers, there is a strong and consistent finding that inattentive and hyperactive behavior is positively related to rejected status by teachers.

Cantrell and Prinz (1984) related teacher evaluations on the Child Behavior Checklist (CBCL) (Edelbrock & Achenbach, 1984) to peer status. The group differences were similar for boys and girls on the Unpopular, Inattentive, Nervous and Overactive, and Aggressive scales. In each case, rejected children had higher scores than either neglected or average children. The last two groups did not differ significantly on any of the scales. Rejected girls also had higher Social Withdrawal scores than the other two groups of girls; however, there was no such finding for the boys. There were no group differences on the Anxiety scale. These results corroborate the findings of the other teacher evaluation studies of this older elementary school group. Rejected children are perceived by teachers as inattentive, hyperactive, and aggressive. Social withdrawal is a characteristic of rejected girls but not of rejected boys.

French and Waas (1985) obtained teacher ratings on popular, neglected, and rejected boys and girls from second- and fifth-grade rural classes using the School Behavior Checklist. Rejected children were rated by teachers as having more behavior problems, particularly aggression and hostile isolation, as well as more academic disability than either popular or neglected children. Neglected children had more behavior problems and academic disability than popular children. Parents of children from the three status groups were asked to complete the CBCL. Rejected children were described as showing more externalizing problems, social withdrawal, hyperactivity, aggression, and delinquency than either popular or neglected children. Neglected children differed from popular children only in greater frequency of obsessive–compulsive behaviors.

In order to examine the relation between peer status and aggression more closely, Coie and Dodge (1988) devised a teacher checklist containing a wide range of peer aggression items that dealt with verbal and physical forms of aggression and did not contain items describing the disruptive, hyperactive, attention-getting, or snobbish behaviors that are sometimes contained in aggression factors. Teachers were asked to rate 339 first- and third-grade boys who belonged to one of five peer status categories (rejected, popular, neglected, average, and controversial) based on positive and negative sociometric nomination totals. Teachers made clear status group distinctions on the Aggression cluster, with rejected and controversial groups being described as the most aggressive and neglected and popular groups being the least aggressive.

Coie and Dodge also included nonaggressive items in their checklist, including lack of skillfulness in joining a group of peers, being actively rejected from group activities, isolating oneself from peers, conformity to rules, and interpersonal sensitivity. For the last two items, rejected children had lower scores than average, neglected, and popular children. The scores of the controversial group were in between those of the rejected group and those of the other three groups. Rejected children were also described by teachers as having more difficulty gaining entry to groups of peers at play than popular children, with the other groups falling somewhere between these two extreme groups. A similar pattern of scores held true for self-isolating behavior and being overtly rejected by peers.

Conclusions

One methodological point can be underscored. Again, the use of positive nomination indices of status results in ambiguous findings for children who are not high on this scale. Positive nomination indices of status are positively correlated with various clusters of prosocial behavior. Low scores on positive nominations are rarely related in any clear way to negative behavior clusters. On the substantive side, the prosocial behavior clusters that are related to peer popularity invariably describe two kinds of behavior, interpersonal sensitivity and rule-following behavior.

There is ample evidence that teachers perceive rejected children as displaying two types of behavior: hyperactivity and disruptiveness, and aggression. Social withdrawal has also been associated with low peer status, but the picture is somewhat complicated. Although active social participation is related to positive status, it is not always clear that low-status children are withdrawn. Rejected children appear to be anxious to be involved, not shy. Where sex differences have been examined, rejected girls appear to be more withdrawn than rejected boys. However, in the most recent work by Coie and Dodge, self-isolating behaviors were described by teachers as being characteristic of rejected boys more than any other group, including neglected boys. Girls were not included in this study.

Direct observational studies

The direct observation of children by unbiased adults is the method of choice for many investigators wishing to understand the behavioral bases of sociometric status (Foster & Ritchey, 1979; Hymel & Rubin, 1985). Adults who are unacquainted with the children are not biased by previous contacts with them and can be more objective in their observations. Trained observers are also capable of coding discrete behaviors as they occur, enabling researchers to understand the behavioral bases of status at a far more discrete and sophisticated level than can be obtained from ratings by peers or teachers (see Cairns & Green, 1979, for a discussion of the relative merits of ratings and discrete coding). Direct observation allows the researchers to define behaviors at an operational, communicable level. To know that a rejected child is "highly aggressive" is not as informative as knowing that the child verbally teases peers at a rate of three times that of other children in the class. Direct observation also enables researchers to understand the sequencing of behavioral events and the contingencies controlling events. With the advent of videorecording, children's social behavior can be studied intensively, both in the laboratory and in naturalistic settings. Most of the existing observational research has been done in naturalistic settings, usually in the school, and involves comparisons of children whose peer status has already been established in these settings. This is the literature that will be reviewed in this section. There is a newer literature describing the relation between social behavior and peer status in newly formed groups. This literature speaks more directly to the behavioral determinants of peer status than the older literature and will be reviewed in a separate section of this chapter.

Unfortunately, unbiased adult observers have been used to report on peer group sociometric status only among the two youngest age-groups for which this review has been organized. In fact, there are very few observational reports on age-groups other than 7- and 8-year-olds. Observation in natural settings is expensive, intrusive, and time-consuming. The social behavior of older children is relatively complex and private, rendering abstraction of meaningful sequences difficult. Cairns, Perrin, and Cairns (1985) have begun to carry out observations of adolescents in which two observers code the social behavior of a child simultaneously (one to code the behavior and one to code the context). These observations may yield informative data about these children, but as of now, they have not been related to sociometric status as defined here.

Studies of preschool and primary school children

Several observational investigations of preschoolers have relied exclusively on positive nominations for a measure of peer status. In the earliest of these, Bonney and Powell (1953) found that high-friendship first-graders conformed to classroom rules, were less disruptive, were more helpful and cooperative, and were less often alone during free play than low-friendship children. Krantz (1982) found a positive correlation ($r = .37$) between positive sociometric nominations and degree of social participation among preschool children using Parten's scale. Similarly, Quay and Jarrett (1984) found a modest positive correlation ($r = .26$) between positive nominations and frequency of positive peer interactions. Greenwood, Walker, Todd, and Hops (1979) obtained correlations ranging from .29 to .39 between positive sociometric scores and rate of prosocial interactions with preschool classmates. In none of the preceding studies were the relations among gender, type of social participation, and peer status clarified. On the other hand, Deutsch (1974) observed 60 preschool females and found no relationship ($r =$ .09) between the total amount of social interaction and number of positive sociometric nominations. One could speculate that Bonney and Powell's data on active participation, for example, applied only to boys, because their low-status group was made up of boys, primarily. If girls are more socially active than boys, then these status group differences in social participation might be an artifact of group composition.

Marshall and McCandless (1957a) found that frequency of associative play, friendly approach, and conversation with peers was positively related to positive sociometric nominations among preschoolers. No relation was found between hostile interaction and positive nominations. In a second paper (1957b), positive nominations were negatively related to adult association ($r = -.59$) and adult hostile interaction ($r = -.51$) but unrelated to friendly adult interaction. Although these results have been interpreted as evidence that highly dependent preschoolers are unpopular with peers, a more plausible explanation is that children who have difficulty following group rules are going to receive teacher reprimands and adult supervision more often than other children and are going to be less well liked by peers for the same reasons.

Moore and Updegraff (1964) found some evidence for a low positive relation ($r = .29$) between dependency on peers (e.g., asking another child for help or attention) and peer social preference. Peer status had low positive correlations with nurturance giving to peers ($r = .30$). There was no relationship between status and adult dependency among preschool groups.

McGuire (1973) also used a social preference score to relate status to observed aggressive behavior among preschoolers. Using the separate distributions of total aggression scores for males and females, he classified children as high or low in aggression (compared with same-gender peers) and examined the distributions of these children among high and low social preference groups. Although there were more aggressive males in the low preference group than in the high preference group (22 vs. 14), there were more aggressive females in the high social preference group than in the low preference group (21 vs. 8). It is interesting to note that the low-aggressive males and the high-aggressive females displayed about the same frequencies of aggression on an absolute scale. These frequencies were greater than those for low-aggressive girls and less than those for high-aggressive boys. Thus, high preference was associated with a moderate absolute level of aggression among both boys and girls.

More differentiated information on observed behavior and peer status among preschool children comes from reports in which both positive and negative sociometric nominations have been employed and analyzed separately. The most influential of these was a study by Hartup, Glazer, and Charlesworth (1967) in which positive and negative behaviors were observed among preschool children. Although positive peer status was strongly positively correlated with the frequency of positive behavior, it had a negligible relation to negative behavior. On the other hand, the negative sociometric score had strong positive correlations with negative behavior and no relation to positive behavior. The fact that a social preference score (positive minus negative nominations) had somewhat lower correlations with each type of behavior suggests that some information about status and behavior is lost by combining positive and negative nominations into a single score as was done by McGuire and by Moore and Updegraff.

Three other investigations of preschool behavior have used positive and negative nominations separately. Gottman's (1977) findings differed from the others and these differences cannot be attributed to small-sample effects, because his was one of the largest observation samples of preschoolers ($n = 113$) reported. Gottman's findings differed from the others in that he found negative nomination scores to be positively correlated with both frequency of peer interaction ($r = .33$) and negative peer interactions ($r = .30$). Positive nominations were unrelated to either variable or with his "tuned out" variable, a measure of time spent off task and alone, usually daydreaming or staring into space. Negative nominations were positively related to being tuned out ($r = .21$). Vaughn and Waters (1981), on the other hand, found positive nominations to be highly related to the frequency of peer interaction ($r = .70$) and amount of talk ($r = .51$). Negative nominations were positively correlated with hazing and teasing ($r = .57$) and hostile behavior ($r = .69$). Masters and Furman (1981) obtained findings similar to those of Hartup et al. and Vaughn and Waters, but of more modest strength of association. Differentiating between whether a behavior was initiated by the subject or directed toward the subject, they found that positive nominations were positively correlated with both giving ($r = .29$) and receiving ($r = .28$) positive behavior, whereas negative nominations were positively correlated with giving ($r = .34$) and receiving ($r = .41$) punishing behavior.

These preschool studies, viewed together, provide consistent evidence that when asked to nominate peers whom they like, preschool children identify peers who display positive behaviors. When asked to name peers whom they dislike, they identify peers who display negative behaviors. How does one reconcile the findings of Gottman (1977), which are discrepant with this picture? One difference between Gottman's study and the others was that his subjects came from lower socioeconomic backgrounds. Another difference was that Gottman related total peer interaction to status, whereas the others differentiated between positive and negative behaviors and did not examine relations between status and total interaction. Those investigators who have examined the total rate of interaction have found no relation to social status (Asher, Markell, & Hymel, 1981). However, given the high ratio of positive to negative interaction events reported in the papers by Hartup et al., Vaughn and Waters, and Masters and Furman, it seems unlikely that a combined interaction variable would have the same relations to peer status as Gottman found. It is possible that a high ratio of negative to positive interaction events in Gottman's low-SES sample could explain these discrepancies.

Two early studies (Koch, 1933; Lippitt, 1941) in which paired-comparison sociometrics were used with small samples of preschool children yielded contradictory findings that may have resulted from a failure to control adequately for gender effects within these small samples. Koch found moderately strong negative correlations ($-.40$ to $-.60$) between aggressive activities and popularity, as well as negative correlations for dawdling ($-.81$) and playing alone ($-.45$). Lippitt, on the other hand, found no relationships between either friendly behavior or hostile behavior and peer popularity.

Several large-sample studies of behavior and social status, as indexed by peer-rating scales, have been focused primarily on the degree of social involvement of children's preschool play activities. In one project (Rubin & Daniels-Beirness, 1983; Rubin, Daniels-Beirness, & Hayvren, 1982), investigators found that negative interactions and solitary play, particularly solitary dramatic play, were negatively correlated with social acceptance among kindergarten subjects. These correlations were quite low, however, accounting for no more than 4% of the variance in social acceptance. Total frequency of positive interactions was positively correlated with social acceptance among both kindergarteners ($r = .31$) and first-graders ($r = .35$). On the other hand, Goldman, Corsini, & de-Urioste (1980) found peer ratings to be negatively related to solitary play ($r = -.34$) but unrelated to total positive peer interaction. Interaction with adults was negatively related to peer ratings ($r = -.35$).

In summary, the observational findings on preschool children are marked by some inconsistencies. They also suffer from the fact that rate of social participation is the only variable that has been investigated by a majority of researchers. The observation categories used to assess behavior vary greatly from study to study. Many of these studies involved samples of fewer than 20 children, and this fact may account for the variability in correlations from one study to another. In many studies, male and female data are combined in correlational analyses. This is a major problem because there is evidence for gender differences on some variables. These differences may exaggerate or suppress relations between peer status and behavior.

Nonetheless, there are some patterns of behavior that do seem to be linked reliably to peer status among preschool children. Following rules and being cooperative and helpful are positively related to social acceptance and high social status. A child's frequency of positive interactions also seems to be positively related to peer status, although the correlations are often quite modest and account for relatively little variance in status.

Solitary behavior appears to be predictive of a lack of social acceptance among preschool children, although the correlations are quite low, generally. Some kinds of solitary behavior, such as being off task, dawdling, daydreaming, or engaging in fantasy behavior, seem to be most closely related to a lack of acceptance and are linked to rejected status. Conversely, the relation between total peer interaction and peer status is less well established. These two statements would seem to be mutually contradictory, and perhaps they are. However, one possible resolution to this seeming contradiction is that only some kinds of solitary behavior are related to peer rejection. Perhaps only solitary behavior that is aimless or inappropriate to the social context is related to rejected status, whereas the simple absence of active social involvement with other children is not related to peer status. The frequency of a child's interaction with adults has not had a consistent relation to peer status, but in some cases a negative relation with acceptance has been found. However, as was argued above, this relation does not necessarily reflect emotional dependency on adults but might reflect the activity of adult caretakers toward children who have difficulty complying with group rules or who are aggressive or off task.

Surprisingly, there are not many findings on aggression and preschool social standing. Three reports show a positive relation between physical and verbal aggression and social rejection, but in one of these the relation seems to hold true only for boys. There is also some evidence linking the frequency of negative peer interactions, disruptiveness, and teasing to rejected peer status. It appears, then, that prosocial, positively reinforcing behaviors contribute to social acceptance among preschool peers but do not predict whether or not a child will be socially rejected. Aggression and negatively reinforcing behaviors contribute to social rejection but do not predict a child's level of acceptance. Once again, a two-dimensional scheme is required to integrate these findings.

Studies of elementary school children

Only recently have there been observational studies of peer group behavior and social status among children older than those in preschool to first grade.

In one study, Gottman, Gonso, and Rasmussen (1975) compared high- and low-status children, based on a median split of positive nomination scores only, with respect to six behavior categories. They found that low-friendship third- and fourth-graders were more often alone and off task than high-friendship children. High-friendship children also received more positive behavior directed at them by other children. No group differences were found in the categories of alone and on task, distributing positive behavior, or distributing or receiving negative behavior.

Peer ratings were correlated with behavior frequencies in a study of mildly mentally retarded children from age 7 to 14 by Morrison, Forness, and MacMillan (1983), but insubstantial correlations were found between social acceptance and attending behavior ($r = .10$) and disruptive behavior ($r = -.13$). Green et al. (1980) correlated peer ratings with behavior among 116 third-graders and found positive correlations between ratings and being alone and on task ($r = .28$) and positive peer interactions ($r = .23$). A nonsignificant negative correlation between peer acceptance and negative peer behavior ($r = -.19$) was also obtained. In each of the preceding three studies, the data for boys and girls were combined for all analyses, so gender effects are not known and could have confounded the reported findings.

In only a few studies has gender been considered explicitly, making possible a clearer interpretation of the findings. Vosk et al. (1982), for example, observed popular and rejected boys and girls in the third grade. The popular boys and girls were more frequently on task in the classroom than rejected boys and girls. Rejected children initiated negative interactions with peers more frequently than did popular children. No group differences were found for total positive peer interactions. There were no effects for gender, indicating that the behavioral correlates of status were similar for boys and girls.

In a recent study, Asarnow (1983) divided fourth- and sixth-grade boys into high-status and low-status groups on the basis of the ratio of total negative class play nominations to total number of class play nominations received. This classification, therefore, was not strictly a sociometric one. High-status boys had higher behavior frequencies on the following variables: on-task behavior, receiving and initiating positive interactions with peers, and reciprocating positive exchanges. Low-status boys had higher frequencies of off-task behaviors, receiving and initiating both negative and neutral peer contacts, and initiating and receiving teacher instructions.

Although the preceding two studies describe behavior differences between high- and low-acceptance children that are reasonably consistent, comparing groups from the two extremes of high and low status contributes to some ambiguity about the relations between social status and behavior. It is not clear whether the differences just described distinguish extremely low-status children from those who are not low status (but are not necessarily of extremely high status) or distinguish extremely high-status children from everyone else. In other words, the behavior patterns that contribute to high acceptance may not necessarily be the polar opposite of those that lead to social rejection. To understand these behavior–status linkages more clearly, Dodge, Coie, and Brakke (1982) conducted two related investigations in which average-status children were contrasted with both popular and rejected groups. In the first study, boys and girls in each of these three status groups were observed in both classroom and playground settings. Dodge et al. found that rejected children were more often alone and off task than the other two groups and less often on task. Rejected children were more aggressive than average and popular children. Rejected children also initiated more social contact with other children in the classroom setting but initiated less contact on the playground; they were also rejected in their social approaches to others more often than popular or average children. Average and popular groups did not differ with respect to these variables. In the second study, a sociometrically neglected group was added to a design in which third- and fifth-grade boys were observed. Rejected boys differed from the other groups in all the ways just described and were also found to be interacting with teachers more than the other groups. Neglected boys were more often alone and on task than other children and made fewer social approaches to others. The robustness of these status group differences is emphasized by the fact that the first sample was from a racially mixed southern population, whereas the boys in the second sample were all white and from a midwestern community.

Ladd (1983) also contrasted popular, rejected, and average groups, as defined by peer ratings, and included both boys and girls. Third- and fourth-grade boys and girls were assigned to groups in equal numbers and observed on the playground at recess. Popular and average groups were observed in cooperative play and social conversation more often than the rejected group. Rejected children argued more often than the other two groups and were more often unoccupied on the playground. Popular children were less often engaged in onlooker behavior than average or rejected children. Two categories reflected status by gender effects. Rejected boys engaged in rough-and-tumble play more than popular or average boys, and rejected girls displayed more parallel play than popular or average girls. No status main effects or interactions in solitary play were observed.

In summary, in contrast to the research on preschool subjects, the last group of investigations provides a high degree of consensus on the behavior patterns associated with social rejection. Rejected children ʳeem to be off task more often and engage in positive interactions with others less often than other children. They are also involved in negative interactions with other children more often, particularly aggressive and argumentative interactions. They initiate interaction as frequently as do other children but are rebuffed at relatively high rates. They also engage in negative interactions with teachers at a high rate. Rejected boys also seem to be frequently engaged in rough-and-tumble play, giving a clue as to why they may be frequent recipients *and* initiators of aversive behavior, because this is the kind of behavior that can easily lead to misunderstanding and conflict. Rejected girls do not engage in this behavior more than other girls, however. Instead, they engage in more parallel play than other children. These facts mirror similar findings among primary grade children, indicating that aggressive behavior is highly relevant to status for boys, whereas social participation is relevant to status for girls.

Popular and average-status children were not very well differentiated from each other in the two studies (Dodge et al., 1982; Ladd, 1983) that included average subjects in their designs. This would suggest that in many of the other studies in which only high- and low-status groups were contrasted, it was the low-status group that was most distinctive from the rest of the population. The one distinction obtained between popular and average children was that reported by Ladd, who found that popular children were less often onlookers to peer activity. It may be that the relative nondistinctiveness of the categories used to record prosocial behavior, coupled with the difficulties of recording more complex verbal interactions in natural settings, has restricted the possibility of identifying behavior patterns that distinguish popular children from average children. It is also possible that children become highly popular for reasons other than their behavioral characteristics.

Only a few reports on the behavior of sociometrically neglected children are available. Neglected boys seem to engage in solitary appropriate activity more than other children, and they make fewer attempts to initiate social interaction. They engage in fewer acts of aggression than rejected children. The consequences of combining children from these two groups into a single low-status group to be compared with a high-status group are obvious.

Multi-age, multi-method studies

The preceding review has been organized according to source of data about behavior relating to social status, and with a few exceptions, there has been little repetition of authorship across these sections. Cantrell and Prinz (1985) employed both peer assessments and teacher ratings, for example. There are a few recent studies in which the issues of method or cross-age comparisons have been dealt with directly. Ladd and Mars (1986) collected behavior data on 63 preschool children using all three sources of data as a way to assess the validity of peer assessments of aggression, prosocial behavior, and solitary play. Peer-rated aggression had a low negative correlation ($-.25$ to $-.20$) with a peer-rating measure of status. Cooperative play was positively related to status (.50), but social conversation was unrelated to status as was teacher-oriented behavior. Solitary play had a moderate negative relation ($-.44$) to peer status. Although correlations between teacher ratings, behavior observations, and peer status were not reported, Ladd and Mars did provide data on the intercorrelations between the three sources of behavior data. Teachers and peers agreed on physical ($r = .54$) and verbal aggression ($r = .41$), but peer ratings and behavior observations showed less agreement ($r = .29$) for physical aggression. The correlations for prosocial behavior were in the low positive range ($r = .28$ to $.39$). Peers and observers agreed highly ($r = .60$) on solitary play.

Beck, Collins, Overholser, and Terry (1985) attempted a multi-age, multi-method study with first- and sixth-grade children; however, they obtained only 10-min samples of observed behavior on each subject. As a result, perhaps, aggressive and negative peer interactions occurred too infrequently for analyses of these behaviors to be carried out. The teacher ratings on the CTRS yielded results similar to those of Vosk et al. cited above.

A more comprehensive multi-age, multi-method study was completed by two of the present authors (Coie & Dodge, 1988) on 141 first-grade boys and 161 third-grade boys who were categorized by sociometric nominations into the five status groups of Coie et al. (1982). Peer assessments, teacher ratings, and 60 min of behavior observations sampled from class and play times were contrasted across these five status groups. The results obtained from peer and teacher sources were quite similar to those found with third-, fourth-, or fifth-grade samples in earlier work (Coie et al., 1982; Coie et al., 1984). There were no significant interaction effects for age and status. Rejected and controversial boys were more aggressive and disruptive than other status groups, and rejected boys were less prosocial. Observers confirmed the greater aggressiveness of rejected and controversial boys at the first-grade level but not at the third-grade level. Third-grade boys were much less frequently observed in aggressive interactions than first-graders – so much so, that it was not possible to make any status group distinctions.

Whereas teachers described rejected boys as the most socially isolated at both grade levels, observers did not find that to be true. Rather, observers described neglected boys as the most solitary during play times, although this solitary play was seen as appropriate to the situation. Rejected boys were no more solitary than average boys, whereas controversial boys were less solitary and more often engaged in prosocial play. Teachers also described rejected boys as having more academic problems, a circumstance that was mirrored in observer reports of greater off-task activity in the classroom by rejected boys.

Several conclusions about methods and age effects can be drawn from this study. One is that there is reasonably good cross-method agreement for aggression variables when the subjects are still young enough to be relatively oblivious to outside observers. By middle elementary school, greater reliance must be placed on inside observers such as peers and teachers. Although observers continue to be able to provide reasonable estimates of activity levels both within the classroom and in play settings, teachers and observers disagree on solitary activity, and as has been suggested earlier in this chapter, different conceptions of this construct may be employed by these two sources.

Observations of behavior within new peer groups

Having a fairly coherent picture of the behavior that distinguishes rejected children from other children makes it tempting to conclude that these are the behaviors that cause rejected children to become rejected by their peers. The problem, as Moore (1967) first pointed out, is that in all of the preceding studies behavior differences associated with status are observed well after status has been achieved, making it difficult to sort out just which differences originally contributed to status and which ones were the result of status.

There are clearly ways in which an acquired status could lead a child to behave differently. For example, peers who come to view a child as well liked or disliked may change their behavior toward that child. Dodge and Frame (1982) have shown that peers become biased in their perceptions of a child and alter their behavior toward that child once they have identified that child as liked or disliked. They may assume a disliked child is blameworthy of negative outcomes, and therefore they may exclude him or her from play activities. Alternatively, they may make it very easy for a liked child to succeed. These behaviors, in turn, may lead the child to respond in ways that perpetuate the peers' perceptions. A disliked child may get angry and aggress in response to unfair treatment or may give up and withdraw. The child's retaliatory behaviors thus may have little to do with the acquisition of his or her status in the first place.

Until recently, this problem presented serious limitations for interpreting all the research dealing with the behavioral correlates of sociometric status. The authors of this chapter, however, have developed a methodology for observing the acquisition of status as it actually unfolds over time. This methodology consists of bringing together previously unacquainted children in free-play situations and allowing them to interact over a long enough period of time for differences in peer status to emerge. Two investigations employing this methodology have been completed thus far. Coie and Kupersmidt (1983) observed the behavior of popular, average, neglected, and rejected fourth-grade boys (as determined by their classroom peers) in play groups made up of either familiar classmates or unfamiliar boys from other schools. The 10 play groups (5 with familiar boys and 5 with unfamiliar boys) met once a week for 6 weeks. Each group was composed of a popular-, an average-, a neglected-, and a rejected-status boy. One feature of the research design was that each boy was driven to and from each group session by a separate adult driver so that all interactions among the boys could be recorded on videotape during the actual group sessions. During the ride home from each session, the driver interviewed each boy about his play preferences among the other members of the group. These responses provided a session-by-session social status ranking that could be related to status in the classroom and to behavior patterns in the group.

The play preference rankings in these groups proved to be highly correlated with status rankings in the classroom. For the familiar groups, this positive correlation emerged by the end of the second session ($r = .56$), and for the unfamiliar groups, this happened by the end of the third session ($r = .54$). The play group rankings and classroom rankings continued to be highly correlated in all subsequent sessions. These findings indicate that status is stable across settings, indicating that it is something about the child that accounts for peer rejection. This is an important point because it indicates that status is not solely reflective of group dynamics or the accident of the group and child interactions.

Analyses of the videotapes of these play groups revealed a number of behavioral differences among boys of different types of social status. In general, the differences between rejected boys and other boys held true across both familiar and unfamiliar groups. Rejected boys made more hostile and aversive comments than did other boys and were more often engaged in physical aggression than all but the average-status boys. Most of the aggressive conflicts took place between the rejected and average-status boys. When asked at the conclusion of the sixth group session who tended to start fights, however, there was a consensus that the rejected boys most often did so. In a subsequent analysis of conflict episodes in the unfamiliar groups (Coie & Benenson, 1983), average and rejected boys were judged by unbiased adult coders to be equally likely to become angry and act aggressively when there appeared to be some justification for their anger. However, only the rejected boys were observed to become angry and assaultive without apparent adequate justification. It was as if the rejected boys found something worth fighting over in situations that the other boys viewed as relatively benign. Given the tendency for rejected, aggressive boys to make attributions that peers are acting in hostile ways even in circumstances that do not warrant these interpretations (Dodge & Frame, 1982), this behavioral pattern is not surprising.

Ladd's (1983) finding that rejected boys are involved in rough-and-tumble play more often than are other boys received some corroboration in this study, although it was both the average and the rejected boys who most often engaged in this activity. Because rough-and-tumble play requires more than one participant, as does physical conflict, the fact that the groups contained only four boys may have contributed to similar frequencies of these kinds of interactions among average- and rejected-status groups. Of the boys available to engage in these kinds of activities with the rejected boy, the average boy would be the most likely prospect. Rejected boys also were observed to talk as much or more so than other boys, and this held true across both familiar and unfamiliar groups.

In general, the rejected boys appeared to be quite interactive in these groups. There was one important exception to this pattern, and it has importance for understanding some of the earlier data on the off-task solitary behavior of rejected children in school settings. In the present study, rejected boys were relatively likely to engage in solitary off-task behavior at times when the rest of the boys were engaged in a structured group task or game. One may be tempted to attribute this behavioral difference to attention deficits that make it difficult for rejected children to stay on task (Milich & Landau, 1984) or to a tendency toward withdrawn behavior that is itself a contributor to peer rejection. However, the onset of this excess of solitary inappropriate behavior was temporally linked to the point when the rejected boys actually began to be rejected by peers in the new group setting. Rejected boys in the familiar groups became rejected after the second session and began to stop participating in the structured group activity significantly more often than others only by the third and fourth weekly sessions. Among the rejected boys in the unfamiliar groups (who came to be rejected after the third session), they did not become significantly more solitary during the structured group activity until the fifth and sixth sessions. These findings suggest that although rejected children may have more difficulty staying on task generally, social factors may contribute in important ways to this type of behavioral withdrawal. Moore's suggestion that children respond to the feelings that other children have about them may be reflected in some of the social withdrawal behavior of rejected children. They lose interest in group activities as the social reinforcement value of these activities diminishes, or they leave them because they have a growing sense that their presence is unwanted by others. Clearly, their withdrawal is primarily a consequence of their acquired status and not an antecedent of it.

Neglected boys appeared to be the most reactive to the group's composition. With familiar classmates they behaved much the way that they do in the classroom (Dodge et al., 1982). They were much less socially active than other boys. They talked less and engaged in fewer prosocial and aversive behaviors. They avoided rough-and-tumble activity. Neglected boys were also the ones that familiar peers rated as shy and isolated. Among unfamiliar peers, however, they became more socially active, in prosocial ways. They showed more supportive behavior than most of the other boys. They were also as involved in rough-and-tumble play as other boys. However, consistent with their style in familiar groups, they refrained from negative, aversive behavior. Thus, the strongest behavioral patterns of the neglected boys across both types of group situations were a minimum of aggressive and hostile activity and a tendency to play alone in socially appropriate activities. These findings suggest that neglected boys may be able to change their status in new groups with relative ease. This is consistent with findings that neglected status is relatively unstable over time (Coie & Dodge, 1983).

A characteristic of the popular boys that emerged in this study is one that may contribute to their status as leaders, noted earlier in the discussion of peer assessment data. Popular boys engaged in more norm setting than other boys. They reminded others of the rules, they provided suggestions and directions for handling difficult or ambiguous situations, and established norms for behavior in the play setting.

This study also provided an insight into one way that concurrent observations of status and behavior may result in misleading conclusions. In the familiar group situation, popular boys were much less often the target of abusive or aversive acts by others. In the unfamiliar group situation, however, they were equally as often the recipients of this kind of behavior as anyone else. In both groups, popular boys directed abusive behavior toward others less frequently than did average or rejected boys. This fact means that they were able to control the impulse to retaliate aggressively in situations where they were just getting to know new boys and were subjected to the normal experience of aversive acts by others. In the familiar peer group they are less often subjected to negative behavior, so it was probably easier for them to avoid conflict. However, they seemed to have earned this privilege by the way they handled themselves in the early stages of the acquaintance process, as demonstrated in the unfamiliar group condition.

In another study of the acquisition of status, Dodge (1983) formed groups of unfamiliar second-grade boys unselected for prior social status. They were observed in play groups of 8 boys that met for eight almost daily sessions. After the last session, each of the 8 boys in each group was interviewed about his positive and negative sociometric choices. Popular, rejected, neglected, controversial, and average-status boys were identified on the bases of sociometric nominations within the group. The earlier behaviors of these five groups were then compared.

Dodge found that boys who came to be rejected in their groups engaged in more inappropriate play, talked more, made more hostile comments than average-status boys, and were observed to hit other boys more than any other group. They also displayed more inappropriate solitary play than any other group except the neglected group. In the early sessions of their groups, the rejected boys made frequent social approaches to other boys but were rebuffed at a high rate. They decreased the frequency of these approaches in the later sessions and became increasingly isolated in their play. It is clear that this study corroborates the Coie and Kupersmidt (1983) finding that social withdrawal in rejected boys occurs only *after* they have had negative experiences with peers and is not a likely contributor to their rejected status.

Popular boys, by contrast, maintained a constant pattern of social approach behavior across the eight sessions and met with frequent positive reactions by the other boys. Popular boys were also less frequently engaged in conversation with the adult leader and were less frequently reprimanded by the leader. The popular boys were, again, named as leaders by their peers in postexperiment interviews.

The consistent picture of popular boys from these two studies is that they are not overly assertive in the early stages of group life. They spend much of their time in active interaction with the group in such a way that they have relatively little contact with adult supervisors. Eventually, they come to be viewed as leaders by their peers.

Neglected boys engaged in fewer aggressive acts than other boys in this second study also. They were more often observed in solitary play than other groups. As was true in the Coie and Kupersmidt study, neglected boys were no less involved in rough-and-tumble play than any but the controversial boys.

Although there were only three controversial boys identified among the total of 48 participants, a proportion (7%) similar to that found by Coie et al. (1982) in a study of 848 children, their observed behavior matched the peer descriptions noted in the Coie et al. study. They were more often involved in cooperative *and* rough-and-tumble play than other groups and less often engaged in solitary play. They talked a lot and made hostile comments more often than other boys. They also were more often reprimanded by the adult leader than other boys.

These two studies have yielded similar patterns of relationship between the social behavior of boys (including aggression, group entry, and leadership) and the emergence of social status in newly established groups. The similarities are striking given the differences in the two samples and in some design characteristics. The Coie and Kupersmidt sample consisted of black, fourth-grade boys from schools in a southern city, whereas Dodge's sample were mostly white, second-grade boys from midwestern small-town schools. In the former study, the boys met only six times at weekly intervals and in groups of 4. Boys in the latter study met almost daily for eight sessions in groups of 8. The two reports provide complementary and congruent pictures of the temporal sequence of social approach, rejection, and social withdrawal among children who become rejected in new peer situations. Both studies indicate that aggressive behavior is clearly associated with the emergence of rejected status.

Using sociometric and behavior data collected on boys in a summer camp program for children referred for behavioral and social problems, Wright, Giammarino, and Parad (1986) have produced some interesting counterpoints to those generated by the two new-group studies just discussed. Wright et al. argue that there are limitations to the search for invariant correlates of peer social status and that similarities between persons and groups need to be considered. They argue that aggression is less likely to be a correlate of rejected status in highly aggressive peer groups than in groups low in aggression. To test this hypothesis the living-group units within which peer status measures were obtained were categorized into high- and low-aggression groups, and individual behavior scores on three variables – aggression, withdrawal, and prosocial behavior – were correlated with social status within each type of group. As predicted, aggression was negatively correlated with status in low-aggression groups but was uncorrelated with status in high-aggression groups. Conversely, withdrawal was negatively correlated with status in high-aggression groups but uncorrelated with status in low-aggression groups. Prosocial behavior was positively correlated with status in both high- and low-aggression groups. These results held true both with a cohort for which positive nominations (acceptance) was the only index of status and with a cohort for which social preference scores were available.

Subjects from this second cohort were categorized into four status groups (popular, rejected, average, and neglected) and univariate analyses of status differences in aggression and withdrawal were performed across all groups and within high- and low-aggression groups. Across all groups significant status effects were found for both aggression and withdrawal, with rejected boys having the highest aggression scores and neglected boys the highest withdrawal scores. In the low-aggression groups, the greater aggressiveness of rejected boys was even more striking, and although neglected boys were clearly the most withdrawn, there was no significant status effect for withdrawal. In the high-aggression groups, however, no significant status effect was obtained for aggression, and the significant status effect for withdrawal reflected greatest withdrawal among rejected boys, followed by neglected boys.

An important point is made by the Wright et al. study regarding the role of group context in determining the relationship between individual behavior and group status. Behavior that deviates seriously from local group norms is more likely to be related to rejection in that group than behavior that violates more general norms but not local norms. This point may serve to explain some of the inconsistencies found in the literature. The fact that Wright et al. studied groups of boys with serious behavior and social problems in their normal school settings must be remembered before generalizing from their findings. Their population may have been more aggressive than normal school samples. In fact, the behavioral data from Coie et al. (1982) look more like the low-aggression group comparisons of Wright et al. than combined-groups comparisons. Thus, while aggression may be a predictor of rejection in most peer groups, it should be recognized that this will not always be true and, in fact, the determinants of rejection may be highly group-specific in many circumstances.

Conclusions

The data from peers, teachers, and observers are quite consistent with respect to the correlates of high status or acceptance among preschool children. High-status children are described as helpful and considerate of others, and they follow the rules, particularly the rules for peer interaction. They are also very actively engaged in positive peer interaction. The findings for 8- to 12-year-olds, as integrated from all three sources, are similar to those for younger children except that greater emphasis is placed on the athletic and academic competence of popular children as children get older. This trend may reflect the increasing emphasis on competence by the school system as children move from primary to middle school grades and the fact that children seem to engage more consciously in social comparisons of achievement as they enter the third- and fourth-grade years (Ruble, Boggiana, Feldman, & Loebl, 1980). The increasing developmental emphasis on competence is also seen in the peer reports of well-liked adolescents. Their peers mention physical and social competence as primary reasons for liking popular adolescents.

Social rejection, on the other hand, is clearly related to aggression, rule violations, hyperactivity, and disruptiveness, in both the youngest and the middle age-groups. However, there is evidence that aggression is more a factor in the rejection of boys than of girls. Less is known about aggression and rejection among adolescents, although overt aggression appears to play a less significant role in peer rejection than among younger age-groups.

Whereas there is only a slight indication of a relation between social withdrawal and rejected status among preschool children, this relation appears much more clearly for the middle school group. However, two important qualifications must be stated about this relation. First, from the standpoint of teachers, the relation is much more true for girls than for boys. That is, rejected girls are withdrawn but rejected boys are not. Second, a closer look at the phenomenon of social withdrawal suggests that social withdrawal may be a consequence of rejection rather than a cause of rejection. In the initial phase of peer interactions, children who ultimately come to be rejected have been observed to approach others frequently. These same children have a higher probability of being rebuffed in their social overtures than do other children, however. When this phenomenon has been observed among groups of children who have just become acquainted for the first time, withdrawal increases in frequency only after these children have become clearly rejected by the group. Furthermore, in those studies in which popularity ratings have been found to be negatively correlated with withdrawal scores, these withdrawal scores have been factor scores that reflect not only isolated activity but hypersensitivity and other forms of social inadequacy. It is possible that these other forms of social inadequacy characterize the rejected children more closely than do the shyness items, because the latter have lower factor loadings than the former. This point is underscored by the adolescent peer assessment data in which the relation between sociometric rejection and being a frequent target of peer group abuse and not being accepted into group activities is particularly evident.

One way to interpret the developmental findings on aggression, withdrawal, and social rejection is in the context of age changes in the relative frequency and nature of aggressive behavior. Among preschool children, aggression is much more commonplace than it is among older children. Children who are overly aggressive and disruptive of group activities are the ones preschool children tend to dislike. The same thing is true in elementary school; however, as the general frequency of physical aggression decreases with age, verbal aggression and disruptiveness of classroom order become the more salient dimensions of the behavior that contributes to peer rejection. Also, because behavior becomes more differentiated as children get older, there may be an increasing number of ways to become rejected, so that aggression by itself becomes relatively less important to the general phenomenon of peer rejection. Withdrawal becomes a correlate of rejection with increasing age because rejected children have a history of being rebuffed and disliked, and because withdrawal can take many different forms as children grow older. Recall that one of the consistent observations of middle-school-aged rejected children is that they are more often off task in the classroom situation. This off-task activity sometimes takes the form of solitary, disruptive behavior (Krehbiel & Coie, 1985) and sometimes involves ineffective attempts at social interaction that are refused (Dodge et al., 1982). One consequence of this nuisance activity by rejected children is that other children begin to let them know that they do not want them around. The rejected children begin to withdraw from group activities and become more alienated from the group. If this cycle is repeated across time, then one would expect this pattern of rejection and avoidance to become increasingly characteristic of the interaction of older rejected children and their peers. As group sentiment coalesces against them, rejected children react by spending more time alone during group activities.

It is also possible, as Rubin, LeMare, and Lollis argue in Chapter 8 of this volume, that some children are rejected because they are consistently withdrawn. Data are not yet available to confirm or deny this contention. One reason for this lack of data may be that this is true for only a small number of rejected children and the behavior of these children is masked when it is included in group comparisons that are dominated by the larger subset of aggressive or disruptive rejected children. It is important to keep in mind, also, that Rubin et al. do not argue that it is solitary behavior per se that leads to rejection but, rather, social withdrawal that is a result of social anxiety and insecurity.

The behavior of socially neglected children is much less easy to characterize. Although these children have definition in sociometric terms, it is appropriate to question whether they have in common any significant behavior patterns. Not surprisingly, because they are defined sociometrically by the absence of notice by their peers, not much is learned about them from peer and teacher report data. There is some evidence that peers see them as shy and withdrawn. This description is corroborated by four observational studies in which they were described as more frequently engaged in solitary play than other children. Also, they have been observed to be much less aggressive than all other children. Under some circumstances they have been found to be noticeably interactive and supportive, but even when more visible in these positive ways, they are still less aggressive than others, even popular boys. These characteristics of neglected children make it clear why failing to separate them from average or rejected children, which occurs in social status comparisons based on a single dimension of peer status, will result in misleading observational findings and inflated variances in the behavior scores of contrasted status groups of subjects.

The status group most unlike the neglected group, the controversial group, has been studied the least. In part, this is because few children in any peer group fit the sociometric criterion of frequent mention on both positive and negative choice items. On the other hand, in every study in which a controversial group has been identified, this group has been the most visible and the behavior patterns associated with this group have been most consistent. Controversial children are the most socially active of all children. They are often engaged in active interaction with peers and are rarely observed in solitary activity. They talk frequently with peers and adults and make the peer group laugh with their humor. They are also among the most aggressive of all children, and because of their disruptive activities, they are most often reprimanded by adult supervisors. They appear to be easily aroused to anger and yet are also seen as much more facilitative in groups than rejected children and are group leaders. It is easy to see why a group could not sustain the presence of too many controversial children.

The neglected and controversial groups have been studied primarily among the 8- to 12-year-old population and so it is not possible to draw conclusions about developmental trends for these groups. More than likely, the same developmental patterns noted for changes in popular and rejected status would hold for these two groups also. In general, the broad correlates of status – cooperation and aggression – hold true for all age-groups. The best available evidence suggests that the behavioral bases for peer status change with age in subtle ways, or at least in ways that are more subtle than the categories with which behavior has been coded thus far. Aggression, for example, becomes less physical and more verbal. It also becomes increasingly less observable to outsiders. This would suggest that the manifestations of unacceptable peer behavior tend to take more complicated forms with age and are more reflective of self-conscious processes.

Directions for the future

This review has been organized in terms of the three major sources of information on children's social behavior. In light of the findings just summarized, some conclusions about the future of each of these approaches can be offered.

Direct observation by unbiased observers generally has been regarded as the standard against which other sources should be evaluated because it is less likely to be contaminated by biases stemming from existing relationships between the observer and the target. Nevertheless, significant restrictions on the potential value of the information to be gained from this source are obvious. One problem is that many potentially interesting subcategories of behavior, such as the distinction between proactive and reactive aggression, occur infrequently in the settings most available to adult observers. The same thing is true for types of socially awkward or anxious behavior that falls short of being blatantly disruptive or hostile. As a result, it is difficult to obtain reliable observer agreement for these categories and it is difficult to make statistically reliable status group comparisons. Thus the investigator is forced to return to more global categories such as "negative interaction" or "active play." Although one could ask peers or teachers to make these finer distinctions in their reports, there is no reason to expect that their accounts would be more reliable or valid. They would be biased by the same effects of infrequent occurrence and a natural tendency to recall behavioral events in terms consistent with one's general evaluative orientation toward the child being described.

One solution to this problem is to observe children in situations that are organized and engineered so that they will increase the likelihood of behavioral events that normally occur less frequently. The study of peer group entry behavior (see Chapter 3, this volume) has frequently relied on this procedure. Similarly, the strategy of organizing groups of children for play in new settings carries with it the possibility of creating settings that engender certain types of interaction. Although this strategy, as utilized by Coie and Kupersmidt (1983) and Dodge (1983), was designed to distinguish the behavior patterns associated with the emergence of social status in new peer groups from those associated with status in long-standing peer groups, to some extent these investigators consciously organized these play situations to increase the occurrence of some forms of problematic behavior. Coie and Kupersmidt, for example, placed a single, electronic, hand-held game in the room to force children to negotiate over the use of a valued toy. They also included in the room inflatable boxing mitts to increase the occurrence of the kinds of rough-and-tumble play that often shift into aggressive encounters. Likewise, the adult supervisor left the room at planned intervals to give the children a sense of freedom from adult constraints and the necessity of managing themselves. If a more differentiated understanding of the relation between behavior and social status is to emerge, it may require the further use of such planned contexts for observation as well as the systematic study of the effects of contexts on behavior.

A second positive consequence to the strategy of organizing new play groups is that social behavior can be videotaped. Tapes can be coded in finer detail than live observation coding systems will permit. Because tapes can be reviewed repeatedly, all of the activities of a group can be coded, in terms of both individual and interactive activity. Low-frequency events can be mined for greater detail, and observer reliability for these events can be improved. All of these advantages will permit greater differentiation among the dependent variables that can be considered, and less reliance on molar-level variables will be necessary.

The strategy of creating new play groups may also enable researchers to study the social behavior of adolescents. Although adolescents are more self-conscious about their social behavior than younger children, carefully constructed peer interaction situations conceivably could be developed to permit an analysis of behavior–status linkages in adolescence based on observed behaviors rather than peer report.

When the behavioral variables used in future observational research become more fine-grained and when direct observations of older subjects become more common, we would expect to see greater evidence for developmental differences in the basis for social rejection than the literature currently reflects. Although the developmental lag hypothesis has been applied to cognitive aspects of social functioning, the possibility that developmental lags in behavior (e.g., assertiveness, peer approach, defending oneself, or negotiating conflict) are responsible for peer rejection has not been explored. Detailed studies of behavior at different ages will make that possible. The implications of having more detailed accounts of the developmental correlates of peer rejection are obvious to those whose purpose is intervention. Rather than having to work toward very global changes in behavior for a targeted age-group, it would be possible to specify age-related goals for intervention.

The preceding review suggests several improvements in the way teachers and peers might be used as informants on the causes of peer rejection. It is clear that these groups are important sources of information and should be exploited more fully in the future. Most of the existing studies utilizing these sources have relied on omnibus assessment instruments, however. Although the factor scores generated from these omnibus questionnaires have the advantage of psychometric stability, the factor scores provide very little differentiated information about the behavior of rejected children. As has been noted, the labels attached to these factor scores can be misleading in some ways. Disruptiveness, showing off, and hyperactivity are confounded with physical and verbal aggression in many Aggression factors, for example. Even more problematic is the combination of solitary behavior, negative affect, and rejection by peers within factors labeled as Isolation or Withdrawal.

One solution to this problem is to place more reliance on peer or teacher ratings for single items rather than factor or cluster scores. There is evidence for the adequate stability of individual peer assessment items (Coie & Dodge, 1983). Thus it is reasonable to consider using fewer items in scales that are carefully constructed to address the relation between particular types of behavior and peer rejection. This strategy could be especially useful with teachers, who could be instructed in the use of the checklist prior to the period of time over which they are asked to report on children in their classes. In other words, just as unbiased observers are trained in a coding system, teachers could be trained to look for specific behaviors on a checklist.

Asher (1983) has observed that behavior studies typically account for a relatively small percentage of the variance in status. That observation is borne out in much of the literature just reviewed. Some of the reasons behind this situation have been discussed. There are problems of access to the important kinds of interaction (such as private conversations) that may contribute to a child's status among peers. The categories used to describe behavior have usually been too broad. The assumption of status group homogeneity is not entirely supportable; children are rejected for different reasons. Factors such as the timing of an act or the interactional context of behavior certainly have significant impact on the way others will interpret behavior, and yet these factors have not been incorporated into observational designs. Likewise, the use of frequency-of-behavior codes often results in the neglect of qualitative differences among behaviors of ostensibly similar content. These are just some of the reasons why the connections between status and behavior are not as powerful as they might be. Still, the general picture provided by the studies reviewed here, covering a broad range of methods and subject groups, is a remarkably coherent one. The recent methodologies involving the observation of children in structured settings or in new groups provide reason for optimism in the continuing search for a behavioral understanding of the processes by which children come to be rejected by their peers.

References

Asarnow, J. R. (1983). Children with peer adjustment problems: Sequential and nonsequential analysis of school behaviors. *Journal of Consulting and Clinical Psychology, 51*, 709–717.

Asher, S. R. (1983). Social competence and peer status: Recent advances and future directions. *Child Development, 54*, 1427–1434.

Asher, S. R., & Hymel, S. (1981). Children's social competence in peer relations: Sociometric and behavioral assessment. In J. D. Wine & M. D. Smye (Eds.), *Social competence* (pp. 125–157). New York: Guilford.

Asher, S. R., Markell, R. A., & Hymel, S. (1981). Identifying children at risk in peer relations: A critique of the rate-of-interaction approach to assessment. *Child Development, 52*, 1239–1245.

Beck, S., Collins, L., Overholser, J., & Terry, K. (1985). A cross-sectional assessment of the relationship of social competence measures to peer friendship and likeability in elementary-age children. *Genetic, Social, and General Psychology Monographs, 3*, 41–63.

Bonney, M. E., & Powell, J. (1953). Differences in social behavior between sociometrically high and sociometrically low children. *Journal of Educational Research, 46*, 481–496.

Bower, E. M. (1960). *Early identification of emotionally handicapped children in school.* Springfield, IL: Charles C. Thomas.

Bukowski, W. M., & Newcomb, A. F. (1984). Stability and determinants of sociometric status and friendship choice: A longitudinal perspective. *Developmental Psychology, 20*, 941–952.

Cairns, R. B., & Green, J. A. (1979). How to assess personality and social patterns: Observations or ratings? In R. B. Cairns (Ed.), *The analysis of social interactions* (pp. 209–226). Hillsdale, NJ: Lawrence Erlbaum.

Cairns, R. B., Perrin, J., & Cairns, B. D. (1985). Social structure and social cognition in early adolescence: Affiliate patterns. *Journal of Early Adolescence, 5*, 339–355.

Cantrell, V. L., & Prinz, R. J. (1985). Multiple perspectives of rejected, neglected, and accepted children: Relation between sociometric status and behavioral characteristics. *Journal of Consulting and Clinical Psychology, 53*, 884–889.

Carlson, C. L., Lahey, B. B., & Neeper, R. (1984). Peer assessment of the social behavior of accepted, rejected, and neglected children. *Journal of Abnormal Child Psychology, 12*, 189–198.

Clifford, E. (1963). Social visibility. *Child Development, 34*, 799–808.

Coie, J. D., & Benenson, J. F. (1983). *A qualitative analysis of the relationship between peer rejection and physically aggressive behavior.* Unpublished manuscript, Duke University, Durham, NC.

Coie, J. D., & Dodge, K. A. (1983). Continuities and changes in children's social status: A five-year longitudinal study. *Merrill-Palmer Quarterly, 29*, 261–282.

Coie, J. D., & Dodge, K. A. (1988). Multiple sources of data on social behavior and social status in the school: A cross-age comparison. *Child Development, 59*, 815–829.

Coie, J. D., Dodge, K. A., & Copottelli, H. (1982). Dimensions and types of social status: A cross-age perspective. *Developmental Psychology, 18*, 557–571.

Coie, J. D., Finn, M., & Krehbiel, G. (1984, September). *Controversial children: Peer assessment evidence for status category distinctiveness.* Paper presented at annual meeting of the American Psychological Association, Toronto.

Coie, J. D., & Kupersmidt, J. B. (1983). A behavioral analysis of emerging social status in boys' groups. *Child Development, 54*, 1400–1416.

Coie, J. D., & Pennington, B. F. (1976). Children's perceptions of deviance and disorder. *Child Development, 47*, 400–413.

Deutsch, F. (1974). Observational and sociometric measures of peer popularity and their relationship to egocentric communication in female preschoolers. *Developmental Psychology, 10*, 745–747.

Dodge, K. A. (1983). Behavioral antecedents of peer social status. *Child Development, 54*, 1386–1399.

Dodge, K. A., Coie, J. D., & Brakke, N. P. (1982). Behavior patterns of socially rejected and neglected preadolescents: The roles of social approach and aggression. *Journal of Abnormal Child Psychology, 10*, 389–410.

Dodge, K. A., & Frame, C. L. (1982). Social cognitive biases and deficits in aggressive boys. *Child Development, 53*, 620–635.

Edelbrock, C., & Achenbach, T. M. (1984). The teacher version of the Child Behavior Profile: I. Boys aged 6–11. *Journal of Consulting and Clinical Psychology, 52*, 207–217.

Elkins, D. (1958). Some factors related to the choice status of ninety eighth-grade children in a school society. *Genetic Psychology Monographs, 58*, 207–272.

Feinberg, M. R., Smith, M., & Schmidt, R. (1958). An analysis of expressions used by adolescents at varying economic levels to describe accepted and rejected peers. *Journal of Genetic Psychology, 93*, 133–148.

Foster, S. L., & Ritchey, W. L. (1979). Issues in the assessment of social competence in children. *Journal of Applied Behavior Analysis, 12*, 625–638.

French, D. C., & Waas, G. A. (1985). Behavior problems of peer-neglected and peer-rejected elementary-aged children: Parent and teacher perspectives. *Child Development, 56,* 246–252.

Goldman, J. A., Corsini, D. A., & deUrioste, R. (1980). Implications of positive and negative sociometric status for assessing the social competence of young children. *Journal of Applied Developmental Psychology, 1,* 209–220.

Gottman, J. M. (1977). Toward a definition of social isolation in children. *Child Development, 48,* 513–517.

Gottman, J. M., Gonso, J., & Rasmussen, B. (1975). Social interaction, social competence, and friendship in children. *Child Development, 46,* 709–718.

Green, K. D., Forehand, R., Beck, S. J., & Vosk, B. (1980). An assessment of the relationship among measures of children's social competence and children's academic achievement. *Child Development, 51,* 1149–1156.

Green, K. D., Vosk, B., Forehand, R., & Beck, S. (1981). An examination of differences among sociometrically identified accepted, rejected, and neglected children. *Child Study Journal, 11,* 117–124.

Greenwood, C., Walker, H., Todd, N., & Hops, H. (1979). Selecting a cost-effective screening measure for the assessment of preschool social withdrawal. *Journal of Applied Behavior Analysis, 12,* 639–652.

Gronlund, N. E., & Anderson, L. (1957). Personality characteristics of socially rejected junior high school pupils. *Education, Administration, and Supervision, 43,* 329–338.

Hartup, W. W. (1983). Peer relations. In E. M. Hetherington (Ed.), *Handbook of child psychology: Vol. 4. Socialization, personality, and social development* (pp. 103–196, 4th ed.). New York: Wiley.

Hartup, W. W., Glazer, J., & Charlesworth, R. (1967). Peer reinforcement and sociometric status. *Child Development, 38,* 1017–1024.

Hunt, J. M., & Solomon, R. L. (1942). The stability and some correlates of group-status in a summer-camp group of young boys. *American Journal of Psychology, 55,* 33–45.

Hymel, S., Freigang, R., Franke, S., Both, L., Bream, L., & Borys, S. (1983, June). *Children's attributions for social situations: Variations as a function of social status and self-perception variables.* Paper presented at the annual meeting of the Canadian Psychological Association, Winnipeg, Manitoba.

Hymel, S., & Rubin, K. H. (1985). Children with peer relationships and social skills problems: Conceptual, methodological, and developmental issues. In G. J. Whitehurst (Ed.), *Annals of child development* (Vol. 2, pp. 251–297). Greenwich, CT: JAI Press.

Koch, H. L. (1933). Popularity in preschool children: Some related factors and a technique for its measurement. *Child Development, 4,* 164–175.

Krantz, M. (1982). Sociometric awareness, social participation, and perceived popularity in preschool children. *Child Development, 53,* 376–379.

Krehbiel, G., & Coie, J. D. (1985). *School-setting behavior of academic achievement-based subtypes of rejected children.* Unpublished manuscript, Duke University, Durham, NC.

Kuhlen, R. G., & Lee, B. J. (1943). Personality characteristics and social acceptability in adolescence. *Journal of Educational Psychology, 34,* 321–340.

Ladd, G. W. (1983). Social networks of popular, average, and rejected children in school settings. *Merrill-Palmer Quarterly, 29,* 283–308.

Ladd, G. W., & Mars, K. T. (1986). Reliability and validity of preschoolers' perceptions of peer behavior. *Journal of Clinical Child Psychology, 15,* 16–25.

Ladd, G. W., & Oden, S. (1979). The relationship between peer acceptance and children's ideas about helpfulness. *Child Development, 50,* 402–408.

La Greca, A. M. (1981). Peer acceptance: The correspondence between children's sociometric scores and teachers' ratings of peer interactions. *Journal of Abnormal Child Psychology, 9,* 167–178.

Lahey, B. B., Green, K. D., & Forehand, R. (1980). On the independence of ratings of hyperactivity, conduct problems, and attention deficits in children: A multiple regression analysis. *Journal of Consulting and Clinical Psychology, 48,* 566–574.

Lesser, G. S. (1959). The relationship between various forms of aggression and popularity among lower-class children. *Journal of Educational Psychology, 50,* 20–25.

Lippitt, R. (1941). Popularity among preschool children. *Child Development, 12,* 305–332.

Livesley, W. J., & Bromley, D. B. (1973). *Person perception in childhood and adolescence.* London: Wiley.

Marshall, H. R., & McCandless, B. R. (1957a). A study in prediction of social behavior of preschool children. *Child Development, 28,* 149–159.

Marshall, H. R., & McCandless, B. R. (1957b). Relationships between dependence on adults and social acceptance by peers. *Child Development, 28,* 413–419.

Masten, A., Morison, P., & Pellegrini, D. (1985). A Revised Class Play method of peer assessment. *Development Psychology, 3,* 523–533.

Masters, J. C., & Furman, W. (1981). Popularity, individual friendship selection, and specific peer interaction among children. *Developmental Psychology, 17,* 344–350.

McGuire, J. M. (1973). Aggression and sociometric status with preschool children. *Sociometry, 36,* 542–549.

McMichael, P. (1980). Reading difficulties, behavior, and social status. *Journal of Educational Psychology, 72,* 76–86.

Milich, R., & Landau, S. (1984). A comparison of the social status and social behavior of aggressive and aggressive/withdrawn boys. *Journal of Abnormal Child Psychology, 12,* 277–288.

Moore, S., & Updegraff, R. (1964). Sociometric status of preschool children related to age, sex, nurturance-giving, and dependency. *Child Development, 35,* 519–524.

Moore, S. G. (1967). Correlates of peer acceptance in nursery school children. In W. W. Hartup & N. L. Smothergill (Eds.), *The young child* (pp. 229–247). Washington, DC: National Association for the Education of Young Children.

Morrison, G. M., Forness, S. R., & MacMillan, D. L. (1983). Influences on the sociometric ratings of mildly handicapped children: A path analysis. *Journal of Educational Psychology, 75,* 63–74.

Newcomb, A. F., & Bukowski, W. M. (1983). Social impact and social preference as determinants of children's peer group status. *Developmental Psychology, 19,* 856–867.

Olweus, D. (1977). Aggression and peer acceptance in adolescent boys: Two short-term longitudinal studies of ratings. *Child Development, 48,* 1301–1313.

Pekarik, E. G., Prinz, R. J., Liebert, D. E., Weintraub, S., & Neale, J. M. (1976). The Pupil Evaluation Inventory: A sociometric technique for assessing children's social behavior. *Journal of Abnormal Child Psychology, 4,* 83–97.

Quay, L. C., & Jarrett, O. S. (1984). Predictors of social acceptance in preschool children. *Developmental Psychology, 20,* 793–796.

Roistacher, R. C. (1974). A microeconomic model of sociometric chance. *Sociometry, 37,* 219–238.

Rubin, K. H. (1984). *Relations between peer and teacher ratings of social competence.* Unpublished manuscript, University of Waterloo, Waterloo, Ontario.

Rubin, K. H., & Clark, M. L. (1983). Preschool teachers' ratings of behavioral problems: Observational, sociometric, and social-cognitive correlates. *Journal of Abnormal Child Psychology, 11,* 273–286.

Rubin, K. H., & Daniels-Beirness, T. (1983). Concurrent and predictive correlates of sociometric status in kindergarten and grade one children. *Merrill-Palmer Quarterly, 29,* 337–352.

Rubin, K. H., Daniels-Beirness, T., & Hayvren, M. (1982). Correlates of peer acceptance and rejection in early childhood. *Canadian Journal of Behavioural Sciences, 14,* 338–348.

Ruble, D. N., Boggiana, A. K., Feldman, N. S., & Loebl, J. H. (1980). Developmental analysis of the role of social comparison in self-evaluation. *Developmental Psychology, 16*, 105–115.

Smith, G. H. (1950). Sociometric study of best-liked and least-liked children. *Elementary School Journal, 51*, 77–85.

Vaughn, B. E., & Waters, E. (1981). Attention structure, sociometric status, and dominance: Interrelations, behavioral correlates, and relationships to social competence. *Developmental Psychology, 17*, 275–288.

Vosk, B., Forehand, R., Parker, J. B., & Rickard, K. (1982). A multi-method comparison of popular and unpopular children. *Developmental Psychology, 18*, 571–575.

Wasik, B. H. (1987). Sociometric measures and peer descriptions of kindergarten children: A study of reliability and validity. *Journal of Clinical Child Psychology, 16*, 218–224.

Wiggins, J. S., & Winder, C. L. (1961). The peer nomination inventory: An empirically derived sociometric measure of adjustment in preadolescent boys. *Psychological Reports, 9*, 643–677.

Winder, C. L., & Rau, L. (1962). Parental attitudes associated with social deviance in preadolescent boys. *Journal of Abnormal and Social Psychology, 64*, 418–424.

Wright, J. C., Giammarino, M., & Parad, H. W. (1986). Social status in small groups: Individual–group similarity and the social "misfit." *Journal of Personality and Social Psychology, 50*, 523–536.

Yarrow, M., & Campbell, J. (1963). Person perception in children. *Merrill-Palmer Quarterly, 9*, 57–92.

Younger, A. J., Schwartzman, A. E., & Ledingham, J. E. (1985). Age-related changes in children's perceptions of aggression and withdrawal in their peers. *Developmental Psychology, 21*, 70–75.

Younger, A. J., Schwartzman, A. E., & Ledingham, J. E. (1986). Age-related changes in children's perceptions of social deviance: Changes in behavior or in perspective. *Developmental Psychology, 22*, 531–542.

3   Children's entry behavior

Martha Putallaz and Aviva Wasserman

The desire to understand the behavioral evolution of peer rejection and to develop effective intervention programs highlights the need for detailed observational information concerning the interaction of children of different levels of sociometric status. However, up until the late 1970s, the principal research approach in this area was to search for global behavioral differences between children of high and low social status. In addition, the exclusive use of real-time observations limited the number of behaviors that could be observed within any one study. For example, among the behaviors considered for their relationship to sociometric status were associative play, friendly approach, conversation, and hostile behavior (Marshall & McCandless, 1957), nurturance-giving and dependency (Moore & Updegraff, 1964), aggression (McGuire, 1973), and total positive and negative reinforcement (Hartup, Glazer, & Charlesworth, 1967). Clearly, the global, disparate nature of these behaviors do not lend themselves readily to integration into a satisfactory, cohesive explanation of peer acceptance. Further, it is unclear how to translate such global results into the types of specific teachable skills necessary for an intervention program (although see Oden & Asher, 1977). Thus, the change in purpose behind the research relating behavior and sociometric status seemed to require a concomitant change in the style of research conducted as well.

Indeed, the nature of the research in this area has changed within the last decade, becoming more sophisticated, both methodologically and conceptually. Probably the most important driving force behind the improved quality of research has been recent improvements in technology. More refined observational procedures have been facilitated by such technological advances as high-quality video equipment, new statistical procedures such as sequential analyses, and an increased use of analogue situations. Thus, researchers in this field not only study global behaviors in real time but also employ molecular and multiple coding systems in controlled situations recorded on videotape.

The authors would like to acknowledge the support of a William T. Grant Faculty Scholar Award to the first author and to thank Blair Sheppard for his comments on an earlier version of this chapter.

Partly because of a focus on discerning teachable skills for intervention and partly as a result of methodological advances, a further trend has appeared in the literature. In addition to the transition from global to more molecular observational coding systems, the behavioral research in this area similarly has begun to move toward the study of sociometric status differences with regard to particular social tasks rather than social behavior in general. Thus, we are in the process of developing midrange theories that concern the relationship between a certain facet of behavior and sociometric status. These midrange theories may, at some later point in time, be integrated to form a comprehensive behavioral theory of social acceptance among children. This situational assessment allows the identification of particular aspects of children's behavior to be targeted for intervention purposes.

One aspect of social interaction, in particular, has been the focus of much recent research attention – namely, children's entry behavior. Here researchers are interested in how children approach and attempt to enter into the ongoing activities of groups of their peers. In fact, the study of children's entry behavior has received more attention than any other social task. The purpose of this chapter is to review the research on entry behavior and its relation to sociometric status in children. Our goals are to discern what we have learned and the implications for the development of a model of effective entry behavior. Thus, the present chapter will (a) outline the reasons for interest in entry behavior, (b) review the relevant literature, and (c) propose a preliminary model of children's entry behavior.

Importance of entry behavior

For many reasons, it is not surprising that children's entry behavior has received so much attention in the literature of late. Researchers interested in the relation between sociometric status and behavior have begun to follow the behavior-analytic assessment approach advocated by Goldfried and D'Zurilla (1969) and consequently to assess competence in terms of skills demonstrated in particular social situations (cf. Dodge, 1986, and Rubin & Krasnor, 1986, for further discussions of this approach). Because the successful initiation of entry into the peer play group is a prerequisite for further social interaction, it is clearly an important task for children to master and a natural first aspect of social interaction to examine in depth.

The critical nature of the entry task for children was recognized earlier than this recent wave of research. One goal of many intervention programs designed to help isolated or unpopular children was to better equip them to enter and become integrated into already-existing peer groups. For example, the modeling film used by O'Connor (1969, 1972) in his intervention program consisted of 11 episodes featuring children's attempts to enter groups of their peers. A narrative track accompanying the film explicitly described each child's entry actions, thus drawing the audience's attention to the relevant behaviors. One of these episodes was narrated as follows: "Now here are two children playing with blocks. Another child wants to play too. She is holding her hands out so they will know she wants to play with them. She comes close and they give her blocks. Now she comes close and plays with the other children. They are having fun because she came close and asked to play." Clear strategies for entry were given to the audience. Yet as Gottman (1977a) pointed out, at the time of O'Connor's (1969, 1972) work, there was no empirical knowledge of how socially competent children at a particular developmental level gained entry into groups. Rather, the entry strategies taught in such intervention programs were generated by the author without considering that children's entry style might, in fact, differ markedly from that used by adults or from what adults imagined children's entry strategies to be.

In addition to instruction in entry skills, the narrative track of the O'Connor film also provided an outcome for each entry episode shown. All entry attempts made by the children in the film were highly successful, making it appear that entering groups was relatively easy if only children were willing to try. The following narrated episode from the O'Connor film is especially illustrative of this point. "Now another child comes up close to watch. She wants to play too. She waits for them to see her. Now she gets a chair. And she sits down with them so they will play with her. She starts to do what they are doing so they will want to play with her. Now they notice her. One of the girls is smiling at her because she is doing what they are doing. They give her some toys because she is playing just like them. Now she has lots of toys and some friends to play with. They are so nice; they want to give her all the toys, but she doesn't want them all. She wants them to keep some so they can all play together. They are happy."

Unfortunately, the type of positive outcome portrayed in the above episode appears to be a very uncommon one indeed. Garvey (1984) recently wrote that the task of entering a group "poses a serious problem, not only to the socially inept or relatively unpopular child, but even to the more socially skilled and popular child" (p. 162). Corsaro (1981) found that among nursery school groups of acquainted 3- and 4-year-olds, 53.9% of all initial entry attempts were rejected by the group. Putallaz and Gottman (1981a) reported that even the entry attempts of popular second- and third-graders were rejected or ignored by their classmates 26% of the time. The example below, illustrating the potential for rejection, is taken from Corsaro's (1981) participant observations. Linda is attempting to join Barbara, Nancy, and Bill Corsaro who are playing with toy animals and building blocks.

Linda watched at a distance for one minute, then entered the block area, sat next to Barbara and began playing with the animals.

Barbara: You can't play!

Linda: Yes, I can. I can have some animals too.

Barbara: No, you can't. We don't like you today.

Nancy: You're not our friend.

Linda: I can play here too.

Barbara: No, her can't – her can't play, right Nancy?

Nancy: Right.

Linda: Can I have some animals, Bill?

Bill: You can have some of these (Offers Linda some of his animals).

Barbara: She can't play, Bill, cause she's not our friend.

Bill: Why not? You guys played with her yesterday.

Nancy: Well, we hate her today.

Linda: Well, I'll tell teacher. (Linda leaves now but returns with a teaching assistant.)

Teacher: Girls, can Linda play with you?

Barbara: No! She's not our friend.

Teacher: Why can't you all be friends?

Barbara: No!

Nancy: Let's go outside, Barbara.

Barbara: Okay. (Barbara and Nancy leave. Linda remains shortly and plays with animals and then moves into juice room.) (pp. 214–215)

On the basis of his observations, Corsaro (1981) cautioned that children must learn that their peers will most probably not accept them immediately. "Often a child must convince others of his or her merits as a playmate, and sometimes he or she must anticipate and accept exclusion" (p. 207). Likewise Putallaz and Gottman's (1981a, 1981b) research concerning children's entry behavior led them to conclude that it appeared crucial that intervention programs provide some sort of "inoculation" for low-status children against being rejected or ignored during their entry attempts. In fact, Putallaz and Gottman further recommended adding a component to intervention programs that would provide a mechanism for increasing the group's likelihood of accepting new members. Clearly, the type of positive entry outcomes portrayed in the O'Connor film are not the expectations that should be conveyed to children. Entry is not only an important social task but a difficult one to accomplish as well. In support of this notion, Dodge, McClaskey, and Feldman (1985) recently reported that the peer group entry situation was identified by both teachers and clinicians as being an especially important and problematic one for children.

A final reason for the increased attention to children's behavior in an entry situation is due to its apparent utility in assessing social competence. The entry situation appears to be highly diagnostic in terms of quickly revealing differences in levels of social skillfulness. Behavioral differences have been detected among children in such short time intervals as 15 min (Burns, Pellegrini, & Notarius, 1985; Gelb & Jacobson, 1985; Putallaz & Gottman, 1981a, 1981b), 10 min (Francis & Ollendick, 1984), and even 6 min (Dodge, Schlundt, Schocken, &

Delugach, 1983) and 5 min (Putallaz, 1983). Clearly, recent research has demonstrated that the entry situation is not only an important and problematic one for children but one that is highly diagnostic of their social skillfulness as well.

Early research on entry behavior

Although all of the research specifically examining the relationship between sociometric status and behavior in the entry situation has been published within the 1980s, the general study of children's entry behavior has been a topic of inquiry for over 50 years. The primary focus of this early research concerned the assimilation of newcomers into groups, although the entry of children into familiar groups of children was also considered. To fully chronicle the development of recent notions concerning entry behavior, this background literature will be reviewed in some detail.

Research on entry of newcomers

With respect to adults, the impetus for the study of the assimilation of newcomers into established groups arose from an increasing awareness of the inherent difficulty of this task for such diverse populations as immigrants (e.g., Eisenstadt, 1951, 1952; Richardson, 1957), foreign college students (e.g., Zajonc, 1952), and new employees (e.g., Wanous, 1977), to name but a few. The interest in child newcomers resulted from both an appreciation of the difficulty involved in beginning school (e.g., Mallay, 1935; McGrew, 1972) and an awareness of the increasing percentage of Americans who move and thus relocate their children to new schools each year (Schaller, 1975).

The findings from this newcomer literature support the notion that a common series of events is associated with the assimilation of all children in groups. From her study of 67 preschoolers ranging in age from 18 to 48+ months, Washburn (1932) proposed that regularity exists in the assimilation process, beginning with a period of inhibition induced by the novel situation and followed by a release of this inhibition. She suggested that the newcomer's behavior progressed as follows: Initially there was a period of alert but passive observation by the child, which was followed by a period of active exploration of either the setting or some particular object. Vocalization usually was found to be the final activity to emerge.

Washburn's (1932) observations have been examined in greater depth and elaborated upon, but basically they have been supported. McGrew (1972), for example, intensively studied the entry of 12 newcomers to nursery school and found a similar pattern of entry to emerge. McGrew described the newcomers on their first day as "inhibited and shy." All were reported to display a great deal of "automanipulation" (e.g., thumb-sucking, playing with one's hair or clothing), and all but one showed immobility during the first few minutes of entry into the novel situation. Passive exploration of the surroundings and of the other children occupied much of the newcomer's time. Typically, the newcomer sat or stood in one location and watched the activities of others but seldom entered into any of them. A few children were described as playing with the first toy given to them by the teacher for the remainder of the morning. McGrew also noted that a tendency to avoid performing conspicuous behavior patterns was evident as was a preference for quiet locations, which the newcomer vacated if other children came near (McGrew & McGrew, 1972). Newcomers responded to requests and queries by silently moving away and avoided competitive or quarrelsome situations. McGrew (1972) summarized the behavior of newcomers as being "the antithesis of aggressive: arms kept down and close to the trunk, face and eyes averted, movements slow, silent" (p. 138). The new children were described as being conspicuously silent, speaking softly and answering many questions with head nods and shakes. Loud vocalizations such as yelling or squealing were not observed.

In addition to describing the behaviors characterizing initial entry, researchers also have considered the progression of assimilation into the group. McGrew (1972) gave some consideration to this issue in his work. He reported that conspicuous changes in the new children's behavior occurred during their first 5 days in nursery school as the children increasingly became assimilated. There was a significant decrease in display of such typical newcomer behaviors as immobility, automanipulation, glancing, and total amount of looking. Follow-up observations made 65 days after their initial introduction revealed the new children to be integrated completely into the group and indistinguishable behaviorally. Thus, it would seem that at least within the nursery school context, the process of assimilation is completed within 2 months of initial introduction to the group. However, what remains unanswered from McGrew's work is (a) the identification of those particular behaviors that facilitate or hinder acceptance into a group and (b) a more precise understanding of the time line by which assimilation into a new group progresses.

Phillips, Shenker, and Revitz (1951) have attempted to explain assimilation as a strategic process by applying the social psychological notions of Newcomb (1950). Primarily, they saw the task of new children in an entry situation as one of reducing the discrepancy between themselves (e.g., their roles, activities) and the group members. They proposed that the new children's most successful strategy for reducing this discrepancy was to determine the "frame of reference" common to the group members (e.g., their activities, goals) and then to establish themselves as sharing in this frame of reference. Phillips et al. (1951) studied the assimilation of 6- and 7-year-old female newcomers into experimentally formed, preacquainted, 3-member groups. The groups met for six 30-min sessions. One striking observation Phillips et al. reported was that it was the new child who attempted to communicate with the other children rather than the effort being reciprocal or in the opposite direction. Rarely did the group as a whole or any of its individual members attempt to put the newcomer at ease, solicit the new child's interests or opinions, or take the new child into account in their activities. Phillips et al. commented, "If assimilation is dependent upon learning to take roles – that is, the perception of oneself in relation to others and the gradual acquisition of commonly shared frames of reference – then, a priori, the movement early in the assimilation process would have to go in the direction: new-child-moving-toward-group. This is true because it is the nucleus group, by virtue of its members' previous associations with each other, that already have common frames of reference; it is up to the new child to find out what these frames of reference may be and to continually test them on a reality basis" (p. 322).

Consistent with the data of Washburn (1932) and McGrew (1972), Phillips et al. noted the initial propensity of newcomers to observe the other children. They asserted that this was a necessary prerequisite to establishing common frames of reference with the nucleus group. They further proposed that the new child's movements toward the group seemed to follow a five-step sequence (although behavior and criteria for success seem somewhat confounded). First, the new child attempted to join the group's activities by imitating the remarks or activities that another child in the group had initiated. Typically, the new child did this last, after the other members had performed. In the second proposed step of the assimilation sequence the new child attempted to initiate, direct, or otherwise influence group activities, but failed in this regard and was ignored by the group. Next, the new child's attempts to initiate group activity met with partial success in that at least one child from the group responded. The fourth step was marked by the new child's inclusion by the group in their activities. In the fifth and final step of assimilation, the new child's attempts to initiate and direct group activities were successful and no longer ignored.

Phillips et al. (1951) noted that only 5% of the new children's activities during the first of the six sessions were successful in influencing the group (i.e., attainment of the fifth level of assimilation). However, by the last session, this figure had risen to 25%, reflecting substantial progress on the part of the new children toward becoming assimilated into the group. In contrast, the group members were successful in influencing their peers 31% of the time at the initial session and 36% by the final session. Although Phillips et al. were not concerned with studying when a child would be fully assimilated into a group, these data seem to indicate that these new children were fairly far along in the assimilation process.

Ziller and Behringer (1961) were more concerned with ascertaining the point at which assimilation could be said to have occurred and thus studied the longitudinal course of assimilation of 28 newcomers to elementary school. They conceptualized the assimilation process as one in which the new child changes from a group member with unknown status to one with an established position in the social hierarchy of the group. The repeated administration of positive sociometric nomination questionnaires served as one index of the degree of assimilation. These questionnaires were completed seven times over the 11-week period as follows: 1st day, 7th day, 14th day, 21st day, 5th week, 7th week, and 11th week. Not surprisingly, degree of assimilation and time in the classroom appeared to be related, with sociometric status apparently stabilizing after 3 to 5 weeks following initial entry. Newcomers tended to be assimilated with greater facility in the early grades, and in addition, girls were assimilated more easily than boys. More importantly, the results indicated that the newcomers' mean popularity during the 11-week period assumed the form of a U-shaped function. There was a slight rise in popularity after the initial day, then a series of drops in the newcomers' popularity, followed by increasing popularity in the last two periods. Interestingly, though, the newcomers' popularity during the first afternoon in the classroom and their popularity 11 weeks later were correlated substantially ($r = .45$). To explain this U-shaped curve, Ziller and Behringer (1961) proposed that initially the newcomer is perceived by the class members more as a guest than as a permanent member of the class. Thus, the newcomer's increased popularity at the end of the first week may be a reflection of a honeymoon period marked by the class's excitement at the initial novelty of the newcomer and their temporary suspension of comparative, and particularly negative, evaluations. However, as the permanency of the relationship is realized, the group exerts pressure on the newcomer to conform to their norms and established protocol. The resulting interpersonal difficulties presumably lead to reduced popularity of the newcomer, whereas the subsequent rise in popularity is hypothesized to reflect the new child's adoption of the group's norms and values (i.e., their frame of reference). Clearly, observational data are necessary to test the assimilation process proposed by Ziller and Behringer (1961).

Thus, it would seem from the work of Phillips et al. (1951) and Ziller and Behringer (1961) that the successful assimilation of newcomers into established groups is dependent upon their ability to determine and adopt the group's frame of reference. Influenced by this conceptualization, Feldbaum, Christenson, and O'Neal (1980) attempted to integrate the work of McGrew (1972), Phillips et al. (1951), and Ziller and Behringer (1961) to understand the process involved in the assimilation of the newcomer to the preschool. The behavior of 12 newcomers and 42 host children ranging in age from 3 years 1 month to 4 years 6 months was observed over a 4-week interval. Similar to McGrew (1972), assimilation was defined as complete when the new children were no longer distinguishable behaviorally from their classmates with greater tenure in the group.

Consistent with descriptions generated by Washburn (1932) and McGrew (1972), Feldbaum et al. (1980) found a behavioral profile that distinguished the newcomers from their more established classmates during their initial week at preschool. Specifically, the new children were more likely than the host children to be off task, spatially isolated, and engage in more on-task but nonsynchronous behaviors. In contrast, their classmates were more likely to talk to each other, play cooperatively, and engage in parallel play requiring proximity and synchronization with the activities of other children. Feldbaum et al. described the newcomers to be both hesitant and nonassertive with regard to their initial interactions with peers as well as their entry attempts into ongoing activities. This behavioral profile was attributed to the new children's uncertainty as to what constituted acceptable behavior under such unfamiliar circumstances. Feldbaum et al. pointed out that in adult groups behavior is often structured and knowledge of acceptable behavior is more readily available to new members by way of explicit guidelines or indoctrination manuals. In contrast, children entering new groups must infer or extract this information from the wide range of activities with which they are confronted, with little help from existing group members. Thus, it is not surprising that new children initially engage in a high frequency of passive spectator behavior. Feldbaum et al. (1980) described the process of assimilation as follows: "It seems plausible that as the newcomer observes his peers interacting, he comes to recognize the behavioral contingencies of inclusion, approval, and acceptance. By relying on the actions of more knowledgeable hosts and the observable consequences of their behavior, new children may learn to act appropriately without having to discover what is positively or negatively sanctioned from direct experience" (p. 507). Later increases in amount of interaction with group members should lead to an accompanying increase in knowledge concerning the group's frame of reference.

In summary, then, there appears to be a clear progression associated with assimilation of the newcomer into the group. Initially, the new child is withdrawn from the established group members and engages in a high frequency of immobility, passive observation, and automanipulation, although this last behavior may be age specific to the nursery school children observed. Over time these behaviors diminish and the newcomer attempts to become more involved with the other children. Via observation, the newcomer gradually learns which activities are sanctioned by the group and begins to engage in these behaviors. This demonstration of sharing in the group's frame of reference appears to be the most effective means of becoming assimilated. Premature attempts to influence the group or violations of their frame of reference appear most likely to be met with rejection or no response at all from the group.

Research on entry into familiar groups

As mentioned previously, prior study of entry behavior also has included attention to entry of children into groups of familiar, rather than unfamiliar, peers. This literature will be reviewed briefly, as it complements the results of the newcomer research and thus provides a further context for the research to be discussed later in this chapter, namely, the study of the relationship between entry behavior and sociometric status.

Probably the earliest work done in this area was by Mallay (1935), who tried to ascertain the techniques or strategies culminating in the establishment of successful social contacts with peer groups. Twenty-one nursery school children, ranging in age from 2 years 0 months to 4 years 9 months, were observed during the fall and spring of the school year. Successful approaches were defined as those that elicited "maintained group contact" (i.e., "those social situations in which the children were moved by a common underlying aim into patterns of behavior which kept them functionally and spatially together" – p. 432). Each approach was coded using one or more of the following behavior categories: Regard (i.e., looking at another child while standing inactive or engaged in an unrelated activity), Vocalization (i.e., verbal statement or laughter), Physical Contact (either directly or through materials), Parallel Activity (i.e., engagement in related activity, similar but independent), and Cooperative Activity (i.e., engagement in related activity, interdependent and supplementing each other toward a common goal).

Mallay (1935) found that the most frequent patterns or sequences of approach behavior were Regard, Regard and Parallel Activity, and Regard and Vocalization, together accounting for 79.2% of the total attempts made. Interestingly, the pattern found to be the most successful in terms of attaining group entry was not one of these but rather consisted of Regard, Vocalization, and Cooperative Activity. This sequence of behaviors resulted in establishing group contact 97.1% of the time. Other entry patterns similarly proving to be successful were Regard and Cooperative Activity (89.7% successful) and Regard, Vocalization, and Parallel Activity (70% successful). In contrast, the most unsuccessful entry strategy was Regard; only 2.9% of such approaches resulted in the establishment of group contact. Also low in terms of leading to successful entry were the behavioral sequences of Regard and Physical Contact (10.1% successful); Regard, Vocalization, and Physical Contact (10.7% successful); and Regard and Vocalization (16.6% successful). Mallay (1935) noted that only 27.3% of all entry approaches resulted in the successful establishment of group contact and that 70.3% of all entry approaches made consisted of these last four unsuccessful entry types.

Because the most successful entry patterns all included either Cooperative Activity or Parallel Activity, Mallay (1935) concluded that they were the important factors facilitating the initiation of successful social contacts. However, at least with respect to Cooperative Activity, this conclusion must be taken with some caution, because Cooperative Activity and the criterion for entry appear somewhat confounded. Both Cooperative Activity and Parallel Activity, though, involved engagement in an activity related to that of the group, whereas the four least successful entry strategies involved engagement in an unrelated activity. Again, consistent with the results of the newcomer research, it appears that the entering child's demonstration of sharing in the group's frame of reference is the critical component leading to acceptance by the group. In addition, the two successful entry patterns also seem to suggest the importance of observing the group prior to engaging in a related activity. Finally, Mallay pointed out that the success of the entry strategies seemed to be independent of such personality or situational variables as age of the children, level of personal adjustment of the children, intelligence, and time of the school year. Thus, success seemed to be more attributable to type of approach and sequencing of behaviors rather than to any particular personality or situational factor.

An unpublished dissertation by Belle (1976; described by Forbes, Katz, Paul, & Lubin, 1982) replicated Mallay's study but combined the Parallel Activity and Cooperative Activity codes into a single Related Activity code. Also included in this new code was any conversation concerning the group's activity. Belle similarly found that the entering child's use of Related Activity behavior was most likely to lead to successful entry into the group.

Corsaro (1979, 1981) also studied naturalistic entry behavior at the preschool level, under the name of "access rituals." Two 25-member groups of nursery school children, ranging in age from 2.10 years to 4.10 years, were observed over the course of the school year. Initially children were observed unobtrusively from a concealed area of the school; later a participant observation methodology was employed. A successful entry sequence was defined as one that led to eventual acceptance into the group's ongoing activity even though there may have been numerous prior negative or nonresponses from the group. In contrast, an unsuccessful entry sequence was marked by either the entering child's termination of an entry attempt, typically by leaving the area without any further attempts at access during the course of the activity, or by a failure to gain acceptance prior to the end of an activity.

Although Corsaro (1979) identified 15 distinct entry strategies, 5 strategies accounted for nearly 80% of the data, namely, (a) Nonverbal Entry (i.e., entering into or near an area where an activity is under way without verbal marking), (b) Encirclement, (i.e., physically circling area where activity is under way without verbal marking), (c) Producing Variant of Ongoing Behavior (i.e., entering into an area where activity is under way and producing similar verbal or nonverbal behavior or both to that under way), (d) Disruptive Entry (i.e., entering into an area where activity is under way and producing verbal or nonverbal behavior or both that physically disrupts ongoing activity), and (e) Making a Claim on Area or Object (i.e., entering into an area where activity is under way and verbally making claim on area or object in the area). As Corsaro (1979) pointed out, it is interesting to note that all (with the exception of Making a Claim on Area or Object) involve the children's production or monitoring of nonverbal cues. However, despite their high frequency of usage by the children, only one of these strategies, Producing Variant of Ongoing Behavior, was even moderately likely to receive a positive response from the group (56% of the time). Corsaro contrasted the children's apparent preference for indirect, nonverbal strategies with their infrequent use of more successful, direct, verbal strategies such as Request for Access (61.5% successful), Questioning Participants (58% successful), and Greeting (50% successful), which he considered to be more adult-like.

The obvious question then that followed from these data was why would children rely on indirect and often nonverbal entry strategies, which had less likelihood of resulting in initial positive outcomes. Corsaro suggested that the key to answering this paradox was recognizing that the children's sequencing of entry strategies was more important than their initial entry behavior. Although these initial strategies did not tend to lead to immediate entry, they often did work if the sequence continued beyond the initial exchange. Corsaro (1979) found that 70% of the entry sequences observed were only one round in length, with nearly half (45.5%) consisting of Nonverbal Entry. This latter strategy by itself led to successful entry only 25.7% of the time. The probability of successful entry increased if the sequence moved beyond one round for all strategies, with the exceptions of Disruptive Entry, where successful entry was always unlikely, and Producing Variant of Ongoing Behavior, where there was a high probability of success regardless of round. For most strategies, the probability of successful entry was highest for sequences of three or more rounds. Thus, generally, the more persistent children were in their efforts to join a group and the less disruptive their attempts, the higher the likelihood of their success.

Corsaro (1979) observed that a child employing Nonverbal Entry and receiving no response from the group would often continue to monitor their ongoing activity. He posited that this careful monitoring led to the acquisition of information that then could be used for the production of other access strategies in later rounds.

Corsaro's data also suggested that indirect entry sequences (e.g., Nonverbal Entry and Producing Variant of Ongoing Behavior; Encirclement and Producing Variant of Ongoing Behavior; Nonverbal Entry and Reference to Affiliation or Offering a Gift) may be favored more than direct strategies because of the higher overall likelihood that entering children will be rejected or ignored by a group rather than accepted (68.4% to 31.7%). Thus, children may opt for indirect and multiple sequences for much the same reasons that Gottman (1983) outlined for children's choices regarding the types of demands they make of their peers. Weaker forms of demands (e.g., "why don't you make that black?") allow children to save face more readily when not met with compliance than do stronger forms of the same demands (e.g., "make that black"). Thus, given the high likelihood of failure, indirect and multiple entry sequences may be providing the opportunity for saving face as well as serving as direct bids for entry.

The initial use of Nonverbal Behavior during entry may also be favored because it allows entering children to monitor the group's behavior and thus to ascertain the behavioral contingencies of the group without directly experiencing them (Feldbaum et al., 1980). If children are eventually to employ such apparently successful entry behaviors as Producing a Variant of Ongoing Behavior (Corsaro, 1979) or Related Activity (Mallay, 1935), careful monitoring of the group's activity would appear an essential preliminary step.

Although not explicitly assessing the effectiveness of children's entry strategies, a study by Forbes et al. (1982) will be reviewed at this point because it contributes some novel conceptual notions regarding children's entry behavior. The major purpose of their research was to explore the developmental and gender differences marking children's planning behaviors as manifested by the way children organized or sequenced their actions when attempting to enter groups of their peers. Twenty-four unfamiliar children, half of whom were age 5 and the other half age 7, were grouped to form four 6-member play groups, homogeneous by age. The groups met for twelve 1-hour sessions over a 3-week period. Videotaped records were used to identify 14 types of entry behavior. These bids were classified as being either opening moves (i.e., initial behaviors in an entry sequence made without benefit of group feedback concerning the group's receptivity to the entering child) or midgame moves (i.e., later behaviors made in an entry sequence following feedback from a group). In addition, all entry behaviors were classified as being either relationally oriented (i.e., those concerning the relation between the entry child and the group, such as acknowledging oneself as having outsider status) or activity oriented (i.e., those concerning the relation between the entry child and the group activity, such as suggesting a role for oneself in the group activity).

Forbes et al. (1982) also examined the qualitative differences among the children's entry behaviors. This research resulted in several interesting findings.

First, in terms of their opening entry moves, boys were more likely to employ "forceful" relationally oriented strategies (e.g., displaying one's own qualities, asserting superiority over group members, or criticizing group members) than were girls, although no sex difference was found regarding opening activity-oriented entry moves. Forbes et al. (1982) further examined whether there were similar sex differences regarding the use of force or pressure by the entry child in response to negative group feedback during the midgame moves of the entry sequence. Again, no differences were found regarding the use of force in terms of activity-oriented strategies. However, once again, a significant sex difference was apparent in the use of forceful relationally oriented midgame entry behaviors. Following negative feedback from the group, boys were more likely than girls to engage in such face-saving behaviors as referring positively to one's own attributes, criticizing the members of the group, or appealing to playroom norms mandating group acceptance. Considering both the greater propensity of boys to employ forceful relationally oriented opening moves and face-saving relationally oriented midgame moves, Forbes et al. (1982) proposed that boys were more likely than girls to be assertive regarding their status vis-à-vis the group in an entry situation. They further suggested that boys appeared more concerned with attaining positive status in the group than with attaining acceptance by the group, although it would seem that either data regarding the effectiveness of different strategies or direct indications of the children's goals would be necessary to draw this conclusion.

In support of this notion, though, Forbes et al. (1982) found a significant decrease from age 5 to 7 in the tendency of boys to accommodate to the group following negative feedback, whereas girls' use of accommodation remained constant across the two age levels. Thus, by age 7, girls were more apt to accommodate to the group following rejection in both the relationally oriented mode (e.g., by asking neutral questions of group members, by making neutral comments about themselves, or by asking permission to join the group) and in the activity-oriented mode (e.g., by retreating from a forceful opening move to a less forceful midgame move). Forbes et al. (1982) interpreted this difference to mean that boys learn not to use the plan of accommodation. Because they speculated that accommodation to the group would be a strategy aimed at attaining acceptance by the group but not at attaining status within the group, these findings are consistent with those reported earlier. Boys may be employing dominant postures in the peer group entry situation primarily for the purpose of status elevation rather than to pursue such instrumental goals as joining a group activity. Forbes et al. identified three means by which this status elevation might be accomplished: (a) by announcing one's own positive attributes, characteristics, and possessions for oneself, the group, and any observers so as to compensate for the rejection, (b) by derogating the group members and devaluing them so that not being included might be viewed more positively, and (c) by asserting control over the group's behavior and forcing inclusion by such means as citing a rule mandating inclusion.

Thus, the work by Forbes et al. (1982) adds several novel conceptualizations to those presented thus far concerning children's entry behavior. First, they have elaborated on the behavioral sequencing notion by introducing the concepts of opening versus midgame moves in the entry sequence. In addition, they have broadened the dimension of directness previously applied to entry behaviors to include the degree of force exhibited by children in their entry attempts. Such entry behaviors as Approaches or Flatters would be low in terms of force, and Appeals to Norms or Suggests New Activity would represent more forceful entry bids.

More importantly, though, Forbes et al. (1982) speculated that often the use of force during entry may be in the pursuit of different goals than those of more accommodative strategies. Like entry behaviors, the goals that children pursue within the entry context may be considered either relationally oriented or activity oriented. For example, some children may wish to be included in the group's activity (an activity-oriented goal) and thus may persist despite encountering initial group opposition. They presumably would demonstrate a preference for entry bids permitting accommodation to the group. These speculations are consistent with the previous literature's finding that persistence and behaving in a manner consistent with the group members are likely to result in eventual acceptance by the group. However, other children may set more relationally oriented goals concerned specifically with status elevation. When attempting entry, these children may be more preoccupied with their relationship or status vis-à-vis the group members than with the instrumental goal of joining the activity. When confronted with a negative response from the group, these children would be more concerned with saving face and recovering their loss of personal status than with persistence. From the previous literature, it would seem that one way for children to save face would be to retreat or withdraw from the situation and only attempt entry through a multiple sequencing of behaviors gradually increasing in terms of their directness and possible risk of rejection. Thus, one means of saving face may be to anticipate continued rejection and restrict it to a minimum by being indirect, thereby providing a ready alternative explanation for continued exclusion other than not being valued (e.g., "they did not see me"; "they were too busy to notice that I wanted to play").

Forbes et al. (1982) have identified a second, more direct means by which children may attempt to save face following rejection in the entry situation. Some children, particularly boys, may directly confront the group following rejection and attempt to elevate their status by equalizing the apparent status differential rather than by continuing to seek inclusion in the group activity. Means to accomplish this status elevation might include highlighting one's positive attributes, devaluing the group members, or attempting to control the group by citing a rule mandating inclusion. Although not mentioned by Forbes et al., involving an authority figure such as a teacher or parent would also seem to serve this last purpose.

Summary

An impressive feature of the entry literature is the remarkable consistency of results spanning five decades of research and involving very different contexts for studying entry behavior. From the entry literature dealing specifically with entry into unfamiliar groups, it is clear that the process of assimilation begins with a period marked by immobility, automanipulation, and passive observation on the part of the newcomer. With time, these behaviors become less frequent and the child is more apt to approach and interact with group members. This initial spectator behavior seems to serve the important purpose of permitting the child to learn the behavioral contingencies of the group without directly experiencing them. Through such observation, then, the entry child can learn the group's norms or frame of reference and can then engage in the entry behavior most likely to lead to successful entry – doing what the group is doing. This behavior appears to convey to the group that the entering child shares their frame of reference, thereby increasing their receptivity to the entry child.

In addition, the proper sequencing of entry bids appears to be critical in terms of attaining group acceptance. One example of a successful entry sequence appears to consist of watching the group and then engaging in an activity similar to that of the group members. Only later, once the child is an integral part of the group, should the child be more directive and attempt to influence or redirect the group activity. To do so too early in the assimilation process is to risk being rejected or ignored. Thus, the most successful sequence of behaviors in terms of optimizing probability of acceptance also seems to represent a sequence of behaviors increasing in risk as well. Passive observation is not likely to lead one to be rejected by the group, but similarly it has a low probability of leading to group acceptance, its most likely consequence being no response. In contrast, attempting to redirect the group prematurely is a high-risk strategy. If successful, the child certainly has become active in terms of the group's leadership, but success is a low-probability outcome, with rejection being the much more probable response. The importance of persistence also is clear from the previous literature. Entry is a difficult task for all children and the prospect of acceptance increases with time.

Finally, it is important to note that there appear to be at least two discrepant goals that children may pursue when confronted with an entry situation, particularly involving a familiar group of peers. In addition to the instrumental goal of joining the group activity, some children may be more preoccupied with their relationship or status vis-à-vis the group members. When confronted with a negative response from the group, these children would be more concerned with saving face and recovering from the attack on their personal status than with persistence. One means by which children may attempt to save face is to anticipate continued rejection and attempt to contain it by using indirect entry behaviors that typically carry a low probability of rejection. At the same time, they would avoid the more direct, higher risk strategies until having received sufficient positive feedback from the group. Thus, they would exhibit a preference for behaviors characteristic of the early segments of the entry sequence. In contrast, a second face-saving strategy for children may be to directly confront the group following rejection and attempt to elevate their status by equalizing the apparent status differential. Children might attempt to effect this status elevation by engaging in a positive portrayal of their own attributes, criticizing the group members, or forcing their way into the group activity by such means as invoking a rule mandating inclusion or involving an authority figure such as a teacher or parent. These face-saving strategies probably would appear quite unsuccessful as measured by their likelihood of leading to group acceptance, but perhaps not in terms of promoting recovery following a loss of personal status inflicted by the group. Recently, Renshaw and Asher (1983) have underscored the importance of understanding children's goals when interpreting their behavior.

Entry behavior and children's sociometric status

An interesting difference between the general entry studies discussed thus far and those concerned specifically with the relationship between entry behavior and sociometric status is that the former group consists primarily of naturalistic entry research (with the exceptions of Forbes et al., 1982, and Phillips et al., 1951) and the latter literature consists mainly of entry analogue studies. Much of this analogue research employs a variant of a contrived entry situation developed by Putallaz and Gottman (1981a, 1981b). Their entry situation involved a pair of children who believed that they were testing a novel word-naming game for its possible use by children their age. These children were videotaped as they played the word game alone in a room for 10 minutes and were not informed that another child would attempt to join them later. The entry child was instructed to enter the room where the others were playing the word game, but no explicit instruction was given to join in the play of the game. As the third child attempted to enter the group, 15 minutes of additional videotaped data were obtained. A child was considered to have gained entry once the child actually began to play the game. Using this definition, all children eventually did secure entry by the end of the observation period. Verbatim transcripts were made from the videotapes and coded using the microanalytic coding system developed by Gottman and Parkhurst (1980), with the addition of one entry code (Bid for Entry) and three group response codes (Accept, Reject, Ignore) to facilitate the coding of the entry sequence.

Putallaz and Gottman (1981a, 1981b) originally used this paradigm to study the entry behavior among familiar peers. The second- and third-graders participating in the research were classified as either popular or unpopular on the basis of a median split of the number of positive sociometric nominations received within each classroom. The four conditions of the study, determined by both the status of the entering child and that of the group entered, involved the entry of a popular or unpopular child into either a popular or an unpopular dyad of same-sex classmates.

The results indicated that regardless of their status, all children were accepted, rejected, and ignored by the groups at some point during their entry attempts. However, unpopular children were less likely to be accepted and more likely to be ignored than popular children. Further, they waited longer before making their first bid for entry and required both more time and more bids to achieve entry than did popular children. Interestingly, there was no indication that unpopular children had an entry skills deficit, as they displayed all of the entry strategies used by popular children with moderately similar probabilities, although the coding system would not have detected any differences in timing or stylistic execution of the entry bids.

It was still possible that the bids most preferred by the unpopular children were not those that would be most effective in terms of gaining them entry. To test this possibility, Putallaz and Gottman (1981a, 1981b) computed a cost–benefit score for each entry behavior as used by popular and unpopular children by calculating the probability of the bid leading to acceptance of the entering child by the group minus the probability of it leading to nonacceptance (i.e., being rejected or ignored by the group). Thus, a high positive score would be indicative of an entry bid that had a high probability of leading to acceptance and a low probability of leading to the group rejecting or ignoring the user, while the converse would be true of a high negative score. Next the correlation between the unconditional probability of each entry bid and its cost–benefit score was computed. This correlation would permit examination of whether the entry bids that had the highest probability of occurring corresponded to those that had the most favorable cost–benefit score. For popular children, this correlation was .74, $p < .05$ for entry into popular groups and .51, $p < .10$ for entry into unpopular groups. For unpopular children, this correlation was $-.06$ for entry into unpopular groups and $-.13$ for entry into popular groups; neither correlation was significant. Thus, popular children appeared to act to maximize their benefits and minimize their costs, but this was not true of unpopular children. These results did not indicate that unpopular children deliberately were intending to be ignored or rejected when attempting to enter groups; however, this was the net effect of their behavior. Of course, these analyses did not rule out the possibility that unpopular children were being ignored or rejected for some reason other than the type of entry bid displayed (e.g., reputation, physical attractiveness). The behavioral differences detected, however, did encourage further investigation of the children's use of entry bids.

Upon further examination, it was clear that there were differences in the frequency with which particular entry bids were used. When entering groups of their classmates, unpopular children were more likely than popular children to disagree, ask informational questions, say something about themselves, and state their feelings and opinions. In their discussion of these results, Putallaz and Gottman (1981a, 1981b) introduced a newcomer hypothesis that drew a parallel between the behavior of unpopular children and the behavior of newcomers. First, they noted that unpopular children waited longer prior to making their first attempt at entry, an indication that during this time the children were hovering on the outskirts of the group. Earlier, Gottman (1977b) had used the term *hovering* to describe the fearful, shy, withdrawn newcomer-like behavior he found characteristic of two groups of sociometrically neglected children identified through a linear typal analysis of behavioral and sociometric data. Also similar to newcomers with outsider status in the initial stages of the assimilation process, Putallaz and Gottman found unpopular children to have a high probability of being ignored when attempting entry. Further, the entry bids more frequently used by unpopular children appeared to reflect a lack of awareness of the group's frame of reference. These children introduced new conversational topics abruptly and directed the conversation to themselves by making self-statements, stating their feelings and opinions, and disagreeing with the group members more than popular children. These tactics seemed to be attempts to divert the group's attention to the user; paradoxically, the net result was most often being ignored or rejected.

In contrast, popular children seemed to employ the more effective entry strategy of attempting to determine the frame of reference common to the group members and then establishing themselves as sharing in this frame of reference. Putallaz and Gottman hypothesized that popular children may be better able than unpopular children to determine the prevailing norms or expectations in a given situation and to act in accordance with those norms. However, when faced with the prospect of entering an unpopular group, the behavior of popular children seemed to reflect a newcomer effect as well. In this situation, they were somewhat more likely to act in ways that increased their chance of being ignored than was true when they entered popular groups.

Thus, the results of this study seemed to support one important principle of successful entry behavior identified earlier (i.e., fitting in with the group's frame of reference) and suggested several key entry behaviors that were related to children's sociometric status. However, due to some limitations to this first study, a second study was conducted by Putallaz (1983) to test this frame-of-reference hypothesis under even more controlled conditions. First, two child confederates were enlisted to serve as the dyad that all subjects attempted to enter. The use of confederates ensured that all subjects confronted a similar entry situation and permitted the group's activity, or frame of reference, to be changed several times. This provided a controlled test of the children's abilities to detect such a switch and change their behavior accordingly.

The use of unfamiliar confederates also ensured that no past history of interaction with the group members would influence the subject's behavior. Asher and Hymel (1981) have suggested that using familiar peers (e.g., classmates) makes it impossible to examine whether the child's behavior caused the low status or whether his or her low status caused the dysfunctional behavior to occur in response to being ignored or treated poorly by classmates. This revised entry context also permitted an examination of the earlier study's findings in a situation requiring children to enter groups of unfamiliar rather than familiar peers, thus testing the generalizability of the previous results.

In addition, the children's entry behavior was assessed during the summer prior to their entry into first grade, and the results of this assessment were used to predict later sociometric status in first grade. The predictive nature of the study provided a stronger test of the role of dysfunctional behavior in determining social status than would a study collecting behavioral and sociometric data at the same point in time. Further, a sociometric rating scale was used rather than positive nominations to assess social status, ensuring that both positive and negative dimensions were included in the sociometric evaluation.

A further limitation of the earlier study was that it included only a behavioral assessment of the children's entry skills and did not consider their perception of the entry situation. Thus, it was impossible to determine whether the observed behavioral differences were due to a differential preference for particular entry bids, a perceptual deficit (i.e., an inaccurate or incomplete perception of the social situation, thereby decreasing the likelihood of selecting the appropriate behavioral response), or a performance deficit (i.e., accurately perceiving the situation, but for some reason, such as anxiety, failing to translate this knowledge into appropriate behavior).

Thus, in order to determine the importance of accurate social perception in the entry situation, a variation of an interview procedure introduced by Forbes and Lubin (1979) was adopted in this study. All subjects were shown their videotapes following their sessions and interviewed to assess the extent to which they were aware of the different activities of the group. The children's perceptions of the situation then could be compared with the group's actual behavior, so that a measure of the accuracy of the children's perceptions could be obtained.

It was predicted that those children who received the highest future sociometric ratings would demonstrate both a tendency to fit into the group's frame of reference (operationalized as the proportion of relevant statements) and an ability to accurately identify what the group was doing. In contrast, children who demonstrated a deficiency in either relevant behavior or perceptual accuracy were predicted to obtain lower sociometric ratings in first grade. These hypotheses were based on the assumption that the ability to fit into the group's frame of reference would be facilitated by an ability to correctly label what the group was doing. That is, it was predicted that the ability to enact successful entry behavior would involve the ability to size up the nature and demands of the social situation and then, based on one's assessment, to choose the appropriate skills from one's behavioral repertoire to enact.

The results of this study were consistent with both central hypotheses. First, children whose behaviors and conversations were generally relevant to the ongoing activities of the group did attain higher social status in first grade than the children whose behaviors were not relevant. Interestingly, the more socially accepted children were not more likely to conform to the group's activities (i.e., actually play the game). Instead, they were simply less likely to act in a manner that redirected the group's attention, and they were more likely to act in a manner related to what the group was doing. Second, the relationship between this type of behavior and sociometric status was strongest for those entering children who accurately perceived the norms of the group.

In addition, the results of this study seemed to qualify two findings from Putallaz and Gottman (1981a, 1981b). First, when attempting to enter groups of unfamiliar peers, hovering was no longer found to be related negatively to sociometric status. In fact, there was a positive, although nonsignificant, relationship between future sociometric rating and time until first entry bid. Thus, in an entry situation involving familiar peers, unpopular children hovered more as if they were outsiders not yet privy to the norms of the group, and in an unfamiliar entry situation, the tendency to hover was not predictive of social acceptance. This finding is not surprising, because all children in the unfamiliar entry situation were equally unacquainted with the group's frame of reference, thus having an equal need to observe the group to learn it. In fact, the design of the Putallaz (1983) study probably maximized the children's propensity to hover because the group's activity changed repeatedly during the session. However, the children who would become more accepted in first grade seemed more adept at discerning what the group was doing, because children's future sociometric ratings were related positively to the relevance of their behavior to the group's activity. Further, similarly to the findings of Putallaz and Gottman (1981a, 1981b), the amount of conversation produced was related negatively to social status and to the relevance dimension. It appears that those children who were to be more highly rated in first grade were more cautious in terms of what or how much they said.

Also, with the exception of feeling statements, Putallaz (1983) found that the correlations between sociometric rating and the remaining entry behaviors identified by Putallaz and Gottman (i.e., informational questions, disagreement, and self-statements) were either marginally significant or in the expected direction, thus supporting the earlier findings. However, the correlations between the entry behaviors and the relevance code were even higher than those between entry behavior and status. These results suggested that the relevance of an entry behavior to the group's behavior may be the factor mediating the relation between entry behavior and sociometric status. In other words, informational questions and self-statements may have induced negative reactions because they frequently were unrelated to the ongoing activity of the group (i.e., irrelevant). Thus, calling attention to oneself may be problematic only if it diverts the group from its ongoing activity or discussion.

Further evidence of differences between the entry strategies of children with different social status comes from the work of Dodge et al. (1983). In an initial study, kindergarteners who were either popular, neglected, or rejected (as defined by Coie, Dodge, and Coppotelli, 1982) each joined two average-status peers from a different classroom. Six minutes of videotaped data were collected on each of the children's entry attempts. The results indicated no differences between any of the status groups with respect to the total number of entry bids made. However, there were differences in the frequency of particular bids employed. Consistent with earlier entry research, popular children were more likely to make group-oriented statements and less likely than the others to engage in entry tactics that brought attention to themselves, such as self-statements or disrupting the group activity. In contrast, rejected children were found to employ disruptive tactics more than any other group, whereas neglected children engaged in more waiting and hovering behavior than the others. Also in keeping with earlier entry results, Dodge et al. (1983) reported that making group-oriented statements was most likely to lead to a positive group response, engaging in disruptive tactics most likely to result in a negative group response, and waiting and hovering behavior most likely to be ignored by the group. Not surprisingly, then, rejected children were more likely than popular children to elicit negative responses from the group; in turn, they were most likely to respond negatively and least likely to respond positively to the host children.

In a follow-up study, Dodge et al. (1983) examined the entry attempts of unacquainted second-grade boys while they were participating in 8-member play groups that met for an hour on eight separate occasions. Like Putallaz (1983), this study was able to assess the role of entry behavior in determining social status, because sociometric status was calculated on the basis of sociometric nominations made following the last session. The boys' entry attempts during the first, third, and fifth sessions were analyzed. Again, consistent with earlier research, the results indicated that making group-oriented statements and mimicking the peer group (both demonstrative of a shared frame of reference) were the behaviors most likely to lead to a positive group response, whereas using attention-getting or disruptive tactics was most likely to lead to a negative response. Once more, waiting and hovering behavior was most likely to be ignored by the group. Further, the group Dodge et al. (1983) referred to as deviant in status (i.e., rejected and neglected children) made more entry attempts and displayed higher proportions of attention-getting behavior, marginally higher proportions of disruptive behavior, and marginally lower proportions of mimicking behavior than the group labeled normal (i.e., popular and average children). Again, rejected children were most likely to be responded to negatively by the other children.

Consistent with Corsaro's (1979) work, sequential analyses revealed that waiting and hovering were most likely to occur at the first step of an entry sequence, and mimicking and making group-oriented statements were less likely to occur at the first step than at later steps. Waiting and hovering behavior was relatively likely to be followed by mimicking, as was making a group-oriented statement. These two sequences occurred the most frequently, accounting for 26% of all multiple-behavior episodes. The most successful entry sequence involved all three of these behaviors (i.e., wait and hover followed by mimicking followed by a group-oriented statement) and had an 82% probability of eliciting a positive response from the other children. Dodge et al.'s normal group (i.e., popular and average children) was three times more likely to use this three-behavior sequence than their deviant group (i.e., rejected and neglected children).

These findings are remarkably similar to those reported earlier. However, it is important to note that they resulted from a more rigorous methodological and statistical approach than was characteristic of the majority of studies from the general entry literature. In addition, Dodge et al. (1983) have expanded the work of Putallaz and Gottman (1981a, 1981b) and Putallaz (1983) by differentiating the behavior of rejected and neglected children in an entry situation. This distinction led Dodge et al. (1983) to suggest a variant of Putallaz and Gottman's newcomer hypothesis. Dodge et al. speculated that the incompetence of neglected and rejected children during entry might be attributable to a failure to have learned the progression from low-risk to high-risk entry strategies. Neglected children seemed to remain at a stage of employing low-risk tactics (i.e., waiting and hovering), and rejected children immediately employed high-risk tactics (i.e., disruptive behavior).

Recently, however, Berndt (1983), in his commentary on the Dodge et al. study, argued that the newcomer hypothesis is problematic as an explanation for low social status on at least four grounds. First, the disagreeable behavior of unpopular children reported by Putallaz and Gottman (1981a, 1981b) and the tendency of rejected children to respond more negatively than others to host children described by Dodge et al. (1983) are not consistent with the parallels drawn between unpopular children and newcomers to a group. Second, in response to the attempt made by Dodge et al. (1983) to account for the disruptive, disagreeable behavior of rejected children, Berndt (1983) pointed out that disruption and disagreeableness seemed less like high-risk tactics to be reserved for the latter part of an entry sequence than like low-success behaviors to be avoided altogether. Third, in reviewing the specific results of the Dodge et al. (1983) study, Berndt noted that the tactics described by the authors as carrying a high risk of failure (e.g., self-statements and attention-getting behavior) did not actually do so in all cases or for all types of children. Finally, Berndt objected to the lack of attention paid by Dodge et al. to the interactional effects of the entry situation on the entering child's behavior. He proposed that certain aspects of more popular children's groups, such as their cliquishness (cf. Ladd, 1983), may contribute to the exclusion of rejected children. Thus, the disruptive behavior characteristic of rejected children may be, in part, a result of the poor treatment received from their peers. Consistent with this notion, Putallaz and Gottman (1981a, 1981b) reported that unpopular children experienced more difficulty entering popular than unpopular groups.

The arguments made by Berndt (1983) are very well taken. It does not appear that low-status children consistently resemble newcomers when entering a group. Indeed, their observed tendency to make disagreeable, disruptive, self-focused statements seems the antithesis of the newcomer behavior they display at other times. However, if one considers Berndt's argument concerning the mutual influence of the group and entering child along with the concept of relational versus instrumental goals developed earlier in this chapter, it may be possible to explain the apparently inconsistent entry behavior of low-status children. As Berndt (1983) suggested, features of the group being entered, as well as the entering child's past experience with the group, may contribute to the continued exclusion of low-status children even when appropriate strategies are employed. From the earlier discussion of the general entry literature, it seems likely that such exclusion will cause children to become concerned with saving face. One means of saving face for children may involve protecting their status by anticipating further rejection and attempting to restrict it to a minimum. In this instance, children would likely act much like newcomers, exhibiting hovering and other low-risk strategies, which only become more direct if responded to positively by the group. Such behaviors provide some, albeit quite modest, chance of gaining entry, but more importantly, they provide a ready alternative explanation or excuse for continued exclusion other than not being valued (e.g., "they were too busy to know I wanted to play"). However, saving face may also take a much more active form to the exclusion of concern for gaining entry into the group's activity. In such instances, the children's goal would be to elevate their personal status vis-à-vis the group members. As Forbes et al. (1982) suggested, this means of saving face typically would involve somewhat disruptive, disagreeable, or self-centered behavior.

The discussion thus far leads to the model of entry behavior presented in Figure 3.1. In an optimal entry situation, a child is not confronted with a rejecting group, recognizes this, and seeks entry into the group by accommodating to the group and by being generally positive. When a child is new to a group or does not know the norms governing a group's interaction, this accommodation would be preceded by hovering, passive observation, and other newcomer-like behavior. However, it is possible for several less optimal scenarios to occur during entry. A child may perceive the group to be hostile or rejecting. Under such circumstances, the goals of (a) protecting or (b) recovering one's status may replace a concern for attaining entry into the group's activity. This change of goal would seem most likely to occur for low-status children, because they are rejected and ignored more by groups (Dodge et al., 1983; Putallaz & Gottman, 1981a, 1981b) and may be more likely both to interpret neutral or ambiguous cues as negative and to expect negative behavior from other children (cf. Dodge, 1986; Dodge & Frame, 1982; Dodge, Murphy, & Buchsbaum, 1984). To protect their status following rejection, children would engage in the type of low-risk entry behaviors characteristic of newcomers. To elevate their status, children would be expected to employ the kind of disagreeable, disruptive, and self-focused entry behavior outlined earlier. The entry behaviors associated with these last two goals would seem quite unsuccessful as measured by their likelihood of leading to group acceptance, but they are perhaps more successful in terms of promoting recovery following a personal loss of status inflicted by the group or protecting against further loss of status.

Summary and conclusions

There is remarkable consistency in the results of entry studies spanning five decades and conducted within a wide array of settings. Effective group entry behavior involves strategic hovering and watching the target group members to learn their frame of reference and then applying this knowledge to perform

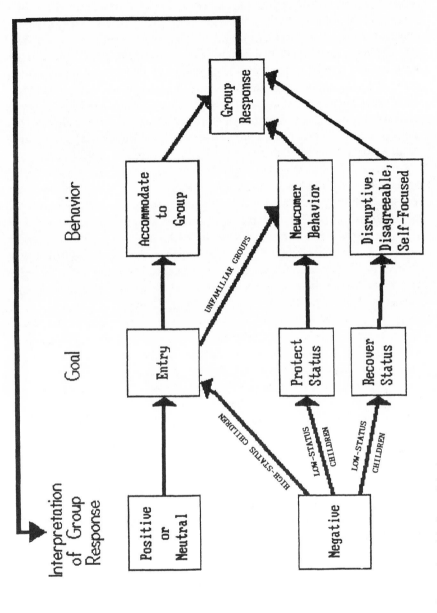

Interpretation
of Group
Response

Goal

Behavior

Figure 3.1. Proposed model of entry behavior.

behavior related to the ongoing activity of the group. Ineffective entry behavior involves either protracted hovering or engaging in disruptive, nonnormative behavior. One conclusion to be drawn from this review is that although these less effective strategies may be attributable to skill differences between children, they may also have a substantial motivational basis. It appears that low-status children may exhibit a greater concern for saving face when responded to negatively by peers than do more accepted children. Such concern for saving face may drive these children to adopt strategies that are unlikely to result in entry or group acceptance. Somewhat paradoxically, it appears that the long-term effect of this concern for saving face or recovering status is continued low status. Entry and resulting interaction appear to be key elements of long-term peer acceptance.

However, it is important to note that the suggestions relating goals to hovering or disruptive behavior are hypotheses awaiting direct test. Research is necessary to evaluate directly the validity of the hypothesis concerning mediating goals and the relationship between sociometric status and concern for saving face. In addition, research also is required to assess the limits of the model suggested in Figure 3.1. For example, it is unclear whether the model pertains equally well to familiar and unfamiliar children in an entry situation. Certainly, initial hovering and the display of other newcomer behavior would be more pronounced in an unfamiliar than in a familiar group entry situation. Further, it would seem that the group's response as well as the interpretation of that response would be greatly affected by the entering child's prior history of interaction with the group members. Further research is necessary to understand other effects the familiarity of the group would have on the model of entry presented in Figure 3.1.

Another possible limit of the model requiring research also concerns the context of the entry situation. At present, it is unclear whether the model applies primarily to competitive tasks or whether it would generalize to other tasks as well. With regard to this issue, Gelb and Jacobson (1985) recently reported that a competitive entry situation seemed to highlight behavioral differences between popular and rejected fourth-grade boys whereas a cooperative situation appeared to mask differences. In particular, the rejected boys' behavior was affected by context: They made more group-oriented statements during the cooperative task but made silly noises, broke rules, and appealed to authority primarily during the competitive situation. Context also affected the host children's behavior. They were more likely under competitive than cooperative circumstances to greet the popular entry boys positively and to react negatively to the rejected boys. Incidentally, Gelb and Jacobson (1985) reported that 75% of the rejected group responded to this initial rebuff by their classmates with a statement appealing to authority, a behavior suggested previously to be aimed at status elevation.

In addition to assessing the limitations of the model, further research is necessary to investigate other elements of effective entry. Such research should be directed at both a strategic level as well as an implementation level. In other words, it is necessary to consider not just what children choose to do during entry (i.e., strategy) but also how well they do it (i.e., implementation). For example, one strategic decision necessary during entry may be the size of the group to target for entry. Recently, Putallaz and Wasserman (1989) observed the naturalistic entry behavior of first-, third-, and fifth-grade children during recess. From their results, it appears that both the size of the group approached as well as developmental differences must be considered when attempting to understand a group's reaction to an entering child's behavior. In terms of research involving implementation issues, Burns et al. (1985) recently examined the effect of nonverbal behavior on entry success. Their findings suggested that affect influenced the group's response to an entry bid. An accompanying positive tone increased the likelihood that an entry bid would elicit acceptance from the group.

Thus, in conclusion, the research on entry is promising in at least two ways. First, although more work remains to be done, relatively firm conclusions can be drawn at this point concerning effective entry behavior, as impressive convergence exists in the literature. Second, the extent of development toward a midrange theory of one aspect of social competence, entry behavior, gives promise that a comprehensive behavioral theory of social acceptance among children is forthcoming.

References

Asher, S. R., & Hymel, S. (1981). Children's social competence in peer relations: Sociometric and behavioral assessment. In J. D. Wine & M. D. Smye (Eds.), *Social competence* (pp. 125–157). New York: Guilford Press.

Belle, D. (1976). *The preschool child's techniques for entering social groups.* Unpublished doctoral dissertation, Graduate School of Education, Harvard University.

Berndt, T. J. (1983). Correlates and causes of sociometric status in childhood: A commentary on six current studies of popular, rejected, and neglected children. *Merrill-Palmer Quarterly, 29,* 439–448.

Burns, T. J., Pellegrini, D. S., & Notarius, C. (1985, April). *Nonverbal group entry behavior and sociometric status in middle childhood.* Paper presented at the biennial meeting of the Society for Research in Child Development, Toronto.

Coie, J. D., Dodge, K. A., & Coppotelli, H. (1982). Dimensions and types of social status: A cross-age perspective. *Developmental Psychology, 18,* 557–570.

Corsaro, W. A. (1979). "We're friends, right?": Children's use of access rituals in a nursery school. *Language in Society, 8,* 315–336.

Corsaro, W. A. (1981). Friendship in the nursery school: Social organization in a peer environment. In S. R. Asher & J. M. Gottman (Eds.), *The development of children's friendships* (pp. 207–241). Cambridge: Cambridge University Press.

Dodge, K. A. (1986). A social information processing model of social competence in children. In M. Perlmutter (Ed.), *Minnesota symposia on child psychology* (Vol. 18, pp. 77–125). Hillsdale, NJ: Lawrence Erlbaum.

Dodge, K. A., & Frame, C. L. (1982). Social cognitive biases and deficits in aggressive boys. *Child Development, 53,* 620–635.

Dodge, K. A., McClaskey, C. L., & Feldman, E. (1985). A situational approach to the assessment of social competence in children. *Journal of Consulting and Clinical Psychology, 53,* 344–353.

Dodge, K. A., Murphy, R. R., & Buchsbaum, K. (1984). The assessment of intention-cue detection skills in children: Implications for developmental psychopathology. *Child Development, 55,* 163–173.

Dodge, K. A., Schlundt, D. G., Schocken, I., & Delugach, J. D. (1983). Social competence and children's social status: The role of peer group entry strategies. *Merrill-Palmer Quarterly, 29,* 309–336.

Eisenstadt, S. N. (1951). The place of elites and primary groups in the absorption of new immigrants in Israel. *American Journal of Sociology, 57,* 222–231.

Eisenstadt, S. N. (1952). The process of absorption of our immigrants in Israel. *Human Relations, 3,* 223–246.

Feldbaum, C. L., Christenson, T. E., & O'Neal, E. C. (1980). An observational study of the assimilation of the newcomer to preschool. *Child Development, 51,* 497–507.

Forbes, D., & Lubin, D. (1979, September). *Reasoning and behavior in children's friendly interactions.* Paper presented at the annual meeting of the American Psychological Association, New York.

Forbes, D. L., Katz, M. M., Paul, B., & Lubin, D. (1982). Children's plans for joining play: An analysis of structure and function. In D. Forbes & M. T. Greenberg (Eds.), *New directions for child development: Children's planning strategies* (pp. 61–79). San Francisco: Jossey Bass.

Francis, G., & Ollendick, T. H. (1984, November). *Peer group entry behavior.* Paper presented at the annual meeting of the American Association for the Advancement of Behavior Therapy, Philadelphia.

Garvey, C. (1984). *Children's talk.* Cambridge: Harvard University Press.

Gelb, R., & Jacobson, J. L. (1985, April). *Popular and rejected children's interactions during cooperative and competitive peer group activities.* Paper presented at the biennial meeting of the Society for Research in Child Development, Toronto.

Goldfried, M. R., & D'Zurilla, T. J. (1969). A behavioral-analytic model for assessing competence. In C. D. Spielberger (Ed.), *Current topics in clinical and community psychology* (Vol. 1, pp. 151–198). New York: Academic Press.

Gottman, J. M. (1977a). The effects of a modeling film on social isolation in preschool children: A methodological investigation. *Journal of Abnormal Child Psychology, 5,* 69–78.

Gottman, J. M. (1977b). Toward a definition of social isolation in childhood. *Child Development, 48,* 513–517.

Gottman, J. M. (1983). How children become friends. *Monographs of the Society for Research in Child Development, 48*(Serial No. 201).

Gottman, J. M., & Parkhurst, J. (1980). A developmental theory of friendship and acquaintanceship processes. In W. A. Collins (Ed.), *Minnesota symposia on child psychology* (Vol. 13, pp. 197–253). Hillsdale, NJ: Lawrence Erlbaum.

Hartup, W. W., Glazer, J. A., & Charlesworth, R. (1967). Peer reinforcement and sociometric status. *Child Development, 38,* 1017–1024.

Ladd, G. W. (1983). Social networks of popular, average, and rejected children in school settings. *Merrill-Palmer Quarterly, 29,* 282–307.

Mallay, H. (1935). A study of some of the techniques underlying the establishment of successful social contacts at the preschool level. *Journal of Genetic Psychology, 47,* 431–457.

Marshall, H. R., & McCandless, B. R. (1957). A study in prediction of social behavior of preschool children. *Child Development, 28,* 149–159.

McGrew, P. L., & McGrew, W. C. (1972). Changes in children's spacing behavior with nursery school experience. *Human Development, 15,* 359–372.

McGrew, W. C. (1972). *An ethological study of children's behavior.* New York: Academic Press.

McGuire, J. M. (1973). Aggression and sociometric status with preschool children. *Sociometry, 36,* 542–549.

Moore, S., & Updegraff, R. (1964). Sociometric status of preschool children related to age, sex, nurturance-giving, and dependency. *Child Development, 35,* 519–524.

Newcomb, T. M. (1950). *Social psychology.* New York: Dryden Press.

O'Connor, R. D. (1969). Modification of social withdrawal through symbolic modeling. *Journal of Applied Behavior Analysis, 2,* 15–22.

O'Connor, R. D. (1972). Relative efficacy of modeling, shaping, and the combined procedures for modification of social withdrawal. *Journal of Abnormal Psychology, 79,* 327–334.

Oden, S., & Asher, S. R. (1977). Coaching children in social skills for friendship making. *Child Development, 48,* 495–506.

Phillips, E. L., Shenker, S., & Revitz, P. (1951). The assimilation of the new child into the group. *Psychiatry, 14,* 319–325.

Putallaz, M. (1983). Predicting children's sociometric status from their behavior. *Child Development, 54,* 1417–1426.

Putallaz, M., & Gottman, J. M. (1981a). An interactional model of children's entry into peer groups. *Child Development, 52,* 986–994.

Putallaz, M., & Gottman, J. M. (1981b). Social skills and group acceptance. In S. R. Asher & J. M. Gottman (Eds.), *The development of children's friendships* (pp. 116–149). Cambridge: Cambridge University Press.

Putallaz, M., & Wasserman, A. (1989). Children's naturalistic entry behavior and sociometric status: A developmental perspective. *Developmental Psychology, 25,* 1–9.

Renshaw, P. D., & Asher, S. R. (1983). Children's goals and strategies for social interaction. *Merrill-Palmer Quarterly, 29,* 353–374.

Richardson, A. (1957). Some psycho-social characteristics of satisfied and dissatisfied British immigrant skilled manual workers in Western Australia. *Human Relations, 10,* 235–248.

Rubin, K. H., & Krasnor, L. R. (1986). Social cognitive and social behavioral perspectives on problem solving. In M. Perlmutter (Ed.), *Minnesota symposia on child psychology* (Vol. 18, pp. 1–68). Hillsdale, NJ: Lawrence Erlbaum.

Schaller, J. (1975). The relation between geographic mobility and school behavior. *Man–Environment Systems, 5,* 185–187.

Wanous, J. P. (1977). Organizational entry: Newcomers moving from outside to inside. *Psychological Bulletin, 84,* 601–618.

Washburn, R. W. (1932). A scheme for grading the reactions of children in a new social situation. *Journal of Genetic Psychology, 40,* 84–99.

Zajonc, R. B. (1952). Aggressive attitudes of the stranger as a function of conformity pressures. *Human Relations, 5,* 205–216.

Ziller, R. C., & Behringer, R. D. (1961). A longitudinal study of the assimilation of the new child into the group. *Human Relations, 14,* 121–133.

4   Preschoolers' behavioral orientations and patterns of peer contact: Predictive of peer status?

Gary W. Ladd, Joseph M. Price, and Craig H. Hart

Considerable evidence has accumulated to suggest that children differ in their behavior toward peers and that some behavioral orientations (i.e., an enduring tendency to act in a particular manner toward peers) are related to social status in the peer group (see Chapter 2, this volume; Ladd & Asher, 1985). Perhaps the most compelling evidence of this relationship comes from recent short-term longitudinal studies of boys' peer-oriented behavior and their emerging social status in small play groups (Coie & Kupersmidt, 1983; Dodge, 1983). Dodge (1983) assembled play groups of unacquainted boys and examined the behavioral histories of those who became unpopular as opposed to accepted by peers. Results indicated that children classified as rejected were more likely to employ rough play and aggressive behaviors with peers and were less likely to engage in positive or prosocial forms of interaction such as cooperative play and social conversation. Coie and Kupersmidt (1983) also explored the development of social status in boys' play groups, but unlike Dodge, these investigators selected boys who were known to occupy varying sociometric strata in school (i.e., popular, average, neglected, rejected) and then charted their behavioral histories and emerging social status in play groups comprised of either familiar or unfamiliar peers. Analyses of the boys' behavior in both types of play contexts revealed that previously rejected boys displayed higher levels of aggression than did popular or neglected peers. Moreover, over time in the play groups, these boys tended to reestablish their prior reputations as rejected peers. Popular boys, in contrast, were seldom aggressive and more often engaged in prosocial norm-setting behaviors.

Taken together, these studies corroborate the findings of previous correlational studies (e.g., Hartup, Glazer, & Charlesworth, 1967; Marshall & McCandless, 1957) and further support the view that individual differences in behavior are responsible for children's social acceptance and rejection in the peer group. Moreover, it is clear that some behavioral orientations (e.g., prosocial or aggressive behavior patterns) are more predictive of children's peer status than others. Thus, in understanding how children come to occupy particular social

90

positions in a peer group, it seems important to consider the behavioral content of their interactions.

It is also important to recognize that children's behavior occurs in specific social contexts. Indeed, it is conceivable that the context of children's interactions may play an important role in both the development and the modification of their peer status. Thus, in addition to measures of the character or orientation of children's behaviors (e.g., the frequency or percentage of time children spend in particular behaviors), it may also be important for researchers to consider the contexts in which these behaviors occur.

It is possible, for example, that the means by which children come to establish a social reputation within a group depends not only on the character of their interactions but also on the pattern with which these interactions are deployed among individual members of the group (cf. Masters & Furman, 1981). For example, regardless of their behavioral orientations, children may differ in the number of group members they have contact with and, thus, vary in the degree to which they are "known" by others or "impact" upon peers' judgments of likability. Variation may also occur in the degree of association children have with the individuals who make up their range of contacts, as in the case where one or more "consistent" play partners can be identified (see Hinde, Titmus, Easton, & Tamplin, 1985; Howes, 1983). If, as Howes (1983) has shown, frequent or maintained companionship provides an important context for the development of social skills, then higher levels of peer acceptance might be anticipated for children who routinely participate in these relationships.

Information about the types of contexts in which children's interactions tend to occur may also be an important consideration in the design and implementation of skill-oriented intervention programs. For example, in teaching children social skills, it may be important to know something about the context in which they are likely to use the skills. Factors associated with social situations, such as the number of peers who tend to be present in an exchange (i.e., average group size) and the types of participants involved (i.e., the age, gender, and social status of one's companions), may affect the appropriateness or effectiveness of children's social skills.

Unfortunately, there has been little effort in the field of peer relations to map both the content and the context of children's behaviors in group settings. As a step in this direction, we were interested in developing a methodology that would yield information about children's (a) behaviors with peers, (b) patterns of contact with group members, and (c) typical interactional contexts. To accomplish this task, we first sought a conceptual foothold that would allow us to define these variables and devise corresponding measures. It seemed to us that literature on the social networks of adults and children might provide such a foothold. Thus, we devote the initial portion of this chapter to an overview of the central concepts and methods employed in past research on adult social networks, and then we consider the utility of these tools in light of our research objectives. Previous efforts to identify and map children's peer networks are also reviewed, along with relevant findings from this literature.

A second purpose of this chapter is to provide empirical data on children's behaviors and contact patterns in peer groups and to explore relations between these variables and measures of children's peer status. Toward this end, we will present the findings of a recent study we have conducted on the relationship between preschoolers' peer status and their behavioral orientations and peer contact patterns, as observed on a school playground. Specifically, the stability of children's behavioral orientations and contact patterns is examined over the course of a school year, and relationships between these measures and children's classroom peer status are explored in terms of both change over time and direction of effect. In addition, findings concerning temporal trends and sex differences in the interpersonal context of children's interactions are presented. We conclude with a discussion of the implications of these findings for intervention research with low-status children.

Social network research: history, concepts, and methods

The roots of systematic research on social networks reach back more than 30 years and are anchored in several disciplines, including social anthropology, sociology, and psychology. The concept of the social network was first employed by social anthropologists and sociologists (e.g., Barnes, 1954; Bott, 1971; J. C. Mitchell, 1969) to map the collection of people (usually excluding family or kin) with whom individuals relate on a regular basis. For example, the British social anthropologist Barnes (1954) first charted the social networks of people living in a Norwegian fishing village by observing the range of fellow inhabitants with whom they interacted. Research on social networks, or "reference groups," was also pursued in the field of psychology during the 1940s and 1950s as researchers became interested in group relations and the impact of groups on individuals. Examples of this focus include studies that proliferated during the 1940s and 1950s based on reference group theory (see Hyman & Singer, 1968) and social comparison theory (Festinger, 1954). Central to these investigations were questions concerning the influence of social groups on the behavior and attitudes of individuals and the extent to which the individual's social field served as a source of motivation, affiliation, and self-understanding (for a detailed review of this literature, see Heller & Swindle, 1983).

In the decades that followed these pioneering efforts, much of the work by social anthropologists and sociologists was devoted to mapping specific network features and norms, often to compare individuals living in differing social contexts or cultures (e.g., Cubitt, 1973; Hammer, 1980). Research by Hammer (1980), for example, suggests that adult networks are typically comprised of 6 to 9 close relationships, approximately 30 others who have regular contact with the subject, between 500 and 1,000 acquaintances, and nearly 1,000 to 2,000 people who are acquainted with the individual's close and regular associates. Another emphasis in this research has been on the psychosocial and environmental factors that contribute to the formation and maintenance of social networks. As an illustration of this focus, environmental studies by psychologists such as Holohan and Wilcox (1978) indicate that college students living on higher dormitory floors differ in their friendship patterns from students living on lower floors. Other researchers, such as Heller, Amaral, and Procidano (1978), stress the importance of psychosocial characteristics, such as a person's social skills, in the formation and maintenance of social networks. More recently, the relationship between social networks and various adjustment and health-related outcomes has become of interest to social anthropologists, physicians, and community psychologists. Within this literature, a number of studies point to a relationship between specific network characteristics (e.g., interconnectedness) and various somatic ailments, including pregnancy complications (Nuckolls, Cassel, & Kaplan, 1972) and heart disease (Medalie & Goldbourt, 1976). Evidence linking network features with both psychiatric disorders, such as schizophrenia (Garrison, 1978; Hammer, 1981) and depression (Brown, Bhrolchain, & Harris, 1975), and social problems, such as child abuse (Salzinger, Kaplan, & Artemyeff, 1983), has also begun to accumulate.

To account for these findings, several causal explanations have been advanced in the literature, including the following hypotheses (see Hammer, 1983): (a) the individual's state of health or adjustment determines the features of his or her network, as might be the case when illness causes immobility and, thus, restricts social contacts; (b) social networks facilitate health and adjustment by fostering participation in health-enhancing activities; (c) social networks are both a source of social support and a buffer for stress, which, in turn, enhances adjustment or health; and (d) social networks facilitate health or adjustment by serving as "staging areas" for the acquisition and refinement of adaptive behaviors and as transmission paths for social information.

Description of social networks

The term *social network* has been imbued with numerous meanings over the past 30 years, often implying different foci and levels of analysis. In attempting to define a common referent, early researchers tended to distinguish between personal and social networks (see J. C. Mitchell, 1969), depending on whether the social field to be charted was that of an individual or a larger social unit (e.g., a family or community), respectively. In recent literature, however, these terms have been used interchangeably, even though the former concept defines much of the work conducted in this field.

Important conceptual distinctions have also evolved as investigators have attempted to map variations in the structure and functions of the individual's social contacts. One such issue concerns the distinction between the concepts of social network and social support (see Heller & Swindle, 1983). Although a consensus has not yet been achieved, it is generally understood that the term *social network* refers to various structural or relational properties, or both, of the person's social field (e.g., number of members and quality of ties between the members), whereas the term *social support* refers to various psychological properties of the network, such as the network's ability to reduce stress or provide companionship. Because the structure of the individual's social contacts within his or her reference group is most relevant to our research purposes, the concept of the social network will be considered in greater detail.

In charting a person's social network, it has been necessary for investigators to delineate the contexts in which social encounters are to be mapped. Data concerning the subject's social contacts (e.g., interactions) or relationships (e.g., "important" people) or both with nonfamily members have typically been used as a means of identifying network members (see R. E. Mitchell & Trickett, 1980), and a variety of social settings such as factories, churches, and even doughnut shops have been employed as contexts for network assessment (see Hammer, 1979/80).

Once the members of the individual's social field have been identified, further description of the network is possible. Recently, theorists have proposed a number of dimensions along which networks may vary, each of which is defined by a related set of variables (for a review, see Marsella & Snyder, 1981; R. E. Mitchell & Trickett, 1980). Among the dimensions that have received the most research attention are those that represent the structural and relational properties of the network. Generally, measures of network structure include the number of network members (i.e., size); the degree to which contacts occur in large, as opposed to small, groups (i.e., extensivity); the linkages between the subject's network members (i.e., interconnectedness); and the types of people who make up the network (i.e., composition). Measures of the relational characteristics of the network have been devised to tap properties of the ties that exist between various network actors, such as the strength, duration, and valence of the ties (i.e., intensity, durability, and affinity), the types or number of functions network members serve (i.e., multiplexity), the degree to which these functions are reciprocated by the subject (i.e., reciprocity), geographic proximity of network members (i.e., dispersion), and frequency of contact (i.e., frequency).

Methods for investigating social networks

The principal task in network research is to map the subject's social contacts and gather various types of information about the relationships between the network actors. Moreover, as in any investigative undertaking, the researcher must ensure that the methods used to gather this information produce reliable and valid information. To achieve these goals, three main types of investigative strategies have been employed, either alone or in combination. These strategies can be seen as differing primarily in terms of the data source employed and the methods used to access network information.

Verbal reports. Methods based on verbal reports are perhaps the most frequently employed data-gathering strategies found in the adult social network literature. Testimony concerning network members and network characteristics has often been obtained directly from the subject, or in cases where the accuracy of self-reports may be in doubt, this information has been solicited from persons who are considered to be knowledgeable about the subject's social activities. As a means of gathering these reports, most researchers have relied on face-to-face interviews (e.g., Hammer, 1980; Salzinger et al., 1983). Within these procedures, various approaches have been employed to identify network members and activities. Network membership, for example, has usually been assessed by asking subjects to list "important" social contacts (e.g., Salzinger et al., 1983) or to name persons with whom they share specific social functions or activities (e.g., Hammer, Gutwirth, & Phillips, 1982). Compared with alternative methodologies, verbal report is perhaps the most convenient data collection strategy and, unlike observation, provides information about the subject's perceptions of various network characteristics. This approach is frequently criticized, however, on the grounds that self-report data may be both unreliable and inaccurate due to a number of potential response biases such as social desirability or retrospective distortion. However, efforts to compare verbal self-reports with data gathered through systematic observation (see Hammer, Polgar, & Salzinger, 1969) reveal that subjects' reports of their social activities are fairly accurate, with most inaccuracies occurring due to a tendency to omit rather than distort network information.

Direct observation. Although less extensively employed, observational methods have also been used to map social networks. Generally, this type of research involves one or more observers who unobtrusively document the subject's social contacts in one or more specific settings (e.g., Hammer, 1979/80). Like other forms of observational research, decisions must be made concerning the focus of observation, locations, sampling techniques, recording procedures, and codes. Typically, the subject's behavior during social contacts and companions' names, ages, and genders are considered essential features of the observational record. These data allow investigators to chart network membership and profile features of the individual's social contacts.

It is important to note that observation as a data-gathering strategy differs in several ways from verbal report methods. Perhaps the primary distinction is that observational data provide a measure of subjects' actual social contacts rather than their perceptions of who are the most important social figures in their lives. Another difference is that because observations are scheduled in the present and conducted on events that can be witnessed by more than one person, it is also possible to estimate their reliability. (Although seldom employed, this does not rule out the possibility that multiple informants could be used to corroborate verbal reports.) Finally, due to pragmatic constraints, observations are usually conducted in a limited number of settings and, therefore, do not provide a complete description of the focal person's social field. Rather, the networks described by this methodology are typically referred to as bounded by the social setting(s) under investigation (see Hammer, 1979/80).

Logs and diary records. This approach to mapping social networks requires subjects (or knowledgeable informants) to "observe" and record their own social activities; thus, it can be seen as a compromise between the previous two methods. Until recently, use of this promising approach in network research was somewhat limited. One example can be found in a study conducted by Hammer et al. (1982) comparing the networks of parents and nonparents. For one of the samples employed, participants were asked to keep records of their regular social activities, including the names of people who had been involved in each documented episode. Names found in the participants' logs were used to define network membership.

Another example of the use of diary records can be found in recent work by Carpenter and Huston (e.g., 1983). Rather than focusing exclusively on social networks, these authors used diaries to investigate children's use of time and the role of adults in the development and maintenance of sex-typed behaviors. In one recent investigation (Carpenter & Huston, 1983), children were trained to keep a diary of their activities after school and on weekends. Children were taught to use 15-min time segments from the time they came home from school until bedtime; children were asked to record the following: (a) where they were,

(b) what they were doing, (c) what persons were present (i.e., adult, sibling, or peer), and (d) whether the persons present were engaged in the same activity.

The use of log and diary records in network research is also illustrated in recent work by W. Furman (personal communication, 1986). The goal of this work is to monitor children's relationships in and across natural settings. Using small handheld computers, children record their activities and the persons with whom they interact (e.g., parent, sibling, or peer) during designated time periods.

Logs and diary records offer several advantages over verbal reports and direct observations. They are easy to administer and less obtrusive than observations and, yet, provide data on actual social contacts and activities. Because subjects are typically asked to report on their social activities soon after their occurrence, many of the problems associated with retrospective verbal reports may be averted. Unlike observations, however, procedures for assessing the reliability and validity of logs and diaries have not been developed.

Adapting network methods to research with children

Developmentalists have only recently begun to contemplate the role of social networks in child development (e.g., Cochran & Brassard, 1979; Lewis & Feiring, 1979), and research on this topic has been limited to mapping children's networks (usually in terms of adult members) and exploring the relationship between network composition and the child's cognitive status (e.g., Feiring & Lewis, 1981). Research on children's peer networks is rare (e.g., Ladd, 1983, 1984; Waldrop & Halverson, 1975).

Many of the methods used in research with adults can be used to gather information about children's social networks. However, in adapting these methods, it is important to recognize that both the subjects and the settings differ from those used in past studies with adults. More importantly, these factors may alter the appropriateness and feasibility of the various data-gathering methods. For example, concerns about the reliability and accuracy of self-report methods, often raised in the adult literature, may be even more at issue in research with subjects who are cognitively less mature, such as children. Although researchers may choose to rely on more reliable sources, such as parents or teachers, to compensate for this problem, the accuracy of their verbal reports or logs may be limited to specific contexts such as the home or classroom where they have opportunities to observe children's interactions. In contrast, observational methods have the advantage of providing more "objective" and potentially reliable data and, in addition, may be more feasible to conduct with children than with adults because children are often with peers for extended periods of time in relatively public places (e.g., in schools or other organized settings).

Another issue that follows from the adult literature is that the choice of the data-gathering strategy will, in part, determine what is investigated. Because investigators who employ observational methods can directly witness children's interactions, they are in an excellent position to gather data on the nature of their peer *contacts* within a given setting. Verbal report methods, on the other hand, may be better suited to mapping network membership across multiple settings or gathering data on children's *perceptions* of their companions (i.e., the degree to which particular peers are seen as important or influential).

Research on children's peer networks and play contacts

Studies that map children's peer networks or identify features of their play contacts in group settings are rare. In an early study conducted by Waldrop and Halverson (1975), mothers of 7-year-olds were asked to keep detailed diaries of their children's neighborhood peer contacts during a 1-week interval. To supplement the information found in the diaries, subsequent in-depth interviews were also employed. Data from the diaries were used to create estimates of the number of hours spent with peers in dyads or groups, the number of different peers seen, and the number of occasions in which the child initiated peer contacts or determined the focus of play activities. Several other measures were derived from the mother's interview responses, including estimates of the number of peers in the child's neighborhood, number of friends, and proportion of same-sex and same-age friends. Data from these sources and from child interviews and behavior observations conducted in a free-play setting were subsequently compiled and used to generate ratings for each child on the following global dimensions: intensiveness (i.e., the tendency to play or relate with peers in dyadic or small-group contexts), extensiveness (i.e., the tendency to play or relate with peers in larger group settings), importance of peers, social ease, and dominance. Factor and correlational analyses revealed that measures of the intensiveness and extensiveness of children's play patterns discriminated between boys and girls. For boys, extensive play styles were correlated with measures of social ease, importance of peers, and hours spent with peers, whereas for girls, the same measures were related to intensive play patterns. Moreover, factor scores representing the weighted combination of variables associated with extensiveness in boys and intensiveness in girls were found to correlate significantly with measures of social maturity, proportion of same-sex friends, and, for girls, proportion of same-age friends.

More recently, Ellis, Rogoff, and Cromer (1981) employed a combination of spot observations and telephone interviews to explore the interpersonal context of children's peer contacts in home and neighborhood settings. Observers gathered information about children's peer companions while traversing predetermined routes through a specific neighborhood. Children from each of six age-groups were observed (1–2, 3–4, 5–6, 7–8, 9–10, and 11–12 years). For each focal child selected, observers recorded the number of companions present and inquired about the age, sex, and kinship status of each associate. Similar data were collected from telephone interviews with parents living in the same neighborhood, and this information was combined with that obtained from the observational records for analyses. Results indicated that the presence of peer, as opposed to adult, companions increased sharply from infancy through the preadolescent years. Data for the combined age samples indicated that children were more likely to be found in the presence of near-age companions (children within 2 years of the subject's age) than with either same-age (within 1 year) or cross-age (more than 2 years) playmates. However, companionship with same-age peers increased significantly with age. With regard to gender, infants and preschool children were equally likely to be observed in the company of opposite-sex as same-sex peers, whereas middle-elementary and preadolescent children were more often found in groups of same-sex companions. The majority of peer contacts documented at each age level contained one or more relatives, although the frequency with which peer contacts occurred among unrelated peers increased with age.

Relationship between contact patterns, interactional contexts, and peer status

Research has also been conducted on the contact patterns of children who differ in sociometric status among classmates. Benson and Gottman (1975; and as reported in Putallaz & Gottman, 1981) observed grade-school children in a classroom context and found that popular children tended to initiate and receive positive interactions primarily with peers of similar sociometric status. This same within-group pattern of reciprocity, but for neutral behaviors, was observed among unpopular children.

Working initially in classrooms, Ladd (1983) identified third- and fourth-grade children from each of three social strata (those whose peer status among classmates was defined as popular, average, or rejected) and then compared features of their peer contacts in the larger school context. Observations of children's playground interactions and peer contacts were conducted during mixed-grade recess periods and used to assess the percentage of time subjects spent in various interactive (e.g., cooperative play and social conversation) and noninteractive behaviors (e.g., solitary play and onlooking) and to chart features of the social context in which children conducted their interactions. More specifically, to represent aspects of the peer ecology, scores were developed to index the average number of peers present in the subject's interactions and the percentage of time spent in interactions with peers of similar and/or differing grade levels, sexes, or statuses. In addition, friendship questionnaires and interviews were administered to children throughout the school, and these data were used to determine which of the subject's frequent playground companions were friends with the subject and with each other. Self-report information about the subject's friendships outside the school setting was also collected and used to explore differences in the nonschool friendships of popular, average, and rejected children.

Analysis of children's playground behaviors revealed that rejected children spent less time engaged in prosocial interactions and more time in agonistic and unoccupied behaviors than did popular or average children and that they paralleled average children in time spent watching others play. These findings replicated those obtained in earlier research in classroom settings (see Chapter 2, this volume, for a review). Analyses performed on the various interactional context measures revealed that a larger proportion of rejected children's interactions, as compared with those of popular and average children, occurred in small groups and were distributed among younger or unpopular companions or both. Differences in the playground contacts of popular, average, and rejected children also emerged with respect to the quality of their social ties with play partners. Popular and average children were named as friends by a greater proportion of their frequent playground companions and tended to have companions that were also friends with each other. With respect to nonschool friendships, children in the three sociometric strata did not differ significantly on measures of the number and duration of reported friendships. However, rejected children mentioned having friends who were significantly younger than those reported by children in the other two status groups.

In sum, most of the research on children's peer networks has been designed to explore the context of their peer contacts and has been conducted at only one point in time. Data from past studies suggest that when assessed concurrently, the interpersonal context of children's social interactions (i.e., the types of peers present during social encounters) often varies depending on their status in the peer group. Less is known, however, about children's contact patterns, such as the range of peers with whom they relate in group settings and the frequency of their association with specific group members. These factors may be especially relevant to research on the development of peer status. For example, children with a broader range of contacts may come to be known by a larger proportion of their peer group. That is, a child who has extensive contacts may provide group members with a history of experiences that, in turn, shape their perceptions or attitudes toward the child. This type of research, however, requires that the relation between peer contact patterns and group status be assessed over time so that potential antecedents (e.g., specific contact patterns) can be distinguished from potential outcomes (e.g., peer group status).

A study of preschoolers' behavioral orientations and peer contacts

To further our understanding of the nature of children's behavioral orientations and peer contacts in group settings and their relationship to peer status, we conducted a short-term, within-year longitudinal study of preschoolers' social connections on a school playground. Our goal was not to define the overall membership of children's peer networks but rather to chart their behavioral orientations and patterns of peer contact within a particular social setting. Thus, one aim of this investigation was to assess not only the character of children's behavior toward peers but also the structure of their peer contacts, including both their range of contact and frequency of association with group members. Toward this end, behavioral observations were conducted on three occasions during the school year to assess the percentage of time children spent in various social and nonsocial behaviors and the range and degree of contact they had with available playground companions. A second purpose of the study was to chart features of the social context in which children's interactions tended to occur. This was accomplished by recording, in addition to the behavioral data, the identities of children's interaction partners. Based on this information, we examined (a) temporal trends and sex differences in both the patterns of contact and the interpersonal contexts that characterized children's interactions, (b) the degree to which individual differences in children's behavioral orientations and peer contact patterns remained stable over time, and (c) the extent to which individual differences in behavioral orientations and peer contact patterns predicted children's social status among classmates at specific points during the school year.

The subjects in this study were 28 preschoolers selected from four half-day nursery school classrooms serving a total of 88 children between the ages of $2\frac{1}{2}$ and $5\frac{1}{2}$ years of age. Only children who fell between the ages of $3\frac{1}{2}$ and $4\frac{1}{2}$ within the combined classrooms were selected for participation, and the sample was balanced with respect to gender, enrollment in morning or afternoon classrooms, and familiarity with the school setting.

To assess children's behaviors and peer contacts, observations were made on a playground, where subjects were free to choose their own play companions and activities. Three trained observers and one reliability judge conducted a total of 90 scans (4–5 s intervals) per child during each of three 6-week intervals scheduled at the beginning (early fall), middle (winter), and end (spring) of the school year. During each interval, observers reliably coded (κ > .86) the subject's behavior into either one of four interactive categories (i.e., cooperative play, social conversation, rough play, or argue) or one of five non-peer-interactive categories (i.e., parallel play, solitary play, onlooking, teacher-oriented, or transition). For each 6-week interval, estimates of the proportion of time a child spent in each type of behavior were calculated by summing the total number of entries within each of the four interactive and five noninteractive categories and dividing by the total number of observations.

Each time a child's behavior was coded into one of the four interactive categories, observers also recorded the names of the children who appeared to be involved in the same interaction or activity. The correlations found between observer's estimates of the number of companions present in children's interactions ranged from .84 to .97 across observers and assessment intervals. The identities of the subject's companions were used to create measures of both the structure of children's peer contacts (i.e., range of contacts or number of frequent play companions) as well as the interpersonal contexts in which their interactions tended to occur (i.e., companions' collective ages, genders, and statuses). The subject's range of contacts was estimated at each time of assessment by determining the number of different companions present in his or her playground interactions. Playmates who were present in more than 30% of the subject's interactions were counted to obtain a frequent-play-companions score. The interpersonal context measures were created as follows. The number of companions present in each interaction was averaged to obtain a group size mean. Three additional context dimensions were created by coding the subject's interactions to reflect, relative to themselves, the collective ages (i.e., older by more than 6 months, younger by more than 6 months, same, or mixed), genders (i.e., same, opposite, or mixed), and statuses (i.e., high, medium, low, or mixed) of their companions. For each of these measures (e.g., age composition), the proportions of sampled interactions that fell into corresponding categories (e.g., older, same, younger, or mixed) served as the subject's scores.

Children's peer status was assessed at the end of each observational interval by individually administering sociometric measures to children within each classroom. Children were asked to provide both positive and negative peer nominations and also to rate classmates on a 3-point likability scale (see Asher, Singleton, Tinsley, & Hymel, 1979). From these data, separate positive and negative nomination scores were created by summing the "votes" children received from classmates for each criterion and then standardizing the scores within classrooms. Following the guidelines set forth by Coie, Dodge, and Coppotelli (1982), these scores were combined to create two additional measures, termed

social preference and *social impact*. A mean peer acceptance score was also created for each subject by averaging and standardizing the ratings received from all classmates on the 3-point likability scale.

Temporal trends and sex differences

One objective of our investigation was to determine whether there were sex differences and temporal changes in children's contact patterns and interactional contexts over the course of the school year. A series of separate analyses of variance, performed on these measures, revealed that the number of different peers with whom children interacted on the playground declined significantly from the beginning to the middle and end of the school year ($M = 18.68$, 14.93, 14.93, respectively). Moreover the average number of companions present in children's interactions (excluding the subject) declined significantly over time ($M = 1.62$, 1.54, 1.48), although males ($M = 1.63$) consistently played in significantly larger groups than did females ($M = 1.46$). Changes in the peer composition of children's interactions were also evidenced in that contacts among both same-sex ($M = .46$, $.54$, $.58$) and same-age companions ($M = .34$, $.44$, $.64$) tended to increase over time, whereas interactions among mixed-sex ($M = .27$, $.16$, $.15$) and older children ($M = .23$, $.25$, $.06$) tended to decline. Data on children's contacts with companions of varying levels of peer status, which were obtained only at the middle and end of the school year, revealed that time spent among high-status associates increased significantly over time ($M = .17$, $.29$, respectively), whereas mixed-status companionship declined significantly ($M = .27$, $.21$).

In sum, it would appear that some aspects of children's peer contact patterns and interactive contexts do change systematically over the course of the school year. In particular, changes in the structure of children's peer contacts were evidenced in that preschoolers tended to interact with a smaller range of individuals and in smaller groups over the course of the year. These data suggest that over time, children became more selective in their choice of play companions and pursued more intensive play styles.

Several shifts were also evidenced in the composition of children's playground companionship. Like the findings of Ellis et al. (1981), our data suggest that the interpersonal milieu for children's interactions became more homogeneous over time with respect to both age and gender. During the latter half of the school year, changes in children's interactive contexts also occurred in relation to peer status. Specifically, children spent more time among high-status peers and less time interacting with mixed-status peers. This pattern of findings suggests that as the year progressed, popular children became more of the focus of children's interactions (cf. Benson & Gottman, 1975). That is, regardless of children's own status, they were more often observed to interact with popular companions over the course of the school year. In addition to these temporal trends, our data suggest that males had more extensive peer contacts (i.e., conducted their interactions in larger groups) than did females. These findings are consistent with previous investigations of children's peer networks (e.g., Ladd, 1983; Waldrop & Halverson, 1975).

Stability of individual differences

Another objective of this investigation was to examine the stability of the individual differences found in children's playground behaviors and peer contacts. This was done to determine whether the behavior and peer contact measures, as potential predictors of peer status, indexed individual differences that were consistent (i.e., reflective of an enduring orientation or pattern) within each assessment interval or across the school year. To address this question, children's scores on each of the behavioral and peer contact measures were calculated both for the first and for the second halves of each 6-week assessment period, as well as for each entire interval. The scores obtained for each measure were then correlated within and across assessment periods to assess short-term and long-term stability.

Results indicated that individual differences in children's playground behaviors (with the exception of those coded as parallel play, transition, and onlooking) were relatively stable within each assessment interval (median r for the remaining six measures = .60). Individual differences in cooperative play and unoccupied behaviors were also found to be stable over the school year (r over 20 weeks = .52 and .69, respectively). Trends were also found suggesting that individual differences in rough play became more stable over the school year (r = .36 from fall to winter, and .53 from winter to spring), whereas declining stability was found for behaviors such as social conversation (r = .61 from fall to winter, and .17 from winter to spring). The correlations obtained for the investigated peer contact measures revealed that individual differences in children's range of contacts and number of frequent play companions were quite stable within assessment intervals (median r = .65 and .66, respectively). Over longer intervals, the stability estimates for these two measures were not as high (r over 20 weeks was .33 for the range-of-contacts and .41 for the frequent-play-companion measures).

These findings provide evidence of moderate stability for some of the differences observed in preschoolers' playground behaviors and peer contacts. A similar conclusion can be drawn with respect to the individual differences found in both measures of children's peer contacts. Differences between children in the

diversity of their peer contacts and the number of frequent play companions they acquired were relatively stable within each assessment occasion.

Predicting children's peer status in the classroom

Our final objective in this investigation was to determine whether stable differences in children's playground behaviors and peer contacts were predictive of their classroom peer status. To address this question, a two-step procedure was used to (a) detect emerging relationships between predictors and criteria and (b) shed light on the direction of these emerging relationships. First, correlations were calculated within assessment occasions (i.e., concurrently) between measures of children's behavioral orientations and peer status. Only measures that were found to reflect stable individual differences in children's playground behaviors were included in these analyses. The resulting correlations were examined to determine whether the relationships obtained between these measures tended to change across the three assessment occasions (i.e., the pattern of association was one of increasing or decreasing magnitude). The correlations calculated for four of the behavioral measures (i.e., cooperative play, rough play, unoccupied, and teacher-oriented) produced trends with one or more of the peer status measures. Across the fall, winter, and spring assessment occasions, cooperative play became increasingly associated with both positive nominations (in order, $r = .19, .35, .38$) and peer impact scores (in order, $r = .01, .36, .44$). Over the same intervals, rough play tended to become negatively related to positive peer nominations ($r = -.10, -.30, -.17$) and social preference scores ($r = -.26, -.43, -.41$), and positively related to negative nominations ($r = .34, .57, .56$) and social impact scores ($r = .19, .21, .24$). For unoccupied and teacher-oriented behaviors, a negative relationship emerged with social impact scores over the course of the school year ($r = .11, -.26, -.35$, and $r = .09, -.57, -.30$, respectively).

Relationships between the measures of peer contact and peer status were assessed in the same manner. The relationship between children's range of peer contacts and positive nominations was near zero at the beginning of the school year, and a larger negative relationship was found between these measures at midyear ($r = -.35$) than at the end of the year ($r = -.14$). A similar pattern of correlations emerged for social preference scores ($r = .09, -.44, -.24$, respectively). The correlations obtained between the range-of-contact and negative nomination measures were positive but, again, were higher at midyear ($r = .39$) than at the beginning ($r = .20$) or end of the school year ($r = .22$). The only trend to emerge in the correlations calculated between the number of frequent play companions and peer status measures was found for peer ratings. The correlations obtained between these measures were somewhat higher at the middle and end of the school year ($r = .80$ and $.77$, respectively) than at the outset ($r = .59$).

To shed light on the possible direction of the emerging relations between these predictors and criteria, a series of multiple regression analyses was performed. The aim of these analyses was to determine whether the emerging relations between children's peer behavior and status could best be accounted for in terms of children's antecedent behaviors or peer reputations. This was addressed by comparing the efficacy of two predictive models for each of the observed trends: one in which past behavior was used to predict current peer status after controlling for former status and current behavior and one in which past status was used to predict current behavior after controlling for past behavior and current status. Thus, the first analysis was designed to determine whether children's emerging peer status was a function of their prior behavior toward peers, after controlling for the potential effects of their current behavior (i.e., the level of the predictor behavior that had evolved by the time the criterion was measured), and their prior reputation in the peer group. The second analysis was intended to explore the degree to which children's emerging behavior was a function of their prior peer status, while controlling for the potential effects of their current reputations (i.e., nature of the reputation that had evolved by the time the behavioral criterion was assessed), and their prior peer behavior. Moreover, because it is conceivable that the direction of the relationship between these variables may change over time, the predictive efficacy of both models was separately evaluated for each half of the school year (i.e., fall to winter and winter to spring) and across the entire school year (i.e., fall to spring). The same method of analysis was also used to explore the trends found between the peer contact and peer status measures.

The results of these analyses supported the view that children's peer status is, in part, a function of their past behavior. That is, whereas efforts to predict current behavior from prior peer status were consistently unsuccessful, attempts to predict peer status from past behavior did produce significant or near-significant findings for several pairs of variables. For example, time spent in cooperative play at the beginning of the school year was a significant or nearly significant predictor of both positive nominations, $F(1, 23) = 4.57, p < .04$, and social impact scores, $F(1, 23) = 4.77, p < .03$, at the end of the school year. Higher levels of rough play at the outset of the school year forecasted lower positive nomination scores, $F(1, 23) = 3.62, p < .07$, and higher social impact scores, $F(1, 23) = 4.29, p < .05$, by midyear. A significant negative relationship emerged between time spent in unoccupied behaviors during the early weeks of school and social impact scores at the end of the year, $F(1, 23) = 4.59, p < .04$.

To identify potential antecedents for the relationships observed between the peer contact and peer status measures, we performed an analogous series of

regression analyses. Findings indicated that children's range of peer contact was both predictive *of* peer status and predicted *by* peer status, depending on the time of assessment and the aspect of status measured. More specifically, the analysis designed to predict children's peer status at midyear from their range of contacts in the first month of school revealed significant or marginally significant findings for both positive nominations, $F(1, 23) = 3.35$, $p < .08$, and social impact scores, $F(1, 23) = 11.75$, $p < .01$. The alternative model, which was designed to predict children's range of peer contacts at the middle and end of the school year from their prior peer reputations, produced significant findings for the negative nominations measure. That is, the number of negative nominations children received at the beginning of the school year predicted their range of peer contacts at midyear, $F(1, 23) = 7.13$, $p < .01$, and the number of negative nominations received at midyear predicted their range of peer contacts at the end of the year, $F(1, 23) = 4.63$, $p < .04$. In both cases, higher negative nomination scores tended to predict a broader range of peer contacts. Finally, the relationship between the frequent play companions measure and children's peer ratings was also explored. Findings revealed that the number of frequent play companions children had at the beginning of the school year predicted their average peer ratings at the end of the year, $F(1, 23) = 7.57$, $p < .01$. In contrast, earlier ratings were not found to predict later frequent play companion scores.

Summary and discussion of the findings

Overall, these findings suggest that both the nature of children's playground interactions (e.g., prosocial vs. agonistic encounters) and the structure of their peer contacts (e.g., range of peer contacts and degree of association with companions) forecast their eventual peer status in the classroom. The method of data analysis employed in this investigation was designed to contrast alternative hypotheses concerning the antecedents of children's peer reputations and behavior in the peer group. Stronger support was found for the hypothesis that children's behaviors contribute to their social status among peers than was found for the hypothesis that children's prior peer reputations influence their subsequent behavior. Specifically, whereas higher levels of peer liking were predicted by cooperative play, lower levels of peer liking were predicted by rough play. Interestingly, these two behaviors, cooperative play and rough play, forecasted greater visibility (i.e., social impact) in the peer group during the first half of the school year. The thrust of these findings is consistent with those reported by Dodge (1983) and Coie and Kupersmidt (1983); the findings point to the importance of both prosocial and aggressive behaviors in the formation and maintenance of children's status in the peer group.

One nonsocial behavior was also found to predict low visibility, or social impact, among peers. Children who spent a greater proportion of their time engaging in aimless solitary or unoccupied behaviors appeared to become neither well liked nor disliked by peers, judging from their tendency to receive lower social impact scores by the end of the school year. This finding, coupled with the fact that children's peer reputations did not predict subsequent nonsocial behaviors, suggests that some children become less known by peers because they consistently spend time alone and uninvolved in any form of constructive activity. These findings are interesting in light of recent work indicating that socially isolated or withdrawn children resemble average-status peers early in their school careers but may become neglected or disliked by their classmates later during grade school (Chapter 8, this volume: Hymel & Rubin, 1985). Our sociometric findings suggest that over the course of a school year, children who seldom interact with peers garner very little in the way of liking or disliking in the peer group and, instead, tend to be "overlooked" by their classmates. This apparent discrepancy in findings may be due to differences in the way children's nonsocial or withdrawn behaviors have been assessed. Much of the research indicating that the relation between withdrawn behavior and peer status emerges in middle to late grade school is based on peer assessments of classmate behavior (e.g., measures such as the Revised Class Play or the Pupil Evaluation Inventory). It is possible, however, that children's awareness of peers' nonsocial behaviors increases with age and is not a reliable source of information with young children (see Ladd & Mars, 1986; Younger, Schwartzman, & Ledingham, 1985). At this age, children who seldom interact with peers may provide classmates with little or no basis for judging their likability, and in turn, peers may pay little attention to the behavioral characteristics of classmates that they do not interact with on a regular basis.

Beyond this examination of the quality of children's behavior, a major purpose of this investigation was to explore the patterns of contacts that children pursue with members of their peer group and the degree to which these patterns predict peer status. We had initially proposed that the range of children's contacts might be related to the degree to which they became known by peers and, depending on the quality of these interactions, likely to establish either positive or negative reputations among group members. Some support for this hypothesis was obtained in that a marginally significant relationship was found between the range of contacts children pursued at the outset of school and the number of positive nominations they received from peers at midyear. Moreover, during these early months of the school year, the extensiveness of children's peer contacts predicted their overall visibility as measured by social impact scores.

An alternative hypothesis considered in this investigation was that children's prior peer reputations were influencing their behavior or peer contacts at later points in time. Evidence in favor of this view was obtained in that peer rejection at the beginning or middle of the school year, as measured by negative nominations, predicted later contact patterns. Thus, being disliked at the outset and middle of the school year was associated with more extensive peer contacts at later points in time. These findings are consistent with the hypothesis that children's emerging reputations in the peer group may affect their subsequent contact patterns.

It would appear that more extensive contact patterns early in the school year function to enhance a child's visibility in the peer group but that extensive contacts at later points in time are a consequence of negative peer reputations. The latter finding is in stark contrast with temporal trends indicating that, in general, children's peer contacts tend to become more selective or focused over time. Perhaps the children who are disliked initially are those who are not only aversive to peers but also less skillful or competent at selectively focusing their social ties. Alternatively, it is also possible that the negative peer reputations these children developed interfered with their ability to form and maintain relationships. That is, once these children became disliked, they may have become marginal group members who were avoided by peers and, thus, forced to search out possible interaction partners among a broad range of peers.

This finding is consistent with the hypothesis that children's emerging reputations in the peer group affect their subsequent interactions (see Chapter 6, this volume). However, it does not appear from our findings that the negative character of children's peer reputations led to subsequent changes in their behavior, such as higher levels of rough play. Rather, our data suggest that children's negative peer reputations were less likely to influence the content of children's behavior than their contacts or choice of associates. Evidence concerning behavior–status relationships clearly supported the view that children's behavior plays an instrumental role in determining outcomes such as group acceptance and rejection.

Based on previous work by Howes (1983), we also proposed that children who developed a larger number of consistent play companions would be better liked by peers. The fact that the number of frequent play companions children had early in the school year predicted later peer acceptance provides some support for this contention. Children who choose to participate in sustained relationships may do so because they possess relationship skills or social goal orientations that engender this type of contact or association. Moreover, as Howes (1983) has suggested, participation in these relationships may further enhance interpersonal competence. These characteristics, in turn, may make children more rewarding and attractive play companions and, thus, facilitate their status in the peer group. Alternatively, sustained relationships may provide a secure base from which children can both meet peers and explore new relationships, thus expanding their network of positive social ties and overall levels of group acceptance.

Implications for intervention

The relationship between children's peer behavior and contacts and their status in the peer group appears to be complex. Whereas the results of our analyses were consistent with the view that children's prior behaviors influenced their eventual peer status, they also suggested children with negative peer reputations were less likely to establish consistent or focused social ties. These trends underscore the need to consider both the nature of children's behavior toward peers and their existing peer reputations when planning interventions aimed at enhancing peer relations.

Recent efforts to improve children's peer relations have frequently taken the form of teaching children social skills, and most of these interventions are based on the assumption that skill deficits (i.e., deficiencies in specific social-cognitive and behavioral abilities) are responsible for children's peer difficulties (for reviews, see Ladd & Mize, 1983; Ladd & Asher, 1985; Mize, Ladd, & Price, 1985; Chapter 12, this volume). Often, the thrust of these programs has been to change children's behavior or increase their rate of skill performance to levels well beyond those observed prior to intervention. In planning the intervention curriculum, investigators have typically chosen prosocial skills that are intended to improve the child's peer relationship in some way (e.g., increase the probability that the child can gain entry into ongoing peer activities).

Although data from the present investigation support this approach to intervention, it is also apparent that in planning social skill interventions for young children, considerable attention should be paid to enhancing relationship formation and maintenance skills. In our study, preschoolers who displayed more extensive peer contact patterns and tended to develop and maintain a larger number of frequent play companions early in the school year (but not later) became more visible and better liked by peers in their classrooms. One interpretation of this finding is that it may be important, early in the history of a peer group, for children to scan or "sample" a variety of potential play partners as a means of identifying peers who can become suitable companions. Children who have difficulty developing focused ties may not attend to peers' characteristics in a way that will allow them to make good judgments about who is likely to share interests, be receptive to their overtures, and so on.

Our data also indicated that children who developed negative reputations early in the school year failed to develop more focused social ties. To further explore this correlational finding, children whose scores on the peer rejection measure fell in the top and bottom quartiles were divided into groups, and their average ranges of peer contacts were compared across the three times of assessment in a 2 (groups: high, low) by 3 (time: fall, winter, spring) analysis of variance. Results revealed significant main effects for group and time and a group-by-time interaction, $F(2, 24) = 3.40$, $p < .05$. Over the course of the school year, children's range of peer contacts declined significantly, but less for those with higher (in order, $M = 19.7$, 18.4, and 14.0), as opposed to lower, peer rejection scores (in order, $M = 16.9$, 10.9, and 12.2). Perhaps once negative peer reputations have been established, it is difficult for children to find willing play partners or consistent playmates. If this is the case, then it may also behoove investigators to develop procedures for modifying peers' perceptions.

The point of these findings is that it may not be helpful to teach children simply to interact more often (cf. Asher, Markell, & Hymel, 1981) or even to interact more positively, if the outcome is that they then implement these skills indiscriminately among peers. Rather, it would seem that young children also need to learn that an important purpose or goal for these skills is to establish and maintain peer relationships. Moreover, it also appears that interventions should be aimed at preventing children from establishing negative peer reputations early in the history of a peer group, because status of this type may interfere with their ability to establish and maintain social ties.

Identifying children who persist at maladaptive behavior patterns may also be an important diagnostic task for social skill investigators, and one that might enable them to prevent eventual peer rejection or neglect. In this investigation, it was apparent that some of our measures tapped relatively stable differences in preschoolers' playground behavior patterns and that some of these differences were predictive of social functioning in the classroom. For example, the hierarchies identified for cooperative play and unoccupied behaviors were quite consistent over the school year, and differences in rough play became more stable over time. Moreover, individual differences in these behaviors were also predictive of peer status in the classroom. High scores for behaviors such as rough play may be descriptive of children who, when left to their own devices, consistently choose to behave in aggressive ways. These behavioral orientations, if left untreated, may place children at greater risk for peer rejection.

Finally, some of the normative trends and sex differences found in our data on children's contact patterns and interactive contexts may be relevant for those who wish to design interventions for preschool children. Our data suggest that in implementing social skill interventions, it may be important to consider the nature of the interpersonal contexts that have evolved in the peer group when formulating training objectives and skill rehearsal contexts. For those working in classrooms, for example, it may be necessary to alter the design of interventions depending on the length of time children have been acquainted. Late in the school year, when more focused and intensive play patterns have emerged, it may be important to place greater emphasis on group entry strategies and teach skills that help children to negotiate small-group dynamics. For example, once peers have developed consistent play companions, it may be important for children to learn to deal with exclusion tactics. Trends in the age, sex, and status composition of children's interactive contexts also argue for engineering rehearsal contexts so that children are increasingly afforded contacts with same-age, same-sex, and high-status companions. Conversely, our data suggest that interventions implemented prior to a new school year or during the early weeks of school should place greater emphasis on meeting and interacting with a broad spectrum of peers and identifying children with similar interests as potential companions. Throughout the school year it may be important to prepare boys to implement their skills in larger groups settings, such as in the context of games or physical activities, because our data suggest that boys' interactions more than girls' tend to be embedded in this type of social context.

In conclusion, the results of this investigation underscore the importance of distinguishing between the content of children's behavior and the structure and context of their peer contacts in group settings. In studying both the antecedents and concomitants of peer status, future investigators should continue to probe specific features of children's peer contacts and interactional contexts. Further work is needed to understand the relationship between early contact patterns in the group's history and the development of peer liking and social impact. For example, by combining measures of behavioral quality and peer contacts, future investigators may be able not only to distinguish between children who pursue extensive versus intensive styles but also between those within each pattern who tend to interact in prosocial, as opposed to antisocial, ways (see Ladd & Price, 1986).

Additional investigations are also needed to explore the process by which children focus their social ties and form sustained peer relationships. As earlier work by Masters and Furman (1981) implies, these variables promise to shed light on important relationship skills and possible connections between events that occur at the dyadic level (e.g., relationship formation) and outcomes that develop in the larger peer group (e.g., group acceptance).

References

Asher, S. R., Markell, R. A., & Hymel, S. (1981). Identifying children at risk in peer relations: A critique of the rate-of-interaction approach to assessment. *Child Development, 52,* 1239–1245.
Asher, S. R., Singleton, L. C., Tinsley, B. R., & Hymel, S. (1979). A reliable sociometric measure for preschool children. *Developmental Psychology, 15,* 443–444.

Barnes, J. A. (1954). Class and communities in a Norwegian Island parish. *Human Relations, 7,* 39–58.

Benson, C. S., & Gottman, J. M. (1975). *Children's popularity and peer social interaction.* Unpublished manuscript, Indiana University.

Bott, E. (1971). *Family and social network: Norms and external relationships in ordinary urban families.* London: Tavistock Publishing.

Brown, G. W., Bhrolchain, M. N., & Harris, T. (1975). Social class and psychiatric disturbance among women in an urban population. *Sociology, 9,* 225–254.

Carpenter, C. J., & Huston, A. C. (1983, April). *Structuring children's time in middle childhood.* Paper presented at the biennial meeting of the Society for Research in Child Development, Detroit.

Cochran, M. M., & Brassard, J. A. (1979). Child development and personal social networks. *Child Development, 50,* 601–616.

Coie, J. D., Dodge, K. A., & Coppotelli, H. (1982). Dimensions and types of social status: A cross-age perspective. *Developmental Psychology, 18,* 557–570.

Coie, J. D., & Kupersmidt, J. B. (1983). A behavioral analysis of emerging social status in boys' groups. *Child Development, 54,* 1400–1416.

Cubitt, T. (1973). Network density among urban families. In J. Boissevain & J. C. Mitchell (Eds.), *Network analysis studies in human interaction* (pp. 67–82). The Hague: Mouton.

Dodge, K. A. (1983). Behavioral antecedents of peer social status. *Child Development, 54,* 1386–1399.

Ellis, S., Rogoff, B., & Cromer, C. C. (1981). Age segregation in children's social interactions. *Developmental Psychology, 17,* 399–407.

Feiring, C., & Lewis, M. (1981, April). *The social networks of three-year-old children.* Paper presented at the Society for Research in Child Development, Boston.

Festinger, L. (1954). A theory of social comparison processes. *Human Relations, 7,* 117–140.

Garrison, V. (1978). Support systems of schizophrenic and non-schizophrenic Puerto Rican migrant women in New York City. *Schizophrenia Bulletin, 4,* 591–596.

Hammer, M. (1979/80). Predictability of social connections over time. *Social Networks, 2,* 165–180.

Hammer, M. (1980). Social access and the clustering of personal connections. *Social Networks, 2,* 305–325.

Hammer, M. (1981). Social support, social networks, and schizophrenia. *Schizophrenia Bulletin, 7,* 45–57.

Hammer, M. (1983). Social networks and the long term patient. In I. Barofsky & R. D. Budson (Eds.), *The chronic psychiatric patient in the community: Principles of treatment* (pp. 49–82). New York: Spectrum Publications.

Hammer, M., Gutwirth, L., & Phillips, S. L. (1982). Parenthood and social networks. *Social Science and Medicine, 16,* 2091–2100.

Hammer, M., Polgar, S. K., & Salzinger, K. (1969). Speech predictability and social contact patterns in an informal group. *Human Organization, 28,* 235–242.

Hartup, W. W., Glazer, J. A., & Charlesworth, R. (1967). Peer reinforcement and sociometric status. *Child Development, 38,* 1017–1024.

Heller, K., Amaral, T., & Procidano, M. (1978, August). *The experimental study of social support: An approach to understanding the indigenous helper.* Paper presented at the meeting of the American Psychological Association, Toronto.

Heller, K., & Swindle, R. W. (1983). Social networks, perceived social support, and coping with stress. In R. D. Felner, L. A. Jason, J. N. Moritsugu, & S. S. Farber (Eds.), *Preventive psychology: Theory, research, and practice* (pp. 87–103). New York: Pergamon Press.

114 GARY LADD, JOSEPH PRICE, AND CRAIG HART

Hinde, R. A., Titmus, G., Easton, D., & Tamplin, A. (1985). Incidence of "friendship" and behavior toward strong associates versus nonassociates in preschoolers. *Child Development, 56,* 234–245.

Holohan, C. J., & Wilcox, B. L. (1978). Residential satisfaction and friendship formation in high and low rise student housing: An international analysis. *Journal of Educational Psychology, 70,* 237–241.

Howes, C. (1983). Patterns of friendship. *Child Development, 54,* 1041–1053.

Hyman, H. H., & Singer, E. (1968). *Readings in reference group theory and research.* New York: Free Press.

Hymel, S., & Rubin, K. H. (1985). Children with peer relationships and social skills problems: Conceptual, methodological, and developmental issues. In G. J. Whitehurst (Eds.), *Annals of child development* (Vol. 2, pp. 251–297). Greenwich, CT: JAI Press.

Ladd, G. W. (1983). Social networks of popular, average, and rejected children in school settings. *Merrill-Palmer Quarterly, 29,* 283–307.

Ladd, G. W. (1984). Expanding our view of the child's social world: New territories, new maps, same directions? *Merrill-Palmer Quarterly, 30,* 317–320.

Ladd, G. W., & Asher, S. R. (1985). Social skill training and children's peer relations. In L. L'Abate & M. Milan (Eds.), *Handbook of social skills training* (pp. 219–244). New York: Wiley.

Ladd, G. W., & Mars, K. T. (1986). Reliability and validity of preschoolers' perceptions of peer behavior. *Journal of Clinical Child Psychology, 15,* 16–25.

Ladd, G. W., & Mize, J. (1983). A cognitive–social learning model of social skill training. *Psychological Review, 90,* 127–157.

Ladd, G. W., & Price, J. P. (1987). Predicting children's social and school adjustment following the transition from preschool to kindergarten. *Child Development, 58,* 1168–1189.

Lewis, M., & Feiring, C. (1979). The child's social network: Social object, social functions, and their relationship. In M. Lewis & L. A. Rosenblum (Eds.), *The child and its family: The genesis of behavior* (Vol. 2, pp. 9–27). New York: Plenum.

Marsella, A. J., & Snyder, K. K. (1981). Stress, social supports, and schizophrenia disorders: Toward an interactional model. *Schizophrenia Bulletin, 7,* 152–163.

Marshall, H. R., & McCandless, B. R. (1957). A study in prediction of social behavior of preschool children. *Child Development, 28,* 149–159.

Masters, J. C., & Furman, W. (1981). Popularity, individual friendship selection, and specific peer interaction among children. *Developmental Psychology, 17,* 344–350.

Medalie, J. H., & Goldbourt, U. (1976). Angina pectoris among 10,000 men: II. Psychosocial and other risk factors as evidenced by a multivariate analysis of a five year incidence study. *American Journal of Medicine, 60,* 910–921.

Mitchell, J. C. (Ed.) (1969). *Social networks in urban situations.* New York: Humanities Press.

Mitchell, R. E., & Trickett, E. J. (1980). Task force report: Social networks as mediators of social support. *Community Mental Health Journal, 16,* 27–44.

Mize, J., Ladd, G. W., & Price, J. M. (1985). Promoting positive peer relations with young children. *Child Care Quarterly, 14,* 221–237.

Nuckolls, K. B., Cassel, J., & Kaplan, B. H. (1972). Psychosocial assets, life crisis, and the prognosis of pregnancy. *American Journal of Epidemiology, 95,* 431–441.

Putallaz, M., & Gottman, J. M. (1981). Social skills and group acceptance. In S. R. Asher & J. M. Gottman (Eds.), *The development of children's friendships* (pp. 116–149). New York: Cambridge University Press.

Salzinger, S., Kaplan, S., & Artemyeff, C. (1983). Mothers' personal social networks and child maltreatment. *Journal of Abnormal Psychology, 92,* 68–76.

Waldrop, M. F., & Halverson, C. F. (1975). Intensive and extensive peer behavior: Longitudinal and cross-sectional analyses. *Child Development, 46,* 19–26.

Younger, A. J., Schwartzman, A. E., & Ledingham, J. E. (1985). Age-related changes in children's perceptions of aggression and withdrawal in their peers. *Developmental Psychology, 21,* 70–75.

Part II

Social-cognitive processes

5 Issues in social cognition and sociometric status

Kenneth A. Dodge and Esther Feldman

Numerous researchers have recently been examining the role of children's social cognitions in the origins of behaviors that are associated with sociometric status. The hypothesis guiding this work is quite simple: Children who are deficient or deviant in the way that they process social information may have a difficult time behaving competently with peers, which, in turn, may lead them to be viewed negatively by the peer group. Indeed, there has been growing support for this hypothesis over the past decade.

This "simple" notion, however, needs to be made more complex for a number of reasons. Four issues seem particularly important and will be the focus of the present chapter. First, children's social-cognitive functioning has been recognized recently not as a single construct but as a series of complex phenomena. Recent theoretical models (e.g., Dodge, 1986; Rubin & Krasnor, 1986) have described distinct aspects of social information processing, including the accurate encoding and interpretation of environmental events and the generation and evaluation of responses to social dilemmas. These aspects are relatively independent. The aspects that are related to sociometric status have not been fully identified yet. A second issue concerns the situations and circumstances in which deviant social cognitions occur. Low-status children do not behave equally ineffectively in all situations (Dodge, Coie, & Brakke, 1982). Likewise, it has been recognized that the quality of a child's cognitions is known to vary across situations (Dodge, McClaskey, & Feldman, 1985). It is not known whether and how social-cognitive differences between high- and low-status groups of children also vary across situations. A major research concern must be identifying those kinds of situations that are most likely to elicit deviant social cognitions from low-status children. A third issue concerns the role of the sex of the child. It is known that patterns of development and behavior differ for boys and girls. Patterns of social cognition also differ between the sexes, but how these differences interact with sociometric status differences is not understood. It is not clear whether the social-cognitive correlates of status are the same for boys and girls. A final issue concerns the relevance of age and developmental level in understanding the social-cognitive patterns of low-status children. It is not known whether differences in social cognition across status groups are similar at all ages. Likewise, the age level at which social cognitions begin to predict sociometric status is not known.

This chapter will describe relevant research findings that begin to clarify these issues. These findings suggest that status groups do differ in social cognitions but that these differences vary across studies, across situations, and across age and gender groups. Whereas popular and rejected children may differ in social cognition in one situation, no differences might be found when social cognition is assessed in another situation. These variations are not spurious or random, however. A review of the literature leads to a general hypothesis regarding sociometric status group differences in social cognition. This hypothesis may be stated as follows. It appears that the strongest and most robust status group differences in social cognition occur in those situations that are especially problematic or crucial for that particular age and gender peer group. By a problematic situation, we mean one that is highly salient and developmentally relevant to a subcultural group at a particular time.

The notion that children become socially rejected because they have global social-cognitive skill deficits simply does not hold in many cases. The social-cognitive correlates of status, like the behavioral correlates, are contingent upon the features of the social group, including the goals and orientation of the group. Social groups vary greatly in terms of goals and relevant emphases. For example, a Little League baseball team may emphasize winning and competition, whereas the same group at lunch in school may emphasize gossip about boy–girl relations. Status in the Little League group may be related to behavioral competence in handling competition, whereas status in the lunch group may depend on competence in handling social conversation. Thus, behavior in those social domains that are considered most important to the peer group may determine status in that group. Likewise, those children who are least equipped to process information adequately about those important social situations will behave ineffectively and will become rejected in that group. One of the implications of this hypothesis is that sociometric status may be a function of the match or fit between a child's social-cognitive capabilities and the situational demands of the peer group. This hypothesis has not been tested fully. Indeed, it emerges from a review of the literature in this area. In this chapter, we guide the reader through the literature to examine aspects of this hypothesis.

One of the first observations to be made from scanning the literature in this area is that most of the studies are correlational. One must be cautious about interpreting such data. In fact, any discussion of the nature of the relation between social-cognitive patterns and sociometric status must consider at least three possible causal pathways. These pathways are not mutually exclusive but have vastly different implications. First, the manner in which a child cognizes the world may lead him or her to behave in ways that cause peers to perceive the child as likable or dislikable. This pathway is quite straightforward and suggests that interventions aimed at changing a child's social cognitions may improve his or her social behavior and, in turn, that child's status among peers. Evidence supporting this pathway comes from experimental studies. These studies consist of efforts to alter systematically a child's cognitions and to observe the effects on behavior and others' perceptions. For example, Dodge, Murphy, and Buchsbaum (1984) presented children with videotaped stimuli depicting provocations performed by a peer with systematically varying intentions and asked children to generate a behavioral response. Children were more likely to respond with aggression to provocations that they interpreted as hostile than to provocations that they interpreted as benign. In turn, Dodge (1986) found that peers who are presented with videotaped vignettes depicting a child behaving aggressively are more likely to dislike that child than another child who is behaving benignly. The combination of these two studies suggests that a child's social cognitions can lead to behavior that alters peers' perceptions. Intervention studies could also be conducted to test the causal role of social cognitions in leading to changes in sociometric status.

The second possible causal pathway is that the acquisition of a particular sociometric status leads a child to cognize the world differently. It is quite possible that a child who has been rejected by peers will experience changes in cognitive patterns, including self-defensive attributions and avoidant patterns of solving problems. Experimental evidence is lacking, but the possibility of this pathway serves as a caution to researchers who, upon finding correlations between children's cognitions and status, wish to implement large-scale interventions to change cognitive patterns.

The third possible causal pathway is that children's social cognitions may serve to maintain and perpetuate a child's sociometric status, without necessarily leading to the acquisition of status in the first place. Dodge (1980) has shown that children who have a reputation as aggressive and rejected among peers are likely to perceive the world as a hostile place. This hostile attributional bias leads them to behave aggressively toward peers, a pattern that is likely to perpetuate their social reputations. Darley and Fazio (1980) have articulated the various cognitive processes implicated in the perpetuation of one's social reputation.

These three causal pathways are not mutually exclusive and may operate in tandem in reciprocally influential ways, as suggested by Bandura (1978). It is also possible that different causal pathways operate for different kinds of social cognitions. The cognitions described thus far (including attributions of intentions, patterns of generating responses to social dilemmas, and skills of self-evaluation) are quite diverse. A discussion of the various cognitions is therefore an appropriate place to begin a literature review.

Social cognition and sociometric status

Initial attempts (Rubin, 1972) to relate children's ability to understand social cues to their social outcomes were based on a Piagetian theory of role-taking ability. It was hypothesized that in order to perform competently in social interactions, a child must be aware of the perspective of others and understand others' viewpoints and thoughts. This ability allows the child to relate to others in a way that they will comprehend. Children who lack these skills may be termed egocentric. A literal translation of this hypothesis led researchers to examine children's skills in understanding the spatial perspective of others, as assessed by Piagetian two-mountain tasks. These studies led to mixed results (Gottman, Gonso, & Rasmussen, 1975), mainly because researchers failed to acknowledge the independence between spatial perspective taking and social perspective taking (Ford, 1979).

Chandler (1973; Chandler, Greenspan, & Barenboim, 1974) began the effort to relate *social* perspective taking to social outcomes. Researchers who assessed the social-perspective-taking skills of children were somewhat successful in establishing positive correlations between these skills and popularity (Jennings, 1975; Rubin, 1972; Rubin & Maioni, 1975). For example, Rubin (1972) found that the correlation between performance on the Glucksberg and Krauss (1967) referential communication task (requiring an accurate perception of another's perspective) and peer acceptance scores, holding IQ constant, was .58 ($p < .01$). Marcus (1980) found a positive correlation between affective perspective taking and popularity.

The theoretical relation between social cognition and socially desirable behavior has been given careful scrutiny recently (e.g., Dodge, 1986; McFall, 1982; Rubin & Krasnor, 1986). This work has led to the formulation of models of how children process social information. The sequential stages identified in these models are distinct; these models describe the separate sequential steps that children follow in processing social information. According to the model, the first steps consist of the encoding, perception, and interpretation of social cues. Once cues have been interpreted, the next step for the child is to generate one or more behavioral responses to the cues. The child then evaluates and selects an optimal response. Finally, the child enacts the selected response and monitors its effects. A review of the relation between social cognition and sociometric status must consider each of these steps separately.

The interpretation process

Accuracy. A number of studies have explicitly focused on the first information-processing step: accurately interpreting a social situation. Goslin (1962) hypothesized that children who could not accurately perceive peers' feelings about them would tend to be isolated or rejected by the peer group. In a study of seventh- and eighth-graders, he found that, indeed, children who were unable to predict how peers perceived them were less accepted by those peers. Of course, a simple alternative explanation of the findings is that all children tend to evaluate themselves as well-liked by peers, so that the more popular children will be more accurate in their evaluations. Goslin showed that because the evaluations across children were highly variable, this was probably not the case. Ausubel (1955) conducted a similar study with high schoolers and found a significant correlation between the accuracy of others' perceptions of self and sociometric status among girls but not among boys.

In an attempt to assess children's accuracy of interpretation of others' cues, some researchers have sought to control for the subject's involvement with the other by presenting standard stimuli. Gottman et al. (1975) presented children of high- and low-friendship status with facial photographs from Izard's (1971) research and asked children to match each picture with various emotions (sad, scared, surprised, disgusted, and happy). They found that the groups did not differ in total accuracy of labeling emotions from these facial expressions. Goldman, Corsini, and deUrioste (1980) did find status group differences on a similar task, however. They used photographs taken from Ekman and Friesen (1975), reversed the task (that is, they asked children to match an emotion with one of three photographs), and separated low-status groups of rejected and neglected children. They found that the rejected group (mean correct = 58%) did not perform as well as the popular group (mean correct = 77%), whereas the neglected group (mean correct = 83%) did not differ from the popular group. It is possible that if Gottman et al. (1975) had separated rejected and neglected groups, they would have found the rejected group to be deficient as well.

These studies of accuracy of cue interpretation have yielded findings of significant, although weak, relations between this social-cognitive skill and sociometric status. Most of the studies, however, have not attended to distinctions in the kinds of cues and situations that are being interpreted. It is possible that more robust status group differences would be found in the interpretation of some kinds of cues and no differences would be found in the interpretation of other kinds of cues.

Dodge et al. (1984) were interested in children's skill in interpreting the intentions of others in a specific social situation, which involved a provocation by a peer. They went beyond the presentation of still photographs to the presentation of specially prepared videorecorded vignettes, in which one child displays a provocation toward a peer. For example, in one vignette a child and a peer are painting pictures and the child spills paint on the peer's picture. The intention of the provocateur was varied; sometimes it was hostile and sometimes it was prosocial, whereas in some cases the action was accidental (a fourth vignette depicted a child who did not even commit the provocation). Because they were interested specifically in the skill of interpreting another's intention, they went to great lengths to avoid confounding the assessment of this skill with that of verbal ability (such as the ability to attach verbal labels to intentions). This was accomplished by presenting children with 12 sets of three vignettes (two depicting one intention and the other depicting a second intention, in all possible combinations) and asking them simply to discriminate among the three by pointing out which vignette differed from the other two. Results indicated that children's performance on this task was internally consistent (coefficient $\alpha = .68$). They also were concerned that the assessment of social cue discrimination could be affected by more general, nonsocial cue discrimination skills, so children were asked to complete a similar task in which they were to discriminate among three geometric shapes. The score on this cognitive discrimination task was used as a covariate in subsequent analyses.

The intention cue discrimination task was presented to popular, average, neglected, and rejected boys and girls aged 5 to 10. It was found that the rejected (mean correct = 55%) and neglected (mean correct = 53%) children (who did not differ) performed significantly more poorly than the average (mean correct = 58%) and popular (mean correct = 63%) children. Average children performed significantly more poorly than popular children. It is clear that the skill of accurately discriminating another's social intentions is correlated with sociometric status and is not an artifact of verbal ability or general cognitive discrimination skills.

Dodge et al. (1984) next wondered what kinds of errors low-status children were making in interpreting others' intentions, so they presented the vignettes one at a time to children and asked them to identify the actor's intention. They found that the low-status children were less accurate than popular children at identifying accidental and prosocial intentions but not in identifying hostile intentions. Also, the errors made by low-status children in response to the accidental and prosocial vignettes were most likely ones of inaccurately presuming a hostile intention. Dodge, Murphy, and Somberg (1983) replicated these findings with groups of rejected, aggressive children and average, nonaggressive children. It was concluded that the intention cue interpretation deficits of low-status children are evidenced most strikingly in particular circumstances (involving accidental or prosocial intentions that inadvertently lead to negative outcomes). It is interesting that both neglected and rejected children displayed biases in presuming hostility in peers. Asher and Fitzgerald (personal communication) have suggested that this biased processing pattern may lead to different behavioral responses for these two groups. They hypothesized that rejected, aggressive children may attribute hostility to peers and then generate retaliatory aggressive responses, whereas neglected children may also attribute hostility to peers, but they then generate passive, withdrawing responses. This hypothesis has not yet been tested fully.

Still other studies have focused on children's reasoning about social cues rather than just the accuracy of their interpretations. Selman (1980) has developed a measure of social reasoning and interpersonal understanding that consists of the presentation (by audiovisual filmstrips) of social dilemmas to a child. Structured clinical interviews are used to probe the child's level of understanding of key issues in social domains and the level of reasoning used in interpreting social cues. Responses are scored according to specified stages of sophistication. Pellegrini (1985) used this measure and found that it correlates significantly and positively with measures of social effectiveness on the Revised Class Play (Masten, Morison, & Pellegrini, 1985). It appears, then, that socially competent children are not only more accurate than others in their interpretations of social cues but are also able to reason about those cues at a higher level.

Attributional biases. In addition to the interpretation of social cues in clearly identifiable circumstances, researchers have studied the interpretations that children make in ambiguous situations, such as following a provocation in which the peer provocateur could have acted with hostile intent or with benign intent. A hypothesis generated by Dodge (1980) was that children who attribute hostile intentions to peers will be likely to retaliate aggressively toward these peers and will be disliked by those peers. Indeed, he found that aggressive, rejected boys (second through sixth grade) were 50% more likely to make such hostile attributions than were nonaggressive, socially accepted boys. The phenomenon of a hostile attributional bias has also been found with socially unpopular children by Aydin and Markova (1979), with socially aggressive adolescents by Nasby, Hayden, and dePaulo (1979), and with socially rejected, aggressive adolescent boys by Steinberg and Dodge (1983). In the last study, aggressive and nonaggressive children built a structure out of blocks and then observed a peer whose intentions were ambiguous knock over this structure. Aggressive children were more likely to attribute hostile intent to the peer than were more nonaggressive children.

Dodge and Frame (1982) examined whether this attributional bias is a global tendency to see others as acting in a hostile manner to all others or is restricted to interpretations of others' behavior toward them. The former tendency would reflect a cynical world view, whereas the latter tendency would reflect a personalized, paranoid view. They presented stories to children in which the peer provocateur directed a negative outcome toward the subject or a second peer. Only when the provocation was directed toward the subject did aggressive rejected children demonstrate the hostile attributional bias, thus supporting the latter hypothesis.

Whether this hostile attributional bias is a cause of peer conflict and social rejection or is a consequence of repeated conflicts with peers is not clear. Richard (1985) has recently shown, however, that children who display hostile attributional biases toward peers whom they have never met are relatively likely to be rejected later by those peers, following actual contact with them.

Attributional style. The tendency to attribute hostility to peers is but one kind of attributional style that has been studied by researchers of sociometric status. In another area, Goetz and Dweck (1980) drew on Dweck's (1975) work on learned helplessness attributions in academic situations. They wondered whether the kind of attribution made by a child following social failure would have an impact on that child's subsequent social behavior and on that child's overall sociometric standing. Specifically, Goetz and Dweck (1980) hypothesized that those children who attribute their social failure to their own incompetence would be less likely to improve their social performance subsequently than those children who attributed their social failure to incompatibility, another's chance mood, a misunderstanding, or the other person. They tested their hypothesis in two sessions with each of a number of fourth- and fifth-grade boys and girls. In the first session, they assessed children's attributional styles by presenting them with hypothetical social failure situations and asking them to make an attribution about the failure; for example, "Suppose someone stops telling you her secrets. Why would this happen to you?" (p. 248). In the second session, they asked children to send a friendship initiation message across a one-way audio transmitter to a potential pen pal. Next, they gave preliminary feedback to the child that the pen pal "isn't so sure (she/he) would like you" (p. 248). They then asked the child to try again, by sending a second message. They found that children who had made a high number of "self-incompetence" attributions were relatively unlikely to improve their message-transmitting performance following failure. That is, these children demonstrated social learned helplessness. In addition, Goetz and Dweck found that unpopular children (defined by low mean play ratings and a low number of friendship nominations) were more likely to display this incompetence attribution orientation than popular children.

A number of other researchers have utilized concepts from the social psychological literature on attributions for success and failure to assess attributional styles in high- and low-status children. Ames, Ames, and Garrison (1977), for example, asked children to attribute hypothetical social successes and failures to external, internal, or neutral causes in a multiple-choice format. They found that popular children were more likely than unpopular children to attribute successes to internal causes and failures to external causes. Such an attributional style may be highly adaptive in that success experiences may bolster one's self-concept when they are internally attributed, and failures will not detract from one's self-concept when they are dismissed as externally caused. Hymel, Freigang, Franke, Both, Bream, and Borys (1983) conducted two studies of the same phenomenon, using an open-ended response format rather than the multiple-choice format. They found a significant correlation between popularity and internal attributions of success in one study ($r = .28$) but not in the other ($r = .05$). The reasons for the inconsistency in these findings are not clear. However, these findings are part of a general trend in this area to obtain effects that are specific to a particular population and that cannot be replicated with other populations or in other contexts.

How might these attributional styles relate to behavioral performance? Further studies of the same processes give some hint of an answer. Sobol and Earn (1985a) found that not only did popular children attribute successes to internal causes, they also expected successes to continue in the future more than did rejected children. Sobol and Earn (1985b) have extended this finding in other studies in which they determined that popular children view outcomes and others' perceptions as more controllable than do rejected children. These kinds of attributions may be hypothesized to lead children to behave in ways that will fulfill their expectations.

Still another approach to the study of attributional style has been taken by Campbell and Yarrow (1961). They asked children simply to describe their peers in an open-ended interview, without any hypothetical story as stimulus. Their goal was to understand the cognitive dimensions that are salient in making attributions about and perceiving peers (such as the use of inferences) and in the organizational quality of children's descriptions. They found no relation between popularity and the content of children's descriptors of peers. That is, both popular and unpopular children used the same content categories, such as aggression and leadership, to describe peers. They did find, however, that popular children gave descriptions that contained more and subtler inferential interpretations. The descriptions by popular children were also more highly organized. For example, an unpopular child might describe a peer by citing an incident in which the peer told others the rules of a game. The popular child might say that the same peer has good leadership abilities. As Campbell and Yarrow concluded, "These findings suggest that it is not so much what the child *selects out* in his (her) perception of others as it is what he (she) *does* with these perceived stimuli which accounts for the link between perception and valuation by others" (p. 9).

As a group, the studies of attributional style indicate that patterns of attributing characteristics to others are indeed related to popularity and social effectiveness. The differences in attributional styles are often subtle, however, and may be detected only in some populations (such as 8- to 10-year-olds) and in some social domains (such as attributing causes of social outcomes). It is doubtful that these attributional style differences are pervasive. It is not clear whether the attributional style differences that are found actually precede or contribute to the acquisition of status, but it is easy to surmise that they help maintain differences in self-concept and lead to behavior that will perpetuate one's status among peers.

Response generation

Generativeness. The pioneering work of Spivack and Shure (1974; Shure & Spivack, 1972) has demonstrated that the manner in which a child generates solutions to hypothetical social problems is related to that child's overall social adjustment. These researchers developed the Preschool Interpersonal Problem Solving Test (PIPS), in which they presented a child with a set of cartoon stimuli depicting social dilemmas (such as one in which the story character wishes to gain access to a toy in another child's possession) and asked the child to generate possible solutions to this dilemma. Responses were scored for quantity and quality. Spivack and Shure (1974) concluded that it is the *quantity* of solutions generated that is most strongly related to social adjustment, and they subsequently developed an intervention program aimed at improving the solution-generating skills of socially maladjusted children.

The skills assessed by Spivack and Shure are similar to the response search step of social information processing (Dodge, 1986). A number of researchers have used variations of the Spivack and Shure measures to assess response search tendencies in children who vary in sociometric status. The first aspect of response search that has been examined is the quantity of responses that children are able to generate. This research has yielded mixed findings (see Krasnor & Rubin, 1981). Richard and Dodge (1982) presented a variation of the PIPS to second- through fifth-grade boys who were either popular, rejected and aggressive, or neglected and shy. Their version of the PIPS contained items that involved friendship initiation or conflict resolution. They found that popular children generated slightly more responses to these stories (14% more) than the two low-status groups, which did not differ. Asarnow and Callan (1985) used similar stories with extreme groups of fourth- and sixth-graders and found that high-status children generated 15% to 18% more responses than did rejected children.

On the other hand, Butler (1978), Krasnor and Rubin (1978), and Sharp (1978) found no differences among status groups in the quantity of responses generated. These studies employed preschool children, used teacher ratings of social status, and less extreme groups; whereas the Richard and Dodge (1982) and Asarnow and Callan (1985) studies employed older children, used peer nominations to select status groups, and studied extreme groups, including aggressive rejected children. That these procedural differences may be important is supported in a study by Gesten and Weissberg (1979), who found positive correlations between the quantity of solutions generated and social adjustment, but only among older (third-grade) subjects. Age and selection criteria differences do not completely clarify the mixed findings, however, when one considers that the first study to find significant differences, by Shure, Spivack, and Jaeger (1971), employed preschoolers and teacher ratings, although their population consisted of disadvantaged, inner-city children.

Quality of responses. A clear consensus has been obtained concerning qualitative aspects of response generation. It has been found consistently that the kinds of responses generated by low-status children are more deviant, aberrant, unique, and incompetent. Asher and Renshaw (1981) asked kindergarten children to generate responses to hypothetical situations involving social tasks such as friendship initiation and conflict management. They found that the responses generated by unpopular children (defined by low mean play rating and low number of positive peer nominations) were less effective and less relationship enhancing than those generated by popular children. In response to the conflict stories, 12% of the responses by unpopular children were aggressive ("Punch him" or "She could beat her up"), compared with only 2% of the responses by popular children. In response to the friendship initiation stories, the responses by unpopular children were relatively likely to be vague or appeals to an authority figure for help.

This pattern has been found in a number of other studies as well. Rubin and Daniels-Beirness (1983) administered the Social Problem Solving Test (SPST) to children in kindergarten and first grade and found positive correlations between positive peer sociometric ratings and the proportion of prosocial and relevant strategies generated. Children with low peer ratings generated a relatively high proportion of agonistic and adult-intervention strategies. Rubin, Daniels-Beirness, and Hayvren (1982) have replicated this finding with kindergarteners, and Dodge (1986) also found that aggressive rejected second- and fourth-graders generated a high proportion of aggressive responses to hypothetical provocations by peers. Asarnow and Callan (1985) found that low-status children generated fewer assertive, mature responses and more intensely aggressive responses than high-status children.

In related work, Ladd and Oden (1979) investigated the responses generated by third- and fifth-grade children to a cartoon stimulus in which one child was in need of help (i.e., the child was being teased or scolded by a peer). Child subjects generated ways of providing help for this child. Ladd and Oden found that children who generated unique strategies (that is, strategies that were not generated by anyone else and were therefore deviant) were likely to be given low ratings from peers in a play sociometric interview.

Richard and Dodge (1982) investigated the sequencing of responses generated by popular, rejected (and aggressive), and neglected (and shy) children to friendship initiation and conflict stories. They found that the effectiveness and quality of the first response generated did not differ across status groups; that is, all groups were able to generate an effective response. When asked to generate another response in case the first one was not sufficient, responses by rejected and neglected children deteriorated, and these children began to generate higher proportions of aggressive and inept responses. Similarly, the concept of "persistence in the face of failure" has been described by Rubin and Krasnor (1986) as differentiating adaptive and maladaptive children. Maladaptive children's response repertoire apparently is limited, and their response search may deteriorate when stressed.

Pellegrini (1985) adapted Shure and Spivack's (1972) Means–End Problem-Solving (MEPS) Test to relate popularity to the quality of children's reasoning during response search. He coded the number of relevant responses generated by children as a measure of response search quality. Beyond this, he also coded children's recognition of obstacles to meeting goals and their recognition that time must pass to reach goals. He found that a summary score of these aspects of response search quality was highly positively related ($r = .56$) to popularity. Likewise, Asarnow and Callan (1985) found that high-status children displayed response search patterns that contained more planning than did those of low-status children.

It is clear from these studies that low-status children are relatively deficient in the quality of the responses that they are able to generate to some hypothetical social dilemma. Their responses are more likely to be aggressive, unique, inept, and vague; they fail to recognize obstacles; they are less planful; and their responding may deteriorate following failure. Low-status children are not always deficient in generating high-quality responses to all situations, however. Rubin and Krasnor (1986), for example, found that unpopular children are deficient in generating responses to stress-inducing peer conflicts, but they are not deficient in generating strategies for nonstressful social initiation. On the other hand, Asher and Renshaw (1981) did find that unpopular children are deficient at generating friendship initiation strategies. Certain situations, particularly ones involving conflict and stress, seem to elicit the most dramatic response search differences between popular and unpopular children.

Is there any evidence that response search inadequacies actually precede and lead to social rejection? Most of the empirical research has been correlational and thus can provide no support in this regard. An exception is the Waterloo Longitudinal Project by Rubin and his associates (Rubin & Daniels-Beirness, 1983;

Rubin, Daniels-Beirness, & Hayvren, 1982; Rubin & Krasnor, 1986). In this project, response search skills were assessed in children during kindergarten, and those children were followed into first grade and beyond. Early results of this project indicated that response search patterns are indeed predictive of later sociometric status. Children who generated a high proportion of agonistic and affect-manipulation (coercive attempts to influence peers by threatening to change affect) strategies and a low proportion of relevant strategies in kindergarten were likely to receive low sociometric play ratings in the first and second grades. One intriguing aspect of this ongoing longitudinal project is that it is one of the first opportunities to examine the relative risk for later maladaptation among children with response search deficiencies. Researchers have been interested in sociometric status because longitudinal studies have indicated that low-status children are at high risk for later maladaptation (see Chapter 10, this volume). Response search deficiencies have been implicated as a major correlate of low status. This project will be able to examine directly the contribution of response search deficiencies (vs. status) to this risk.

Response evaluation

Far less research has been conducted on children's skill in evaluating the consequences and outcomes of solutions. This skill constitutes another step of social information processing and is distinct from response generation skills. Richard and Dodge (1982) related children's sociometric status to their skill in recognizing competent solutions as effective and aggressive and passive solutions as ineffective. They found no relation but were cautious in their conclusions because the great majority (88%) of responses were accurate, suggesting that the task as devised by those authors was relatively easy. Dodge (1986) developed a more difficult task for children involving the presentation of solutions by videotape; he found some indication (though relatively weak) that low-status (aggressive rejected) children were less accurate at evaluating consequences than high-status children. Specifically, they evaluated competent solutions as having less positive outcomes and aggressive and passive solutions as having more positive outcomes than did high-status children. Deluty (1983) obtained similar results using a self-report measure of social status, a measure that he found to be correlated with actual peer assessments (Deluty, 1984). Asarnow and Callan (1985) also found that high-status children evaluated positive responses more favorably and aggressive responses less favorably than did low-status children. Perry, Perry, and Rasmussen (1986) and Crick and Ladd (1987) obtained similar findings. The consensus from these studies is that low-status children are indeed deviant in evaluating possible responses, relative to high-status children, particularly when it comes to evaluating aggressive responses to peer conflicts.

Enactment

The final step of social information processing consists of the behavioral enactment of the response selected by the child. This step is distinct from preceding steps in that this step requires verbal and motor skills to execute a behavioral response that has already been selected. Very few studies have examined children's enactments independently of preceding steps. For example, Gottman et al. (1975) asked popular and unpopular children to role-play friendship initiation, with the experimenter playing the part of a peer. Skill was evaluated according to the degree to which the child greeted the "peer," asked for information, extended inclusion, and gave information. They found that popular children performed more skillfully at this task than unpopular children. However, this score reflects not only enactment skills but also response search and evaluation skills, because the child was free to select any response.

Mouton, Bell, and Blake (1956) conducted one of the first studies of enactment, or role-playing, skill. They asked adolescent subjects to role-play three kinds of responses, including those of a sad friend, an angry playmate, and a mischievous student, and had adult observers evaluate their performance. They found that high-status children were judged to be acting with more assurance and interest and displayed greater clarity in expression and more overall effectiveness than low-status children. The low-status children displayed more hesitation, anxiety, and difficulty at this task.

Burleson (1985) recently administered six different enactment skill tasks to popular, rejected, and neglected first- and third-graders. These tasks included measures of referential communication, persuasion of a peer, and comforting ability. He found that all of these measures distinguished among the groups in at least one grade level and that enactment of comforting behavior was consistently the most powerful discriminator among status groups. In related work, Rubin (1972) assessed children's enactments of referential communications and found a negative relation between accuracy of the child's verbal communications and a rating-scale measure of popularity. Goldman, Corsini, and deUrioste (1980) used a similar procedure and found that rejected children, but not neglected children, performed poorly. Dodge, McClaskey, and Feldman (1985) asked children to enact responses to six different social situations and rated the competence of those enactments. They found that aggressive rejected children enacted incompetent responses (relative to average children) to social failure (teasing) and provocation situations, but the groups did not differ in enactments in other situations, such as peer group entry and responding to success. These findings are similar to those for response search, in that the responses of unpopular children are deficient in stress-inducing situations but not in nonstressful situations.

All of these studies suggest that the enactments of low-status children are less competent than the enactments of average- and high-status children. However, most of these studies confound enactment skill with other social-information-processing steps such as response search and evaluation. A low score on one of these tasks could result from deficits in any of these skills, as well as other task-specific communication skills. A recent study by Perry et al. (1986) examined another aspect of enactment, that is, children's confidence in their ability to enact particular behaviors. They found that aggressive children responded with greater confidence than nonaggressive children that they could enact aggressive behaviors in specific situations.

Conclusions and synthesis

Assessments of children's social cognitions – including social cue interpretations and attributions, response search and evaluation, and enactment skills – have yielded significant differences between children of high- and low-sociometric status. Unpopular children are less skillful at interpreting cues, they are biased in their attributions of others, and they attribute social failures to internal causes. They also generate more deviant responses to interpersonal dilemmas, their skill in evaluating responses is relatively deficient, their enactments of responses are more incompetent, and their confidence in aggressive responses is quite great. Caution must be expressed about these conclusions, however. Many of the findings have not been duplicated in different social situations. Also, in each study, the proportion of unpopular children displaying a social-cognitive deficiency is relatively small. The amount of variance in popularity accounted for by the social-cognitive measure is significant but also typically small, suggesting a good deal of divergence in social-cognitive functioning within the popular and unpopular groups.

One reason that the proportion of variance in status accounted for has been so small may be that in actual social interactions multiple cognitive processes are involved. To behave competently, one must perform skillfully at each and every step of social information processing. Typical studies have assessed only a single step. Because these steps may be independent of each other, it is possible that a comprehensive assessment of all steps would yield a more powerful prediction of status. Dodge, Pettit, McClaskey, and Brown (1986) used this reasoning to examine the relation between social information processing and actual behavioral patterns. Children were administered measures of each of five steps of processing about a peer group entry situation and then were observed engaging in actual peer group entry, both in the laboratory and on the playground. As previous studies have found, individual processing measures were significantly correlated with competent social behavior, at levels in the range of .25 to .40. The combined assessment (evaluated by multiple regression), however, yielded a more powerful prediction of behavior (multiple $R = .66-.82$). Dodge et al. repeated their assessments with a second situation type, that of responding to a provocation by a peer. Again, individual processing measures were moderately correlated with actual behavior in this situation, but the combined assessment predicted behavior more strongly (multiple $R = .74$). These studies clearly show that there *is* a strong relation between social information processing and behavioral patterns, as long as an aggregated and comprehensive assessment of processing is conducted.

Another reason that findings of status group differences in social cognition often seem inconsistent is that the type of situation that serves as the stimulus has varied between studies. Patterns in one situation may not hold in a second situation. It has been found, for example, that low-status children are relatively deficient in response search skills in object acquisition situations but not in peer group entry situations (Rubin & Krasnor, 1986). Just as research has revealed a great deal of cross-situational variation in an individual's social-behavioral patterns (Mischel, 1968), so too it seems that children vary across situations in their social-cognitive patterns. Also, the relation between social cognition in one situation and social-behavioral patterns in a second situation has been found to be relatively weak. In the Dodge et al. (1986) study, even though the multiple correlations between social cognition and social behavior were quite high within situations, the multiple correlations between cognition in one situation and behavior in a second situation were not nearly as high and were statistically nonsignificant (multiple $R = .45$ and $.56$). Thus, it seems that a comprehensive assessment of social information processing in one situation will lead to an accurate prediction of social behavior in that situation, but it will predict little about social behavior in a different type of situation. As a corollary point, whether or not *social-cognitive* patterns in a particular situation will distinguish status groups is likely to be a function of whether or not *social-behavioral* patterns in that situation distinguish the groups.

A related point is that individual differences among unpopular children must be considered. One unpopular child may display a deviant social-cognitive pattern in one area, whereas another unpopular child may display a deviant pattern in another area. When all aspects of social cognition are assessed in all relevant situations, a powerful discrimination between status groups might be found. In causal terms, it may be that one child becomes unpopular for one reason (such as a response search deficit in how to acquire objects), whereas another child becomes unpopular for another reason (such as a self-defeating attributional style in response to a provocation). The heterogeneity in social-cognitive deficits of unpopular children must not be overlooked.

A final caution concerns the fact that the findings reviewed thus far have often varied according to the gender and age of the child. Findings that hold for one gender and age-group may not hold for another group. This point is important for a theory of the relation between social cognition and sociometric status because it suggests that there are few universal relations between social cognition and status. Rather, most relations are population specific. Any theory of social cognition and sociometric status must explain why one set of relations holds for one population and another set holds for a second population. This point is also important for clinicians. Clinicians must be sure that the empirical foundations for their social-cognitive interventions with low-status children are based on findings obtained with a population that is similar to the one that they are serving. Because sex and age seem to be important moderators of the relation between social cognition and status, these factors will be considered next.

Sex, social cognition, and sociometric status

Sex differences in psychopathology and deviance have been noted for some time. At a young age, boys have been overrepresented in almost every category of disorder, including adjustment reactions (Anthony, 1970), learning difficulties (Rutter & Yule, 1977), hyperactivity (Cantwell, 1977), antisocial behavior disorders (Wolff, 1977), psychoses (Rutter & Lockyear, 1967), and neuroses (Gove & Herb, 1974). The same is true with deviant sociometric status: Boys are more likely than girls to be rejected (Coie, Dodge, & Coppotelli, 1982), although this finding seems to vary across populations. These findings are in stark contrast with the adult literature, in which overall rates of psychopathology are similar for males and females (Gove & Herb, 1974), and females are actually overrepresented in several categories, including neuroses and depression (Dohrenwend & Dohrenwend, 1974). These findings suggest that the developmental paths to adult psychopathology may be different for males and females.

Most of the longitudinal studies of developmental psychopathology have been focused on males (e.g., Roff, 1961; Robins, 1966). The bulk of this literature has demonstrated that among males, social rejection and overt antisocial behavior are powerful predictors of many forms of adult psychopathology (Kohlberg, La-Crosse, & Ricks, 1972), whereas social withdrawal and shyness are not predictors (Michael, Morris, & Soroker, 1957).

Among females, the predictors are less clear. Robins (1966) found that whereas antisocial behavior was much less common in girls than boys (by a ratio of 1 to 4), when it did occur, it predicted adult sociopathy just as it had for boys. On the other hand, John, Mednick, and Schulsinger (1982) found that childhood aggression and conduct problems predicted later schizophrenia among boys but not among girls.

Even though the behavioral predictors of maladaptive outcomes may differ for boys and girls (partly because of base rate differences in the kinds of deviant behaviors displayed by each sex), the construct of social status may be a unifying risk factor for both sexes. Both boys and girls who have difficulty in relating to peers and are rejected by peers seem to be at risk. The data by Cowen, Pederson, Babigian, Izzo, and Trost (1973) indicate that low-status children are at risk for later mental health problems. Because the analyses were not conducted separately for girls and boys, we can only guess that the finding held for each sex. Kupersmidt (1983) found that rejected boys and girls are both at risk for later juvenile delinquency. Thus sociometric status may be a useful risk indicator for both sexes.

Even though sociometric status may be a unifying risk indicator, the behavioral correlates of status differ for boys and girls. Aggressive behavior has been found to be a major correlate of rejection among boys (Coie et al., 1982; Hartup, Glazer, & Charlesworth, 1967); however, it is not clear that aggression is correlated with status among girls. McGuire (1973) found that girls who displayed high frequencies of aggressive behavior (relative to other girls) tended to be popular rather than unpopular. La Greca (1981) found that peer acceptance ratings were negatively correlated with teachers' ratings of aggression and withdrawal among boys. Among girls, only the withdrawal ratings were negatively correlated with peer acceptance. These findings suggest that low-status boys are aggressive, whereas low-status girls are withdrawn. Findings by Achenbach and Edelbrock (1981), using parent checklists, also indicate that clinic-referred boys tend to display externalizing behavior, whereas clinic-referred girls tend to display internalizing behavior. Coie et al. (1982) examined peer perceptions of boys and girls in each of several sociometric status groups (popular, average, neglected, rejected, and controversial). They found that rejected boys *and* rejected girls were rated as highly aggressive, relative to their same-sex peers. However, a significant interaction between sex and status indicated that aggression was a stronger discriminator of status groups among boys than among girls. On the other hand, peer assessments of cooperativeness were a better discriminator of status groups among girls than among boys.

Given these sex differences in the behavioral correlates of status, it is reasonable to speculate that social-cognitive correlates of status might also differ between sexes. Surprisingly, very few studies have explicitly examined this question. Most studies have included only male samples to study the social-cognitive correlates of status, so the general conclusions in the literature apply for boys but not necessarily for girls. Studies of social cognition in boys and girls, ignoring sociometric status, have demonstrated interesting patterns of sex differences in skill levels (Shantz, 1983). It appears that boys are superior in nonsocial spatial perspective taking (Coie & Dorval, 1973) but that girls are superior in social perspective taking and in affective empathy (Feshbach, 1978; Zahn-Waxler, Radke-Yarrow, & Brady-Smith, 1977). The implications of these differences for studies of the cognitive correlates of status in boys and girls have been examined systematically in relatively few studies.

One aspect of social information processing in which sex interactions with behavioral status have been studied is that of empathy, which is the cognitive and affective understanding of another's emotional perspective. Feshbach and Feshbach (1969) examined the relation between empathy and peer-directed aggression. They found that boys who were deficient in empathy were more aggressive than boys who were highly empathic. There was not a significant correlation between empathy and aggression among girls, although the direction of the relation suggested that highly empathic girls were *more* aggressive than less empathic girls. Although this study did not examine peer sociometric status, it is consistent with behavioral studies of status in that aggression is related to social deficiencies in boys but not in girls.

Ladd and Oden (1979) examined sex effects on the relation between status and children's response search patterns, using story stimuli that called for helpful responses by the subject (such as to a peer who is hurt). They found that the uniqueness and the flexibility of response search were positively correlated with status for both boys and girls, but the magnitude of the relation was stronger among girls than boys. The social-cognitive variables accounted for 7% of the variance in status among boys and 29% of the variance in status among girls. This is one of the few studies to find a stronger relation between social cognition and behavioral outcomes in girls than in boys. It is striking that this finding occurred using stimuli that called for a prosocial, helpful response, a dimension of behavior that is similar to the cooperativeness dimension of behavior that differentiated status groups more strongly in girls than in boys.

We propose that, as with behavior, social-cognitive assessments that relate to aggression (either using aggression as a stimulus or using stimuli to which aggression is a likely response) will discriminate sociometric status groups more strongly among boys than among girls. This is consistent with the hypothesis that aggression and its control are more salient issues for boys than girls (Parke & Slaby, 1983). On the other hand, social-cognitive assessments that relate to cooperativeness and helpfulness (either as stimuli or as responses) will discriminate status groups more strongly among girls than among boys, because these dimensions may be more salient for girls than boys (Taylor & Asher, 1984). In other words, we are predicting that triple interactions among situation type, sex of child, and sociometric status group will be found when tested. These interactions will be orderly in that only sex-relevant situations will distinguish status groups for a particular sex group. These proposals are strictly hypotheses at this point because very few empirical findings have been generated.

Age, social cognition, and sociometric status

Numerous studies have demonstrated increasing sophistication and skill in social cognition with advancing age (reviewed by Shantz, 1983), but little is known about the interaction of age and sociometric status. The focus of this section is on the types of status differences in social cognitions that emerge or disappear at different ages. This focus is central to a theory of the development of sociometric status (is social-cognitive skill an antecedent of high status or an outcome?) and to the planning of interventions for low-status children. Interventions aimed at improving social-cognitive skills in low-status children of a particular age must be predicated on empirical findings demonstrating that those skills are relevant to status at that age (Ladd, 1981).

This discussion must build on the fact that sociometric status itself is unreliably measured prior to the age of 4 (Hymel, 1983), so social-cognitive correlates are not likely to be evidenced prior to this age. One could, however, envision social-cognitive variables at early ages being predictors of status that emerges later. Behavioral deviations occur more frequently at young ages than older ages (Garber, 1984), but many of these deviations are temporary and sporadic and are not likely to be related to stable social-cognitive factors.

Also, it must be noted that the methods for assessing social-cognitive patterns vary with respect to age, and an age-appropriate method must be adopted to examine status group differences within age-groups. Harter and Pike (1984), for example, have developed a reliable scale of perceived self-competence for pre-schoolers that differs from Harter's (1982) scale for older children.

It must also be recognized that different social-cognitive skills are relevant to behavioral development at various ages (Piers & Harris, 1964). Piaget (1965), for example, hypothesized that empathy and social perspective taking will be related to behavioral outcomes, especially during the concrete operational period (ages 6 through 8). This period is a time of rapid growth in these skills, and delays in development may have important effects on behavior at this time. In one of the few studies of referential communication and popularity that included multiple age-groups, Rubin (1972) found that referential communication accuracy correlated positively with popularity in kindergarten and second grade but not in the fourth and sixth grades. On the other hand, Gottman et al. (1975) found significant positive correlations among third- and fourth-grade children. However, Gottman et al.'s study was conducted with low-socioeconomic-status children who performed poorly as a group and may have been at the developmental level of Rubin's second-graders. We hypothesize that a particular social-cognitive skill will be most strongly related to sociometric status during the developmental period when this skill is undergoing crucial change. The notion of a *critical age* for the relevance of particular social-cognitive skills to sociometric status is a useful one here. There may be different critical ages for different social-cognitive patterns.

Higgins, Ruble, and Hartup (1983) have pointed out that relevant social tasks will also vary across stages of development, so the situations in which social-cognitive patterns should be assessed will also vary with age. Rubin and Krasnor (1986) note that proximity seeking and attention getting are significant tasks for toddlers, whereas friendship initiation and information gathering are more critical for elementary school children. Heterosexual behavior is less likely to be relevant until adolescence. Ruble (1983) has noted that social comparison is not relevant to children until they find themselves in the competitive setting of elementary school. We hypothesize that sociometric status groups are likely to differ in social-cognitive patterns only in situations that are relevant at a particular age.

A final reason for attending to age in assessments of social-cognitive patterns in high- and low-status children is to explore the hypothesis that low-status children are lagging in the development of social-cognitive skills relative to their peers (Garber, 1984). By comparing age trends with status differences, the hypothesis that low-status children perform similarly to younger children can be tested. This developmental lag hypothesis has been supported in some domains (such as encoding search [Dodge & Newman, 1982] and intention cue detection accuracy [Dodge et al., 1984]) but not in others (such as attributional biases [Dodge, 1980]). Because attributional biases do not follow a simple developmental course, the concept of developmental lag does not hold.

There also is evidence that certain social-cognitive processes are relevant at all ages. For example, Spivack, Platt, and Shure (1974) accumulated evidence to show that response search patterns relate to social adjustment at all ages of children and adults. Their approach was decidedly void of developmental theory, however, and so they did not attend closely to interactions of age and adjustment (Rubin & Krasnor, 1986). The evidence supports their conjectures to some extent, in that sociometric status differences in response generation have been reported for many age-groups, from kindergarteners through adults. The data are less clear concerning children younger than kindergarten age. Rubin et al. (1982) found status differences among kindergarteners but no differences during preschool. Likewise, Asher and Renshaw (1981) found differences among kindergarteners, whereas Sharp (1978) found no differences among preschoolers. It may be that patterns of responding and status may be insufficiently reliable at the preschool age to yield status differences.

It also has been reported that status differences in response generation have *not* been obtained for children of various age-groups (e.g., Butler, 1978). Rather than implicate the construct of response generation as an unreliable discriminator of status groups, we choose to interpret these mixed findings as being due to the types of social situations used as stimuli. Consistent with the discussion earlier, it may be that some situations are especially relevant to children at one age but not another. We expect that sociometric status differences in response generation are most likely to be found when age-appropriate situations are used as stimuli. This hypothesis is consistent with the call for age-specific task-analytic approaches to assessment by Goldfried and D'Zurilla (1969).

In sum, investigators of sociometric status group differences in social cognition must attend to the possibility that patterns of findings will vary across different ages. No status differences have been found prior to the age of 4. Beyond that age, it appears that status differences are most likely to be found when the following conditions are met: (a) The situational stimuli used are relevant to the social functioning of children at the age of assessment, and (b) the social cognitions being assessed are important to children or are undergoing transition during the age period of assessment. Finally, attention to age-appropriate norms in social cognition is required, because it may be that high-status children perform in age-appropriate ways whereas low-status children may be out of synchrony with the majority of their peers.

Social situations and sociometric status

In this chapter, we have highlighted the importance of the social situation. We will refer to two aspects of the term *situation*. First, we will discuss the effects of the contextual features of an assessment (e.g., the laboratory, the playground). Second, we will discuss how the content of social situations themselves (such as conflict vs. initiation situations) may influence cognition. Both aspects merit attention.

Contextual and mood factors

In their studies of children's response generation skills, Rubin and Krasnor (1986) discuss the many differences between generating responses in hypothetical situations and generating responses in actual interactions. They conclude that in some cases a child's level of social-cognitive sophistication appears greater in actual practice than in laboratory tests, "in keeping with the Piagetian perspective that knowledge is first constructed through action and only later emerges in hypothetical–reflective thought" (p. 12). In other cases, the laboratory-assessed level of social cognition may appear more sophisticated than the child's actual behavioral competence, because the child's pattern of cognitive response happens to match the demands of the testing environment. For example, a child who is rigidly stuck in perceiving the world as a hostile place may perform more accurately than others in those cases in which the stimulus is actually hostile. Selman (1980) has concurred with the conclusions of Rubin and Krasnor (1986) and has noted further that distinctions exist not only in the situational stimulus as hypothetical versus real life but also in the format for responding as naturalistic versus reflective. Naturalistic responding includes spontaneous statements about cognitions, whereas reflective responding includes those responses that are carefully considered after solicitation.

Elias (1982) has listed a number of contextual factors that affect the level of social-cognitive response, including (a) the context of the assessment administration (individual or group; a rationale provided or not), (b) the mode of stimulus presentation (oral, written, pictorial, or live actors), (c) the response format (verbal, written, or behavioral), (d) the degree of structure (immediate vs. delayed responding; fast vs. slow responding), and (e) the relative emphasis on competent performance versus other goals, such as completing the task quickly and without questions.

Another contextual factor is the affective state of the child during the assessment. Intelligence test administrators have long known that a child's performance may be adversely affected when the test is administered under nonoptimal circumstances or when the child is anxious. Recently, Dodge and Somberg (1987) examined whether the disruption caused by having to respond under adverse circumstances would be equally great for aggressive- and average-status children. They presented children with the Dodge et al. (1984) test of social cue interpretation accuracy under relaxed and anxiety-provoking circumstances and found that the status differences were greater under anxiety-provoking conditions than under relaxed conditions. The anxiety-provoking circumstances (in this case, involving a potential conflict with a peer) had a negative effect on the aggressive children but no effect on average children.

Differences across situations

The content of the social cues about which children's behavior and cognitive patterns have been assessed have varied greatly across studies and have also had strong effects on social-cognitive performance. In early studies, the situational cues were not felt to be relevant, and many studies were conducted in which the cues were not even social at all (such as tests of status differences in spatial perspective taking). More recently, researchers have recognized the interaction between status and situation and have sought to assess status differences in social cognition in situations that are thought to be relevant to social functioning. Typically, researchers have selected the focal situations on an intuitive basis. For example, Dodge (1980) was interested in the attributions of another's intention made by aggressive rejected boys and their average peers. It appeared to him that situations involving *being the object of a provocation* (such as being struck by a peer) both were important to children and might differentiate the status groups. He was right on the latter account (and did not assess the former account directly). Other researchers also have targeted a provocation situation for analyses of social cognitions, including Elias (1982) and Aydin and Markova (1979).

A survey of the situations used as the content for assessment in the existing literature reveals that these situations are typically highly interpersonal and range from overt conflict to relationship-enhancing, nonconflict situations. *Responding to a blatant exclusion by peers* has been studied by Elias, Larcen, Zlotlow, and Chinsky (1978), who found that children's problem-solving competencies are impaired under circumstances involving an obstacle to social cooperation, such as the exclusion situation. Goetz and Dweck (1980) studied children's responses to a temporary exclusion from a pen pal club and found that children vary in the degree to which they attribute failure to internal versus external causes. Rubin and Krasnor (1986), Putallaz (1983), and Richard and Dodge (1982) studied response generation following temporary setbacks, such as exclusion from play with peers. It appears that children vary greatly in their cognitions about such conflicts.

The cognitions of children during the *resolution of a conflict* have been studied by Renshaw and Asher (1982) in a study of children's goal selection. They found that low-status children are more likely than others to select avoidant goals and are less likely than others to select relationship-enhancing goals in this situation, although the strength of this finding was affected by the age of children being assessed.

Other researchers have examined children's social cognitions in situations in which the child hopes to exert some sort of influence over another child. Rubin and Krasnor (1986), Richard and Dodge (1982), and Spivack and Shure (1974) found that the problem-solving patterns of high- and low-status children differ in a situation involving the *acquisition of a peer's object,* such as a toy. Elias (1982) also has studied this type of situation, as well as children's attempts to elicit information from a peer. Closely related are studies by Burleson (1985), Rubin and Borwick (1984), Richard and Dodge (1982), and Wheeler and Ladd (1982), in which children's cognitions about *persuasion and peer manipulation* situations were examined. Status differences in problem solving, persuasion skill, and perceived self-efficacy have been found in this situation.

Situations involving *social comparisons,* or the difference in performance among children, apparently become important when children enter school and other competitive settings (Ruble, 1983). Parkhurst and Asher (1985) note that the selection of goals in social comparison situations is relevant to social outcomes. For example, children who perceive that friendship maintenance is important may strive for equality in social comparisons with a peer, whereas children who have dominance goals may derogate peers in social comparison situations.

The *initiation of friendships* is a nonconflict situation that has been studied perhaps more than any other. Gottman et al. (1975) were the first to find that popular children are more skillful at generating solutions in this circumstance than are unpopular children. Putallaz (1983; Putallaz & Gottman, 1981) and Dodge (1986) have found that high- and low-status groups differ in their actual behavior in this situation, but the results of other attempts to document differences in cognitive problem solving skills have been mixed (Dodge, 1986; Richard & Dodge, 1982; Rubin & Krasnor, 1986). Rubin and Krasnor (1986) doubted that social initiations are problematic for children, concluding that "it would seem that situations involving peer confrontation are more problematic than situations involving social initiations for rejected children to think about" (p. 38).

Still other studies have examined children's social cognitions about situations involving *maintaining and enhancing relationships* (e.g., Asher & Renshaw, 1981). One way to enhance a relationship is through accurate referential communication, and this skill has been related to sociometric status in several studies (Goldman et al., 1980; Gottman et al., 1975; Rubin, 1972). Ladd and Oden (1979) found that popular children have a more sophisticated understanding of how to be helpful to peers than do less accepted children. Similarly, Burleson (1985) found that comforting skills are more advanced in popular than unpopular children.

Unresolved issues

The range in social situations studied by researchers indicates the diversity of the social contents and contexts in which children operate and points toward the need to develop a more coherent understanding of the role of context in social cognition, as advocated by Higgins, Ruble, and Hartup (1983). Two issues seem particularly pressing.

First, researchers must clarify who defines a situation as a situation and what parameters are its boundaries. Parkhurst and Asher (1985) have perceptively pointed out that the task of defining a situation is actually part of social cognition itself. When presented with an array of social cues, the child organizes those cues into a meaningful set, called a situation. The same cues may represent different situations to different children. To assume the situation exists as an entity apart from the child's social cognizing misses the point. One might attempt to measure children's varying construals given a fixed array of cues, as Renshaw and Asher (1982) have done, but then the standard meaning would be that meaning applied by the researchers. Accuracy would be defined as consistency with the researchers' meaning.

A second issue concerns the selection of critical situations for use as stimuli. Often, researchers have used intuition or casual observation to make selections, with mixed results. Goldfried and D'Zurilla (1969) have proposed a systematic empirical method for generating situational taxonomies relevant to a particular population. The method consists of asking "experts" to generate a large number of critical situations and then paring down the list by consensus. The experts might include teachers, clinicians, and the children themselves. This method is not only systematic and comprehensive but also leads to the identification of situations that have meaning for the participants. This method is unlikely to lead to the generation of situations that are too molar (e.g., growing up) or too molecular (e.g., differentiating situations according to the weather or time of day) to have meaning for the participants. It is likely, however, to lead to the generation of situations that are especially relevant in the eyes of those who are involved.

McFall and his colleagues have used the Goldfried and D'Zurilla method to generate taxonomies of problematic situations for adolescent boys (Freedman, Rosenthal, Donahoe, Schlundt, & McFall, 1978a, 1978b) and girls (Gaffney & McFall, 1981). These taxonomies were then used as stimuli to assess problem-solving skills. The situational stimuli in those inventories were worded as hypothetical problems, such as the following:

You're visiting your aunt in another part of town, and you don't know any of the guys your age there. You're walking along the street and some guy is walking toward you. He is about your size. As he is about to pass you, he deliberately bumps into you, and you nearly lose your balance. What do you do or say now? (Freedman et al., 1978a, p. 2)

The 44 situations for males and 32 situations for females used in these studies include provocations by peers, social failure, group acceptance, social pressure, heterosocial relations, authority pressure, and moral questions.

Dodge, McClaskey, and Feldman (1985) recently used a similar method to generate a taxonomy of problematic social situations for elementary school boys and girls. Their taxonomy consisted of 44 situations that empirically grouped into six factors: Group Entry, Responding to Provocation, Responding to Success, Responding to Failure, Peer Social Expectations, and Teacher Expectations. Problem-solving responses of high- and low-sociometric-status children differed only in the provocation and failure situations. It appears that only in these stressful situations did low-status children perform deviantly. Elias et al. (1978) also applied the Goldfried and D'Zurilla approach to generate three major types of problematic situations: object acquisition, exclusion from a group of peers, and being unjustly blamed by a teacher. Asarnow and Callan (1985) similarly used this task-analytic approach and found that the great majority of problematic situations identified by children involved acts of verbal and physical aggression or being excluded by peers. Obviously, as Freedman et al. (1978b) have noted, more taxonomic research is necessary both to determine the kinds of situations relevant for various populations and to understand better the concept of the social situation. Still, it appears that five kinds of problematic situations have emerged most frequently across studies: responding to threats, teasing, or insults;

responding to actual provocation; being excluded from play; initiating friend-ships; and fulfilling peer group norms (such as helping).

A study of situation, sex, age, and status effects on social cognition

A serious problem in making conclusions about the role of situation, sex, and age on social-cognitive patterns of high- and low-status children is that these effects have not been examined within the same study. Differences noted may be confounded with other procedural differences across studies. We (Feldman & Dodge, 1987) decided to examine these effects systematically in a study that integrates these issues.

The first step in this research was to generate the social situations that would serve as stimuli for the assessment of social cognitions. Following Goldfried and D'Zurilla's (1969) behavior-analytic technique, elementary school teachers and clinicians were asked to identify frequently occurring social situations that often lead to peer relationship problems among boys and girls aged 5 to 12. The resulting Taxonomy of Problematic Social Situations (TOPS) for children (Dodge, McClaskey, & Feldman, 1985) contained 44 situations that could be classified into six mutually exclusive and exhaustive content categories.

Teachers were asked to designate each situation as one that is more likely to lead to a conflict among girls than among boys, among boys than among girls, or equally among both sexes. One situation type was clearly selected as more frequently being a problem for girls than boys, that of "having problems with initiating entry into a group of peers." This finding is consistent with Berndt's (1983) contention that friendship boundaries are more salient for girls than boys and with Coie et al.'s (1982) findings that cooperating in a group is a salient dimension for girls. A second situation type was selected as more problematic for boys than girls, that of "responding to a peer's ambiguous provocation." Given that aggression is a common retaliatory response in this situation and that control of aggression is a salient and difficult task for boys (Coie et al., 1982; Parke & Slaby, 1983), this finding is not surprising. Finally, a third situation type, "responding to being teased or laughed at for being different," was selected as especially problematic for both sexes. These three situations were therefore selected to be the stimuli for the assessment of social-information-processing patterns in this study.

The assessments were designed to measure four aspects of social information processing described earlier (cue interpretation, response search, response evaluation, and response enactment) in each of the three social situations. For each situation, the child heard an audiotape, accompanied by cartoon visual aids, in which a female narrator told a hypothetical story in which the subject imagined being the protagonist. The narrator described the situation and then asked the child questions designed to assess the child's cognitions about the situation. For each situation, 12 measures were collected, as assessments of various steps of social information processing. These scores were subjected to multivariate and univariate analyses of variance for each situation. The independent variables were children's sociometric status (popular, average, neglected, or rejected), age (first, third, or fifth grade), and sex.

Age effects

As expected, children's patterns of processing information were more sophisticated among older than younger children. Other developmental patterns reflected changing subcultural norms with advancing age. Significant effects were found in all three situations. In response to being teased or identified as different, older children generated a higher proportion of competent responses than younger children. They also became more likely to endorse aggressive responses, a rather surprising finding. In response to an ambiguous provocation, they generated more responses than younger children and were less likely to endorse ineffective withdrawal responses. At the same time, they became more vigilant, in that they were more likely to attribute hostility to the hypothetical peer provocateur. This, too, was a surprising finding. In the peer group entry situation, children became more sophisticated in their evaluations of responses as they got older. They became less likely to endorse all ineffective responses, including aggression, withdrawal, passivity, and authority intervention, and relatively more likely to endorse competent responses. Their enactments of a response in this situation also became more skilled. The findings in these three situations reflect increasing skill in generating, evaluating, and enacting responses with advancing age, consistent with a score of previous studies. The findings also reflect a changing subculture, in that it becomes more acceptable to aggress in response to teasing and less acceptable to withdraw in response to a provocation.

Sex effects

A significant multivariate main effect of sex was found, but only in the situation involving the ambiguous provocation. The findings suggest that boys' difficulty in behaving competently in this situation relative to girls (as noted by Parke & Slaby, 1983, as well as the teachers in this study) may occur as a function of their patterns of processing information in this situation. Boys were more likely than girls to attribute hostile intentions to the peer provocateur. They generated fewer responses to this situation, but their responses were twice as likely to be aggressive and only half as likely to be passive as were those by girls. Girls also were more likely to evaluate withdrawal responses more positively than boys did. Each of these findings suggests that boys process provocation information in a way that is likely to escalate a conflict, whereas girls process information in a way that will minimize a conflict.

Status effects

A significant multivariate main effect of status was found in the situation involving being teased but not in the other two situations. Low-status children (rejected and neglected) in this situation were twice as likely as high-status children (average and popular) to attribute hostility to the hypothetical peer provocateur. They also generated a higher proportion of aggressive responses and a lower proportion of competent responses than did the high-status children. Finally, the rejected group endorsed aggressive responses more than each of the other three status groups. These findings demonstrate that low-status children are more vigilant in their interpretations of peers' intentions, and they generate and evaluate responses in a way that is likely to lead them into conflict with peers. When no conflict is apparent (as in the peer group entry situation), the status groups did not differ in processing patterns. The findings of status group differences in social cognition in a threatening, conflict situation but not in a group entry situation are identical to the patterns found by Rubin and Krasnor (1986). Clearly, the threatening situation should be targeted for further research and intervention, because it is critical to deviant processing by low-status children.

Status and sex interactions

Next, we examined whether status differences in processing were similar for boys and girls. Significant multivariate and univariate interactions of status and sex also were found in the situation involving being teased. These interactions, depicted in Figure 5.1, suggest that subgroups of unpopular children (rejected and neglected) differ in their processing patterns but these differences vary according to the sex of the child. Among boys, the rejected group generated fewer responses than the neglected group, and more of their responses were aggressive. Rejected boys also evaluated aggressive responses more favorably than did neglected boys. Neglected boys, on the other hand, generated a higher proportion of passive responses to being teased than did rejected boys. These processing differences are consistent with behavioral differences between rejected and neglected boys (Coie & Kupersmidt, 1983; Dodge, 1983), in that rejected boys behave inappropriately aggressively and neglected boys behave passively among

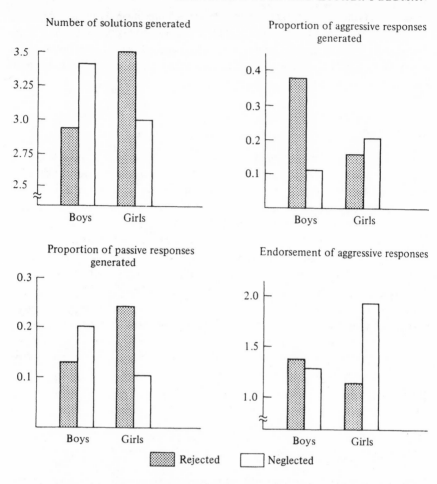

Figure 5.1. Processing patterns in rejected and neglected girls and boys in response to being teased. Data from Feldman & Dodge (1987).

peers. Although their processing patterns differ, both rejected and neglected boys are deviant in processing relative to average and popular boys.

The processing patterns among rejected and neglected girls were just the opposite. That is, neglected girls performed similarly to rejected boys, and rejected girls performed similarly to neglected boys. Specifically, neglected girls generated fewer responses to the teasing situation than did rejected girls. More of the responses of neglected girls were aggressive, whereas more of the responses of rejected girls were passive. Neglected girls were more likely than rejected girls to endorse aggressive responses. Because there are only a few observational studies of rejected and neglected girls, it is difficult to evaluate whether these differences mirror behavioral patterns. Two recent studies indicate that rejected girls are more withdrawn (Cantrell & Prinz, 1984) and engage in more parallel play (Ladd, 1983) than neglected girls, so these findings are consistent with the few studies in which girls have been observed or in which sex differences have been noted.

Discriminant function analysis conducted separately for girls and boys indicated that the magnitude of status differences in processing was stronger among boys than among girls. Although these findings are tentative, they are consistent with previous findings indicating stronger relations between processing and behavior in boys than in girls (e.g., Feshbach & Feshbach, 1969). Why this should be so is not certain.

Status and age interactions

Status differences in processing were found to vary according to the age of the child in all three situations. None of the interactions affected differences between high- and low-status children. Several significant differences were found between rejected and neglected children, however. At the younger ages (first and third grades), the rejected children were more deviant in processing than the neglected children. They generated a higher proportion of aggressive responses to being teased, and they were less skillful in enacting competent responses to a provocation. At the oldest age (fifth grade), the pattern reversed, in that neglected children responded more deviantly than rejected children. One parsimonious explanation of these findings is that processing patterns in a child remain fixed over time, but that children who are deviant in processing are actively rejected at the early ages and become ignored (neglected) at older ages, when, following failure, they withdraw from the peer group. Obviously, longitudinal inquiry into these patterns is required to support this explanation.

Age differences also were found in the comparisons between popular and average children. For example, at the first-grade level, popular children were more likely than average children to endorse passive responses in the group entry situation. At the third- and fifth-grade levels, they were less likely to endorse passive responses. Given that passive responses in this situation received more negative evaluations as children grow older (a strong developmental effect among all status groups), it appears that popular children are more likely than average children to endorse age-appropriate responses at *all* ages. Because the age-appropriate response changes with age, the evaluations by popular children change as well, whereas the evaluations by average children change less and are less responsive to age-appropriate norms. As with previous findings, awareness of the cultural norms for a particular age-group is helpful for interpreting status differences in the way children process social information.

General conclusions

The literature reviewed in this chapter and the findings reported here suggest three general conclusions concerning the relation between social cognition and children's sociometric status. First, there are consistent differences in social cognition between high- and low-status children in ways that reflect less sophisticated and more deviant patterns among low-status children. Low-status children attribute intentions in biased and inaccurate ways and display deficits in response search, evaluation, and enactment. The causal relation between these deviant patterns and status is not clear, because almost all of these studies are correlational.

A second conclusion is a restriction on the first conclusion. The status differences reported vary with the age and sex of the children being assessed and with the situational cues that are the stimuli for the assessments. Little evidence has accumulated that low-status children have general intellectual or processing deficits; rather, their deficits and processing biases appear to be specific to particular situations, especially situations that are potentially stressful or threatening and are relevant to social functioning for their particular age and sex subculture group.

The final conclusion is a suggestion for future work. Intervention efforts and further empirical inquiry should note the restricted conditions in which social-cognitive deficits and biases are likely to be found among low-status children. Empirical inquiry should also examine systematically the development of these conditions. Many interventions are aimed at changing the social cognitions of low-status children as a way of altering their behavior and improving their status. These interventions must focus on social-cognitive patterns that have been found to be critical to effective social functioning for the relevant age and sex peer group. Without attention to these conditions, interventions are likely to be ineffective in achieving a change in sociometric status.

References

Achenbach, T. M., & Edelbrock, C. S. (1981). Behavioral problems and competencies reported by parents of normal and disturbed children aged four through sixteen. *Monographs of the Society for Research in Child Development, 46*(1, Serial No. 188).

Ames, R., Ames, C., & Garrison, W. (1977). Children's causal ascriptions for positive and negative interpersonal outcomes. *Psychological Reports, 41,* 595–602.

Anthony, J. (1970). Behavior disorders. In P. Mussen (Ed.), *Carmichael's manual of child psychology* (Vol. 2, pp. 667–764). New York: Wiley.

Asarnow, J. R., & Callan, J. W. (1985). Boys with peer adjustment problems: Social cognitive processes. *Journal of Consulting and Clinical Psychology, 53,* 80–87.

Asher, S. R., & Renshaw, P. D. (1981). Children without friends: Social knowledge and social skill training. In S. R. Asher & J. M. Gottman (Eds.), *The development of children's friendships* (pp. 273–296). New York: Cambridge University Press.

Ausubel, D. P. (1955). Socioempathy as a function of sociometric status in an adolescent group. *Human Relations, 8,* 75–84.

Aydin, O., & Markova, I. (1979). Attribution tendencies of popular and unpopular children. *British Journal of Social and Clinical Psychology, 18,* 291–298.

Bandura, A. (1978). The self-system in reciprocal determinism. *American Psychologist, 33,* 344–358.

Berndt, T. J. (1983). Social cognition, social behavior, and children's friendships. In E. T. Higgins, D. N. Ruble, & W. W. Hartup (Eds.), *Social cognition and social development: A sociocultural perspective* (pp. 158–192). New York: Cambridge University Press.

Burleson, B. (1985, April). *Communicative correlates of peer acceptance in childhood.* Paper presented at the biennial meeting of the Society for Research in Child Development, Toronto.

Butler, L. (1978, June). *The relationship between interpersonal problem-solving skills and peer relations and behavior.* Paper presented at the annual meeting of the Canadian Psychological Association, Toronto.

Campbell, J. D., & Yarrow, M. R. (1961). Perceptual and behavioral correlates of social effectiveness. *Sociometry, 24,* 1–20.

Cantrell, V. L., & Prinz, R. J. (1984, November). *Multiple perspectives of rejected, neglected and accepted children: Relationships between sociometric status and behavioral characteristics.* Paper presented at the annual meeting of the Association for the Advancement of Behavior Therapy, Philadelphia.

Cantwell, D. (1977). Hyperkinetic syndrome. In M. Rutter & L. Hersov (Eds.), *Child psychiatry* (pp. 524–555). Oxford, England: Blackwell Scientific.

Chandler, M. J. (1973). Egocentrism and antisocial behavior: The assessment and training of social perspective-taking skills. *Developmental Psychology, 9,* 326–337.

Chandler, M. J., Greenspan, S., & Barenboim, C. (1974). Assessment and training of role-taking and referential communication skills in institutionalized emotionally disturbed children. *Developmental Psychology, 10,* 546–553.

Coie, J. D., Dodge, K. A., & Coppotelli, H. (1982). Dimensions and types of social status: A cross-age perspective. *Developmental Psychology, 18,* 557–570.

Coie, J. D., & Dorval, B. (1973). Sex differences in the intellectual structure of social interaction skills. *Developmental Psychology, 8,* 261–267.

Coie, J. D., & Kupersmidt, J. (1983). A behavioral analysis of emerging social status in boys' groups. *Child Development, 54,* 1400–1416.

Cowen, E. L., Pederson, A., Babigian, H., Izzo, L. D., & Trost, M. A. (1973). Long-term follow-up of early detected vulnerable children. *Journal of Consulting and Clinical Psychology, 41,* 438–446.

Crick, N. R., & Ladd, G. W. (1987, April). *Children's perceptions of the consequences of aggressive behavior: Do the ends justify being mean?* Paper presented at the biennial meeting of the Society for Research in Child Development, Baltimore.

Darley, J. M., & Fazio, R. H. (1980). Expectancy confirmation processes arising in the social interaction sequence. *American Psychologist, 35,* 867–881.

Deluty, R. H. (1983). Children's evaluations of aggressive, assertive, and submissive responses. *Journal of Clinical Child Psychology, 12,* 124–129.

Deluty, R. H. (1984). Behavioral validation of the Children's Action Tendency Scale. *Journal of Behavioral Assessment, 6,* 115–130.

Dodge, K. A. (1980). Social cognition and children's aggressive behavior. *Child Development, 51,* 162–170.

Dodge, K. A. (1983). Behavioral antecedents of peer social status. *Child Development, 54,* 1386–1399.

Dodge, K. A. (1986). A social information processing model of social competence in children. In M. Perlmutter (Ed.), *Minnesota symposia on child psychology* (Vol. 18, pp. 75–127). Hillsdale, NJ: Lawrence Erlbaum.

Dodge, K. A., Coie, J. D., & Brakke, N. P. (1982). Behavior patterns of socially rejected and neglected preadolescents: The roles of social approach and aggression. *Journal of Abnormal Child Psychology, 10,* 389–409.

Dodge, K. A., & Frame, C. L. (1982). Social cognitive biases and deficits in aggressive boys. *Child Development, 53,* 620–635.

Dodge, K. A., McClaskey, C. L., & Feldman, E. (1985). A situational approach to the assessment of social competence in children. *Journal of Consulting and Clinical Psychology, 53,* 344–353.

Dodge, K. A., Murphy, R. M., & Buchsbaum, K. (1984). The assessment of intention-cue detection skills in children: Implications for developmental psychopathology. *Child Development, 55,* 163–173.

Dodge, K. A., Murphy, R. M., & Somberg, D. (1983, November). *Assessment of intention-cue detection skills in socially deviant children.* Paper presented at the World Congress on Behavior Therapy, Washington, DC.

Dodge, K. A., & Newman, J. P. (1982). Biased decision making processes in aggressive boys. *Journal of Abnormal Psychology, 90,* 375–379.

Dodge, K. A., Pettit, G. S., McClaskey, C. L., & Brown, M. (1986). Social competence in children. *Monographs of the Society for Research in Child Development, 51*(2, Serial No. 213).

Dodge, K. A., & Somberg, D. (1987). Hostile attributional biases are exacerbated under conditions of threats to the self. *Child Development, 58,* 213–224.

Dohrenwend, B., & Dohrenwend, B. (1974). Social and cultural influences in psychopathology. In M. Rosenweig & L. Porter (Eds.), *Annual Review of Psychology* (Vol. 25, pp. 417–452). Palo Alto, CA: Annual Reviews.

Dweck, C. S. (1975). The role of expectations and attributions in the alleviation of learned helplessness. *Journal of Personality and Social Psychology, 31,* 674–685.

Ekman, P., & Friesen, W. V. (1975). *Unmasking the face.* Engelwood Cliffs, NJ: Prentice-Hall.

Elias, M. J. (1982, September). Assessment of cognitions and behaviors that accompany problematic interpersonal situations. In G. Spivack (Chair), *Prevention and mental health promotion: The Interpersonal-Cognitive Problem Solving (ICPS) Model.* Symposium conducted at Research Planning Workshop, NIMH, Rockville, MD.

Elias, M. J., Larcen, S. W., Zlotlow, S. F., & Chinsky, J. M. (1978, August). *An innovative measure of children's cognitions in problematic interpersonal situations.* Paper presented at the annual meeting of the American Psychological Association, Toronto.

Feldman, E., & Dodge, K. A. (1987). Social information processing and sociometric status: Sex, age, and situational effects. *Journal of Abnormal Child Psychology, 15,* 211–227.

Feshbach, N. D. (1978). Studies of empathic behavior in children. In B. A. Maher (Ed.), *Progress in experimental personality research* (Vol. 8, pp. 1–47). New York: Academic Press.

Feshbach, N. D., & Feshbach, S. (1969). The relationship between empathy and aggression in two age groups. *Developmental Psychology, 1,* 102–107.

Ford, M. E. (1979). The construct validity of egocentrism. *Psychological Bulletin, 86,* 1169–1188.

Freedman, B. J., Rosenthal, L., Donahoe, C. P., Jr., Schlundt, D. G., & McFall, R. M. (1978a). *Adolescent problems inventory raters manual.* Unpublished manuscript, Madison, WI.

Freedman, B. J., Rosenthal, L., Donahoe, C. P., Jr., Schlundt, D. G., & McFall, R. M. (1978b). A social-behavioral analysis of skills deficits in delinquent and non-delinquent adolescent boys. *Journal of Consulting and Clinical Psychology, 46,* 1448–1462.

Gaffney, L. R., & McFall, R. M. (1981). A comparison of social skills in delinquent and non-delinquent adolescent girls using a behavioral role-playing inventory. *Journal of Consulting and Clinical Psychology, 49,* 959–967.

Garber, J. (1984). Classification of childhood psychopathology: A developmental perspective. *Child Development, 55,* 30–48.

Gesten, E., & Weissberg, R. (1979, September). *Social problem-solving training and prevention: Some good news and some bad news.* Paper presented at the annual meeting of the American Psychological Association, New York.

Glucksberg, S., & Krauss, R. M. (1967). What do people say after they have learned how to talk? Studies of the development of referential communication. *Merrill-Palmer Quarterly, 13,* 309–316.

Goetz, T. E., & Dweck, C. S. (1980). Learned helplessness in social situations. *Journal of Personality and Social Psychology, 39,* 246–255.

Goldfried, M. R., & D'Zurilla, T. J. (1969). A behavior-analytic model for assessing competence. In C. D. Spielberger (Ed.), *Current topics in clinical and community psychology* (Vol. 1, pp. 151–198). New York: Academic Press.

Goldman, J. A., Corsini, D. A., & deUrioste, R. (1980). Implications of positive and negative sociometric status for assessing the social competence of young children. *Journal of Applied Developmental Psychology, 1,* 209–220.

Goslin, D. A. (1962). Accuracy of self-perception and social acceptance. *Sociometry, 25,* 283–296.

Gottman, J. M., Gonso, J., & Rasmussen, B. (1975). Social interaction, social competence, and friendship in children. *Child Development, 46,* 709–718.

Gove, W. R., & Herb, T. R. (1974). Stress and mental illness among the young: A comparison of the sexes. *Social Forces, 53,* 256–265.

Harter, S. (1982). The perceived competence scale for children. *Child Development, 53,* 87–97.

Harter, S., & Pike, R. (1984). The pictorial scale of perceived competence and social acceptance for young children. *Child Development, 55,* 1969–1982.

Hartup, W. W., Glazer, J. A., & Charlesworth, R. (1967). Peer reinforcement and sociometric status. *Child Development, 38,* 1017–1024.

Higgins, E. T., Ruble, D. N., & Hartup, W. W. (1983). *Social cognition and social development: A sociocultural perspective.* New York: Cambridge University Press.

Hymel, S. (1983). Preschool children's peer relations: Issues in sociometric assessment. *Merrill-Palmer Quarterly, 29,* 237–260.

Hymel, S., Freigang, R., Franke, S., Both, L., Bream, L., & Borys, S. (1983, June). *Children's attributions for social situations: Variations as a function of social status and self-perception variables.* Paper presented at the annual meeting of the Canadian Psychological Association, Toronto.

Izard, C. E. (1971). *The face of emotion.* New York: Appleton-Century-Crofts.

Jennings, K. D. (1975). People versus object orientation, social behavior, and intellectual abilities in preschool children. *Developmental Psychology, 11,* 511–519.

John, R. S., Mednick, S. A., & Schulsinger, F. (1982). Teachers' reports as predictors of schizophrenia and borderline schizophrenia: A Bayesian decision analysis. *Journal of Abnormal Psychology, 91,* 399–413.

Kohlberg, L., LaCrosse, J., & Ricks, D. (1972). The predictability of adults' mental health from childhood behavior. In B. B. Wolman (Ed.), *Manual of child psychopathology* (pp. 1217–1284). New York: McGraw-Hill.

Krasnor, L., & Rubin, K. H. (1978, June). *Preschoolers' verbal and behavioral solutions to social problems.* Paper presented at the annual meeting of the Canadian Psychological Association, Ottawa.

Krasnor, L. R., & Rubin, K. H. (1981). The assessment of social problem-solving skills in young children. In T. Merluzzi, C. Glass, & M. Genest (Eds.), *Cognitive assessment* (pp. 452–476). New York: Guilford.

Kupersmidt, J. B. (1983, April). Predicting delinquency and academic problems from childhood peer status. In J. D. Coie (Chair), *Strategies for identifying children at social risk: Longitudinal correlates and consequences.* Symposium conducted at the biennial meeting of the Society for Research in Child Development, Detroit.

Ladd, G. W. (1981). Effectiveness of a social learning method for enhancing children's social interaction and peer acceptance. *Child Development, 52,* 171–178.

Ladd, G. W. (1983). Social networks of popular, average, and rejected children in school settings. *Merrill-Palmer Quarterly, 29,* 283–307.

Ladd, G. W., & Oden, S. L. (1979). The relationship between peer acceptance and children's ideas about helpfulness. *Child Development, 50,* 402–408.

La Greca, A. M. (1981). Peer acceptance: The correspondence between children's sociometric scores and teachers' ratings of peer interaction. *Journal of Abnormal Child Psychology, 9,* 167–178.

Marcus, R. F. (1980). Empathy and popularity of preschool children. *Child Study Journal, 10,* 133–145.

Masten, A. S., Morison, P., & Pellegrini, D. (1985). A Revised Class Play method of peer assessment. *Developmental Psychology, 21,* 523–533.

McFall, R. M. (1982). A review and reformulation of the concept of social skills. *Behavioral Assessment, 4,* 1–35.

McGuire, J. (1973). Aggression and sociometric status with preschool children. *Sociometry, 36,* 542–549.

Michael, C. M., Morris, D. P., & Soroker, E. (1957). Follow-up studies of shy, withdrawn children: Relative incidence of schizophrenia. *American Journal of Orthopsychiatry, 27,* 331–337.

Mischel, W. (1968). *Personality and assessment.* New York: Wiley.

Mouton, J. S., Bell, R. L., & Blake, R. R. (1956). Role playing skill and sociometric peer status. *Group Psychotherapy, 9,* 7–17.

Nasby, W., Hayden, B., & dePaulo, B. M. (1979). Attributional bias among aggressive boys to interpret unambiguous social stimuli as displays of hostility. *Journal of Abnormal Psychology, 89,* 459–468.

Parke, R. D., & Slaby, R. G. (1983). The development of aggression. In E. M. Hetherington (Ed.), *Handbook of child psychology: Vol. 4. Personality and socialization processes* (pp. 547–641, 4th ed.). New York: Wiley.

Parkhurst, J. R., & Asher, S. R. (1985). Goals and concerns: Implications for the study of children's social competence. In B. Lahey & A. E. Kazdin (Eds.), *Advances in clinical child psychology* (Vol. 8, pp. 199–228). New York: Plenum.

Pellegrini, D. (1985). Social cognition and competence in middle-childhood. *Child Development, 56,* 253–264.

Perry, D. G., Perry, L. C., & Rasmussen, P. R. (1986). Aggressive children believe that aggression is easy to perform and leads to rewards. *Child Development, 57,* 700–711.

Piaget, J. (1965). *The moral judgment of the child.* London: Kegan Paul.

Piers, E., & Harris, D. (1964). Age and other correlates of self-concept in children. *Journal of Educational Psychology, 55,* 91–95.

Putallaz, M. (1983). Predicting children's sociometric status from their behavior. *Child Development, 54,* 1417–1426.

Putallaz, M., & Gottman, J. M. (1981). Social skills and group acceptance. In S. R. Asher & J. M. Gottman (Eds.), *The development of children's friendships* (pp. 116–149). New York: Cambridge University Press.

Renshaw, P. D., & Asher, S. R. (1982). Social competence and peer status: The distinction between goals and strategies. In K. H. Rubin & H. S. Ross (Eds.), *Peer relationships and social skills in childhood* (pp. 375–395). New York: Springer-Verlag.

Richard, B. A. (1985, April). *The development of attributional biases in children's peer groups.* Paper presented at the biennial meeting of the Society for Research in Child Development, Toronto.

Richard, B. A., & Dodge, K. A. (1982). Social maladjustment and problem solving in school-aged children. *Journal of Consulting and Clinical Psychology, 50,* 226–233.

Robins, L. N. (1966). *Deviant children grown up.* Baltimore: Williams & Wilkins.

Roff, M. (1961). Childhood social relations and young adult bad conduct. *Journal of Abnormal Social Psychology, 65,* 333–337.

Rubin, K. H. (1972). Relationship between egocentric communication and popularity among peers. *Developmental Psychology, 7,* 364.

Rubin, K. H., & Borwick, D. (1984). The communicative skills of children who vary with regard to sociability. In H. Sypher & J. Applegate (Eds.), *Social cognition and communication* (pp. 152–170). Hillsdale, NJ: Lawrence Erlbaum.

Rubin, K. H., & Daniels-Beirness, T. (1983). Concurrent and predictive correlates of sociometric status in kindergarten and grade one children. *Merrill-Palmer Quarterly, 29*, 337–352.

Rubin, K. H., Daniels-Beirness, T., & Hayvren, M. (1982). Social and social-cognitive correlates of sociometric status in preschool and kindergarten children. *Canadian Journal of Behavioural Science, 14*, 338–348.

Rubin, K. H., & Krasnor, L. R. (1986). Social-cognitive and social behavioral perspectives on problem solving. In M. Perlmutter (Ed.), *Minnesota symposia on child psychology* (Vol. 18, pp. 1–68). Hillsdale, NJ: Lawrence Erlbaum.

Rubin, K. H., & Maioni, T. L. (1975). Play preference and its relationship to egocentrism, popularity, and classification skills in preschoolers. *Merrill-Palmer Quarterly, 21*, 171–179.

Ruble, D. N. (1983). The development of comparison processes and their role in achievement-related self-socialization. In E. T. Higgins, W. W. Hartup, & D. N. Ruble (Eds.), *Social cognition and social development: A sociocultural perspective* (pp. 134–157). New York: Cambridge University Press.

Rutter, M., & Lockyear, L. (1967). A five to fifteen year follow-up study of infantile psychosis: I. Description of sample. *British Journal of Psychiatry, 113*, 1169–1182.

Rutter, M., & Yule, W. (1977). Reading difficulties. In M. Rutter & L. Hersov (Eds.), *Child psychiatry* (pp. 556–575). Oxford, England: Blackwell Scientific.

Selman, R. L. (1980). *The growth of interpersonal understanding: Developmental and clinical analyses.* New York: Academic Press.

Shantz, C. (1983). Social cognition. In J. H. Flavell & E. M. Markman (Eds.), *Handbook of child psychology: Vol. 3. Cognitive development* (pp. 495–555, 4th ed.). New York: Wiley.

Sharp, K. (1978, August). *Interpersonal problem-solving capacity and behavioral adjustment.* Paper presented at the annual meeting of the American Psychological Association, Toronto.

Shure, M. B., & Spivack, G. (1972). Means–ends thinking, adjustment, and social class among elementary school–aged children. *Journal of Consulting and Clinical Psychology, 38*, 348–353.

Shure, M. B., Spivack, G., & Jaeger, M. (1971). Problem-solving thinking and adjustment among disadvantaged preschool children. *Child Development, 42*, 1791–1803.

Sobol, M. P., & Earn, B. M. (1985a). Assessment of children's attributions for social experience: Implications for social skills training. In B. H. Schneider, K. H. Rubin, & J. E. Ledingham (Eds.), *Children's peer relations: Issues in assessment and intervention* (pp. 93–110). New York: Springer-Verlag.

Sobol, M. P., & Earn, B. M. (1985b). What causes mean: An analysis of children's interpretations of the causes of social experience. *Journal of Social and Personal Relationships, 2*, 137–149.

Spivack, G., Platt, J. J., & Shure, M. B. (1974). *Social adjustment of young children: A cognitive approach to solving real life problems.* Washington, DC: Jossey-Bass.

Spivack, G., & Shure, M. B. (1974). *The problem solving approach to adjustment.* Washington, DC: Jossey-Bass.

Steinberg, M. D., & Dodge, K. A. (1983). Attributional bias in aggressive adolescent boys and girls. *Journal of Social and Clinical Psychology, 1*, 312–321.

Taylor, A. R., & Asher, S. R. (1984, April). *Children's interpersonal goals in game situations.* Paper presented at the annual meeting of the American Educational Research Association, New Orleans.

Wheeler, V. A., & Ladd, G. W. (1982). Assessment of children's self-efficacy for social interactions with peers. *Developmental Psychology, 18*, 795–805.

Wolff, S. (1977). Nondelinquent disturbances of conduct. In M. Rutter & L. Hersov (Eds.), *Child psychiatry* (pp. 484–509). Oxford, England: Blackwell Scientific.

Zahn-Waxler, C., Radke-Yarrow, M., & Brady-Smith, J. (1977). Social perspective-taking and prosocial behavior. *Developmental Psychology, 13*, 87–88.

6   Reputational bias: View from the peer group

Shelley Hymel, Esther Wagner, and Lynda J. Butler

Underlying much of the research on children's peer rejection is the assumption that rejected children are the "architects of their own difficulties" (Ladd, 1985, p. 243). For example, under the social skill deficit hypothesis (Asher & Renshaw, 1981; Asher, Renshaw, & Hymel, 1982; Curran, 1979; Ladd & Mize, 1983), differences in the interpersonal skills of popular and unpopular children* are conceptualized as deficiencies on the part of less popular children that are presumed to account for their poor social status. Consistent with this model are results of numerous studies that demonstrate behavioral and social-cognitive differences between popular and unpopular children (see Chapters 2 and 5, this volume, and Hymel & Rubin, 1985, for reviews). Identified differences in social competence have, in turn, provided a focus for subsequent social skills interventions aimed at improving the peer acceptance of unpopular children. In effect, such an individual deficit model assumes that deficiencies in social functioning are the primary cause of unpopular children's social difficulties and that modification of these shortcomings will result in greater peer acceptance.

Intervention studies based on the social skill deficit model, however, have yielded mixed results. For example, some studies employing a coaching intervention procedure have demonstrated concomitant behavioral and sociometric improvement as a result of training (e.g., Ladd, 1981). However, others have demonstrated increased peer acceptance in the absence of observed behavioral change (e.g., Gottman, Gonso, & Schuler, 1976; Hymel & Asher, 1977; Oden & Asher, 1977) and some studies have demonstrated behavioral improvements but no change in peer acceptance (e.g., La Greca & Santogrossi, 1980; Whitehall, Hersen, & Bellack, 1980). Although results of these studies provide some support for the social skill deficit hypothesis, the modest success of these interventions suggests that improved social skills are no guarantee of sustained increases in peer acceptance. Peers appear to be resistant to altering their stance toward rejected children even when the behavior of the rejected children improves.

---

*Throughout this chapter, we use the terms *popular* and *unpopular* to refer to children who are accepted or high in social status among their peers versus poorly accepted, rejected, or neglected by peers. The use of these terms is merely an attempt to simplify descriptions of subsamples of children identified across studies on the basis of various sociometric procedures.

In the present chapter, we argue that the predominance of the social skill deficit model has resulted in a rather limited view of the phenomenon of peer rejection. The individual deficit model assumes that inadequate social skills are the primary reason for peer rejection when, in fact, there may be multiple factors that cause and maintain status, including nonbehavioral characteristics (e.g., names, physical appearance) and group processes (e.g., ethnic bias, stereotyping). Moreover, the individual deficit model has led researchers to emphasize behavior change on the part of the target child as the primary vehicle for improving peer relations when, in fact, there may be multiple avenues for intervention, including modification of peer group responsivity.

As a counterbalance to the prevailing emphasis on individual deficits, the present chapter considers peer rejection from a different perspective, one that emphasizes the contribution of the peer group to a child's social difficulties. This perspective considers the impact of the social structure of children's peer groups and the operation of biases related to prior reputation or social status. In particular, we focus on the peer group as a social system with an ingroup and an outgroup in which the social status quo is maintained by biased peer responses to popular (liked) versus unpopular (disliked) children. We contend that a child's social status or reputation, once established, strongly influences how peers respond to that child, because children, like adults, are inclined to maintain reputation-congruent perceptions of others. Popular children acquire a "positive halo" and unpopular children acquire a "negative halo," which color how their behavior is perceived, evaluated, and responded to by others. Biased perceptions serve to maintain positive and negative reputations of popular and unpopular children, ensuring that status distinctions are preserved.

The proposition that peer group structure influences the status of individual children is not new. Moreno (1934) argued that peer social status was a condition imposed on the child as a result of group structure (see Ladd, 1985). Nevertheless, the operation of peer group processes in the maintenance of peer rejection in children has largely been ignored. In resurrecting this perspective, we begin by examining theoretical formulations and recent empirical research on intergroup behavior, impression formation, person perception, memory for social information, and attributional processes that are consistent with a group process perspective on peer rejection. Although a comprehensive review of these literatures is beyond the scope of this chapter, we highlight theory and evidence that have direct implications for social perception processes within children's peer groups. Much of this research has been conducted with adults. However, there is evidence (to be reviewed below) to suggest that the elementary school peer group may be a prime arena in which social perception biases operate. We will then present several recent studies of preadolescent children that have directly examined biases in peers' perceptions of a child's social behavior as a function of affect (liking) toward or status of the other child or both. Finally, our discussion will focus on implications of this work for research on childhood peer rejection.

Evidence for reputational bias

There is a growing body of evidence that social behavior is perceived in a biased fashion as a function of prior attitudes and beliefs about the actor. These biases may operate at the dyadic level as a function of prior affect toward the actor or at the group level as a function of stereotypic beliefs about the actor based on his or her group membership. Research on biases in social perception is based on constructivist or information-processing theories of interpersonal attraction (e.g., Ajzen, 1977), which posit that individuals actively process information about others and do so in such a way as to maintain consistency between prior beliefs and present behavior. These notions were first described by Heider (1958) in his theory of balance. Heider suggested that individuals attempt to maintain evaluative consistency between prior attitudes and behavior and attempt to avoid evaluative inconsistency. Evaluative inconsistency can occur at the dyadic level, when a disliked actor performs a positive action (or a liked actor performs a negative action), or at the intergroup level, when an actor from a negatively perceived group performs a positive behavior (or an actor from a positively perceived group performs a negative behavior).

When a perceiver is faced with an evaluatively inconsistent situation, there are several means by which the discrepancy can be resolved. Heider (1958) noted three major alternatives: (a) modification of existing attitudes toward the individual to make them more consistent with observed behavior; (b) creation of a more integrated, bivalent conception of the other, including both positive and negative qualities; or (c) reinterpretation of the underlying causes of behavior. The first alternative, that of modifying existing attitudes, is one that is expected by interventionists who attempt to improve the social behavior and social acceptance of rejected or unpopular children. However, as we will see, both adults and children can employ a variety of cognitive strategies that effectively eliminate evaluative inconsistency but leave prior attitudes and beliefs intact.

Social perception biases have been found to be characteristic of intergroup relations. Almost three decades ago, Sherif and his colleagues (e.g., Sherif, Harvey, White, Hood, & Sherif, 1961) conducted pioneering work on the nature of group interactions that suggested that intergroup relations were determined by functional (goal) relationships. Competition between groups leads to intergroup hostility and intragroup cohesion. In contrast, intergroup cooperation in the service of mutual or superordinate goals leads to more favorable attitudes and interactions between groups. More recently, however, studies by Tajfel and his colleagues (Billig & Tajfel, 1973; Tajfel & Billig, 1974; Tajfel, Billig, Bundy, &

Flamant, 1971; Tajfel & Turner, 1979) have demonstrated that social categorization alone (categorizing the social world into "us" and "them") is sufficient to produce ingroup favoritism and outgroup discrimination in reward allocation among adults. What is fascinating about these studies is that the groups considered were formed randomly or on the basis of arbitrary criteria. The paradigm has come to be referred to as the minimal intergroup situation (see Brewer, 1979, for a review). Other researchers using the minimal intergroup situation have demonstrated that an individual tends to assign more positive traits to ingroup members (Doise, Csepeli, Dann, Gouge, Larsen, & Ostell, 1976; Rabbie & Horowitz, 1969) and assume that ingroup members' beliefs are more similar to his or her own than are outgroup members' beliefs (Allen & Wilder, 1979).

Tajfel and Turner (1979) have suggested that intergroup biases operate in the service of achieving or maintaining positive social identity, an important aspect of a positive self-image. A positive social identity derives from identification with a group that is positively differentiated through favorable social comparisons with some relevant outgroup. Tajfel and his colleagues also suggest that when there are differences in status between groups, the higher status group may behave differently from the lower status group in order to enhance social identity. High-status group members will work to maintain their group's positive distinctiveness from the low-status outgroup. In contrast, low-status group members, to achieve positive identity, may attempt to join the higher status group (if upward mobility is possible), may attempt to emulate high-status group members, may reinterpret their own "negative" characteristics more positively, or may simply stop comparing themselves with the high-status group.

Once an ingroup and an outgroup are distinguished, intergroup differentiation is enhanced by positive and negative stereotypic beliefs about people as a function of group membership. Stereotypic beliefs about groups are highly resistant to change because they are maintained by biased perceptions (Cooper & Fazio, 1979; Nisbett & Ross, 1980). Biased perceptions may be reflected in (a) biased evaluation of behavior, (b) selective recall of information that is congruent with expectations, and (c) biased attributional interpretations. In the following sections we will review relevant empirical evidence in each of these areas that demonstrates that biases in social perception processes operate at both dyadic and group levels among both adults and children.

Biased evaluations of behavior. Biases in the evaluation and interpretation of the behavior of others may stem from a number of different factors. Studies of impression formation have generally confirmed the power of first impressions in influencing evaluations of subsequently presented information (see Nisbett & Ross, 1980). As early as 1946, Asch demonstrated that overall evaluations of a stimulus person were more favorable when positive descriptors were presented earlier than negative descriptors. Positive and negative global evaluations (halo effects) also result in more favorable and unfavorable evaluations of other specific behaviors, respectively (e.g., Nisbett & Wilson, 1977). Evaluative bias also operates as a function of group membership, including stereotypic evaluations made on the basis of gender (see Ashmore, 1981; S. E. Taylor, 1981) and race (see Crosby, Bromley, & Saxe, 1980; Milner, 1981). For example, in an intergroup context, Duncan (1976) found that white subjects were more likely to perceive an ambiguous shove as "aggressive" when the actor was black and as "horsing around" when the actor was white. Thus, initial impressions and prior expectations, including stereotypic beliefs, influence how social behavior is interpreted and evaluated.

A number of studies have demonstrated that children also evaluate others in a biased fashion as a function of group delimiters, including race (Rosenfield & Stephan, 1981), sex (Martin & Halverson, 1981), and social class (Hartup, 1983) as well as salient physical characteristics such as physical disabilities (Richardson, Goodman, Hastorf, & Dornbusch, 1961) and attractiveness (Kleck, Richardson, & Ronald, 1974; Langlois & Stephan, 1981). It is noteworthy that some group delimiters that provoke stereotyping (e.g., race, sex, attractiveness) are also correlates of peer popularity (see Hartup, 1983). Thus, biases in children's perceptions of the behavior of popular and unpopular peers may be mediated, in part, by biases provoked by these salient, nonbehavioral personal characteristics.

Memory bias. There is a growing body of evidence indicating that memory for social attributes and behavior is affected by expectations about the stimulus person. Most of these studies are based on the notion that people use conceptual schemas to organize, structure, and store information (Bartlett, 1932). Conceptual schemas have variously been thought to have an impact on memory at the encoding stage by providing a framework into which schema-relevant information is more readily assimilated (Cantor & Mischel, 1977), at the retrieval stage by serving as cues for reconstructing previously presented information (Snyder & Uranowitz, 1978), or by eliciting schema-congruent guessing in the absence of memory (Bellazza & Bower, 1981).

Several studies have indicated that schema-congruent information is more likely to be remembered or falsely recognized (e.g., Cantor & Mischel, 1977; Rothbart, Evans, & Fulero, 1979; Snyder & Uranowitz, 1978). In contrast, other studies have demonstrated that behaviors that were incongruent with previous expectations are better recalled (e.g., Hastie & Kumar, 1979). It appears that although schema-congruent information is generally better remembered, incongruent information, if it is highly distinctive by virtue of its unexpectedness, may at times be better recalled (see Butler, 1984, for an extended discussion).

The few studies that have examined schema-based memory bias in children have been concerned primarily with sex-role and occupational-role expectancies (see Martin & Halverson, 1981, for a review). For example, Koblinsky, Cruse, and Sugawara (1978) found that fifth-grade children remembered behavior congruent with sex stereotypes better than incongruent behavior. Mapley (1978) found that first- through sixth-graders recalled with greater accuracy actions that were congruent with the actors' occupational roles. More recently, Gershman and Hayes (1985) examined preschool children's ability to recall incongruent versus congruent characteristics used to describe hypothetical peers. In both immediate and long-term (5-month) recall, preschoolers' memory for congruent attributes was superior to that for incongruent attributes. Overall, then, the evidence suggests that adults and children tend to exhibit better memory for schema-congruent information. Again, such tendencies would contribute to reputation maintenance in that reputation-congruent characteristics and behaviors would be remembered more often than those that were incongruent.

Attributional biases in social perception. The extensive literature on attributional processes (see Shaver, 1975, and Ross & Fletcher, 1985, for reviews) is concerned with how individuals explain the causes of events and has its theoretical roots in the writings of Heider (1958), Jones (e.g., Jones & Davis, 1965; Jones & McGillis, 1976), and Kelley (e.g., 1967, 1972). Briefly, attribution theorists argue that individuals' causal interpretations of events aid them in understanding behavior and interacting effectively with others. Further, attribution theorists assume that individuals' causal attributions are more or less logically determined on the basis of available information and that such attributions can be reliably classified along particular dimensions, including internality (i.e., locus of control; Heider, 1958; Rotter, 1966), stability (e.g., Weiner, 1974), intentionality (e.g., Elig & Frieze, 1975a, 1975b; Heider, 1958), and responsibility (Butler, 1984; Shaver, 1975).

In his balance theory, Heider postulated that the selective use of various attributional inferences helps to maintain consistency between events and prior beliefs, attitudes, or expectations. Consistent behavior is typically viewed as internally caused, whereas inconsistent behavior may be interpreted as accidentally, rather than intentionally, caused (Heider, 1958) or may be attributed to external factors instead of to the motives or dispositions of the actor (O'Keefe, 1980).

Studies with adults provide ample empirical support for the notion that attributional bias functions to maintain consistency between prior attitudes and behavior (see Regan, 1978). For example, Regan, Straus, and Fazio (1974) found that success and prosocial behavior were viewed as internally caused for liked actors and as externally caused for disliked actors.

Attributional biases also maintain stereotypic intergroup perceptions. Pettigrew (1979) describes how attributional mechanisms may be used to explain away positive behaviors performed by members of a disfavored outgroup. In such situations, instead of modifying attitudes toward the outgroup member in a more positive direction, the perceiver posits causal explanations that maintain both attitude–behavior congruency *and* the prevailing negative stereotype. The perceiver might view the actor as an exceptional case or attribute his or her success to luck, special advantages, other external (situational) factors, or inordinate motivation or effort.

Pettigrew's hypotheses are supported in several studies with adult subjects. For example, in the Duncan (1976) study cited earlier, white subjects more often attributed an ambiguous shove by a black actor (perceived as "aggressive") to dispositional causes. The same behavior by a white actor (perceived as "horsing around") was attributed to situational factors. D. M. Taylor and Jaggi (1974), in a study of cultural intergroup bias, compared Hindu subjects' causal attributions for positive and negative behaviors committed by ingroup (Hindu) and outgroup (Muslim) members. For ingroup actors, positive behavior was more likely to be attributed to dispositional causes and negative behavior to situational causes. For outgroup actors, the reverse attributional pattern was more likely.

These studies clearly demonstrate that among adults attributional bias operates in the service of maintaining congruency between behavior and prior affect and stereotypic beliefs determined by group membership. Although there is ample evidence that children utilize many of the same principles of causal attributions as adults (for reviews see Kassin, 1981; Sedlack & Kurtz, 1981), there are few studies that specifically examine attributional biases in children. However, those studies that do exist clearly support the contention that children, like adults, will reinterpret the causes of behavior as a function of prior beliefs or attitudes toward the actor. For example, Stephan (1977) demonstrated attributional biases for fifth- and sixth-grade children as a function of ethnic group membership. In this study, Anglo, Chicano, and black children provided attributions for positive and negative behavior performed by members of their own and the other two ethnic groups. Results indicated a general tendency to attribute positive behavior to internal causes and negative behavior to external causes. However, Chicano and, to a lesser extent, Anglo children clearly biased their attributional interpretations in favor of their own ethnic group, whereas black children did not.

Summary. The preceding review demonstrates that both adults and elementary-school-age children process social information about others in a biased fashion in accordance with their prior attitudes and stereotypic beliefs based on group membership. Such biases are reflected in several social perception processes, including differential evaluations of behavior, selective recall of information, and biased causal attributions.

In concluding this section, we would like to underscore several points. First, social perception is not a passive process. Rather, it involves active organization and interpretation of information that is often inherently ambiguous. Accordingly, it is vulnerable to bias as a function of preconceptions about and attitudes toward other individuals and groups. In short, perceivers, to some degree, construct their own social reality. Second, identification with a group, however defined, typically promotes favoritism toward ingroup members and discrimination against outgroup members. As Tajfel and Turner (1979) suggest, such intergroup bias may emanate from an individual's need to maintain a positive social identity. Regardless of the underlying cause, however, the operation of biases in social perception is clear.

Implications for the elementary school peer group

There are several factors making the middle elementary school peer group a prime arena in which biases in social perception can be expected to operate. First, the elementary school years are an important time for establishing a social identity outside the family (Hartup, 1983; Sullivan, 1953). Because positive social identity is in part linked to identification with a positively differentiated social group (Tajfel & Turner, 1979), one would expect that elementary school children would be motivated to perceive ingroup members positively and outgroup members negatively. This may be particularly true in the case of higher status, popular children.

A second but related factor is the social structure of elementary classroom peer groups, which have been shown to consist of various social subgroups, distinguished in terms of social status (e.g., Benson & Gottman, as cited in Putallaz & Gottman, 1981b; Glidewell, Kantor, Smith, & Stringer, 1966; Ladd, 1983; Wagner, 1986). For example, in an observational study of the social networks of elementary school children, Ladd (1983) found that popular and average-status children were involved in larger and more cliquish social networks of mutual friends, whereas unpopular children interacted in smaller groups with other unpopular peers or younger children.

Wagner (1986) evaluated the social structure in sixth-grade classrooms using self-report measures of friendship in which children rated the degree of friendship they had with each classmate. Mutually high friendship ratings for any given pair of children were considered indicative of a friendship bond. Results indicated, not surprisingly, that popular children had more friends, overall, than did unpopular children. Average-status females were comparable to popular females, and average-status males were comparable to unpopular males in terms of overall number of friends. Moreover, popular children appeared to form a rather cohesive subgroup, characterized by significantly more friendships *within* their own status subgroup (versus across status lines) than was the case for average-status or unpopular children.

The results of studies by Ladd and Wagner suggest that the classroom peer group consists of a relatively cohesive subgroup of popular children and a less cohesive subgroup of unpopular children. Unpopular children may be characterized as a collection of "outliers" or as a group of ostracized, disliked, relatively unaffiliated children who are perceived as having negative attributes. Evidence that popularity is associated with social dominance (e.g., Lippitt & Gold, 1959) suggests that popular children enjoy a superior position within this social structure. Moreover, there is evidence that by the middle to late elementary school years, children are aware of their own and others' social position within the peer group (e.g., Ausubel, Schiff, & Gasser, 1952; Glidewell et al., 1966; Wagner, 1986). Thus, children's awareness of status differences within a group and the typical elementary school social structure, consisting of subgroups of children differing in social status, can be expected to contribute to intergroup bias.

A third factor contributing to the operation of social perception biases is the cognitive limitations of children in this age range that affect person perception. Within the developmental person-perception literature, researchers have consistently demonstrated that with age, children are increasingly able to conceptualize others in terms of more abstract dispositional or traitlike characterizations. This developmental trend is evident both in children's spontaneous descriptions of others (e.g., Barenboim, 1981; Livesley & Bromley, 1973; Peevers & Secord, 1973; Scarlett, Press, & Crockett, 1971) and in their abilities to predict behavioral consistency in others on the basis of previous information (e.g., Rholes & Ruble, 1984, 1986; Rotenberg, 1982). Indeed, research by Livesley and Bromley (1973), Rotenberg (1982), and Rholes and Ruble (1984, 1986) indicates that social-cognitive changes emerging somewhere around the second-grade level permit children to evaluate the behavior of others in terms of stable patterns of behavior and stable personality characteristics. These data suggest that reputational effects and biases may be especially likely to emerge during the elementary school period.

At the same time, children's ability to both differentiate and integrate inconsistent or bivalent (positive and negative) information about others does not appear to be fully developed. For example, studies examining children's spontaneous descriptions of others indicate that younger children perceive others in a global, undifferentiated fashion and do not appear to consider different or uncorrelated attributes in others (e.g., Barenboim, 1981; Livesley & Bromley, 1973; Peevers & Secord, 1973). More recent studies have relied less on verbally demanding methodologies to assess children's ability to differentiate attributes in others. Results of these studies also demonstrate that young children evidence little differentiation in their characterizations of peers and that even partial differentiation begins to appear only at the fourth-grade and, especially, the sixth-grade levels (Lockman & Trejos, 1985; Moely & Johnson, 1985). Moreover, the developmental person-perception literature has indicated that children's descriptions and impressions of others tend to be highly univalent and evaluatively consistent (Livesley & Bromley, 1973; Peevers & Secord, 1973). With age, children appear to become increasingly able to recognize and integrate inconsistent or bivalent information about others (Biskin & Crano, 1977; Gollin, 1958; Rosenbach, Crockett, & Wapner, 1973), although throughout middle childhood, children's descriptions of others remain primarily univalent and evaluatively consistent (Peevers & Secord, 1973). The combination of perceiving others in terms of stable traits and the limited ability to integrate bivalent information about others would appear to make preadolescent children maximally susceptible to the influence of prior reputation or affect on their perceptions of peers.

A fourth factor, which is not exclusive to this age range but which also contributes to social perception biases, is prior expectations about peer behaviors. Newcomb and Rogosch (1982) demonstrated that among elementary-school-age children, social reputations provided a basis for forming expectations of how peers would behave in hypothetical social situations. In particular, they found that children expected more negative behavior from rejected peers than from other peers. Such expectations are probably based, in part, on children's prior social interactions (which would be more negative in the case of unpopular peers and more positive in the case of popular peers) and, in part, on over-generalizations from these interactions.

Evidence for reputational bias in children's peer groups

Perhaps because of the prevailing emphasis on social skill deficits as the primary cause of peer rejection, there has been little direct investigation of reputational bias in children's peer groups. Nevertheless, there is some evidence, buried within the literature on the behavioral correlates of peer status, that is consistent with a peer group process perspective on peer rejection. A brief review of this evidence follows.

First, there is some evidence to suggest that within established peer groups, children respond differently to popular and unpopular peers. Popular children have been shown to receive more visual attention and social initiations from peers than do unpopular children (Rubin, Daniels-Beirness, & Hayvren, 1982; Vaughn & Waters, 1980, 1981). Similarly, research by Putallaz and Gottman (1981a) and by Dodge, Schlundt, Schocken, and Delugach (1983) has suggested that peers respond more favorably to popular than unpopular children's entry overtures, even when they employ similar entry strategies. Other studies have indicated that children are more positive and more socially responsive in interactions with friends than with nonfriends (Foot, Chapman, & Smith, 1979; Masters

& Furman, 1981; Newcomb & Brady, 1982; Newcomb, Brady, & Hartup, 1979). Because unpopular children are less likely than popular children to be friends with their peers (Ladd, 1983; Wagner, 1986), they may be less likely to be the recipients of positive interactions.

More generally, research has also indicated that popular children *receive* (as well as dispense) more positive reinforcement, whereas unpopular children *receive* (as well as dispense) more negative reinforcement in their interactions with peers (Gottman, Gonso, & Rasmussen, 1975; Hartup, Glazer, & Charlesworth, 1967). These data are usually interpreted as reflecting reciprocity in the behaviors directed toward and received from peers. However, given that these findings are based on correlational data, it is not clear how such positive and negative cycles are initiated. Although positive and negative behavior may *cause* differential peer responses, it is equally plausible that such behaviors are *provoked* by differential peer behavior directed toward popular versus unpopular children. A recent study by Asarnow (1983) addressed this issue of reciprocity directly using sequential analyses to evaluate observed interactions involving boys with positive or negative peer reputations. Among other things, Asarnow found that peers responded reciprocally to positive and neutral behavior initiated by boys with either positive or negative reputations. Responses to negative initiations, however, varied with reputation. Negative behavior initiated by boys with negative reputations was most likely to be reciprocated with negative behavior. In contrast, negative behavior initiated by boys with positive reputations was more likely to be followed by neutral responses from peers. These data suggest that peers respond in a biased fashion to negative behavior as a function of the positive or negative reputation of the initiator.

Studies of newly formed peer groups have also yielded indirect evidence of biased peer responses to children who became popular or unpopular. In a study of emerging status among children in a summer camp setting, Campbell and Yarrow (1961; Yarrow & Campbell, 1963) found that peer status was established very quickly within the group and that peers perceived popular children as more friendly and less aggressive than unpopular children even when their respective actual rates of friendly and aggressive behavior (as observed by adults) were controlled for. In two recent studies of emerging peer status (Coie & Kupersmidt, 1983; Dodge, 1983), acquired popularity status was clearly related to behavioral differences. However, peers were also found to respond differently to popular and rejected children. For example, Coie and Kupersmidt (1983) noted that in groups of familiar peers, rejected and average-status boys were the recipients of aversive behavior more often than were popular boys. This was not true of groups of unfamiliar boys. Dodge (1983) noted that although the quality of peer responses was generally related to the quality of the target's behavior, peer responses, overall, were more positive and less negative toward boys who became popular than toward boys who became rejected, *even when they engaged in similar behaviors.* Dodge also noted that social approaches by unpopular boys were rebuffed more frequently by peers than were approaches made by average-status boys.

In the remainder of this chapter, we review a number of studies in which the primary focus was the investigation of potential biases in social perceptions in children's peer groups. Specifically, the purpose of these studies was to examine whether children's perceptions and interpretations of and responses to the *same* peer behavior differed significantly as a function of reputation, prior attitudes (liking) toward the actor, or the actor's status group membership (popularity). Evidence that social perceptions vary even though behavior remains constant would reflect the operation of reputation effects in children's interpersonal relations and would begin to shed light on how the social status quo is maintained in children's peer groups and why peers are resistant to altering their stance toward rejected children even when their behavior improves.

Bias as a function of aggressive reputation

Research by Dodge and his colleagues (Dodge, 1980; Dodge & Frame, 1982) has examined attributional biases as a function of children's specific reputations for aggressiveness versus nonaggressiveness. Second-, fourth-, and sixth-grade children's explanations for negative behaviors supposedly performed by peers with either aggressive or nonaggressive reputations were evaluated for attributions of hostile intent on the part of the peer actor. Results indicated that peers with aggressive reputations were more often perceived as behaving with hostile intent than were peers with nonaggressive reputations. Moreover, although such attributional bias was evident at all grade levels, Dodge (1980) noted that these biases were stronger among the older children, suggesting increasing reputation effects with age. The relevance of these studies to our understanding of how peer rejection is maintained derives from the fact that children with aggressive reputations are often rejected by their peers. Results of research by Dodge and his colleagues indicate that a child's prior reputation colors peers' perceptions of his or her behavior.

Bias as a function of affective attitude

Two recent studies (Hymel, 1986; DeLawyer & Foster, 1986) examined the operation of affective bias in children's perceptions of peer behavior at the level of dyadic interpersonal relations. In other words, these studies considered how children varied their interpretations of peer behavior in response to whether a *particular* actor was liked or disliked by the perceiver. These studies, then, follow directly from adult research (e.g., Regan et al., 1974), which has demonstrated that perceptions of behavior differ considerably as a function of affective bias toward individuals. The relevance of these studies to understanding the maintenance of peer rejection stems from the fact that unpopular children are by definition disliked individuals.

Hymel (1986) examined attributional biases in children's interpretations of peer behavior as a function of prior affect (liking vs. disliking) toward peers. Popular and unpopular children (second-, fifth-, and tenth-grade) were asked to explain why liked or disliked classmates performed actions that had either a positive or a negative outcome for the perceiver (e.g., being invited or not invited to a party). Each subject was presented with four different hypothetical situations in which a liked or disliked classmate behaved either positively or negatively. The protagonists in these hypothetical situations were *known* peers, selected on the basis of previous sociometric data as either extremely liked or extremely disliked by the subject. For each situation, subjects were asked to explain why the behavior occurred. These explanations were later coded in terms of attributional dimensions of internality (whether the behavior was attributed to the actor or to factors external to the actor), stability (whether the behavior was attributed to stable, unchangeable causes or to temporary, changeable causes), and responsibility (the degree to which the actor was credited vs. denied credit for positive behavior or blamed vs. excused for negative behavior).

The results of this study indicated that regardless of age, sex, or social status, subjects varied their interpretations of peer behavior as a function of both their affect toward the actor (liked vs. disliked) and the valence of the behavior described (positive vs. negative). Positive behavior was attributed to more stable causes when performed by liked peers than by disliked peers. In contrast, negative behavior was attributed to more stable causes when performed by disliked peers than by liked peers. Consistent with attribution theory, then, negative behavior on the part of disliked peers and positive behavior on the part of liked peers would be expected to recur, given the perceived greater stability of the underlying causes. Interpretive bias was particularly evident when children's perceptions of responsibility were considered. Children were more willing to credit liked peers for positive behavior and to minimize liked peers' responsibility for negative behaviors. In contrast, disliked peers were viewed as equally responsible for positive and negative behavior. Moreover, when peer actors were described as having performed the same negative behaviors, children were significantly more likely to deny or minimize actor responsibility when the actor was a liked peer than when the actor was a disliked peer. In interpreting these results, Hymel suggested that liked peers appear to be given the "benefit of the doubt" in peer interpretations of their behavior. Even in rather ambiguous, hypothetical social situations, positive behaviors by liked peers were viewed as caused by more stable factors, and liked peers' responsibility or accountability for negative behaviors was more often denied or minimized through the selective use of various causal explanations. In contrast, disliked peers were perceived as having greater responsibility (blame) for negative behaviors. This perceived blame, in turn, may influence subsequent peer behavior and the likelihood of retaliation, creating a cycle serving to maintain negative interactions between disliked children and their classmates. It should be noted that this pattern of results was obtained across grade levels, suggesting that such interpretive biases were evident as early as the second grade and persisted into early adolescence.

Although the results of Hymel's (1986) research demonstrate social perception biases in children's interpretations of peer behavior, they do not indicate how such bias might influence subsequent attitudes or behavior. A recent study of affective bias among fifth-grade children conducted by DeLawyer and Foster (1986) does address this issue. In this study, liked, disliked, neutral, and unfamiliar peers were named as actors in a series of hypothetical vignettes describing either positive or negative interactions between the subject and the peer actor. For each vignette, subjects were asked to describe what they would "say or do" subsequently (behavioral reaction) and to rate how they would feel when the situation occurred and how much they would like the named peer at that time. Behavioral reactions were later rated in terms of three dimensions, derived from Asher and Renshaw (1981): active versus passive responses, relationship enhancement, and effectiveness. Results indicated that negative behaviors performed by disliked peers provoked responses that were judged to be more active (taking initiative, confident, or dominant) than those elicited when the same behaviors were performed by liked, neutral, or unfamiliar peers. Behavioral reactions did not differ as a function of prior affect in the case of positive behaviors. In terms of subjects' affective ratings, girls reported feeling worse about interactions involving disliked peers than about interactions involving other peers, and at the time of the incident, both boys and girls reported less liking for disliked peers than for other peers, regardless of behavior exhibited. Thus, even when disliked peers supposedly performed positive behaviors, they evoked more negative emotional responses from their peers than did more liked actors.

Taken together, results of research by both Hymel and by DeLawyer and Foster indicate that interpretations and reactions to peer behavior vary as a function of prior attitudes or affect. Disliked peers appear to be held more accountable for negative behaviors than are liked peers (Hymel, 1986) and, perhaps as a result, are likely to evoke more active behavioral responses and more negative emotional responses from peers than would liked peers performing the same behaviors (DeLawyer & Foster, 1986). Such biases appear to facilitate the maintenance of positive relationships with liked peers and to inhibit the modification of negative attitudes toward disliked peers.

Bias as a function of status group membership

In light of evidence presented in the preceding section, it seems clear that children are likely to vary their interpretations and responses to peer behavior as a function of attitudes, or affect, toward particular individuals. The next four studies to be reviewed investigated whether social perception biases also operate at the group level, as a function of whether the target child is considered to be popular or unpopular among his or her peers.

A study by Singleton (1981) was designed to examine potential biases in boys' ability to recognize behavior change (from uncooperative to cooperative) in unfamiliar peers who were either initially described as popular or unpopular or for whom no reputational information was provided. Singleton found that the reputation of the target did not significantly influence subjects' perceptions of the targets' behavior or recognition of behavior change on the part of the target. Instead, children's perceptions were found to be generally veridical, and liking for the target corresponded to the quality of behavior. These results could be interpreted as indicating that peer reputation has little effect on how behavior is perceived and that improved behavior leads to increased liking. However, such an interpretation must be judged cautiously in light of the methodology employed in this study. The shift from uncooperative to cooperative behavior was blatantly depicted, and subjects were asked directly whether a change had occurred. Furthermore, the targets were unfamiliar peers, and it is not clear whether children would be as responsive to more subtle changes in behavior on the part of familiar peers with whom they have had long-standing histories of interaction under real-life conditions.

In two studies of preadolescent children, Butler (1984) demonstrated that social information about a hypothetical same-sex peer was processed differently as a function of subjects' prior expectations about the peers' popularity or social status. In the first study, popular, average-status, and unpopular sixth-graders were interviewed about their impressions of a hypothetical peer actor in one of three conditions. For two of the three conditions, initial descriptions of the peer actor effectively induced subjects to believe that the child was either popular or unpopular among his or her classmates. In a third, control condition, no prior expectations about the actor's peer status were induced. Subjects in all three conditions were presented with the same series of descriptions of the actor, which included an equal number of positive, neutral, and negative behaviors supposedly performed by the actor in interactions with classmates over the course of a week at school. Subsequently, in an unexpected recall task, subjects were asked to remember as much information as they could about the actor and were then asked about their own impressions of the actor.

Results indicated that subjects recalled significantly more positive behaviors performed by the popular actor than by the unpopular or control actors, despite the fact that the same information had been provided about each of the three actors. No significant differences were found in terms of the overall amount of negative behaviors recalled for the three actors. However, considering the relative recall of positive versus negative behaviors for the three actors, there was a marginally significant interaction between target popularity and the ratio of positive/negative behaviors recalled. Subjects remembered *proportionately* more negative than positive behaviors in the case of the unpopular and control actors, but not in the case of the popular actor. Consistent with evidence reviewed previously on biases in memory, then, subjects displayed memory bias consistent with prior reputational expectations.

Social perception biases were even more evident in the case of subjects' subsequent impressions of the actors. For example, subjects evaluated the popular actor more positively and the unpopular actor more negatively than they did the control actor on a number of status and social competence dimensions. Moreover, subjects expected more positive than negative future behaviors from the popular actor but expected more negative than positive future behaviors from the unpopular actor. No differences in expectations for future positive versus negative behaviors were found for the control actor. Children also expressed less desire to associate with the unpopular actor than with the popular or control actor. Subject (perceiver) sex or popularity did not greatly influence this process, although there was some indication that unpopular subjects were somewhat more negative than were popular subjects, recalling more negative behaviors and perceiving the social competence of actors more negatively, overall.

In a second study, Butler investigated attributional bias among fifth-grade subjects as a function of prior status expectations for a same-sex hypothetical peer. Popular, average-status, and unpopular subjects were randomly assigned to one of two peer reputation conditions, popular or unpopular. The children in both conditions were then presented with a series of vignettes in which a hypothetical popular or unpopular actor was described as involved in positive and negative interactions with peers. In half of the situations, the actor initiated the positive or negative behavior, and in the other half, the actor was the recipient of positive or negative behavior from another peer. For each situation, subjects were asked to choose one of four alternative explanations for the actor's behavior (i.e., actor personality, temporary motive, external factors, or reinterpretations of the actor's motive), which were ordered along a dimension of responsibility. In addition, subjects were asked to evaluate the actor on several dimensions including global ratings of the actor's responsibility (credit or blame) for the action described.

Butler found that, across situations, children displayed more positive attributional bias in the case of the popular actor than in the case of the unpopular actor. In effect, subjects credited the popular actor for positive acts and excused the popular actor for negative acts more than was the case for the unpopular actor. More specifically, the popular actor was typically given credit for positive outcomes, as evidenced by attributions to positive personality characteristics or motives. In contrast, in the case of the unpopular actor, credit for positive outcomes was more often minimized by attributing the outcome to external causes or was discounted by reinterpreting the actor's motive as negative. In negative outcome situations, subjects were highly excusing of the popular actor, more often attributing the act to external causes or reinterpreting the actor's motive as positive. However, when the unpopular actor performed negative acts, subjects were more likely to attribute the behavior to negative personality characteristics. This positive attributional bias in favor of the popular actor was most marked in situations when the actor initiated negative behavior toward peers. Subjects' global ratings of actor responsibility were generally consistent with attributional biases, with the popular actor rated as more responsible for positive outcomes and less responsible for negative outcomes than was the unpopular actor. In addition, subjects' impressions of the peer actor were more positive for the popular actor than for the unpopular actor, and they expressed more liking for the popular versus unpopular actor.

Butler's studies demonstrate that social perception biases as a function of the social status or popularity of the actor are evident in preadolescent subjects. These biases were demonstrated using a brief, experimental manipulation of the social status of an unknown, hypothetical peer actor and were evident in selective memory, overall impressions, and attributional interpretations of behavior. One might question, however, whether similar biases occur in existing peer groups, when known, rather than hypothetical, peer actors are considered.

A recent study by Wagner (1986) examined social perception bias in existing sixth-grade peer groups. Wagner first demonstrated that the children in her sample were aware of status distinctions within their classroom peer group and that a popularity-based subgroup structure was reflected in friendship patterns that existed in these peer groups. Subsequently, Wagner examined whether intergroup biases as a function of popularity membership group were operating. More specifically, Wagner evaluated differences in children's perceptions of and reactions to hypothetical entry behavior of known, same-sex peers as a function of both the popularity of the perceiver and the popularity of the actor. Popular, average-status, and unpopular subjects responded to three different situations involving either popular, average-status, or unpopular actors. In all cases, the subject's *perception* of the actor's popularity status was consistent with the actor's *actual* status. Each situation depicted an ambiguous entry overture on the part of the peer actor, with the protagonist's actions described in nonevaluative behavioral terms. For example, one of the situations involved a group dodgeball game in which the onlooking peer actor retrieves a missed ball, throws it back to the group, and enters into the playing circle.

For each situation, subjects were first asked to choose between a positive versus negative interpretation of the actor's behavior (e.g., "joined into the play" versus "butted into our game"). Next, subjects were asked to evaluate (a) their own and (b) others' approval of the actor's behavior on a 5-point scale (i.e., how much they, or the other children, would like it if the peer really did that). Then, subjects were asked to explain why the peer actor would perform the behavior described. Causal explanations were subsequently rated in terms of internality, valence, and attributional bias (the extent to which the action was interpreted as reflecting positively or negatively on the actor) and for awareness that the actor's behavior was, in fact, an entry overture. Finally, subjects were asked to describe how (a) they themselves and (b) other peers would respond to the actors' behavior. Reactions were subsequently rated in terms of their favorableness (ranging from most punitive to most favorable) and their likelihood of permitting entry into the activity (ranging from clear exclusion to clear inclusion).

Wagner found significant differences as a function of the popularity of the peer actor for most of the dependent variables considered. First, relatively ambiguous entry overtures on the part of popular actors were almost invariably interpreted in a positive light and were accorded more personal and peer approval. In contrast, the same entry behaviors when performed by unpopular actors were almost equally likely to be interpreted as negative rather than positive behavior and were accorded less personal and peer approval. Average-status actors were perceived as falling between these two extremes. Differences as a function of actor popularity were also evident in terms of valence and attribution bias in subjects' causal explanations for the described behavior. Explanations of entry overtures by popular actors were more positive, generally, and reflected more positively on the actor than explanations of entry overtures by unpopular actors. Finally, subject reactions also varied as a function of the actors' popularity status, with popular actors perceived as more likely to receive favorable reactions from both subjects and peers and to be included in the group as a result of their entry bid than were unpopular actors. For average-status actors, reactions were generally more favorable than for unpopular actors and, on some measures, as favorable as for popular actors. It should also be noted that the obtained differences emerged in a context of equal recognition that the actors' behavior was indeed an entry overture for all status groups.

Perceiver (subject) sex did not significantly influence children's perceptions and reactions to peer behavior. The absence of significant sex-of-perceiver effects suggests that findings are applicable to both male and female peer groups. Similar findings (or lack thereof) were evident in the Hymel (1986) research and, with some exceptions, in Butler's (1984) work, described previously. Significant differences as a function of the popularity of the perceiver were also generally absent (with a few exceptions), suggesting that children at all three status levels share similar biases, perceiving the behavior of popular peers more positively than the behavior of unpopular peers. From an intergroup perspective, these data would suggest that popular children favor ingroup members (i.e., other popular peers) and average and unpopular children do not. Such a conclusion is consistent with Pettigrew's (1979) speculations that ingroup favoritism might be more characteristic of higher status groups. Alternatively, average-status and unpopular children may have weaker membership group identifications given their relative lack of group cohesiveness as reflected in their friendship patterns.

In summary, results of the Wagner (1986) and Butler (1984) research indicate that popular children may be at a considerable advantage and unpopular children at a considerable disadvantage as they negotiate their way in the peer group. Peer perceptions of social behavior are clearly biased in accordance with the social status of the actor. Behavior that is perfectly acceptable to peers when enacted by popular children is somehow less acceptable and less memorable when enacted by unpopular children. There appears to be a double standard in the peer group that ensures that popular children will continue to be viewed positively and that unpopular children will continue to be viewed negatively, regardless of actual behavior. Taken together with the studies by Dodge and his colleagues (Dodge, 1980; Dodge & Frame, 1982) on differential perceptions of the behavior of children with aggressive versus nonaggressive reputations and the studies by Hymel (1986) and by DeLawyer and Foster (1986) on differential perceptions of the behavior of liked versus disliked actors, these findings seem to indicate that in the peer group it is not only *what* you do but also *who* you are that counts.

Summary and conclusions

The present chapter has emphasized the contribution of the peer group to a child's rejection by peers. In particular, we have examined evidence concerning how reputation and expectations within the peer group serve to maintain peer rejection. We focused on the peer group as a social system with an ingroup and an outgroup in which social status distinctions are maintained by biased peer responses. In support of this perspective is a large body of social psychological research demonstrating the existence of social perception biases in both adults and children. These biases have been shown to operate at both dyadic and group levels to maintain prior attitudes and beliefs about others, regardless of actual social behavior, and may be manifested in differential impressions and evaluations of behavior, selective recall of expectancy-congruent information, and biased attributional interpretations of behavior.

Perhaps as a result of the prevailing emphasis on social skill deficits within the peer relations literature to date, the contribution of such social perception biases to the maintenance of peer rejection has largely been ignored. However, even within the literature on the behavioral correlates of status, there is some evidence, albeit indirect, that the peer group may be less positive in their responses to unpopular or disliked children even when they exhibit behaviors similar to those of high-status children. More recent studies that have directly examined the operation of social perception biases in children clearly demonstrate that such biases do indeed play a role in children's social relations, both at the dyadic level, as a function of prior affect toward others (liking vs. disliking), and at the group level, as a function of status group membership (popular vs. unpopular). These findings, however, are based on research involving verbally presented, hypothetical social situations, and their generalizability to real-life behavior remains a question for future research.

The research reviewed in this chapter underscores the need to consider the contribution of the peer group and the impact of social reputation in understanding the process of peer rejection in childhood. Although the prevailing emphasis on social skill deficits within this literature has contributed much to our understanding of children's social difficulties, the predominance of this perspective has resulted in a rather limited view of the phenomenon of peer rejection. It is our conviction that a fuller understanding of children's social difficulties will be achieved by taking into account both individual deficits and the contribution of the peer group. Consideration of both perspectives, however, has important implications for future research endeavors within this area. A discussion of these implications follows.

First, increasing recognition of the contribution of the peer group may result in modifications of our interpretation of previous research. The predominance of the social skill deficit hypothesis to date has led to a biased consideration of research findings. For example, within the behavioral correlates literature, there has been a tendency to emphasize differences between popular and unpopular children and to downplay or minimize similarities. Not all studies have demonstrated status differences (e.g., Benson & Gottman, as cited in Putallaz & Gottman, 1981a; Gottman et al., 1975; Green, Forehand, Beck, & Vosk, 1980; Oden & Asher, 1977; Wagner, 1979), and such results have often been viewed as negative findings, that is, failure to find significant differences. Moreover, when both differences and similarities are found, there has been a tendency to emphasize differences and to ignore or minimize the similarities when discussing implications for understanding children's peer relations (e.g., Asher & Renshaw, 1981; Dodge et al., 1983; Putallaz & Gottman, 1981a). The significance of demonstrated similarities has typically been given little consideration and sometimes merely attributed to insensitive measures (e.g., Dodge et al., 1983). Although an emphasis on differences rather than similarities is understandable, given investigators' goals of identifying potentially ameliorable skill deficits, it may discourage speculation about why status distinctions are maintained despite similarities. As a result, other factors that may also contribute to a child's social problems are not considered.

A second implication of considering both social skill deficits and group processes concerns the design of future research. Most studies to date have examined the relationship between social status and behavior using a correlational methodology. Correlational data do not readily lend themselves to causal interpretations. As Moore (1967) pointed out several years ago:

> To know that popular children perform a preponderance of friendly behaviors is not to say that their friendliness is the "cause" of their popularity. It is just as reasonable to hypothesize that being well liked inspires a child to perform friendly behaviors as it is to hypothesize that performing the behaviors causes the child to be well liked. (p. 236)

More recently, Asher (1983) has suggested that marginal group members, in response to feeling rejected or ignored by peers, may behave in negative ways that do not necessarily reflect their true social competence. Despite these cautions, an implicit causal interpretation has resulted. More recent studies employing alternative methodologies that more readily lend themselves to causal interpretations have provided evidence for a mutual influence of social behavior and reputation. For example, Asarnow (1983), using sequential analyses of observational data (reported earlier), found that although reciprocity characterized interactions following positive or neutral initiations, reputation effects were also evident in the case of interactions following negative initiations. Bukowski and Newcomb (1984), using a LISREL model to examine the causal linkages between reputation and sociometric status in a longitudinal study, found that reputational indices such as perceived aggression were causally related to later sociometric evaluations. Finally, recent studies by Coie and Kupersmidt (1983) and Dodge (1983) and their colleagues have provided innovative alternatives to exploring the direction of causality by studying the emergence of status in play sessions with unfamiliar peers rather than considering behavioral differences in established or familiar peer groups, settings in which reputation effects would be expected to operate maximally. In both studies, there was evidence that some behaviors appeared to develop in response to peer rejection rather than cause peer rejection. Specifically, observed inappropriate solitary behavior of rejected boys (Coie & Kupersmidt, 1983) and observed decreases in social approach behavior of rejected boys (Dodge, 1983) were seen as consequences rather than causes of peer rejection. Consideration of both social skill deficits and reputation effects, then, may require modification of traditional research methodologies.

A third implication of the group process perspective concerns modification of our current conceptions of the problems of socially rejected children. Under the prevailing social skill deficit hypothesis, the rejected child is viewed as the primary cause of his or her social difficulties. With its implicit assumption that the rejected child must be doing something wrong or failing to do something right, the individual deficit model, in effect, has placed a large part of the responsibility for peer rejection on the target child. We contend that such an emphasis represents a one-sided view of social rejection that minimizes the complexity of children's peer relations by ignoring the potential role of peer perceptions and behavior in maintaining a child's status within the peer group. For many rejected children, low social status may indeed be established as a result of poor social skills or inappropriate social behavior. However, once negative status is established, reputation effects may begin to operate and serve to exacerbate the child's social difficulties. Studies of emerging peer status that examine behavioral differences as they develop among previously unacquainted children lend some support to this notion. As noted previously, research by Coie and Kupersmidt (1983) and by Dodge (1983) suggests that although status differences are clearly related to some observable behavioral differences evident even in initial play sessions, other behavioral differences appear to emerge gradually once status distinctions are made. Similarly, Richard (1985) studied the development of attributional bias among previously unacquainted aggressive and nonaggressive boys and found that the tendency to exhibit biases in attributions of hostile intent toward aggressive boys (following Dodge, 1980; Dodge & Frame, 1982) emerged only after previously identified aggressive boys had displayed aggressive behavior during play and that such biases appeared to increase over time. Studies of emerging status or reputation, then, indicate that initial social behavior *and* reputation-based peer responses mutually influence one another. In such cases, social perception biases clearly contribute to the maintenance of peer status, status established initially as a result of social skill deficits.

For some children, however, reputation may play a more causal role in the development of social difficulties. We speculate here that social perception biases may contribute to the *origins* as well as the maintenance of peer status. Darley and Fazio (1980) suggest that social interaction begins with the formation of an expectancy about another person's behavior, which influences subsequent behavior toward that person as well as interpretations of his or her behavior. Expectancies, of course, may stem from previous behavior directed toward the perceiver by the target, as in the above scenario. However, Darley and Fazio suggest that expectancies may also be derived more indirectly, through observations of the target's behavior toward *others* or from stereotypes about the class of individuals to which the target is assumed to belong (including those evoked by salient nonbehavioral characteristics such as race, ethnic group, physical attractiveness or appearance, or mental or physical handicaps). Finally, initial expectancies might also be based on information derived from third-party agents. In regard to this source, it is interesting to note that Gottman and Mettetal (1987), in evaluating the content of peer conversations across the school years, found that gossip (especially negative gossip) about others increased substantially during the middle-childhood years and appeared to function in the service of establishing solidarity between friends in the form of "we against them." Newcomers may be particularly vulnerable to this form of initial labeling prior to actual interaction with peers. It is clear that all of these more indirect sources of information do not stem from actual behavior directed by the target toward perceivers. Instead, expectancies or initial reputations may contribute directly to negative peer status, setting the stage for all subsequent interactions. Positive initial expectancies may lead to more favorable interactions, whereas negative initial expectancies may lead to less favorable interactions. Moreover, as Asher (1983) has suggested, negative social behavior may occur in response to initial peer group rejection. Research with adults has shown that biased expectations can create self-fulfilling prophecies, with actors coming to behave as expected by perceivers (e.g., Snyder, Tanke, & Berscheid, 1977; Word, Zanna, & Cooper, 1974). Thus, observed negative behavior may be induced by biased peer expectations and responses. If, indeed, social perception biases can contribute to the origins of status, the prevailing emphasis on individual deficits within the literature may constitute an unwarranted blaming of the victim for his or her current social difficulties. Future research on the origins of reputation is clearly needed.

Finally, the research reviewed in the present chapter has important implications for future intervention research with socially rejected children. Even when a social skills intervention program has improved the behavior of an unpopular child, there is no guarantee that changes in peer perceptions and attitudes will follow. Future intervention efforts, then, must take into account not only the social skills of the target child but also the receptivity of the peer group in order to maximize effectiveness.

Previous intervention efforts have demonstrated that more appropriate social skills can be learned by unpopular children (see Chapter 11, this volume, and Asher, 1985, for reviews). Our discussion, then, will focus on several different avenues by which intervention efforts can more effectively consider the impact of peer group attitudes. One important approach might be to prepare the target child for the likelihood of negative peer responses despite improved behavior. As Putallaz (1982) has suggested, unpopular children may require training in ways to anticipate and cope with potential rejection from peers when they first try out their newly acquired social skills. To date, such an approach has been absent in intervention programs.

A second approach is to design intervention programs that indirectly or directly influence peer group attitudes toward the unpopular child. One possibility here is to directly increase peer involvement in intervention efforts. For example, in initial coaching intervention studies (e.g., Oden & Asher, 1977), the inclusion of a variety of different peers as part of the practice opportunity constituted a major component of the coaching intervention. The importance of this tactic was demonstrated in a recent coaching intervention study conducted by Bierman and Furman (1984). In this study, both individual and group (involving peers as well as the target) coaching procedures were compared with group involvement only and no treatment controls. Although both coaching procedures resulted in improved social behavior, improvements in sociometric status were evident only for those children whose intervention had included peer group involvement. In a subsequent, process analysis of these treatment effects, Bierman (1986) further demonstrated that those unpopular children who exhibited the greatest improvement in coached skills *and* who received more positive peer reaction during treatment were the most likely to generalize these skills to other settings (lunchroom interaction) and were most likely to gain in peer acceptance following treatment. Bierman suggests that in these cases peer partners provided a more positive peer environment for the unpopular child, exhibiting greater responsivity to the socially skilled behaviors produced by the child. Including peers directly in intervention efforts may afford them an opportunity to get to know a rejected child on a one-to-one basis in a benign social context in which the target child's more positive qualities and skills are highlighted.

Another possibility is to increase peer involvement more indirectly by structuring activities in which popular and unpopular children are required to function as a group. As demonstrated in the work of Sherif et al. (1961), bringing previously hostile parties together in the service of cooperating to achieve a mutual or superordinate goal resulted in more favorable attitudes and interactions among group members. Once social skill deficits of the unpopular child have been ameliorated as a result of social skills intervention, such cooperative involvement may facilitate peer group responsivity to his or her behavior change.

A final suggestion involves interventions designed to directly facilitate greater responsivity on the part of the peer group. This could be accomplished through adult-administered rewards for increased receptiveness or for cooperative behavior and attitudes toward others. Alternatively, it may be possible to minimize social perception biases through direct educative efforts, by teaching children to see others in a more differentiated way. A recent study by Langer, Bashner, and Chanowitz (1985) is illustrative in this regard. In this study, Langer and his colleagues demonstrated that training sixth-grade children to pay more attention to the specific features and abilities of handicapped people led to less overall discrimination as children came to view handicaps as function-specific rather than person-specific. A parallel effort in the social arena that sensitized children to see the positive and negative aspects of both accepted and rejected peers might result in more realistic peer perceptions. A related intervention might involve teaching children to make more charitable attributions about the behavior of rejected children.

We offer these suggestions in full recognition that existing attitudes and intergroup biases are not easily countered. However, it is our conviction that to continue to focus intervention efforts solely on the rejected child will result in addressing only part of the problem. It is hoped that the present chapter will stimulate future research on the origins, maintenance, and amelioration of peer rejection based on a broader perspective of children's social success and failure in the peer group, one that considers both social skill deficits of the rejected child and the contributions of the peer group.

References

Ajzen, I. (1977). Information processing approaches to interpersonal attraction. In S. W. Duck (Ed.), *Theory and practice in interpersonal attraction* (pp. 51–78). London: Academic Press.

Allen, V. L., & Wilder, D. A. (1979). Group categorization and attribution of belief similarity. *Small Group Behavior, 10,* 73–80.

Asarnow, J. R. (1983). Children with peer adjustment problems: Sequential and nonsequential analyses of school behavior. *Journal of Consulting and Clinical Psychology, 51,* 709–717.

Asher, S. R. (1983). Social competence and peer status: Recent advances and future directions. *Child Development, 54,* 1427–1434.

Asher, S. R. (1985). An evolving paradigm in social skill training research with children. In B. H. Schneider, K. H. Rubin, & J. E. Ledingham (Eds.), *Children's peer relations: Issues in assessment and intervention* (pp. 157–171). New York: Springer-Verlag.

Asher, S. R., & Renshaw, P. D. (1981). Children without friends: Social knowledge and social skill training. In S. R. Asher & J. M. Gottman (Eds.), *The development of children's friendships* (pp. 273–296). New York: Cambridge University Press.

Asher, S. R., Renshaw, P. D., & Hymel, S. (1982). Peer relations and the development of social skills. In S. G. Moore & C. R. Cooper (Eds.), *The young child: Reviews of research* (Vol. 3, pp. 137–158). Washington, DC: National Association for the Education of Young Children.

Ashmore, R. D. (1981). Sex stereotypes and implicit personality theory. In D. L. Hamilton (Ed.), *Cognitive processes in stereotyping and intergroup behavior.* Hillsdale, NJ: Lawrence Erlbaum.

Ausubel, D., Schiff, H. M., & Gasser, E. B. (1952). A preliminary study of developmental trends in socioempathy: Accuracy of perception of own and others' sociometric status. *Child Development, 23,* 111–128.

Barenboim, C. (1981). The development of person perception in childhood and adolescence: From behavioral comparisons to psychological constructs to psychological comparisons. *Child Development, 52,* 129–144.

Bartlett, F. C. (1932). *Remembering: A study in experimental and social psychology.* London: Cambridge University Press.

Bellazza, F. S., & Bower, G. H. (1981). Person stereotypes and memory for people. *Journal of Personality and Social Psychology, 41,* 856–865.

Bierman, K. L. (1986). Process of change during social skills training with preadolescents and its relation to treatment outcomes. *Child Development, 57,* 230–240.

Bierman, K. L., & Furman, W. (1984). The effects of social skills training and peer involvement on the social adjustment of preadolescents. *Child Development, 55,* 151–162.

Billig, M., & Tajfel, H. (1973). Social categorization and similarity in intergroup behaviour. *European Journal of Social Psychology, 3,* 27–52.

Biskin, D. S., & Crano, W. (1977). Structural organization of impressions derived from inconsistent information: A developmental study. *Genetic Psychology Monographs, 95,* 331–348.

Brewer, M. B. (1979). In-group bias in the minimal intergroup situation: A cognitive–motivational analysis, *Psychological Bulletin, 86,* 307–324.

Bukowski, W. M., & Newcomb, A. F. (1984). Stability and determinants of sociometric status and friendship choice: A longitudinal perspective. *Developmental Psychology, 20,* 941–952.

Butler, L. J. (1984). *Preadolescent children's differential processing of social information in the peer group.* Unpublished doctoral dissertation, University of Waterloo, Waterloo, Ontario.

Campbell, J. D., & Yarrow, M. R. (1961). Perceptual and behavioral correlates of social effectiveness. *Sociometry, 24,* 1–20.

Cantor, N., & Mischel, W. (1977). Traits as prototypes: Effects on recognition memory. *Journal of Personality and Social Psychology, 35,* 38–48.

Coie, J. D., & Kupersmidt, J. B. (1983). A behavioral analysis of emerging social status in boys' groups. *Child Development, 54,* 1400–1416.

Cooper, J., & Fazio, R. H. (1979). The formation and persistence of attitudes that support intergroup conflict. In W. G. Austin & S. Worchel (Eds.), *The social psychology of intergroup relations.* Monterey: Brooks/Cole.

Crosby, F., Bromley, S., & Saxe, L. (1980). Recent unobtrusive studies of black and white discrimination and prejudice: A literature review. *Psychological Bulletin, 87,* 546–563.

Curran, J. P. (1979). Social skills: Methodological issues and future directions. In S. S. Bellack & M. Hersen (Eds.), *Research and practice in social skills training.* New York: Plenum Press.

Darley, J. M., & Fazio, R. H. (1980). Expectancy confirmation processes arising in the social interaction sequence. *American Psychologist, 35,* 867–881.

DeLawyer, D. D., & Foster, S. L. (1986). The effects of peer relationship on the functions of interpersonal behaviors of children. *Journal of Clinical Child Psychology, 15,* 127–133.

Dodge, K. A. (1980). Social cognition and children's aggressive behavior. *Child Development, 51,* 162–170.

Dodge, K. A. (1983). Behavioral antecedents of peer social status. *Child Development, 54,* 1386–1399.

Dodge, K. A., & Frame, C. L. (1982). Social cognitive biases and deficits in aggressive boys. *Child Development, 51,* 620–635.

Dodge, K. A., Schlundt, D. G., Schocken, I., & Delugach, J. D. (1983). Social competence and children's sociometric status: The role of peer group entry strategies. *Merrill-Palmer Quarterly, 29,* 309–336.

Doise, W., Csepeli, G., Dann, H. D., Gouge, C., Larsen, K., & Ostell, A. (1976). An experimental investigation into the formation of intergroup representations. *European Journal of Social Psychology, 34,* 590–598.

Duncan, E. L. (1976). Differential social perception and attribution of intergroup violence: Testing of the lower limits of stereotyping of blacks. *Journal of Personality and Social Psychology, 34,* 590–598.

Elig, T., & Frieze, I. H. (1975a). Measuring causal attributions for success and failure. *Journal of Personality and Social Psychology, 37,* 621–634.

Elig, T., & Frieze, I. H. (1975b). A multidimensional scheme for coding and interpreting perceived causality for success and failure events: The CSPC. *JSAS Catalogue of Selected Documents in Psychology, 5*, 313.

Foot, H. C., Chapman, A. J., & Smith, J. R. (1979). Friendship and social responsiveness in boys and girls. *Journal of Personality and Social Psychology, 35*, 401–411.

Gershman, E. S., & Hayes, D. S. (1985, April). *Preschoolers' asymmetrical recall of congruent and incongruent attributes associated with hypothetical peers.* Paper presented at the biennial meeting of the Society for Research in Child Development, Toronto, Ontario.

Glidewell, J. C., Kantor, M. B., Smith, L. M., & Stringer, L. A. (1966). Socialization and social structure in the classroom. In L. W. Hoffman & M. L. Hoffman (Eds.), *Review of child development research* (Vol. 3, pp. 221–256). New York: Russell Sage.

Gollin, E. S. (1958). Organizational characteristics of social judgement: A developmental investigation. *Journal of Personality, 26*, 139–154.

Gottman, J., Gonso, J., & Rasmussen, B. (1975). Social interaction, social competence, and friendship in children. *Child Development, 46*, 709–718.

Gottman, J., Gonso, J., & Schuler, P. (1976). Teaching social skills to isolated children. *Journal of Abnormal Child Psychology, 4*, 179–197.

Gottman, J., & Mettetal, G. (1987). Speculations about social and affective development: Friendship and acquaintanceship through adolescence. In J. M. Gottman & J. G. Parker (Eds.), *The conversations of friends: Speculations on affective development* (pp. 192–240). New York: Cambridge University Press.

Green, K. D., Forehand, R., Beck, S. J., & Vosk, B. (1980). An assessment of the relationships among measures of children's social competence and children's academic achievement. *Child Development, 51*, 1149–1156.

Hartup, W. W. (1983). The peer system. In E. M. Hetherington (Ed.), *Handbook of child psychology: Vol. 4. Socialization, personality, and social development* (pp. 103–196, 4th ed.). New York: Wiley.

Hartup, W. W., Glazer, J. A., & Charlesworth, R. (1967). Peer reinforcement and sociometric status. *Child Development, 38*, 1017–1024.

Hastie, R., & Kumar, P. A. (1979). Person memory: Personality traits as organizing principles in memory for behaviors. *Journal of Personality and Social Psychology, 37*, 25–38.

Heider, F. (1958). *The psychology of interpersonal relations.* New York: Wiley.

Hymel, S. (1986). Interpretations of peer behavior: Affective bias in childhood and adolescence. *Child Development, 57*, 431–445.

Hymel, S., & Asher, S. R. (1977, April). *Assessment and training of isolated children's social skills.* Paper presented at the biennial meeting of the Society for Research in Child Development, New Orleans (ERIC Document Reproduction Service No. ED 136 930).

Hymel, S., & Rubin, K. (1985). Children with peer relationships and social skills problems: Conceptual, methodological, and developmental issues. In G. Whitehurst (Ed.), *Annals of child development* (Vol. 2, pp. 251–297). Greenwich, CT: JAI Press.

Jones, E. E., & Davis, K. E. (1965). From acts to dispositions: The attribution process in person perception. In L. Berkowitz (Ed.), *Advances in experimental social psychology* (Vol. 2, pp. 220–266). New York: Academic Press.

Jones, E. E., & McGillis, D. (1976). Correspondent inferences and the attribution cube: A comparative reappraisal. In J. H. Harvey, W. J. Ickes, & R. F. Kidd (Eds.), *New directions in attribution research* (Vol. 1). Hillsdale, NJ: Lawrence Erlbaum.

Kassin, S. M. (1981). From laychild to "layman": Developmental causal attributions. In S. Brehm, S. Kassin, & P. Gibbons (Eds.), *Developmental social psychology* (pp. 169–190). New York: Oxford University Press.

Kelley, H. H. (1967). Attribution theory in social psychology. In D. Levine (Ed.), *Nebraska symposium on motivation* (Vol. 15). Lincoln: University of Nebraska Press.

Kelley, H. H. (1972). Causal schemata and the attribution process. In E. E. Jones et al. (Eds.), *Attribution: Perceiving the causes of behavior* (pp. 151–174). Morristown: General Learning Press.

Kleck, R. E., Richardson, S. A., & Ronald, L. (1974). Physical appearance cues and interpersonal attraction to children. *Child Development, 45,* 305–310.

Koblinsky, S. G., Cruse, D. F., & Sugawara, A. I. (1978). Sex role stereotypes and children's memory for story content. *Child Development, 49,* 452–458.

Ladd, G. W. (1981). Effectiveness of a social learning method for enhancing children's social interaction and peer acceptance. *Child Development, 52,* 171–178.

Ladd, G. W. (1983). Social networks of popular, average, and rejected children in school settings. *Merrill-Palmer Quarterly, 29,* 283–308.

Ladd, G. W. (1985). Documenting the effects of social skills training with children: Process and outcome assessment. In B. H. Schneider, K. H. Rubin, & J. E. Ledingham (Eds.), *Children's peer relations: Issues in assessment and intervention* (pp. 243–269). New York: Springer-Verlag.

Ladd, G. W., & Mize, J. (1983). A cognitive-social learning model of social-skill training. *Psychological Review, 90,* 127–157.

La Greca, A. M., & Santogrossi, D. A. (1980). Social skills training with elementary school students: A behavioral group approach. *Journal of Consulting and Clinical Psychology, 48,* 220–227.

Langer, E. J., Bashner, R. F., & Chanowitz, B. (1985). Decreasing prejudice by increasing discrimination. *Journal of Personality and Social Psychology, 49,* 113–120.

Langlois, J. H., & Stephan, C. W. (1981). Beauty and the beast: The role of physical attractiveness in the development of peer relations and social behavior. In S. Brehm, S. Kassin, & F. Gibbons (Eds.), *Developmental social psychology* (pp. 152–168). New York: Oxford University Press.

Lippitt, R., & Gold, M. (1959). Classroom social structure as a mental health problem. *Journal of Social Issues, 15,* 40–49.

Livesley, W. J., & Bromley, D. B. (1973). *Person perception in childhood and adolescence.* London: Wiley.

Lockman, J. J., & Trejos, L. M. (1985, April). *Differentiation of peers' social attributes.* Paper presented at the biennial meeting of the Society for Research in Child Development, Toronto, Ontario.

Mapley, G. E. (1978, August). *Children's distortion of incongruous behavior: Primacy effect or stereotypes?* Paper presented at the 86th annual meeting of the American Psychological Association, Toronto, Ontario.

Martin, C. L., & Halverson, Jr., C. F. (1981). A schematic processing model of sex typing and stereotyping in children. *Child Development, 52,* 1119–1134.

Masters, J. C., & Furman, W. (1981). Popularity, individual friendship selection, and specific peer interaction among children. *Developmental Psychology, 17,* 344–350.

Milner, D. (1981). Racial prejudice. In J. C. Turner & H. Giles (Eds.), *Intergroup behaviour* (pp. 102–143). Oxford: Blackwell.

Moely, B. E., & Johnson, T. D. (1985, April). *Differentiation of peers' ability attributes by elementary school children.* Paper presented at the biennial meeting of the Society for Research in Child Development, Toronto, Ontario.

Moore, S. G. (1967). Correlates of peer acceptance in nursery school children. In W. W. Hartup & N. L. Smothergill (Eds.), *The young child* (pp. 229–247). Washington, DC: National Association for the Education of Young Children.

Moreno, J. L. (1934). *Who shall survive? A new approach to the problem of human interrelations.* Washington, DC: Nervous and Mental Disease Publishing.

Newcomb, A. F., & Brady, J. E. (1982). Mutuality in boys' friendship relations. *Child Development, 53,* 392–395.

Newcomb, A. F., Brady, J. E., & Hartup, W. W. (1979). Friendship and incentive condition as determinants of children's task-oriented social behavior. *Child Development, 50,* 878–881.

Newcomb, A. F., & Rogosch, F. A. (1982). *The influence of social reputation on the social relations of rejected and isolated children.* Unpublished manuscript, Michigan State University.

Nisbett, R. E., & Ross, L. (1980). *Human inference: Strategies and shortcomings of social judgement.* Engelwood Cliffs, NJ: Prentice-Hall.

Nisbett, R. E., & Wilson, T. D. (1977). The halo effect: Evidence for unconscious alteration of judgements. *Journal of Personality and Social Psychology, 35,* 250–256.

Oden, S., & Asher, S. R. (1977). Coaching children in social skills for friendship making. *Child Development, 48,* 495–506.

O'Keefe, D. (1980). The relationship of attitudes and behavior: A constructivist analysis. In D. P. Cushman & R. D. McPhee (Eds.), *Message–attitude–behavior relationships: Theory, methodology, and application* (pp. 117–148). New York: Academic Press.

Peevers, B. H., & Secord, P. F. (1973). Developmental changes in attribution of descriptive concepts to persons. *Journal of Personality and Social Psychology, 27,* 120–128.

Pettigrew, T. F. (1979). The ultimate attribution error: Extending Allport's cognitive analysis of prejudice. *Personality and Social Psychology Bulletin, 5,* 461–476.

Putallaz, M. (1982, November). *The importance of the peer group for successful intervention.* Paper presented at the annual meeting of the Association for the Advancement of Behavior Therapy, Los Angeles.

Putallaz, M., & Gottman, J. M. (1981a). An interactional model of children's entry into peer groups. *Child Development, 52,* 986–994.

Putallaz, M., & Gottman, J. M. (1981b). Social skills and group acceptance. In S. R. Asher & J. M. Gottman (Eds.), *The development of children's friendships* (pp. 116–149). New York: Cambridge University Press.

Rabbie, J. M., & Horowitz, M. (1969). Arousal of ingroup–outgroup bias by a chance win or loss. *Journal of Personality and Social Psychology, 13,* 269–277.

Regan, D. T. (1978). Attributional aspects of interpersonal attraction. In J. H. Harvey, W. Ickes, & R. F. Kidd (Eds.), *New directions in attribution research* (Vol. 2, pp. 207–233). Hillsdale, NJ: Lawrence Erlbaum.

Regan, D. T., Straus, E., & Fazio, R. (1974). Liking and the attribution process. *Journal of Experimental Social Psychology, 10,* 385–397.

Rholes, W. S., & Ruble, D. N. (1984). Children's understanding of dispositional characteristics of others. *Child Development, 55,* 550–560.

Rholes, W. S., & Ruble, D. N. (1986). Children's impressions of other persons: The effects of temporal separation of behavioral information. *Child Development, 57,* 872–878.

Richard, B. A. (1985, April). *Attributional bias in children's peer groups.* Paper presented at the biennial meeting of the Society for Research in Child Development, Toronto, Ontario.

Richardson, S. A., Goodman, N., Hastorf, A. H., & Dornbusch, S. A. (1961). Cultural uniformity in reaction to physical disabilities. *American Sociological Review, 26,* 241–247.

Rosenbach, D., Crockett, W. H., & Wapner, S. (1973). Developmental level, emotional involvement, and the resolution of inconsistency in impression formation. *Developmental Psychology, 8,* 120–130.

Rosenfield, D., & Stephan, W. G. (1981). Intergroup relations among children. In S. Brehm, S. Kassin, & F. Gibbons (Eds.), *Developmental social psychology* (pp. 271–297). New York: Oxford University Press.

Ross, M., & Fletcher, G. O. (1985). Attribution and social perception. In G. Lindzey & E. Aronson (Eds.), *Handbook of social psychology* (3rd ed., Vol. 2, pp. 73–122). Reading: Addison-Wesley.

Rotenberg, K. J. (1982). Development of character constancy of self and other. *Child Development, 53,* 505–515.

Rothbart, M., Evans, M., & Fulero, S. (1979). Recall for confirming events: Memory processes and the maintenance of social stereotypes. *Journal of Experimental Social Psychology, 15,* 343–355.

Rotter, J. B. (1966). Generalized expectancies for internal versus external control of reinforcement. *Psychological Monographs, 80* (1, Whole No. 609), 1–28.

Rubin, K. H., Daniels-Beirness, T., & Hayvren, M. (1982). Social and social-cognitive correlates of sociometric status in preschool and kindergarten children. *Canadian Journal of Behavioral Science, 14,* 338–348.

Scarlett, H. H., Press, A. N., & Crockett, W. H. (1971). Children's descriptions of peers: A Wernerian developmental analysis. *Child Development, 42,* 439–453.

Sedlack, A. J., & Kurtz, S. T. (1981). A review of children's use of causal inference principles. *Child Development, 52,* 759–784.

Shaver, K. G. (1975). *An introduction to attribution processes.* Cambridge: Winthrop.

Sherif, M., Harvey, O. J., White, B. J., Hood, W. R., & Sherif, C. W. (1961). *Intergroup conflict and cooperation: The Robbers Cave experiment.* Norman: University of Oklahoma Press.

Singleton, L. C. (1981, August). *The influence of reputation on children's perception of behavioral change.* Paper presented at the annual meeting of the American Psychological Association, Los Angeles.

Snyder, M., Tanke, E. D., & Berscheid, E. (1977). Social perception and interpersonal behavior: On the self-fulfilling nature of social stereotypes. *Journal of Personality and Social Psychology, 35,* 656–666.

Snyder, M., & Uranowitz, S. W. (1978). Reconstructing the past: Some cognitive consequences of person perception. *Journal of Personality and Social Psychology, 36,* 941–950.

Stephan, W. G. (1977). Stereotyping: The role of ingroup–outgroup differences in causal attributions for behavior. *Journal of Social Psychology, 101,* 255–266.

Sullivan, H. S. (1953). *The interpersonal theory of psychiatry.* New York: W. W. Norton.

Tajfel, H., & Billig, M. (1974). Familiarity and categorization in intergroup behavior. *Journal of Experimental Psychology, 10,* 159–170.

Tajfel, H., Billig, M., Bundy, R., & Flamant, C. (1971). Social categorization and intergroup behaviour. *European Journal of Social Psychology, 1,* 149–178.

Tajfel, H., & Turner, J. (1979). An integrative theory of intergroup conflict. In W. G. Austin & S. Worchel (Eds.), *The social psychology of intergroup relations.* Monterey: Brooks/ Cole.

Taylor, D. M., & Jaggi, V. (1974). Ethnocentrism and causal attribution in a South Indian context. *Journal of Cross-Cultural Psychology, 5,* 162–171.

Taylor, S. E. (1981). A categorization approach to stereotyping. In D. L. Hamilton (Ed.), *Cognitive processes in stereotyping and intergroup behavior.* Hillsdale, NJ: Lawrence Erlbaum.

Vaughn, B. E., & Waters, E. (1980). Social organization among preschool peers: Dominance, attention, and sociometric correlates. In D. R. Omark, F. F. Strayer, & D. G. Freedman (Eds.), *Dominance relations: An ethological view of human conflict and social interaction* (pp. 359–379). New York: Garland.

Vaughn, B. E., & Waters, E. (1981). Attention structure, sociometric status, and dominance: Interrelations, behavioral correlates, and relationships to social competence. *Developmental Psychology, 17,* 275–288.

Wagner, E. (1979, April). *Interpersonal behavior and peer status.* Paper presented at the biennial meeting of the Society for Research in Child Development, San Francisco.

Wagner, E. (1986). *Bias in preadolescent children's responses to ambiguous social information about peers.* Unpublished doctoral dissertation, University of Waterloo, Waterloo, Ontario.

Weiner, B. (1974). *Achievement motivation and attribution theory.* Morristown: General Learning Press.

Whitehall, M. B., Hersen, M., & Bellack, A. S. (1980). Conversation skills training for socially isolated children. *Behavior Research and Therapy, 18,* 217–225.

Word, C. O., Zanna, M. P., & Cooper, J. (1974). The nonverbal mediation of self-fulfilling prophecies in interracial interaction. *Journal of Experimental Social Psychology, 10*, 109–120.

Yarrow, M. R., & Campbell, J. D. (1963). Person perception in children. *Merrill-Palmer Quarterly, 9*, 57–72.

Part III

Parent–child relations and peer rejection

7   Parent–child interaction

Martha Putallaz and Anne Hope Heflin

The study of parental influence on children has a long history in developmental psychology (see Maccoby & Martin, 1983, for a recent review). Yet, little of this research has concerned whether and in what manner parents play a role in the origins of their children's social status among peers. This lack of research comes as no surprise, however. As both Asher (1983) and Hymel and Rubin (1985) have observed, the recent growth of the sociometric status literature represents a by-product of the shift from the emphasis of Freudian theory on the parent–child relationship to a recognition of peers, among others, as important socialization agents. The resulting lack of attention to parents in the recent sociometric literature was probably necessary to ensure that the role of peers in the socialization process received its proper recognition.

Given that this recognition now exists, however, it is appropriate to begin considering the influence parents might have with respect to the development of their children's social status. Other factors also seem to underscore the need to study the parental role in the development of children's social status. First is the presence of indirect evidence suggesting that parents do indeed play an important role. Investigators have reported a relation between sociometric status and social behavior and social knowledge in children as young as preschool and kindergarten age (e.g., Asher & Renshaw, 1981; Hartup, Glazer, & Charlesworth, 1967; Marshall & McCandless, 1957; Putallaz, 1983; Rubin & Daniels-Beirness, 1983). Because of the very early appearance of this relation between social status and social behavior, it is quite likely that parents do influence the development of their children's social competence and acceptance level among peers. If such social behavior is learned, at least in part, through early family interaction, then a further motivation for studying the parental role is the potential to develop preventive interventions that can be implemented before children experience the many negative consequences of social rejection. Further, if parents do play an important role in the development and maintenance of children's social behavior

The authors would like to acknowledge the support of a William T. Grant Faculty Scholar Award to the first author and to thank Blair Sheppard for his comments made on an earlier version of this chapter.

related to social status, then any theory of the origins of peer acceptance not incorporating parental influence would be incomplete. Similarly, any interventions not including parents would seem likely to have their potential success compromised in the long run.

Thus, the major purpose of this chapter is to explore the potential parental contribution to the development of children's social behavior and status in the peer group. Toward this end, the chapter has been divided into the following parts. First, those studies within the general parent–child literature focusing on the relation between parent–child interaction and children's social behavior will be reviewed. The focus of this review will be on delineating the parental behaviors that appear related to children's social behavior and the possible means of transmission from parent to child. The following four areas within the general parent–child literature will be reviewed: (a) characteristics of parents' psychological and interpersonal functioning related to their children's social behavior, (b) general parenting styles (i.e., dimensions that characterize parents' manner of interacting with their children), (c) parental disciplinary techniques, and (d) quality of infant–parent attachment. This portion of the chapter, although not focused specifically on social competence or sociometric status, does serve to provide a general context for the research to be presented in later portions of the chapter. Furthermore, as will be seen, research within this general socialization research tradition can be used to inform our understanding about links between parental behavior and children's peer relationships. Indeed, in the second part of the chapter, those studies pertaining directly to the parental role in the development of social status will be discussed in light of this broader literature. The chapter will conclude with a theoretical discussion of the implications of these results for understanding the origins of children's social behavior and status.

Parental behavior and children's social behavior

Interpersonal characteristics of parents

The first area within the larger parent–child literature to be explored is the extent to which characteristics of parents' psychological and interpersonal functioning have been related to their children's social characteristics. Several studies (e.g., Becker, Peterson, Hellmer, Shoemaker, & Quay, 1959; Glueck & Glueck, 1950; Sameroff & Seifer, 1983) have demonstrated that general characteristics of psychological functioning such as parental level of adjustment and degree of mental illness are related to children's social behaviors, including aggression, shyness, low self-esteem, and depression. These researchers did not delineate a specific model to account for these relations between parent and child characteristics. However, in all three studies, a general suggestion was made that parents who are poorly adjusted themselves or who suffer from some degree of mental illness may be unable to provide an optimal environment in terms of security and stimulation for their children's social and emotional development. Sameroff and Seifer (1983) further suggested that parents who are mentally ill may not adequately buffer their children in times of stress and may not provide sufficient social support for them.

A number of researchers also have reported relations between more specific characteristics of parents' psychological and interpersonal functioning and their children's social behavior. For example, a positive association has been reported between level of aggression in parents and children (e.g., Bandura & Walters, 1959; Becker et al., 1959; Glueck & Glueck, 1950; McCord & McCord, 1958). Eron (1982) reported that parental aggression, as measured by the Minnesota Multiphasic Personality Inventory (MMPI), was positively related to boys' aggressiveness. Similarly, Becker et al. (1959) found that parents who vented their emotions in an uncontrolled manner tended to have children who behaved in aggressive, uncontrolled ways. Glueck and Glueck (1950) also reported that parents of delinquent adolescents were more likely to have had criminal records themselves than were parents of nondelinquent children. To explain the association between parent and child aggression, a modeling theory has most often been employed. Both Bandura and Walters (1959) and Eron (1982) reported that parents of aggressive children were more likely to use physical punishment with their children than were parents of nonaggressive children. Thus, the parents of aggressive children may be providing models of aggressive behavior for their children. Glueck and Glueck (1950) employed a similar modeling notion to explain their results by suggesting that the parents of their delinquent sample were unable to provide sound moral standards for their children to follow.

In addition to modeling, response evocation has been proposed as a mechanism to explain the relation between parent and child aggression. Researchers have found that more subtle forms of parental aggression are associated with children's aggressiveness (Bandura & Walters, 1959; Eron, 1982; Lefkowitz, Eron, Walder, & Huesmann, 1977). Results of these studies indicated that parents who were highly critical, disapproving, and generally rejecting of their children tended to have children who behaved in hostile and aggressive ways. Supposedly, the parental rejection caused the children to feel angry and frustrated and thus was an instigating factor in evoking the children's aggressive behavior.

A second fairly specific characteristic of parental interpersonal functioning that has been related to children's social behavior is level of altruism. Hoffman (1975) found that altruistic children had at least one parent, usually the same-sex parent, who had altruistic values. Again, a modeling theory was used to account for the relation between altruism in parents and children. Hoffman asserted that parents communicate these values in words and actions and that their children assume these values through an identification process.

A final example of a parental interpersonal characteristic that has been related to children's social behavior is the orientation of parental communication. Bearison and Cassel (1975) found that children who could better accommodate their communication to a listener's perspective were more likely to have mothers who communicated in a person-oriented fashion (focusing on a person's feelings, thoughts, needs, or intentions) rather than in a position-oriented fashion (focusing on general rules governing behavior). The authors theorized that in person-oriented families it is necessary that the speaker be able to understand and attend to the listener's perspective as well as his or her own. Thus, children from those families learn to communicate more effectively. The authors did not specify how that learning occurs; however, as they described the process, it seems likely that parents in person-oriented families model effective communication for their children.

General parenting styles

The second area within the parent–child literature to be examined is the association between parenting styles and children's social behavior. Much of the research in this area has been based on variations of several basic dimensions of parenting behavior. Symonds (1939) proposed two such dimensions, acceptance–rejection and dominance–submission. Acceptance–rejection has been studied under such different labels as warmth–hostility and warmth–coldness; and dominance–submission has been studied under various labels including restrictiveness–permissiveness, control–autonomy, and high demandingness–low demandingness (see Maccoby & Martin, 1983, for further discussion).

Although the findings regarding these dimensions have not always been consistent, one fairly constant conclusion has been that the most socially competent children have parents who have received high ratings on both warmth and control. In one of the most influential series of studies in this area, Baumrind (1967, 1971, 1973) identified and studied three patterns of parenting: authoritarian (high control, low warmth), authoritative (high control, high warmth), and permissive (low control, high warmth). The authoritarian parents were highly controlling in accordance with an absolute set of standards, tended to discourage verbal communication with their children, and sometimes rejected their children. These parents typically had children who were highly dependent with only average social responsibility scores. Authoritative parents (i.e., also fairly controlling but with higher scores in terms of their maturity demands, democratic ways, and encouragement of verbal give and take) were likely to have socially successful children who were independent and socially responsible. The final set of parents, the permissive parents, exercised little control over their children, made few maturity demands, and were generally accepting of their children. Their children exhibited little social responsibility and were only moderately independent. Results of a later study (Baumrind, 1977, reported in Maccoby, 1980) indicated that children who exhibited high social agency (i.e., were active participants and leaders in group activities and were comfortable and outgoing in peer interactions) at age 8 or 9 years were likely to have had authoritative parents as preschoolers.

Other researchers have provided support for the conclusion that parental warmth and at least some degree of control are crucial in terms of the development of children's social competence. For example, Hinde and Tamplin (1983) found that authoritarian mothers (i.e., below the median score on warmth and gentle control but above on inhibition) tended to have hostile children who were below the median for friendliness to peers, whereas children of authoritative mothers (i.e., above the median score on warmth and on gentle control) tended to be above the median for friendliness. Further support for the importance of parental warmth has also accrued as researchers have reported parental acceptance and affection to be related to children's prosocial behaviors (e.g., Brody & Shaffer, 1982; Hoffman, 1963, 1975; Jensen, Peery, Adams, & Gaynard, 1981) and maternal responsiveness to be related to children's social ability (e.g., Bakeman & Brown, 1980; Bryant & Crockenberg, 1980).

The most common theoretical explanations given for these relations between parent and child behavior include the following. First, children whose own needs are effectively met by their parents are less preoccupied with themselves and thus are better able to be responsive to others. In addition, such children typically have positive relationships with their parents, and the resulting positive affective social orientation generalizes to other people. Finally, parental warmth enhances parental effectiveness as a model of positive social behavior (Brody & Shaffer, 1982; Bryant & Crockenberg, 1980; Hoffman, 1963, 1975).

Probably the most comprehensive explanation regarding the possible manner of transmission from parent to child in this area has been offered by Baumrind (1967, 1971, 1973). First, she maintained that authoritative parents were more effective in teaching their children the social behaviors they desired than were authoritarian or permissive parents. Because authoritative parents were nurturing, they made better use of affection and approval as positive reinforcement than did authoritarian parents. Additionally, authoritative parents were able to use punishment more effectively than authoritarian parents because their disapproval was more powerful. Similarly, authoritative parents could use punishment more effectively than permissive parents because they were more consistent and more committed to the punishment than permissive parents, who were ambivalent and often unintentionally nullified the effects of the punishment.

Second, Baumrind asserted that authoritative parents taught their children to be self-assertive and affiliative by modeling those behaviors in their interactions with their children. In contrast, permissive parents were not good models of self-assertive behavior, and authoritarian parents were poor models of affiliative behavior. In addition, the combination of warmth and power exercised by authoritative parents should lead to increased imitation of them by their children (e.g., Hetherington & Frankie, 1967).

The children of authoritative parents also tended to be self-reliant and goal directed because their parents placed high maturity demands on them and were nurturing and encouraging as the children attempted to meet those demands. The children were persistent in their efforts because they were motivated by their parents' continued approval. Eventually, the children's successful achievements served as positive reinforcers in themselves, encouraging more self-reliant behavior and higher aspirations. Permissive parents, on the other hand, came to the children's aid as soon as they became frustrated. Thus, their children learned to seek adult help in order to relieve frustration rather than relying on their own problem-solving behaviors. In contrast, authoritarian parents punished their children's dependent behaviors but failed to reward their children's independent efforts at problem solving. Their children did attempt to avoid punishment by avoiding any display of dependent behavior; however, they did not learn to associate work with pleasure. Thus, they were less self-reliant and goal directed than the children of authoritative parents.

Finally, authoritative parents communicated more clearly with their children, because they combined a directive with a rationale and identified for the children the consequences of their behavior. They also allowed their children to express their thoughts and feelings openly. Baumrind suggested that such open communication prevented the buildup of frustration and aggression in the children and helped them develop a stronger control system within themselves.

Parental disciplinary techniques

Another important aspect of parent–child relations associated with children's social behaviors is parental disciplinary techniques. The following three general categories of parental discipline have been used to discuss the literature in this area: (a) power assertion: the use of commands, physical power, or deprivation of privileges; (b) love withdrawal: the use of negative techniques that threaten the love received from the parent (e.g., ridicule, expressions of dislike or disappointment, isolation of the child from the parent); and (c) induction: the use of reason so that the child can understand the rationale underlying the parent's response and the parent's reasons for engaging in certain actions or prohibitions (Brody & Shaffer, 1982).

Much of the parent–child research investigating disciplinary techniques has focused on parental power assertion. Typically, power assertive disciplinary techniques have been found to be associated with high levels of aggression in children (Becker, 1964) and with children's hostility toward peers and own use of power assertion methods in attempting to influence other children (Hoffman, 1960). Becker (1964) identified the following three hypotheses that possibly account for the relation between power assertive techniques and child aggression. (a) This type of punitive discipline is frustrating to the child and thus provokes anger and aggression (i.e., response evocation). (b) Parents are providing an aggressive model for their children and implicitly sanctioning such behavior (i.e., modeling). (c) Parents may be directly rewarding aggressive behavior in their children by encouraging them to fight for their rights with other children (i.e., positive reinforcement). The comparative merits of these three hypotheses remain to be tested.

Much less is known concerning the relation of the other disciplinary methods to children's social behavior. Although it has been speculated that love withdrawal techniques might be associated with neurotic, inhibited behaviors (e.g., Simonds & Simonds, 1981), others have found little support for that hypothesis (e.g., Martin, 1975). In a comparative study of the disciplinary techniques, Hoffman (1963) reported that maternal use of love-withholding techniques was related to nurturance seeking in children and that this association was not evident in children whose mothers frequently used power assertive techniques. Further, maternal use of a type of inductive discipline called other-oriented discipline (i.e., focusing on the consequences of the child's behavior for another child) was related to children's consideration of others. Hoffman (1963, 1975) hypothesized that disciplinary techniques that emphasize the harmful consequences of the child's behavior for someone else teach children to consider other people's thoughts or feelings and eventually to allow that consideration to guide their future behavior. A positive relation between inductive discipline techniques and children's prosocial behavior has been documented in children as young as two years of age (Zahn-Waxler, Radke-Yarrow, & King, 1979). However, Hoffman (1963) found the nature of that association to differ according to the frequency with which power assertion techniques were used. There was a positive relation between other-oriented discipline and children's consideration of others if mothers seldom used power assertion techniques, while the reverse was true if mothers frequently used these techniques. Hoffman theorized that the frequent use of power assertion techniques may elicit hostility which will provoke children into rebelling against the parent regardless of other disciplinary techniques used.

Infant–parent attachment

The final area within the general parent–child literature to be examined in this chapter is the relation between parental behavior and the quality of infant attachment. In an early series of studies assessing infant–mother attachment, Ainsworth and her colleagues (Ainsworth, 1967; Ainsworth & Bell, 1969; Ainsworth, Bell, & Stayton, 1971) proposed a typology of attachment based primarily upon their observations of infant responses in the Strange Situation. Briefly, this situation involves the separation and reunion of infants and their mothers in an unfamiliar laboratory setting as well as the introduction of a strange adult. The three types of attachment proposed were (a) Type A, or avoidant (i.e., not particularly distressed by separation from the mother and as easily comforted by a stranger as by the mother); (b) Type B, or securely attached (i.e., neither avoidant nor resistant in terms of displayed behavior toward mother either prior to or following separation); and (c) Type C, or resistant (i.e., ambivalent or inconsistent behaviorally with respect to attachment to mother).

Researchers using this typology of attachment have identified different behaviors exhibited by the mothers of these three types of infants during their interactions with their children. Mothers of infants classified as secure in their attachment have been judged more sensitive and responsive to their infants' signals and communications (Ainsworth, Bell, & Stayton, 1971; Ainsworth, Blehar, Waters, & Wall, 1978; Clarke-Stewart, 1973), more warm and accepting (Ainsworth et al., 1971; Clarke-Stewart, 1973; Louderville & Main, 1981), more cooperative rather than interfering with or controlling of their infants (Ainsworth et al., 1971), more supportive (Matas, Arend, & Sroufe, 1978), more involved in social stimulation of their infants (Clarke-Stewart, 1973), and more likely to be accessible to their infants rather than to ignore them when not engaged in caretaking tasks (Ainsworth et al., 1971) than mothers of insecure infants. In contrast, mothers of avoidant infants have been judged as more rejecting of their infants and insensitive to their signals, and the mothers of resistant infants similarly have been reported to be rejecting but, in addition, to be high either on interfering with their infants' behavior or on ignoring their infants (Ainsworth et al., 1971).

Quality of attachment during infancy has, in turn, been related to social competence in children. Secure infants, for example, have been observed to relate better to unfamiliar adults (Main & Weston, 1981; Thompson & Lamb, 1983) and unfamiliar peers (Easterbrooks & Lamb, 1979; Lieberman, 1977; Pastor, 1981) than infants judged as insecure in their attachment. In fact, quality of infant attachment has been used successfully to predict social competence in nursery school (Waters, Wippman, & Sroufe, 1979) and kindergarten (Arend, Gove, & Sroufe, 1979). Other researchers (e.g., Bakeman & Brown, 1980; Clarke-Stewart, VanderStoep, & Killian, 1979) have not found such a relation, but that difference may be due to differences in assessment techniques. Thus, there appears to be a connection not only between parental behavior and the quality of infant–parent attachment but between this attachment and children's social behavior as well.

Most of the investigators cited above offered two hypotheses to account for the relation between infant–parent attachment and children's social behavior. First, they theorized that the mother–child relationship establishes for the child a social orientation that is likely to generalize to other relationships. Thus, a securely attached infant develops a positive social orientation to the mother that generalizes to other people (e.g., Easterbrooks & Lamb, 1979; Lieberman, 1977; Pastor, 1981; Thompson & Lamb, 1983). In addition, a secure early attachment enables the infant to actively explore and eventually master his or her environment. This tendency toward greater exploration and competency is evident in the area of social relationships; a securely attached infant is likely to be more active in exploring new relationships and is likely to feel more confident about his or her success in those explorations than an insecurely attached child. In contrast, a child lacking a secure parental attachment is likely to approach social relationships with timidity and anxiety (Easterbrooks & Lamb, 1979; Lieberman, 1977; Matas et al., 1978; Thompson & Lamb, 1983; Waters et al., 1979).

Summary

To summarize thus far, there does seem to be ample evidence from the general parent–child literature that parents, whether it be in terms of their personal characteristics, parenting styles, disciplinary techniques, or the quality of their attachment to their infants, influence the social behavior of their children. Although many specific parental behaviors have been discussed, there appear to be several general dimensions that summarize many of these findings. First, parental warmth appears to receive overwhelming support as a major contributor to the development of children's social competence. Second, some degree of gentle parental control seems to relate positively to children's peer competence, although the exertion of too much control without warmth appears to reverse this effect. Third, the extent to which parents are sensitive, responsive, and involved with their children appears to influence positively their children's peer relationships. Finally, a favorable influence on their children's social competence also appears to result when parents use a democratic and inductive-reasoning approach with their children.

The theories that have been offered to account for the parental influence on children's social behavior can similarly be summarized. First, parents who demonstrate the characteristics described above tend to foster a sense of security and self-confidence in their children. Because these children feel secure in their relationships with their parents and feel good about their own abilities, they are able to explore new relationships with more confidence. Furthermore, they are more likely to be successful in those relationships because they can be responsive to other people without being preoccupied with their own needs. These children have a positive orientation toward social relationships in general that is based in their positive relationships with their parents. Second, parents demonstrating the above characteristics also tend to be effective teachers. These parents are quite successful in their attempts to explicitly teach their children appropriate social behaviors because they communicate clearly and use a democratic and inductive-reasoning approach. Additionally, their combined warmth and control enable them to use positive reinforcement and punishment effectively. Third, these parents influence their children by serving as models of appropriate social behaviors. Finally, these parents behave in ways that induce styles in their children that later generalize to interactions with peers.

Recently, Rubin and Sloman (1984) proposed a more formal typology for organizing and examining the ways in which parents might influence their children's friendships and peer relationships. Three of their five proposed categories involve modes of transmission discussed in our literature review. The authors used descriptive data gathered from semistructured interviews with parents (mostly mothers) of 4-year-old ($N = 18$) and 5-year-old ($N = 1$) children to illustrate their theoretical types of parental influence. First, Rubin and Sloman proposed that parents influence their children through the "home base" they provide. Citing the attachment literature, they theorized that secure family relationships provide children not only with a secure base from which to explore their social environment but also with a positive orientation toward social relationships. Second, parents influence their children by coaching or explicitly teaching them about social behaviors through suggestions, instructions, or expressions of approval or disapproval. Third, children's peer relationships are affected by the manner in which their parents engage in social interaction and social relationships (i.e., modeling). Fourth, Rubin and Sloman proposed that parents influence their children by "setting the stage" for their social interactions, because they determine their children's neighborhood, day-care program or school, and even the people with whom they interact. These social contexts affect the structure of the peer interaction (e.g., highly structured activities vs. free play) as well as the number of potential playmates children have, their ages, sexes, socioeconomic status, and ethnic backgrounds. Fifth, Rubin and Sloman suggested that parents influence their children's peer relationships by "arranging social contacts," such as parties, visits with friends, or organized educational and sports activities. The manner in which these last two modes of parental influence may affect children's social behavior was not explored by the authors.

Although the purpose of this chapter is to examine the potential parental contribution to the development of children's social behavior and status, it is important to note that the flow of influence also occurs from children to parents. Bell's (1968) classic article underscored the importance of recognizing the bidirectionality of influence in the parent–child relationship. The reader is directed to work by Bell and Harper (1977) and Maccoby and Martin (1983), which discusses the effects of children's characteristics on parental behaviors in some detail.

Parental behavior and children's sociometric status

Although parental behavior and children's social behavior do appear related, there is very little research that has examined the role played by parents in the development of their children's social status. The few investigators that have examined this relation, however, have found evidence for such an association. For example, Kolvin et al. (1977) found that the mothers of rejected (who received many negative sociometric nominations) and isolated children (who received few sociometric nominations) had significantly lower sociability scores (as measured by a questionnaire assessing sociability toward neighbors) than mothers of popular children. Further, the parents of rejected children relied more on physical punishment and deprivation of privileges and less on inductive disciplinary techniques than did the other parents. Armentrout (1972) found that high-popular elementary school children reported significantly greater acceptance by their parents than did their low-popular peers. Their two measures of parental control (i.e., covert intrusiveness and overt rule making) did not differentiate between the children in terms of popularity. However, Winder and Rau (1962) reported that parents of "likable" elementary school boys tended not to be aggressive or punitive with their children and had low demands for aggression. The mothers reportedly had high self-esteem and were well adjusted, and the fathers expressed high regard for their sons and evaluated them as competent. Elkins (1958) also reported a positive relationship between the level of satisfaction parents had with their eighth-grade children and the sociometric scores of the children. Thus, once again both parental warmth and acceptance as well as use of inductive rather than power assertive disciplinary techniques emerge as important variables, this time with respect to children's social status.

Evaluation of previous literature

Clearly, the results of the studies discussed thus far suggest that parents play an important role in the development of their children's social status in the peer group. However, it is important at this point to note the shortcomings that have marked much of the parent–child literature to date in order to guide both the interpretation of this work as well as its implications for future research. First, with few exceptions, the predominant form of data collection characterizing this literature has been self-report questionnaires and interviews. Very little actual behavioral data have been collected, which is surprising given that it is the relation between parental behavior and children's social behavior that has been the focus of investigation. Although there are certainly benefits to self-report questionnaires and interviews, there are also disadvantages to solely using these techniques. For example, some of the most common criticisms of these methods are that (a) parental responses may be influenced by a desire to appear socially appropriate, (b) parental responses may be unreliable because parents may have difficulty remembering dates and events accurately, (c) parents may vary considerably in their use of subjective descriptive terms, and (d) parents may be unaware of subtle aspects of their own behavior or the behavior of their children (Maccoby & Martin, 1983).

Second, historically, the rating and coding systems employed by researchers in this area have been fairly global in nature. Although such molar analyses are valuable in identifying fairly general and stable characteristics, they may also ignore some important but more molecular aspects of behavior. As Eckerman and Stein (1983) have indicated, the additional use of molecular constructs would permit detailed tracing of clear antecedents and consequences of social interaction. Additionally, a shift from simple frequency counts of behavior to sequential analyses of both parental and child behavior would probably better capture the interactional relation between the behavior of the participants. This is consistent with Hartup's (1979) suggestion that the main measures of such studies reflect interaction rather than the actions of parents and their children as individuals.

Finally, the behavior of parents and children typically has not been examined across situations or social spheres. In particular, little research has been conducted by observing behavior in both the family socialization and peer socialization situations. Indeed, Hartup (1979) stated, "Quite possibly the most serious oversight in the literature on social development is the absence of information concerning the interdependencies existing between experiences in one social world and experiences in others" (p. 944). MacDonald and Parke (1984) and Rubin and Sloman (1984) also have emphasized the potential interdependence of the family and peer social systems. What little research there is on the relation between these two social spheres has concerned primarily the impact of infant–parent attachment on later social competence with peers. A neglected area of study has been the potential opportunities existing within the family for children to learn socially skillful behavior that later may be applied to the peer social context.

Drawing on this methodological evaluation as a guide, then, it would seem important for research exploring the relation between parental behavior and children's social status and behavior to incorporate the following design features. Clearly, the description of the parent–child interaction should encompass actual behavioral observations in addition to information derived from questionnaires, interviews, or classification typologies (e.g., attachment types). Further, the variables studied should be less global in nature and should adequately capture the interactional pattern of parent–child behavior. Finally, the children should be observed interacting with their peers as well as their parents in order to assess the relations between parent–child interaction, peer interaction, and sociometric status. Recently, two studies have examined the relation between parental behavior and children's social status while following the methodological suggestions just described. Therefore, these two studies, one by MacDonald and Parke (1984) and the other by Putallaz (1987), will be reviewed in some detail to assess the contribution of parental behavior to the development of children's social status and the utility of this advocated research approach.

Two recent studies

The study by MacDonald and Parke (1984) focused upon the comparison of social behavior exhibited by 27 preschoolers across several social spheres, namely, playing in a dyadic situation with their mothers, their fathers, and their peers. The children were videotaped playing individually with their parents for 20 min each. The parent–child observations were coded for the following: (a) the number of 10-s blocks in which the parent and child engaged in physical play together, (b) the degree of positive affect exhibited by the child during each 10-s block of play as rated on a 4-point scale ranging from neutral affect to intense laughter, (c) the frequency of parental directives or commands, (d) the number of time blocks characterized by active involvement of the parent with the child, and (e) the number of times the parent spoke to the child.

The children also were videotaped in 12-min dyadic play sessions with 3 same-sex classmates. The children's behavior was rated on nine 7-point scales, which intercorrelations revealed to form the following four clusters: (a) an abrasive interaction cluster composed of ratings of irritability, negative affect, and acrimony; (b) a dominance cluster composed of a dominance rating and a rating involving taking initiative, directing, and making suggestions; (c) a relaxed cluster composed of ratings of being relaxed and secure; and (d) a harmonious interaction cluster comprising ratings concerning coordination of interaction and display of high agreement. Additional assessments of the children's social competence were obtained in two ways. First, teachers ranked the children in terms of their popularity (i.e., the frequency and extensiveness with which they were sought out by classmates). Second, teachers completed the California Q-sort (Baumrind, 1968), which provided descriptions of specific aspects of the children's social behavior. Although no peer sociometric measures were obtained in this study, the teacher rankings of popularity do provide an estimate of the children's social status among their peers.

The written report of this research encompasses a tremendous amount of data, which is impressive in its scope and difficult to summarize adequately. Thus, only the portions of the research relevant to the purposes of this chapter will be reviewed here. The reader is referred to the original report by MacDonald and Parke (1984) for a more comprehensive description of this study.

To ascertain the relation between parental behavior and children's social behavior, three sets of correlations were computed. First, the relations between the parent variables and the teacher rankings of popularity were examined. Boys assessed as more popular by their teachers had mothers and fathers who were rated high on engagement in play with their child and on eliciting positive affect from their child during the course of their play. In addition, the mothers of the more popular boys were verbally stimulating, and their fathers were low in terms of their directiveness but were physically playful with their sons. Similarly, the more popular girls had parents who were physically playful and affect-eliciting, mothers who were high on directiveness, and fathers who were less directive.

In the second set of analyses, the parental behaviors found previously to be most highly related to popularity (i.e., paternal engagement, paternal physical play, paternal directiveness, maternal verbal interchange, and maternal directiveness) were correlated with the teacher Q-sort items assessing the children's social behavior. Boys showed a consistent array of positive characteristics associated with their fathers' engagement and physical play and with their mothers' frequency of verbal interchange. Although a factor analysis of these data was not performed by MacDonald and Parke, it seems intuitively that many of these items could be grouped into four meaningful clusters: (a) thoughtfulness and helpfulness toward peers, (b) physical competence, (c) goal directedness and involvement, and (d) leadership. In contrast, a variety of negative attributes that would seem less likely to be related positively to social status were related to paternal directiveness for boys. At least two clusters of these negative individual attributes seem to be evident: a grouping of anxious and hesitant behaviors and a set of items reflecting adult orientation. The results for girls were somewhat different from those just discussed for boys. A consistent set of positive characteristics was associated with paternal physical play and, to a lesser degree, maternal directiveness. These characteristics seemed to group into at least four clusters of positive items, specifically: (a) creativity and curiosity, (b) adult orientation, (c) expressiveness, and (d) engagement.

The final manner in which the relation between parental behavior and peer competence was assessed was through the correlations between parental behavior and the ratings of the children's behavior during the peer interaction situation. For boys, the same parental behaviors appeared to be related most highly and in the same direction with the children's social competence as had been reported in the two previous sets of analyses. Maternal verbal behavior and paternal physical play and engagement were associated with a child behavior pattern of harmonious, relaxed, and dominant interaction with peers. In addition, paternal directiveness was related to an abrasive interaction pattern for boys. For girls, paternal verbal behavior was correlated positively with the rating of peer interactions as harmonious and relaxed. However, paternal physical play and paternal engagement were related to abrasive and dominant peer interaction, whereas paternal verbal interchanges were negatively related to this style of peer interaction. Maternal directiveness was associated with an abrasive interaction pattern for girls. Maternal verbal behavior was correlated negatively with peer interactions characterized as being both relaxed and dominant.

The results of the MacDonald and Parke (1984) study are in many ways consistent with the findings of the more general parent–child literature discussed earlier. Again, positive affect (although this was examined as the parents' ability to elicit positive affect from their child rather than their own level of warmth conveyed), parental involvement (engagement) with the child, and the degree of parental control (directiveness) exhibited appeared to be important in terms of child social behavior. For both parents, the tendency to elicit positive affect from their child was related positively to their child's popularity. Parental engagement and physical play generally appeared to be associated positively with peer acceptance, although there were some apparent sex differences. Paternal engagement and maternal verbal interchange were correlated positively with social competence for boys, whereas the converse relation was true for girls. Generally, parents' physical playfulness was related positively to peer acceptance for both boys and girls. Finally, maternal directiveness was associated positively with children's social competence, but paternal directiveness was not. This again appears consistent with the findings of the earlier parent–child literature. Typically, some degree of gentle control seemed important in terms of children's social competence, but the use of excessive control tended to have the reverse effect. As MacDonald and Parke (1984) pointed out, the fathers in their study exhibited significantly more directive behavior than did the mothers. Therefore, they hypothesized that moderate levels of directiveness exhibited by either parent probably would be related positively to children's peer acceptance.

MacDonald and Parke offered several explanations as to why these behaviors might relate to children's social competence. All appear to stem from their conceptualization of the family socialization process as one that provides opportunities for children to learn certain interactional skills and behaviors that then carry over to their peer interactions. First, they proposed that moderately directive parents provide their children with opportunities to learn and practice how to regulate an interaction (i.e., how to control its direction, tempo, and content), whereas highly controlling parents limit these opportunities for their children. Similarly, through physical play, parents (especially fathers) help their children learn affect recognition and regulation. Specifically, children learn the social impact of their own affective displays, how to accurately decode the social and affective signals of others, and how to use these signals to regulate the social behavior of others. Regarding the relation between social competence and parents' ability to generate positive affect in their children, MacDonald and Parke suggested the following explanation. The tendency of children to be affectively expressive during parent–child interactions carries over to their interactions with peers, which is a behavior previously found related to peer competence (e.g., Sroufe, Schork, Motti, Lawroski, & LaFreniere, 1983). Although not mentioned by MacDonald and Parke, it also seems conceivable that this ability to elicit positive affect is simply one measure of the warmth of the parent–child relationship, which relates to the type of social orientation the child will develop and ultimately to his or her degree of social competence. Finally, MacDonald and Parke proposed that children learn verbal strategies for initiating and maintaining peer interaction from parental verbal behavior (especially true for mothers and sons).

In summary, then, the results reported by MacDonald and Parke (1984) are in keeping with the findings of the more general parent–child literature reviewed earlier. Parental involvement, warmth, and moderate control appear to be important factors in terms of children's social competence. Within the social context of their family, children appear to learn certain interactional skills and behaviors that then transfer to their interactions with peers. Further, the MacDonald and Parke work reveals some interesting nuances concerning the different influence of mothers and fathers with respect to the peer acceptance of their sons and daughters. In addition to the differences discussed previously, daughters appeared to have fewer parental behaviors significantly related to their social status, and those relations were less consistent across the three sets of analyses than those of sons. Clearly, the impressive work of MacDonald and Parke highlights not only the utility but also the need to examine the social behavior exhibited by children across several social spheres in order to study the origins of their social competence and status.

As with the MacDonald and Parke study, a major purpose of the Putallaz (1987) research was to explore the potential link between the social behavior of parents (in this case mothers) and the behavior and status of their children. Also similar to MacDonald and Parke (1984), the behavior of the participating children was examined in a second social sphere, namely, interacting with their peers, in this case an unfamiliar age-mate. In this manner, the children's interactional style with their mothers could be compared with their behavior when interacting with peers. A similar pairing of the children's mothers also allowed an initial examination of the mothers' own interactional style with peers. Thus, the mothers' behavior in a situation somewhat analogous to that of their children could be explored and compared. A brief description of these aspects of this study will now be presented.

Each session involved 4 participants: 2 unacquainted first-grade children of the same sex, race, and level of social status (i.e., summed standardized positive nomination and rating scores) and their mothers. First, each mother–child pair was videotaped for 15 min while they played the same word-naming game used by Putallaz and Gottman (1981). Use of this game facilitated comparison of the study's results with those from earlier peer interaction research. In the second part of the study, the two children were videotaped playing together with a variety of toys for 15 min. Meanwhile, their mothers (in a separate room) were videotaped discussing, if they chose to, a suggested set of general issues related to children's social development.

Verbatim transcripts were made of all videotaped interactions between mother–child, child–child, and mother–mother pairs and then coded using a microanalytic system developed by Gottman, Parkhurst, and Bajjalieh (1982). This system consists of 42 content codes contained within the broader categories of demands, demands for the pair, inclusion, self-focus, emotive, social rules, and information and message clarification statements. These codes were developed to describe children's conversations exhaustively and to facilitate the study of social processes thought to be relevant to friendship. Thus, use of this coding system would facilitate the task of empirically deriving dimensions on which maternal behavior might be related to children's sociometric status and behavior. Further, because this coding system had been employed in prior work regarding children's social relationships (e.g., Gottman, 1983; Putallaz & Gottman, 1981), its use permitted comparison of the present study's results with those of earlier investigations. A lumping scheme introduced by Gottman (1983) was employed as a means of reducing the data to 18 codes. To further reduce the number of codes employed as well as to manage the potential problem of interdependence among the summary codes, principal component factor analyses were conducted separately for the mother–child, child–child, and mother–mother interaction data. The 42 children and their mothers for whom complete data were available across all three social contexts were included in these analyses.

To examine the relation between the behavior exhibited by the children during the mother–child interaction situation and their sociometric status, the children's factor scores were correlated with their social status scores. Both the Disagreeable factor, reflecting the children's disagreeableness and negative affect, and the Self-focused factor were related negatively to social status. Thus, consistent with previous peer research (e.g., Coie & Kupersmidt, 1983; Dodge, 1983; Putallaz & Gottman, 1981), the use of self-statements (talking about oneself) and disagreeableness was more characteristic of lower status than of higher status children when interacting with their mothers. Interestingly, the factor encompassing the children's attempts to influence their mothers' behavior in such indirect and socially acceptable ways as weak (face-saving) demands, jokes, and little questioning was related positively to their social status among peers. Only the Feeling factor, reflecting the children's tendency to focus on their own feelings and those of their mothers, was not significantly related to sociometric status.

To complete the picture of the mother–child interaction situation, the factors summarizing the mothers' interactions with their children were correlated with their children's social status scores. The Agreeable/Feeling factor was related positively to status, and there was a negative association with the Disagreeable/ Feeling factor. Thus, the mothers of higher status children seemed more apt to interact in a positive and agreeable manner with their children and to be more concerned with feelings, both their own as well as those of their children, than were mothers of lower status children. In contrast, mothers of lower status children exhibited more negative and controlling behavior with their children than did the mothers of higher status children. Only the factor encompassing the mothers' tendency to ask their children questions, both questions in general as well as questions concerning their feelings and opinions, was not correlated significantly with social status.

As with the mother–child interaction data, the factors generated from the child–child interaction data were correlated with the children's social status scores. Consistent with the peer interaction literature, there was a strong negative association between the Disagreeable factor and the children's social status, with the children displaying more of this disagreeable behavior having lower status. Neither of the other two factors, the Self-focus/Demand factor and the Feeling factor, correlated significantly with the children's social status scores.

Finally, the last set of behavioral factors, those derived from the mother–mother interaction, were correlated with the children's social status scores. Only one of the mother–mother factors was related significantly to the children's social status scores. Mothers of higher status children were more likely to discuss their feelings and opinions with another mother than were mothers of lower status children. The remaining factors, which reflected the mothers' tendency to talk a lot and their tendency to exchange information, were not associated with their children's status.

Thus, the results of the Putallaz (1987) research are also consistent with those discussed earlier. Again, parental warmth and control emerged as important dimensions in terms of children's social competence. Mothers of higher status children appeared to be more positive and agreeable and less disagreeable and demanding when interacting with their children than mothers of lower status children. In addition, as Baumrind (1967) suggested, maternal concern for feelings and open communication seemed to play a critical role. Mothers of higher status children were more concerned with soliciting and expressing feelings with their children than were mothers of lower status children. Even when interacting with another adult, mothers of higher status children seemed to discuss their feelings and opinions more than did mothers of less accepted children. Further, the behavior mothers exhibited with their children was highly related to the manner in which their children acted, both with them and with peers. Taken together, these results are consistent with (although, as will be discussed later, clearly not a confirmation of) a model suggesting that children acquire at least some of their social behavior repertoire through interaction with their mothers and that the character of such interaction, in turn, influences their sociometric status.

If mothers are influencing their children's behavior, then at least two possibilities concerning the nature of the influence of maternal behavior on children's behavior seem to suggest themselves from the Putallaz study for testing in future research. First, the results are consistent with the notion of modeling in that children in their interactions with peers seemed to model their mothers' general affective dispositions. Positive, agreeable mothers had positive, agreeable children, mothers who focused on feelings had children who focused on feelings, and disagreeable mothers had disagreeable children. This tendency to reflect their mothers' affective behavior was generally as strong when children were interacting with another child as it was when they were interacting with their mothers. It is also possible that these results reflect the secure home base notion in that the warmth of the mother–child relationship affects the child's social orientation toward peers.

There is also evidence in the present study that maternal behavior may be evoking responses that induce a complementary style in their children. For example, the mothers most likely to have children who attempted to influence their behavior were high on the Agreeable/Feeling factor rather than the factors involving greater display of control (i.e., the Disagreeable/Demanding factor or the Questioning factor). This result suggests that children's autonomy or assertiveness may be an induced derivative of autonomy-giving by mothers rather than a modeling of maternal behavior. In contrast, mothers high on the Disagreeable/Demanding factor tended to have children who were relatively high on the Disagreeable factor and Self-focused factor during their interactions with both mothers and peers, perhaps reflecting some degree of defensiveness on the children's part or need to protect their interests. Clearly, further research is needed to clarify the processes through which maternal behavior may be influencing child behavior, but both general modeling and response evocation appear to be likely possibilities.

The preceding discussion presumed that maternal behavior, at least in part, influenced children's social behavior. However, it is important to note that in actuality the direction of influence is unclear from these data. It may be indeed that disagreeable mothers cause their children to squabble with them or that positive mothers model this behavior for their children and that these behaviors subsequently transfer to interactions with peers. However, it is equally likely that difficult, squabbling children cause their mothers to respond to them in a disagreeable, demanding manner, or similarly, it may be easy for mothers to be positive with pleasant, compliant children. Regardless, there clearly does appear to be a relation between the behaviors mothers display when interacting with their children and the manner in which their children behave, both with their mothers and with peers.

Conclusion: A model of parental influence on sociometric status

The research reviewed in this chapter appears to converge in suggesting two general forms of parental influence on the development of children's sociometric status. The first form of influence is to directly affect children's acquisition of social behavior and social skills, and the second form of influence is more indirect and involves providing opportunities for children to be exposed to social interaction. These two types of parental influence will be discussed in turn.

Direct parental influence

The means by which parents directly influence children's social behavior can be summarized in terms of four forms of learning: modeling, operant conditioning, classical conditioning, and coaching. As suggested by the results of the literature previously reviewed, the simplest manner by which children may learn socially skillful behavior is through observing the behavior of their parents. It appears that such behaviors as altruism, aggression, communication style, as well as positive and negative social behaviors, can be acquired through a direct modeling process. Further, it seems that modeling may be involved in the acquisition of a general orientation toward social interaction through imitation, for example, of a parent's generally positive, approach-oriented interactional style or generally negative, avoidant social orientation (e.g., Putallaz, 1987; Rubin & Sloman, 1984). Of course, it is difficult to disentangle specific skill modeling from modeling of a social orientation in some instances. For example, it may be that lower status children seem more disagreeable because they are lacking skills to keep their disagreements from escalating, thus making their social interactions appear generally negative. Conversely, it is possible that peers or parents interacting with generally positive children behave in ways that evoke more agreeable, skillful behavior.

A second form of learning, classical conditioning, may also be involved in the development of general orientations toward social interaction. Several researchers (e.g., Baumrind, 1973; Hoffman, 1975; Easterbrooks & Lamb, 1979) have suggested that warm parents tend to have more socially effective children. Similarly, MacDonald and Parke (1984) and Putallaz (1987) found that parents who were more agreeable and warm had higher status children than parents who scored lower on this dimension. One possible explanation for these results (e.g., Easterbrooks & Lamb, 1979; Lieberman, 1977; Rubin & Sloman, 1984; Thompson & Lamb, 1983) is that children develop, through a process similar to classical conditioning, strong positive or negative associations with social interactions based upon their relationships with their parents. Thus, children of warm, positive parents would be expected to develop a generally positive approach orientation to social interaction, and children of negative parents would be expected to develop a generally negative and avoidant association with social interaction.

The third form of learning by which parents may influence the development of their children's social competence is operant conditioning, which apparently operates in several ways. For example, parents may directly reward socially desirable behavior and either punish or ignore socially inappropriate behavior. However, as Baumrind (1973) suggested, this form of operant learning is not independent of the classical conditioning notions just described. As a result of their positive interactions with their children, warm parents supposedly would be more effective reinforcement agents than more negative, cold parents, whose personal regard would be less valued by their children. Another form of operant process involves the evocation of desirable or undesirable behavior in children as a response to particular parental behaviors or styles. For example, several investigators (e.g., Eron, 1982; Lefkowitz et al., 1977) suggested that rejecting parents evoke hostile and aggressive behavior in their children. Supposedly, their actions make their children angry and frustrated, and the release of this frustration in the form of aggressive behavior results in tension reduction for the children, a form of reinforcement. Similarly, Putallaz (in press) reported that agreeable parents had children who utilized more appropriate methods to influence others than less

Mode of Parental Influence

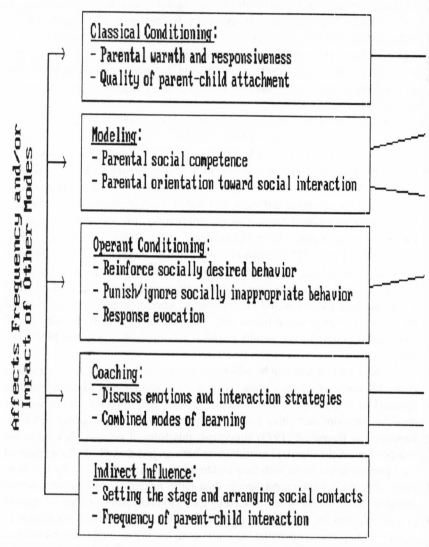

Figure 7.1. Proposed model of parental influence on sociometric status.

Effect on Child

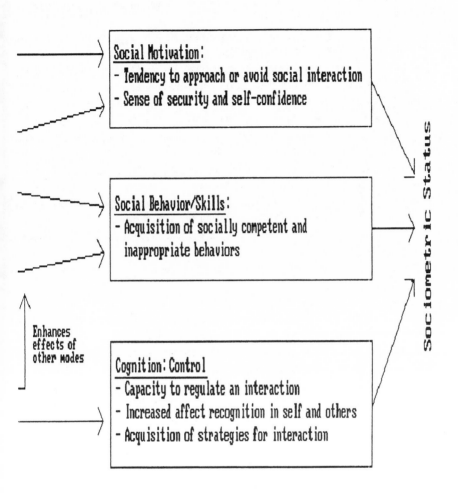

agreeable parents, whose children were more likely to be bossy and self-focused. One explanation for these results is that children of agreeable parents anticipate agreement and thus use more subtle, less directive influence styles than do children expecting disagreement.

In addition to these three forms of learning, it also appears that parents of socially effective children have conscious strategies for coaching their children. One aspect of such strategic coaching involves the combined utilization of the three learning processes just discussed in that parents attempt to have positive relationships with their children, model socially appropriate behavior, and reward socially desirable behavior while punishing or ignoring socially inappropriate behavior. A second aspect of such coaching attempts involves parent–child discussions concerning the behavior of the interactants as well as the children's emotional reactions during the interaction. As MacDonald and Parke (1984) suggested, such active discussion not only may increase the effectiveness of the learning that occurs during the interaction but also may help children learn to accurately assess their own reactions during the interaction as well as those of others and to develop appropriate responses to these reactions, a sort of metacognitive learning.

Indirect parental influence

A more indirect form of parental influence in the development of children's social behavior and social status also is suggested by the research reviewed in this chapter. The basic notion underlying such strategies is to provide an environment maximizing the probability that social interaction and appropriate skill acquisition will occur. Thus, for example, a friendly, warm, yet instructive home environment is likely to be one in which children engage in and discuss social interactions, thus increasing their opportunities for learning effective social behavior. In addition, parents may attempt to directly manipulate both the frequency and the type of social interactions in which their children engage, in the hope that the correct social behavior will be learned (Rubin & Sloman, 1984). Both of these strategies are indirect in the sense that the specific nature of the behavior in which the children engage is not controlled. However, such indirect influences should increase the probability of interaction and of the right type of interaction occurring.

Summary

The sorts of parental influence and the factors each is likely to affect in children are presented in the preliminary model portrayed in Figure 7.1. The purpose of this model is to provide a summary of the findings reported in this chapter. As can be seen, parental activities are portrayed as affecting the children's (a) general social orientation or social motivation, (b) social behavior or skills, and (c) cognitive understanding of social interaction, all of which in turn affect children's sociometric status. In other words, the children's own behavior is hypothesized to mediate the relation between parental behavior and children's social status. Also delineated in this model are hypothesized relations between the forms of direct parental influence and the types of behavior they affect in the child. For example, it is suggested within the figure that classical conditioning primarily affects children's social motivation or orientation, whereas modeling affects their acquisition of social behaviors. The more indirect forms of parental influence are hypothesized to affect the frequency of these direct parental influence modes or the strength of their impact on the children or both.

Thus, the model does more than summarize the sorts of parental styles and activities that have been shown to be related to children's social competence and sociometric status. It also presents a summary of the hypothesized mechanisms through which these styles and activities may have their effect. However, these are only hypotheses that require direct testing. In fact, the literature in this area has focused almost entirely on establishing relations between behaviors of parents and children. The nature of the relations and the processes through which they are established have been largely ignored. Such research is necessary and should form the focus of future efforts in this area. Fortunately, there is a strong base of consistent empirical findings from which to develop this research. Thus, the model presented in Figure 7.1 should be considered an invitation to future research, not a finished product.

References

Ainsworth, M. D. S. (1967). *Infancy in Uganda: Infant care and the growth of attachment.* Baltimore: Johns Hopkins University Press.

Ainsworth, M. D. S., & Bell, S. M. (1969). Some contemporary patterns of mother–infant interaction in the feeding situation. In A. Ambrose (Ed.), *Stimulation in early infancy* (pp. 133–170). New York: Academic Press.

Ainsworth, M. D. S., Bell, S. M., & Stayton, D. J. (1971). Individual differences in strange-situation behavior of one-year-olds. In H. R. Schaffer (Ed.), *The origins of human social relations* (pp. 17–57). London: Academic Press.

Ainsworth, M. D. S., Blehar, M., Waters, E., & Wall, S. (1978). *Patterns of attachment.* Hillsdale, NJ: Lawrence Erlbaum.

Arend, R., Gove, F., & Sroufe, L. A. (1979). Continuity of individual adaptation from infancy to kindergarten: A predictive study of ego-resiliency and curiosity in preschoolers. *Child Development, 50,* 950–959.

Armentrout, J. A. (1972). Sociometric classroom popularity and children's reports of parental child-rearing behaviors. *Psychological Reports, 30,* 261–262.

Asher, S. R. (1983). Social competence and peer status: Recent advances and future directions. *Child Development, 54,* 1427–1434.

Asher, S. R., & Renshaw, P. D. (1981). Children without friends: Social knowledge and social skills training. In S. R. Asher & J. M. Gottman (Eds.), *The development of children's friendships* (pp. 273–296). New York: Cambridge University Press.

Bakeman, R., & Brown, J. V. (1980). Early interaction: Consequences for social and mental development at three years. *Child Development, 51*, 437–447.

Bandura, A., & Walters, R. H. (1959). *Adolescent aggression.* New York: Ronald.

Baumrind, D. (1967). Child care practices anteceding three patterns of preschool behavior. *Genetic Psychology Monographs, 75*, 43–88.

Baumrind, D. (1968). *Manual for the preschool behavior Q-sort.* Berkeley: Institute of Human Development, University of California.

Baumrind, D. (1971). Current patterns of parental authority. *Developmental Psychology Monograph, 4*(1, Pt. 2).

Baumrind, D. (1973). The development of instrumental competence through socialization. In A. D. Pick (Ed.), *Minnesota symposia on child psychology* (Vol. 7, pp. 3–46). Minneapolis: University of Minnesota Press.

Baumrind, D. (1977, March). *Socialization determinants of personal agency.* Paper presented at the biennial meeting of the Society for Research in Child Development, New Orleans.

Bearison, D. J., & Cassel, T. Z. (1975). Cognitive decentration and social codes: Communication effectiveness in young children from differing family contexts. *Developmental Psychology, 11*, 29–36.

Becker, W. C. (1964). Consequences of different kinds of parental discipline. In M. L. Hoffman & L. W. Hoffman (Eds.), *Review of child development research* (Vol. 1, pp. 169–208). New York: Russell Sage Foundation.

Becker, W. C., Peterson, D. R., Hellmer, L. A., Shoemaker, D. J., & Quay, H. C. (1959). Factors in parental behavior and personality as related to problem behavior in children. *Journal of Consulting Psychology, 23*, 107–118.

Bell, R. Q. (1968). A reinterpretation of the direction of effects in studies of socialization. *Psychological Review, 75*, 81–95.

Bell, R. Q., & Harper, L. V. (1977). *Child effects on adults.* Hillsdale, NJ: Lawrence Erlbaum.

Brody, G. H., & Shaffer, D. R. (1982). Contributions of parents and peers to children's moral socialization. *Developmental Review, 2*, 31–75.

Bryant, B. K., & Crockenberg, S. B. (1980). Correlates and dimensions of prosocial behavior: A study of female siblings with their mothers. *Child Development, 51*, 529–544.

Clarke-Stewart, K. A. (1973). Interactions between mothers and their young children: Characteristics and consequences. *Monographs of the Society for Research in Child Development, 38*(Serial No. 153).

Clarke-Stewart, K. A., VanderStoep, L. P., & Killian, G. A. (1979). Analysis and replication of mother–child relations at two years of age. *Child Development, 50*, 777–793.

Coie, J. D., & Kupersmidt, J. B. (1983). A behavioral analysis of emerging social status in boys' groups. *Child Development, 54*, 1400–1416.

Dodge, K. A. (1983). Behavioral antecedents of peer social status. *Child Development, 54*, 1386–1399.

Easterbrooks, M., & Lamb, M. (1979). The relationship between quality of infant–mother attachment and infant competence in initial encounters with peers. *Child Development, 50*, 380–387.

Eckerman, C. O., & Stein, M. R. (1983). The toddler's emerging interactive skills. In K. H. Rubin & H. S. Ross (Eds.), *Peer relationships and social skills in childhood* (pp. 41–71). New York: Springer.

Elkins, D. (1958). Some factors related to the choice status of ninety eighth-grade children in a school society. *Genetic Psychology Monographs, 58*, 207–272.

Eron, L. D. (1982). Parent–child interaction, television violence, and aggression of children. *American Psychologist, 37*, 197–211.

Glueck, S., & Glueck, E. T. (1950). *Unraveling juvenile delinquency.* Cambridge: Harvard University Press.

Gottman, J. M. (1983). How children become friends. *Monographs of the Society for Research in Child Development, 48*(Serial No. 201).

Gottman, J. M., Parkhurst, J., & Bajjalieh, S. (1982). *Children's social speech during play: A coding manual.* Unpublished manuscript, University of Illinois at Urbana–Champaign.

Hartup, W. W. (1979). The two social worlds of childhood. *American Psychologist, 34,* 944–950.

Hartup, W. W., Glazer, J. A., & Charlesworth, R. (1967). Peer reinforcement and sociometric status. *Child Development, 38,* 1017–1024.

Hetherington, E. M., & Frankie, G. (1967). Effects of parental dominance, warmth, and conflict on imitation in children. *Journal of Personality and Social Psychology, 6,* 119–125.

Hinde, R., & Tamplin, A. (1983). Relations between mother–child interaction and behavior in preschool. *British Journal of Developmental Psychology, 1,* 231–257.

Hoffman, M. L. (1960). Power assertion by the parent and its impact on the child. *Child Development, 31,* 129–143.

Hoffman, M. L. (1963). Child-rearing practices and moral development: Generalizations for empirical research. *Child Development, 34,* 295–318.

Hoffman, M. L. (1975). Altruistic behavior and the parent–child relationship. *Journal of Personality and Social Psychology, 31,* 937–943.

Hymel, S., & Rubin, K. H. (1985). Children with peer relationship and social skills problems: Conceptual, methodological, and developmental issues. In G. J. Whitehurst (Ed.), *Annals of child development* (Vol. 2, pp. 251–297). Greenwich, CT: JAI Press.

Jensen, L., Peery, C., Adams, G., & Gaynard, L. (1981). Maternal behavior and the development of empathy in preschool children. *Psychological Reports, 48,* 879–884.

Kolvin, I., Garside, R., Nicol, A., MacMillan, A., Wolstenholme, F., & Leitch, I. (1977). Familial and sociological correlates of behavioural and sociometric deviance in 8-year-old children. In P. J. Graham (Ed.), *Epidemiology of childhood disorders* (pp. 195–222). New York: Academic Press.

Lefkowitz, M., Eron, L., Walder, L., & Huesmann, L. (1977). *Growing up to be violent: A longitudinal study of the development of aggression.* New York: Pergamon Press.

Lieberman, A. (1977). Preschoolers' competence with a peer: Relations with attachment and peer experience. *Child Development, 48,* 1277–1287.

Louderville, S., & Main, M. (1981). Security of attachment, compliance, and maternal training methods in the second year of life. *Developmental Psychology, 17,* 289–299.

Maccoby, E. (1980). *Social development: Psychological growth and the parent–child relationship.* New York: Harcourt Brace Jovanovich.

Maccoby, E., & Martin, J. (1983). Socialization in the context of the family: Parent–child interaction. In E. M. Hetherington (Ed.), *Handbook of child psychology: Vol. 4. Socialization, personality, and social development* (pp. 1–101, 4th ed.). New York: John Wiley.

MacDonald, K., & Parke, R. (1984). Bridging the gap: Parent–child play interaction and peer interactive competence. *Child Development, 55,* 1265–1277.

Main, M., & Weston, D. (1981). The quality of the toddler's relationship to mother and to father: Related to conflict behavior and the readiness to establish new relationships. *Child Development, 52,* 932–940.

Marshall, H. R., & McCandless, B. R. (1957). A study in prediction of social behavior of preschool children. *Child Development, 28,* 149–159.

Martin, B. (1975). Parent–child relations. In F. D. Horowitz (Ed.), *Review of child development research* (Vol. 4, pp. 463–540). Chicago: University of Chicago Press.

Matas, L., Arend, R. A., & Sroufe, L. A. (1978). Continuity of adaptation in the second year: The relationship between quality of attachment and later competence. *Child Development, 49,* 547–556.

McCord, J., & McCord, W. (1958). The effects of parental models on criminality. *Journal of Social Issues, 14*, 66–75.

Pastor, D. L. (1981). The quality of mother–infant attachment and its relationship to toddlers' initial sociability with peers. *Developmental Psychology, 17*, 326–335.

Putallaz, M. (1983). Predicting children's sociometric status from their behavior. *Child Development, 54*, 1417–1426.

Putallaz, M. (1987). Maternal behavior and sociometric status. *Child Development, 58*, 324–340.

Putallaz, M., & Gottman, J. M. (1981). An interactional model of children's entry into peer groups. *Child Development, 52*, 402–408.

Rubin, K. H., & Daniels-Beirness, T. (1983). Concurrent and predictive correlates of sociometric status in kindergarten and grade 1 children. *Merrill-Palmer Quarterly, 29*, 337–351.

Rubin, Z., & Sloman, J. (1984). How parents influence their children's friendships. In M. Lewis (Ed.), *Beyond the dyad* (pp. 223–250). New York: Plenum Press.

Sameroff, A., & Seifer, R. (1983). Familial risk and child competence. *Child Development, 54*, 1254–1268.

Simonds, M. P., & Simonds, J. F. (1981). Relationship of maternal parenting behaviors to preschool children's temperament. *Child Psychiatry and Human Development, 12*, 19–31.

Sroufe, L. A., Schork, E., Motti, F., Lawroski, N., & LaFreniere, P. (1983). The role of affect in social competence. In C. Izard, J. Kagan, & R. Zajonc (Eds.), *Emotions, cognitions, and behavior* (pp. 289–319). New York: Plenum Press.

Symonds, P. M. (1939). *The psychology of parent–child relationships*. New York: Appleton-Century-Crofts.

Thompson, R. A., & Lamb, M. E. (1983). Security of attachment and stranger sociability in infancy. *Developmental Psychology, 19*, 184–191.

Waters, E., Wippman, J., & Sroufe, L. A. (1979). Attachment, positive affect, and competence in the peer group: Two studies in construct validation. *Child Development, 50*, 821–829.

Winder, C. L., & Rau, L. (1962). Parental attitudes associated with social deviance in preadolescent boys. *Journal of Abnormal and Social Psychology, 64*, 418–424.

Zahn-Waxler, C., Radke-Yarrow, M., & King, R. A. (1979). Child-rearing and children's prosocial initiations toward victims of distress. *Child Development, 50*, 319–330.

8 Social withdrawal in childhood: Developmental pathways to peer rejection

Kenneth H. Rubin, Lucy J. LeMare, and Susan Lollis

During the 1960s and the early 1970s, many North American psychologists participated in a cognitive development revolution. The rediscovery of Piaget's theory and the accompanying notion that intellectual development occurs via active experience with the physical, impersonal environment led to a burgeoning of laboratory experiments concerning the development of cognitive skills (see Elkind & Flavell, 1969, and Sigel & Hooper, 1968, for classic examples).

Interestingly, Piagetian theory also played a critical role in stimulating research in the 1970s and 1980s on peer relations and social skills. One of the earliest psychological statements implicating peers in normal social development emanated from Piaget's (1926, 1932) early work concerning communicative development and the growth of moral judgmental skills. In his writings, Piaget noted that it is the cooperation and mutuality engendered in peer relationships that allow children to gain broader cognitive perspectives about their own social worlds. Piaget considered very young children to be egocentric and neither willing nor able to appreciate the viewpoints, intentions, and feelings of their social partners. However, he suggested that with the onset of peer play, a unique opportunity occurs to establish egalitarian and reciprocal relationships, as well as to experience conflict and negotiation. Such conflict and negotiation, whether centered around objects or different perspectives of the social world, were thought to hold the power of eliciting compromise and reciprocity. These encounters with peers were thought to bring about the realization that positive and productive social interaction is gained through cooperation with and sensitivity to one's social partner.

Sullivan (1953) also considered peer relationships to play a significant role in development. The major tenet of Sullivan's interpersonal theory of psychiatry

Preparation of this chapter and the collection of the data reported herein were supported, in part, by grants from Health and Welfare Canada and the Ontario Mental Health Foundation. We would like to thank Jay Belsky and Al Cheyne for their helpful, constructive criticisms of earlier drafts of this chapter.

The section "Sociometric Nominations" was coauthored by Kevin Murphy.

was that an individual's personality was shaped by that individual's social relationships. Peers first became implicated as shaping agents in the juvenile stage (elementary school years). During this stage, peers were suggested to play causal roles in building the framework for the child's gradual understanding of (a) social rules for cooperation and competition and (b) social roles such as deference and dominance. In the next stage, preadolescence, Sullivan speculated that children's peer, and particularly chumship, relationships fostered "genuine" development in the conceptualization of equality, mutuality, and reciprocity as central, defining characteristics of intimate relationships.

Learning and social-learning theorists and researchers also have extolled the benefits of childhood peer interaction. Peers serve as control agents for each other, punishing or ignoring nonnormative behaviors and reinforcing culturally appropriate activities. Prosocial, aggressive, and sex-typed behaviors, among others, can be modified by exposure to peer models (see Hartup, 1983, for a review). Furthermore, peers can serve directly as cognition and behavior change agents; peer tutoring has been shown to promote developmental advances in the areas of altruism (Staub, 1975), self-esteem, and academic prowess (East, 1976).

The perspectives described above lead, naturally, to the conclusion that peer interaction and peer relationships are important forces in the development of competence during childhood. Furthermore, one could well posit that children who do not interact with their peers, who withdraw from their social community, may be at risk for problems in the social-cognitive and social-behavioral domains. It is this group of withdrawn, isolated children who represent the focus of our chapter.

In this book, contributors are concerned with the correlates and consequences of rejection from the peer group. Our chapter focuses on children who are behaviorally inhibited and who refrain from interacting with peers. It is our belief that this group of children may be at risk for peer rejection as well as for other difficulties of a socioemotional nature.

The clinical literature extant reveals a variety of views concerning whether or not childhood withdrawal represents a risk factor. Some psychologists suggest that withdrawal in childhood is not especially problematic (e.g., Kohlberg, La-Crosse, & Ricks, 1972); others indicate that child social "isolates," however identified, are sufficiently deviant from their childhood peer group to merit close attention and intervention (e.g., Strain & Kerr, 1981). One purpose of this chapter is to address this controversy. In so doing we will review the literature concerning the concomitant and predictive correlates of social withdrawal in childhood, drawing largely, though not exclusively, from the findings of the Waterloo Longitudinal Project.

A second issue to be addressed concerns the identification of socially withdrawn children. One method that researchers often use to identify children experiencing peer relationship difficulties is sociometry. Other chapters in this volume will attest to the wide employment of this technique for identifying *rejected* children. Although sociometric status is one viable method of identifying rejected children with peer relationship problems, we believe that one cannot rely on this method to identify withdrawn children. The theoretical positions presented above implicate peer *interaction* in healthy development. However, we will demonstrate that there is no one-to-one correspondence between any sociometric category and behavioral indices of social withdrawal. Thus, the second aim of this chapter is to consider the procedures typically used to identify socially withdrawn children and discuss their relative strengths and weaknesses.

A final purpose of the present chapter is to propose and explore a developmental connection between social withdrawal and peer rejection. We will present two possible ways by which children eventually become identified as withdrawn *and* rejected. The central point is that these pathways lead to seemingly similar characterizations of children as withdrawn and rejected; yet, the development of withdrawn and rejected status and the outcomes or prognoses for these two groups of children are quite different. Because these developmental pathways provide a conceptual framework for our chapter, we present them first.

Social withdrawal in childhood: A conceptual framework

In this chapter we will use the terms *socially withdrawn children* and *social isolates* interchangeably to describe those children who interact with their peers much less frequently than is the norm for their particular age-group. Of course, we recognize that there are many possible reasons for the development of social withdrawal in childhood. We suggest two possibilities. These two possible pathways are described, in greater detail, in Rubin and Lollis (1988).

From the outset, we want to make clear that the pathways we propose are highly speculative. Indeed, our intention in outlining these pathways is to provide researchers with some useful, conceptual heuristics from which active, longitudinal research programs concerning peer relations may emerge.

Setting conditions

Drawing from the seminal work of Bronfenbrenner (1979; Bronfenbrenner & Crouter, 1983) concerning the significance of ecological factors in human development, both of our pathways begin by suggesting that negative environmental circumstances provide important setting conditions for the development of familial and extrafamilial relationships. Thus, we speculate that strains on financial resources and stresses brought on by living under difficult conditions (e.g., urban poverty, crowding) may have a negative impact on the ways that mothers interact with their newborn infants. Being poor, living in crowded quarters, and not having access to desired goods must assuredly result in maternal feelings of stress and frustration, which can be transferred to the budding mother–infant relationship (Belsky, Robins, & Gamble, 1984). We speculate further that these socioecological conditions have a striking impact on familial relations throughout the course of childhood. Loss of income or employment, domestic resettlement, and loss of life-supporting resources may all negatively influence marital and parent–child relations not only in the child's infancy but also at other points during childhood (e.g., Alvarez, 1985; Belsky, 1980; Elder, 1974; Kemper & Reichler, 1976).

Acting in concert with these socioecological setting conditions are *personal–social setting conditions*. These conditions, which include variables like parental mental health (e.g., depression, schizophrenia) and the availability of familial and extrafamilial support networks (friends, community agencies), may exacerbate or inhibit the negative impact of certain socioecological settings. Thus, one can envision an interactional model whereby the presence of negative socioecological conditions *and* negative personal–social conditions has a more deleterious impact on parent–child and other familial relations than the presence of negative conditions of only one sort. On the other hand, it has been found that mothers living in poverty feel less stress and are less punitive and authoritarian in their relations with their children when they receive socioemotional support from husbands or boyfriends, friends, and relatives (Colletta, 1979; Zur-Szprio & Longfellow, 1981). And, in the opposite case, the presence of personal–social stressors in the absence of poor socioecological conditions can and does seem to exact a toll from the parent–child relationship. Current work on divorce, separation, and marital hostility (e.g., Hetherington, 1979) and on parental mental health status (Zahn-Waxler, Cummings, McKnew, & Radke-Yarrow, 1984) is suggestive of the impact of negative personal–social conditions.

A final setting condition that likely influences the establishment and maintenance of parent–child relations stems from the parents' personal belief system concerning children in general and child rearing in particular. At the very general level, a parent who did not want a baby to begin with may not provide the infant with an emotionally responsive and sensitive environment during infancy. This negative attitudinal set is likely to have ramifications for the development of the parent–child relationship.

Parental beliefs as reflected in statements like "spare the rod, spoil the child" or "children should be seen, not heard" are also likely to influence the parent–child relationships as well as the child's development of social skills. Clearly, when negative attitudes and beliefs are crossed with negative socioecological and personal–social setting conditions, the family environment will not be optimal for the healthy development of children.

To summarize, we propose that the establishment of positive parent–child relationships is affected by the setting conditions described above. We propose further that positive changes in these setting conditions can alter negative developments in personal relationships and social skills. Alternatively, negative changes in setting conditions may change the quality of previously positive relationships. Needless to say, these statements, although supported by a number of studies, require further investigation.

Prior to describing the first pathway, we remind the reader again that our developmental scenarios are speculative. Our goal is to make conceptual links between many disparate areas of inquiry. As we see it, the pathways represent sets of "if–then" causal statements that require direct study in the future.

Pathway 1

Our first developmental scenario begins with an infant who is perceived by his or her parents as being of difficult temperament (see Figure 8.1). Although it would be unreasonable to suggest that all such babies are at risk, one might predict that fussy, overactive, difficult-to-soothe babies born into undesirable situations such as those described above may receive early socialization experiences that are less than optimal (e.g., Sameroff & Chandler, 1975). Consistent with this position is the recent work of Vaughn, Taraldson, Crichton, and Egeland (1981) and Booth (1985), who studied samples of low-income, high-risk mothers. These investigators reported that temperamentally difficult infants were being raised by mothers who were more aggressive, less nurturant, more anxious, and less responsive than mothers of nondifficult babies. The setting conditions described above may be critical mediating factors in the developing relationship between mothers and their temperamentally difficult infants. It is reasonable to suggest that mothers of temperamentally difficult infants who have social and financial support will be less likely to react negatively to their babies than will "high-risk" mothers (Crockenberg, 1981) such as those studied by Vaughn et al. (1981) and Booth (1985). Thus, for some families, the *interaction* between endogenous temperamental characteristics of infants and socioecological and personal–social setting conditions may promote parental socialization practices that result in the establishment of insecure, perhaps hostile, early infant/toddler–parent relationships.

The research of Egeland and Farber (1984) lends some support for this hypothesis. These investigators have reported that poor maternal caretaking practices are associated with and predictive of insecure, *avoidant* attachment status. Similarly, Ainsworth, Bell, and Stayton (1971) have argued that mothers of avoidant, insecure babies are likely to reject their infants and to be more abrupt and interfering in the handling of their babies. Once again, it is very important to note that these negative maternal socialization practices are often associated with

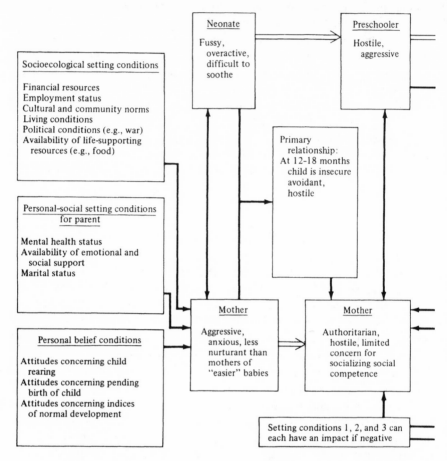

Figure 8.1. Pathway 1.

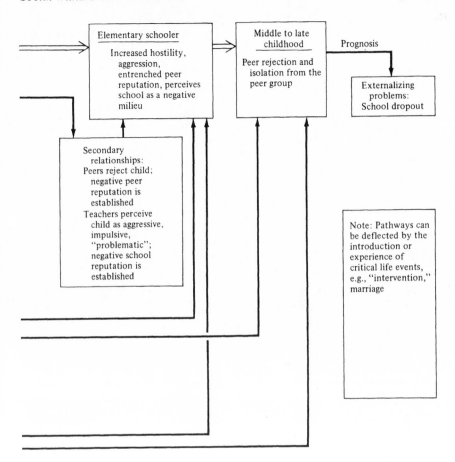

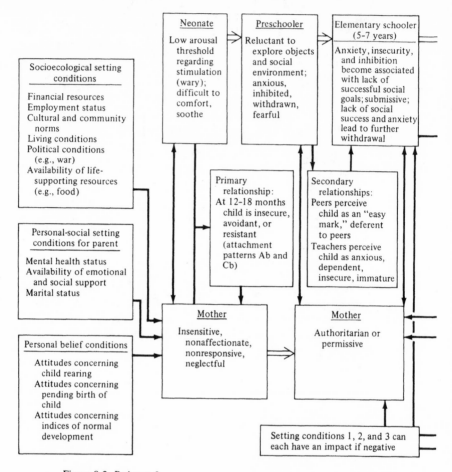

Figure 8.2. Pathway 2.

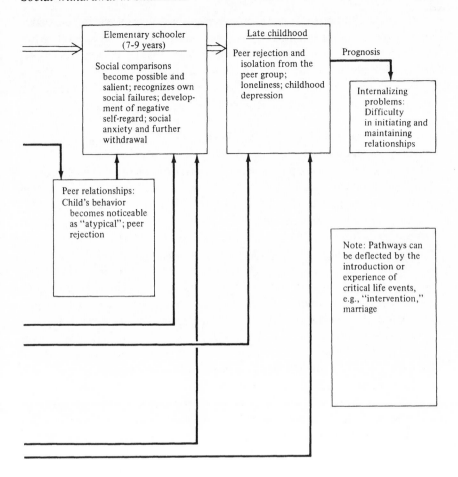

environmental and personal stressors such as poverty, unemployment, premature birth of the infant, or maternal depression. Indirect evidence in support of this reasoning includes recent research by Crockenberg (1981), who noted that mothers' perceptions of social support are associated with security of infant attachment. Crockenberg revealed further that such support was especially important when the infants were irritable or when the mother–child dyads were under stress.

Taken together, the results of the aforementioned studies suggest that there may be a group of infants and toddlers who at 12 or 18 months are experiencing insecure and/or hostile relationships with their primary caregivers. Psychologists (e.g., Main, 1981; Sroufe, 1983) have suggested that these babies (labeled *insecure avoidant*) harbor hostile feelings toward their mothers. Their "felt insecurity and anger" is demonstrated by their avoidance of the mother, their seeming independence in novel settings, and their lack of affect and proximity-seeking behavior when they are left alone in "strange [i.e., novel] situations" (Ainsworth, Blehar, Waters, & Wall, 1978). The anger and frustration with their primary caregivers become evident (and perhaps displaced) in later years when avoidant babies are observed interacting with their peers. Researchers have shown that these infants, when they reach the toddler and preschool years, demonstrate hostile, aggressive behavior patterns in the company of their agemates (Jacobson, Tianen, Wille, & Aytch, 1987; Pastor, 1981; Sroufe, 1983). From these data it is not difficult to speculate that because aggressive behavior is a salient, aversive, and stable phenomenon, it can lead to peer rejection (e.g., LaFreniere & Sroufe, 1985). Indeed, one of the most common predictors of social rejection in the early and middle childhood years is the display of aggressive behavior (e.g., Coie & Kupersmidt, 1983; Rubin & Daniels-Beirness, 1983). It follows, logically, that children who are rejected by their peers may soon become isolated from their community of age-mates (Coie, 1985). That is, the peers of rejected children may refuse to play with them. Thus, following the establishment of negative peer reputations, children may be found to play alone significantly more often than was the case prior to rejection.

One can envision further that those children who are hostile, aggressive, and rejected by peers will become more noticeable to their preschool and elementary school teachers (e.g., Rubin & Clark, 1983). Teachers who are sufficiently concerned with these children would be likely to provide the parents with negative feedback about aggressive, in-school behaviors. These external appraisals, in concert with the already hostile home environment, may lead the parents to become more controlling, demanding, and authoritarian in efforts to counter their children's oppositional, coercive, and aggressive behaviors (Baumrind, 1967). Authoritarian parents are known to use commands and directives that focus on direct control of their children's ongoing behaviors rather than using teaching techniques that focus on the consequences of aggressive, impulsive behaviors for others in the social environment (Sigel, 1982). In short, a cycle of family coercion can be predicted, with the aggressive child being subjected to great parental control efforts, which serve only to exacerbate the child's frustration and hostility within the familial milieu (e.g., Patterson, 1976).

To summarize, one developmental pathway to social isolation may stem from the interactions between temperament factors, socialization factors, and setting condition factors that promote the development of hostile primary relationships. The negative affect fostered by these early parent–child relationships may result in inappropriate, negative, and aggressive interchanges with peers. These interchanges, in turn, may result in peer rejection and the exclusion of the aggressive child from the peer group. Rejection and exclusion may then result in higher-than-normal frequencies of nonsocial, solitary activities in the focal child. This first developmental scenario, then, results in a sociometrically rejected *and* socially withdrawn child. In this case, however, social withdrawal or isolation from the community of peers may be an imposed consequence rather than due to traitlike dispositions such as behavioral inhibition or wariness (Garcia-Coll, Kagan, & Reznick, 1984). Keeping this last statement in mind, we move to our second developmental pathway.

Pathway 2

Our second scenario (Figure 8.2) begins with an infant who, from the outset, may be biologically predisposed to have a lower threshold for arousal when confronted with social stimulation and novelty (e.g., Buss & Plomin, 1984; Kagan, Reznick, Clarke, Snidman, & Garcia-Coll, 1984). When faced with novelty or uncertainty, these babies may be very difficult to soothe and comfort. It is possible that some mothers (and fathers) may find such displays aversive and thus may react to their babies with hostility, insensitivity, lack of affection, nonresponsivity, or neglect or some combination of these responses. Interestingly, all of these parental behaviors are predictive of insecure attachment relationships at 12 and 18 months (e.g., Ainsworth et al., 1978; Belsky, Rovine, & Taylor, 1984). This interplay of temperamental, socialization, and early-relationship factors will, in all probability, be mediated by the setting conditions described earlier. In cases where support systems are absent, the child will be living in an already-insecure family environment. For the dispositionally inhibited infant, the familial circumstances may lead to an exaggerated sense of insecurity in toddlerhood and early childhood. For these children, their felt insecurity may further exacerbate behavioral wariness and inhibition in novel social and impersonal settings.

The behavioral wariness and inhibition in the face of novelty describes the play behaviors of specific subsets of both A (avoidant) and C (resistant) babies (Pastor, 1981; Sroufe, 1983); it also describes the behaviors of toddlers who have been identified by parents and psychologists as "behaviorally inhibited" (Garcia-Coll et al., 1984; Kagan et al., 1984). In novel settings these babies cling to their parents and refrain from exploring both persons and objects (Kagan et al., 1984; Waters, Vaughn, & Egeland, 1980). One can speculate that these children will avoid the peer milieu when they first enter school, and as such, they may be those whom psychologists identify as socially withdrawn during the preschool and kindergarten years (Reznick, Kagan, & Snidman, 1985; Rubin, 1982b; Rubin & Borwick, 1984).

Reticence to explore novel, out-of-home settings may preclude establishing normal social relationships and developing those social and cognitive skills presumably encouraged by these relationships. It is easy to envision a circular effect, with the failure to develop social and cognitive skills leading to further anxiety and withdrawal from the social arena. These speculations are entirely consistent with attachment theory (Sroufe, 1983) and Sullivan's (1953) personality theory. In short, it is conceivable that social isolation and personal feelings of anxiety and insecurity may become increasingly exacerbated through their interplay.

We should point out that during the preschool and early elementary school years, teachers may express some concern for these initially withdrawn and anxious children. Indeed, parents may receive feedback concerning the "problems" being evidenced. Such disclosures may prompt the initially nonaffectionate, insensitive, or hostile parent to maladaptive courses of action. On the one hand, a parent may recognize that the inhibited child has developed deficiencies in dealing with the academic or social milieu. Such recognition may motivate the parent to teach directly and autocratically those skills deficient in the child's repertoire. To use terms familiar to those who study socialization processes, the parent may become increasingly authoritarian and directive (Baumrind, 1967). A second option that may be taken by parents is the adoption of a laissez-faire or permissive attitude (Baumrind, 1967). Presumably such a parental response would be guided by an attempt to place the blame for the child's failures on sources external to the parent. Choice of this option and the parent's attempt to attribute the child's difficulties to supposedly inalterable, endogenous variables may result in increased parental neglect of the child's problems. Such an attribution might lead parents to distance themselves psychologically and physically from their children. Interestingly, at this time there is a virtual lack of knowledge concerning parental attributions for their children's successful and unsuccessful development of social skills and relationships (one notable recent exception is the work of Dix and Grusec, 1985). However, one can reasonably posit that attributing the causes for a child's incompetence to the child, to oneself as parent, or to other factors ought to lead to different parental socialization responses.

At any rate, the result of the interplay between familial relationships and teacher perceptions might be reinforcement of the child's own feelings of anxiety and insecurity. Such feelings could lead to exaggerated rates of withdrawal from the peer milieu. It is important to note that during the early years of childhood, solitary or nonsocial activity is quite normal (Rubin, Fein, & Vandenberg, 1983); consequently, there is little reason for nonsocial players to be singled out by their peers as displaying behaviors deviant from age-group play norms. However, children do become increasingly sociable, or interactive, with age (Greenwood, Todd, Hops, & Walker, 1982; Parten, 1932). Thus, it may be that during the middle and later years of childhood, individuals who are behaviorally inhibited, who continue to remain on the periphery of the peer group, and who are insecure and anxious may become increasingly salient to their age-mates (Younger & Boyko, 1987). Their deviance from age-appropriate social and emotional norms may well result in the establishment of negative peer reputations. It appears, then, that our second developmental scenario, like the first scenario, could lead to a socially withdrawn *and* sociometrically rejected child. In this second pathway, however, withdrawal is linked to dispositional inhibition and insecurity; rejection occurs when the child's behavioral withdrawal and emotional insecurity become salient to the peer group.

Possible prognoses

The developmental pathways described suggest that the sources of behavioral isolation in childhood can differ in individual cases. Furthermore, the problems associated with these different cases also may vary. For Pathway 1, the child's rejection is associated with hostile, aggressive behavior; for Pathway 2 rejection is associated with anxious, insecure, withdrawn behavior. Following our first scenario, one might predict that the aggressive child who is rejected by his or her peers may react with increased hostility. One possible outcome for this child may be the development of externalizing disorders (e.g., delinquency; Kupersmidt, 1983).

From the second scenario, one might predict that the anxious, inhibited child who is rejected by the peer group may react with further withdrawal from the social milieu. Self-recognition that she or he is rejected or is failing with regard to the social world may elicit feelings of distress and despair in the child. Furthermore, if the child's parents react to his or her feelings and behavior in the manners described, the child's negative perceptions of self-competence may become heightened. We might, therefore, predict that the logical outcomes for the child who follows Pathway 2 are problems of an internalizing nature (e.g., depression, anxiety disorders).

In keeping with the focus of this chapter, our primary interest is with the child in the second scenario: the behaviorally inhibited child who from the early years of life interacts minimally with peers. We focus on the initially withdrawn child because, as we noted earlier, the notion that the withdrawn/anxious/inhibited behavioral syndrome comprises a risk factor is a controversial one. Some psychologists have suggested that socially withdrawn children may be at risk for adolescent or adult psychopathology (e.g., Achenbach & Edelbrock, 1981; Strain & Kerr, 1981; Wanlass & Prinz, 1982). Indeed, social withdrawal has been implicated in three DSM III categories of psychological disturbance: shyness disorder, adjustment disorder with withdrawal, and introverted disorder. Other psychologists, however, drawing on retrospective data or on follow-through studies of clinically identified samples of children, indicate that social withdrawal is not a risk factor (e.g., Michael, Morris, & Soroker, 1957; Robins, 1966).

The fact that controversy exists concerning the predictive significance of childhood withdrawal emanates from the paucity of data concerning the phenomenon. Simply put, the correlates and consequences of childhood social withdrawal are virtually unknown. This lack of data is problematic on two accounts. First, the controversy concerning withdrawal as a risk factor will remain unsettled until methodologically strong and conceptually based longitudinal programs of research provide relevant information. Second, despite the controversy and lack of empirical data, large numbers of psychologists are developing intervention programs designed to ameliorate the negative concomitants and effects of social withdrawal (e.g., Furman, Rahe, & Hartup, 1979; Strain & Kerr, 1981; Strain, Kerr, & Raglund, 1982).

In the remaining sections of this chapter, we will review research concerning the correlates and consequences of social withdrawal in childhood. First, however, we will describe those procedures that are being used to identify withdrawn children.

Identifying socially withdrawn children

Four procedures have been used to identify children who researchers believe are withdrawn. These procedures are peer nominations on sociometric measures, peer and teacher assessments of social behavior, and behavioral observations concerning rate and quality of peer interaction. These four procedures are also used to identify children to whom other social status or behavioral labels might apply, for example, rejected, popular, or aggressive children. In this section we describe and compare procedures used to identify withdrawn children and address the distinctions between social withdrawal and the other categorical labels that these procedures yield.

Hymel and Rubin (1985) give three basic reasons for utilizing information from peers to learn about children who are experiencing social difficulties. First, peers are "inside" sources of information, and as such, they can identify or judge behaviors and characteristics that are important to those who determine a child's integration within the peer group. Second, information from peers is based on many extended and varied experiences with the target child. Thus, for example, peers may be aware of infrequent but psychologically significant events that lead to particular social reputations. Third, information from peers is obtained from multiple observers with whom a target child has likely had different relationships and who, therefore, view the child from a variety of perspectives. Taken together, these reasons provide ample justification for using peers as sources of information concerning children's reputations and behaviors.

Sociometric nominations

The use of sociometric nominations to study children's peer relations is accelerating; however, it is certainly not a new methodological development. From the time of Moreno's (1953) original work (see also Thompson, 1962), investigators have suggested implicitly that sociometric nominations can be used to identify children who lack friends or who are socially isolated. The wisdom of inferring that sociometric nominations can be employed to identify children who are isolated or withdrawn in the behavioral sense is a point we shall return to; first, we will describe the procedures generally used to gather nomination data.

Traditionally, children are required to name a number of classmates (usually three to five) with whom they *do* and *do not* like to play or work. Typically, children who receive very few positive and negative nominations are regarded as "neglected" (e.g., Coie, Dodge, & Coppotelli, 1982; Gronlund, 1959; Peery, 1979). This group can be distinguished from those who receive many positive nominations only ("popular" children) and those who receive many negative nominations only ("rejected" children). Thus, conceptually, a distinction is made between sociometrically rejected and neglected children; the former group is thought to be actively disliked, whereas the latter group is represented as being overlooked or ignored by peers.

It is probable that researchers who have used nomination data to identify neglected children have never explicitly equated this sociometrically targeted group with children who are behaviorally isolated or withdrawn. Yet, the literature is full of suggestions to this effect. A perusal of relevant publications indicates that the aforementioned equation requires only a small inferential step.

Consider the following examples. Thompson (1962) in a review of the nomination literature wrote that "a child who was chosen by no other member of the group on any basis would be considered a social 'isolate'" (p. 483). Moore (1967, p. 232) has referred to sociometrically neglected children as "isolates." More recently, Coie, Dodge, and Coppotelli (1982) wrote that these children "are sometimes referred to as *isolates* and sometimes as neglected children" (p.

558; italics added), reinforcing the belief that isolation and neglect are inter-changeable terms. Dodge, Murphy, and Buchsbaum (1984) have written that children "who respond with *withdrawal* have a high probability of achieving *neglected* status among peers" and "that the characteristic behavior of *neglected* children is *withdrawal*" (p. 171; italics added). Indeed, the first author of the present chapter, in a recent review written with Hymel (Hymel & Rubin, 1985), wrote that there appears to be "some commonality between neglected and with-drawn" children (p. 289) and that "neglected children tend to exhibit more withdrawn patterns of behavior" (p. 290).

Finally, the ease with which researchers and psychologists may infer that sociometric neglect and withdrawal are equivalent phenomena is demonstrated in the following quotation:

These two facts about neglected boys – that they rarely offend others and that they seem to be able to become socially outgoing in new, small-group situations – may account for the evidence that they are not a group that is at long-term risk because of their social adjustment. In a follow-up study of socially withdrawn and isolated children who had originally been referred to the Dallas Child Guidance Clinic but not treated, Morris, Soroker, and Burrus (1954) found that these children were not significantly at risk for psychiatric disorder. (Coie & Kupersmidt, 1983, p. 1415)

It seems clear to us that there is a danger of inferring equivalence between sociometric and behavioral prototypes. We present the equation as a danger because of the suggestions made in describing our second developmental path-way (Figure 5.2). We *do* believe that severely withdrawn children who are insecure and anxious are at risk, even though we agree with others (e.g., Coie, 1985) that sociometrically neglected children are neither concurrently nor pro-spectively problematic.

Is there any empirical evidence to support the conceptual equation of so-ciometric neglect and social withdrawal? In their work on the determinants of sociometric status, Coie and Kupersmidt (1983) did not find that neglected children interacted less frequently with their peers than did "average" children. Dodge (1983) did find, however, that neglected children played alone more often than average children; however, his neglected group engaged in as much solitary play as rejected children. Furthermore, rejected children have been found to display more solitary "inappropriate play" than both neglected and average children (Coie & Kupersmidt, 1983). Finally, Dodge, Coie, and Brakke (1982) found that neglected children demonstrated more solitary task-appropriate ac-tivity than any other sociometric group. Rejected children engaged in more solitary task-inappropriate activity than all other groups. Thus, both neglected and rejected children appeared to display greater amounts of solitary activity than other sociometric groups. Dodge et al. (1982) further demonstrated that the neglected group was the least likely of any of the sociometric groups to initiate prosocial approaches. These data, especially the observation that neglected children engage in a high frequency of solitary task-appropriate activity, led the authors to suggest that neglected children are best described as shy in their peer interactions. However, it is extremely important to note that the data show that neglected children were as likely as all other groups to receive initiations from others. Indeed, they were approached more often (although not significantly so) than all groups other than the popular group! Because approachability is not suggestive of neglect, the conceptual meaning of this sociometric category begins to escape us. In short, given the three studies described above, the data do not allow one to conclude unequivocally that sociometric neglect can be equated with social withdrawal (for further discussion see Rubin, Hymel, LeMare, & Rowden, 1989).

Neither the conceptual analyses nor the data extant make a strong case for inferring that sociometrically neglected children are socially withdrawn. Although we recognize that it may not have been the intent of researchers to create such an equation, the potential of the sociometric nomination method for inappropriate inferences makes it unsuitable for the identification of withdrawn children.

Peer assessments of behavior

A number of procedures have been designed to assess children's perceptions of their peers' behaviors. Typical of these measures are the Pupil Evaluation Inventory (PEI) (Pekarik, Prinz, Liebert, Weintraub, & Neale, 1976) and the Revised Class Play (Masten, Morison, & Pellegrini, 1985). On these tasks, children are asked to nominate peers on the basis of a variety of behavioral roles or character descriptions (e.g., one item on the Revised Class Play is, "Choose someone in your class who could play the part of a person who is a good leader"). A number of behavioral or character descriptions (30 on the Revised Class Play and 35 on the PEI) are presented to children, and in general, the measures yield similar factor structures. The PEI, for example, consists of separate Likability, Aggression, and Withdrawal factors, and the Revised Class Play produces Sociability/Leadership, Aggressive/Disruptive, and Sensitive/Isolated factors. In both cases, it is argued that target groups of sensitive/ isolated/withdrawn children can be identified as those who receive extremely high numbers of nominations on those items dealing with the relevant factors.

Recently, Hymel and Rubin (1985) examined the relations between peer assessments of behavior on the Revised Class Play and sociometric ratings of likability. Their analyses revealed that the relation between sociometric status and peer-assessed sensitivity/isolation increased with age from the second grade to the sixth grade; the relation between status and aggression, however, decreased with age. Related research by Younger, Schwartzman, and Ledingham (1986) has indicated that children's responses to the withdrawal items on the PEI become increasingly cohesive over time and increasingly distinct from the aggressive items with age. Taken together, these data suggest that the sensitivity/isolation dimension becomes more identifiable as nonnormative as children move through the elementary school years. Furthermore, these findings address a speculation posited in our introductory remarks: In the middle to late years of childhood, those who remain on the periphery of the peer group may become increasingly conspicuous, and their deviance from group norms may result in the establishment of negative peer reputations.

Despite the usefulness and advantages of peer assessments of behavior, surprisingly few researchers have exploited their potential. Many of the data extant on the correlates of peer-assessed isolation come from our own laboratory and are, as yet, unpublished. We have found that the Sensitive/Isolated factor of the Revised Class Play (Masten et al., 1985) is moderately stable between second and third grade, $r(69) = .49$, $p < .001$. Furthermore, scores on the Sensitive/Isolated factor correlate significantly, in both second and third grades, with teacher ratings of Anxiety/Fearfulness. However, this factor correlates significantly with observations of solitary behavior for boys only ($r = .45$, $p < .001$). The tentative conclusion is that the Revised Class Play Sensitive/Isolation factor appears to more strongly assess sensitivity than isolation in second- and third-grade children.

It is possible, of course, that we have been using peer assessment of behavior developmentally earlier than should be the case. Thus, it may be that as children become more astute, their assessments of the peer milieu will prove more meaningful and reliable. One hint that this is the case stems from the research of Serbin, Lyons, Marchessault, and Morin (1983), who found that peer ratings of withdrawal (on the PEI) in the fifth and sixth grades correlated strongly and significantly with observations of solitary playground activity. We await the collection of similar data on the Revised Class Play.

Teacher assessments of behavior

Teachers, like peers, spend a large amount of time with children. Consequently, they may be useful informants about infrequent but critical events that relate to a child's status in the peer group. One advantage of having teachers assess behavior is that the data-gathering procedure can be more efficient, faster, and more economical than when using children as informants. The major potential disadvantages are (a) teachers provide us with an "adult" perspective on peer status and behavior; (b) the typical teacher assessment derives data from only one observer rather than from numerous judges, as is the case with peer ratings; and (c) teachers may be good judges of aggressive behavior, but they may not be able to identify generally well-behaving, nondisruptive but withdrawn children (Ledingham & Younger, 1985; Strain & Kerr, 1981). Research is needed on whether teacher assessments of behavior agree significantly with other assessments such as peer nominations and behavioral observations. Several teacher rating scales of social behavior exist, but the psychometric strengths of the measures (especially construct validity) remain unknown.

Nevertheless, teacher assessments are used in research to identify withdrawn children. For young children, the Preschool Behavior Questionnaire (PBQ) (Behar & Stringfield, 1974) and the Hahnemann Preschool Behavior Rating Scale (Shure, Newman, & Silver, 1973) include items that concern childhood social withdrawal. For older children, relevant scales include the Children's Behavior Questionnaire (Rutter, 1967), the Devereaux Child Behavior Rating Scale (Spivack & Spotts, 1966), the Walker Problem Behavior Identification Checklist (Walker, 1970), the Conners Teacher Rating Scale (Conners, 1969), the Child Behavior Profile (Edelbrock & Achenbach, 1984), and the Kohn Social Competence Scale and Kohn Problem Checklist (Kohn, 1977). All of these scales produce factors similar to those found for the peer behavioral assessment measures and distinguish withdrawn, sensitive, anxious, or shy children from all or some of the following: aggressive/conduct-disordered children, hyperactive/impulsive children, and children who are sociable, likable, and have leadership qualities.

The only relevant data on the connection between teacher-rated withdrawal or anxiety and observed solitary behavior appear to be from our longitudinal research. We found that the Anxious/Fearful factor of the PBQ (Behar & Stringfield, 1974) correlated with the observed incidence of nonsocial, unoccupied behavior in preschool. In first grade a factor analysis of the PBQ was computed, resulting in a two-factor solution. These factors were labeled Internalization Difficulties and Externalization Difficulties (see also Tremblay, Desmarais-Gervais, Gagnon, & Charlebois, 1985). Teacher ratings on the Internalization factor, which included items concerning anxiety, fearfulness, and solitude, correlated significantly and positively with observations of solitary activity and negatively with social activity (Rubin, Moller, & Emptage, 1987). Although the correlations were statistically significant, they were nevertheless only moderate in magnitude. Thus, although these data do support our contention that high frequencies of peer withdrawal are associated with anxiety and fearfulness, the overlap between the two variables is not a perfect one. With this in mind, we would suggest that children who are characterized as withdrawn are those who are not only infrequent interactors but also rated by teachers (and peers) as anxious, fearful, and withdrawn.

In summary, it is obvious that a good deal more work must be done to validate teacher rating scales of social withdrawal. Teacher ratings must be significantly correlated with observations of isolate activity; furthermore, they must be correlated with those variables cited in our introductory remarks as being conceptually related to the construct of childhood withdrawal (e.g., anxiety and insecurity). One particularly noteworthy point to make is that many of the psychologists who assume that withdrawn children are not at risk for later psychopathological or emotional disorders (e.g., Kohlberg, LaCrosse, & Ricks, 1972; Robins, 1978) have identified shy–withdrawn children by using teacher and other adult rating scales that have undetermined reliability and validity (Fischer, Rolf, Hasazi, & Cummings, 1984). From our perspective, these conclusions negating the significance of social withdrawal are premature and unsubstantiated.

Behavioral observations of social withdrawal

We believe that behavioral observations represent the standard against which all other forms of assessment of withdrawn behavior must eventually be compared. Yet, despite the growing literature on the causes, correlates, and treatment of social isolation (e.g., Wanlass & Prinz, 1982; Conger & Keane, 1981), the observational method of selecting withdrawn children is not often used (see Rubin, 1982b, for a relevant discussion). The reasons for the relative neglect of observational assessments are quite understandable; the method requires weeks, if not months, of data collection. This time frame does not compare favorably with the few hours required to administer teacher and peer assessment measures. Moreover, researchers find that naturalistic observations of children's behavior are especially difficult to obtain in elementary schools, where free-play periods are not part of daily classroom routines. Recently, however, this latter problem has been overcome by observing children during recess (e.g., Ladd, 1983), gym (e.g., Asarnow, 1983), or in free-play environments created in mobile trailer laboratories (e.g., Coie & Kupersmidt, 1983; Dodge, 1983; Rubin & Krasnor, 1986).

The typical observational procedure used to study withdrawal involves the use of event- or time-sampling methods; children observed to display low rates of social interaction are identified as socially withdrawn (e.g., Greenwood, Walker, Todd, & Hops, 1979). Unfortunately, the definition of a low rate of interaction varies considerably from study to study. In some reports, children who are observed to interact with peers less than 15% of the time are identified as withdrawn (e.g., O'Connor, 1972); in other studies withdrawn children have interaction rates that range up to 50% of the time (Keller & Carlson, 1974)! These various selection criteria have led some investigators to critically evaluate rate-of-interaction approaches on both empirical and conceptual grounds (e.g., Asher, Markell, & Hymel, 1981; Rubin, 1982a, 1982b). Empirically, the different rates employed to select withdrawn children make comparison across studies virtually impossible. Conceptually, the inclusion of many forms of activity under one general label, "nonsocial" or "solitary play," precludes the possibility of making qualitative distinctions between different forms of isolate behavior. The dilemma raised by this conceptual issue may be illustrated by referral to Rubin's (1982a) finding, for preschool children, that the frequencies of solitary-sensorimotor and solitary-dramatic play but *not* solitary-constructive play correlate negatively with various indices of social and social-cognitive competence.

Finally, on both conceptual and empirical grounds, it seems inappropriate to discuss, evaluate, and define the phenomenon of social withdrawal in children without reference to developmental, age-group norms. Yet, this is exactly what has transpired in most of the extant literature (noteworthy exceptions are the work of Furman et al., 1979, and Greenwood et al., 1982). Despite observations that preschool- and kindergarten-age children spend much, if not most, of their free-play time not interacting with others (e.g., Parten, 1932), some researchers have identified young children as withdrawn if their social interaction rates make up less than one-half to one-third of all observed behavior. Such arbitrary, non-norm-based selection procedures no doubt lead to some normal youngsters being identified as socially withdrawn and at risk.

Given these concerns, Rubin and his colleagues have recently developed a norm-based procedure for identifying socially withdrawn children (Rubin, 1982b, 1985, 1986; Rubin & Borwick, 1984; Rubin, Daniels-Beirness, & Bream, 1984; Rubin & Krasnor, 1986; Rubin & Lollis, 1988). In this work, preschool, kindergarten, and first-grade children were observed for six 10-sec time samples each day, during free play, over a period of 6 weeks. When the children were in the second grade and then in the fourth grade, their behaviors were similarly time-sampled over four 15-min, specially structured free-play sessions. These sessions involved observations of focal children in same-sex, same-age quartets. The quartets varied in composition such that the child's playmates differed in each of the four sessions (e.g., Rubin, 1985; Rubin & Krasnor, 1986).

Behaviors were coded on a checklist that included the cognitive play categories described originally by Smilansky (1968): functional-sensorimotor, constructive and dramatic play, and games-with-rules. These categories were nested within the social participation categories described by Parten (1932) and revised recently by Rubin (e.g., 1982b, 1986): solitary, parallel, and group activities. In addition, the frequencies of unoccupied and onlooker behaviors, reading or being read to, rough-and-tumble play, exploration, conversations with teachers or peers, and transitional activities (moving from one activity to another or making preparations for an activity) were recorded.

After coding play behavior, the names of the observed child's play or conversational partners and the affective quality (positive, negative, or neutral) of their interactions were recorded. *Isolate* play consisted of the total of solitary plus unoccupied plus onlooker behaviors. *Sociable* play consisted of group play plus conversations with peers.

Isolated preschool, kindergarten, and first-grade children were identified as those whose nonsocial behavior was 1 standard deviation (SD) above the entire group mean and 10% above their class mean. These children engaged in sociable behavior (group play and conversations) that was 1 SD below their age-group mean and 10% below their class mean. In the second and fourth grades the classroom criteria (10% above or below class means) were dropped, because all observations were carried out in a single setting in which the effects of available materials, room size, and numbers of children in the room were controlled. These stringent criteria result in the identification of approximately 15% of all children as isolates. In short, the procedure results in the norm-based selection of a fairly extreme group of withdrawn children. In preschool through second grade, isolates tended to engage in peer-related social behavior only 12% of the time.

The stability of behavioral withdrawal was assessed in two ways. First, we correlated total observed isolate behavior in kindergarten with that in second grade, $r(59) = .37$, $p < .01$. We also found that observed isolate behavior in kindergarten and second grade correlates negatively with observed sociable behavior both within and between grades. *Within* kindergarten and second grade, the correlations between isolate and sociable behaviors are $r(111) = -.47$, $p < .001$ and $r(83) = -.67$, $p < .001$, respectively. The increase in the magnitude of the correlations is consistent with Younger et al.'s (1986) argument that solitary behavior becomes increasingly distinctive with age. Between the grades, kindergarten isolate activity negatively correlates with second-grade sociable play, $r(59) = -.34$, $p < .01$, and kindergarten sociable activity is a negative correlate of second-grade isolate play, $r(59) = -.22$, $p < .05$.

Our second procedure for examining the stability of observed social isolation stems from the extreme groups targeting procedure we described above. We were able to observe 12 children during second-grade free play who were identified as isolates in kindergarten. Eight of these children were identified as isolates in second grade; that is, 66.7% of the original group of extremely withdrawn kindergarteners available for study in second grade were similarly identified 2 years later. These data are clearly supportive of the stability of extreme withdrawal in the early years of childhood.

Summary

In summary, we have examined four means by which researchers attempt to identify withdrawn children: sociometric measures of peer neglect, peer assessments of withdrawal, teacher assessments of withdrawal, and observations of isolate behavior. Clearly, the first three procedures would prove extremely valuable and economical if we could ascertain that they corresponded well with direct observational data. At this time, however, we are not sufficiently confident in these procedures to suggest that psychologists use them exclusively to identify withdrawn children. One reason for our concern is that most peer assessment and teacher assessment measures have not been studied in relation to observations of withdrawn behavior; such analyses are the acid tests of validity. Second, those measures that have been examined in relation to behavioral observations exhibit moderate to very low correlations. Finally, correlations between peer assessment and teacher assessment measures are, at best, of a moderate nature.

Taken together, the data extant suggest that further research must be carried out to develop new, strengthen old, and test the validity of all peer and teacher assessments of childhood withdrawal. This psychometric research must also examine the agreement among the results of the various assessment procedures at different developmental points in childhood.

Naturally, behavioral assessment, itself, could be improved. In addition to our suggestion that age-related norms be used to identify withdrawn children, research is also needed concerning the generalizability of social isolation in childhood. Are children observed to be withdrawn in the classroom likewise isolated on the playground, in their neighborhoods, or in other formal groups (Sunday schools, scouts, etc.)? The only data collected thus far are suggestive of a generalizable phenomenon. In Rubin's (1982b; Rubin & Borwick, 1984) work with preschool- and kindergarten-age children, extremely withdrawn children, as identified in classroom settings, were less sociable than their nonisolate playmates when observed in specially arranged free-play dyads formed from classroom members. More generalizability data should be gathered at different ages and in different venues.

Finally, at this stage in our understanding, it would seem that the identification of withdrawn children should take one of two forms. If the researcher is interested in examining Pathway 1, then observations of solitude along with teacher or peer ratings of aggression might be merited. If the researcher is interested in Pathway 2, then observations of solitude plus teacher or peer ratings of anxiety, insecurity, or sensitivity might be prescribed. Clearly, benefits would accrue from studying both pathways within the same study.

The concomitants of observed socially withdrawn behavior in childhood

In this section, we are concerned with those variables that are associated with the production of high frequencies of observed isolated play. From the outset, we should note that there has been very little research in which the antecedents, concomitants, and consequences of social withdrawal have been explored. In part, this lack of data may reflect the traditional clinical treatment of withdrawal; it appears as if the phenomenon has been considered a problem in and of itself. Consequently, most efforts have centered on the amelioration of withdrawal; little effort has been given to discover why and how children become withdrawn, if they experience related difficulties, and if they do, what the nature of the difficulties is.

The literature on social withdrawal in childhood thus strikes us as having certain peculiar features. It is commonplace to provide intervention for socially withdrawn children, yet we do not know if anything is "wrong" with these children! Is the withdrawn child rejected by his or her peers, socially anxious and insecure, unhappy or lonely, or deficient in social and social-cognitive skills? If socially withdrawn children do not evidence problems in these areas, is there any reason to intervene on their behalf? These questions are obviously important to answer; we attempt to address them in the following discussion of the correlates of observed social withdrawal.

In the Waterloo Longitudinal Project, Rubin and his colleagues studied those variables associated with observed social withdrawal in the early and midyears of childhood. The data suggest the following.

In preschool and kindergarten, extremely withdrawn children are observed to display less mature forms of play and they receive fewer social overtures from peers than their more sociable age-mates (Rubin, 1982b). Their immature play patterns are mirrored by their lower mental age scores as computed on a measure of receptive vocabulary, the Peabody Picture Vocabulary Test.

During specially arranged dyadic free play with a more sociable age-mate, isolate children emit more egocentric speech and direct more of their utterances to imaginary companions or inanimate objects than do their nonisolate counterparts (Rubin, 1982b). When they do address their playmates, isolate children produce fewer direct (imperative) requests, and their requests, whether uttered in the imperative or in a nondirective fashion (e.g., declaratives, interrogatives) are more likely to result in failure (Rubin & Borwick, 1984). The goals of young, isolate children's verbal requests also appear to vary from those of more sociable children. Withdrawn preschoolers and kindergarteners are more likely to attempt to gain their playmate's attention and less likely to attempt to acquire objects or to elicit action from the partner. The last two request forms require greater expenditure of resources and personal energy on the part of the target child (Rubin & Borwick, 1984). Yet, despite producing less costly social requests, isolate children's overtures are more likely to result in failure. These children also are more likely to comply or give in to the assertive demands of their more sociable dyadic play partners. Taken together, the preschool and kindergarten data present isolated children as less mature, less assertive, and more compliant or deferential than their more sociable age-mates.

A second set of findings that has emerged from the Waterloo Longitudinal Project concerns the social-cognitive correlates of observed withdrawal. Rubin et al. (1984) have recently reported that withdrawn kindergarten children produce fewer relevant solutions and fewer flexible alternatives to hypothetical object acquisition problems. Moreover, withdrawn preschoolers and kindergarteners are more likely to suggest that an adult intervene on the part of hypothetical child protagonists to aid in the solution of object acquisition dilemmas (Rubin, 1982b; Rubin et al., 1984). For example, when asked what a cartoon character could do or say to acquire a desired object from another character, isolate children were more likely to suggest "adult intervention" strategies, which might denote adult dependency and social anxiety. Clearly, these findings are in keeping with the observations that preschool and kindergarten isolates are less assertive and less successful in influencing their peers' behaviors than are more sociable children. The data also suggest that young, withdrawn children lag behind their more sociable age-mates in their social-reasoning skills.

Interestingly, much of what is known about the correlates of observed social withdrawal stems from data concerning 3-, 4-, and 5-year olds (e.g., Greenwood et al., 1982; Rubin, 1982b; Rubin & Borwick, 1984). Very little is known about the correlates of withdrawal during the middle and later years of childhood. Given that isolate activity decreases with age (Greenwood et al., 1982; Parten, 1932), one would expect that this form of behavior, if regularly displayed at 6, 8, or 10 years of age, would carry with it more negative associations than it does during the early years of childhood, when it is not perceived as being particularly abnormal.

There is also an unfortunate lack of information concerning the characteristics of children who remain consistently withdrawn in childhood. It seems likely that a withdrawn preschooler who is no longer isolated in kindergarten would be less at risk than the child whose isolate status is stable from one year to the next. Along these lines, Rubin (1985) and Rubin and Krasnor (1986) have compared children who were identified as extremely withdrawn in second grade as well as in either or both of kindergarten and first grade with those who were identified as (a) withdrawn in kindergarten or first grade or both but *not* second grade, (b) average in all 3 years, and (c) sociable in second grade and average or sociable in the previous 2 years. The data indicated that children who were identified as continuously withdrawn were no less popular and performed as well as the three comparison groups on hypothetical-reflective problem-solving tests concerning object acquisition and friendship initiation. However, despite their sociometric status and social-cognitive skills, continuously withdrawn children perceived themselves as lacking in social, cognitive, and physical competence and general self-worth relative to the sociable group. Using Harter's (1982) self-concept measure, consistently withdrawn children were also more negatively self-disposed in the cognitive, social, and general areas relative to the inconsistently withdrawn group, and in the physical domain relative to the average group. Finally, a total self-perception score calculated across all competency domains revealed that the consistently withdrawn children had significantly lower scores than each of the other groups.

The first two sets of findings alone (i.e., those concerning sociometric status and social problem-solving skills) would seem to support the claim that withdrawal is not a risk factor. However, caution in reaching this conclusion is warranted. Perhaps, in second grade, isolate/withdrawn activity is not conspicuous to the peer group as a nonnormative form of behavior, and thus peer rejection might not be a consequence of withdrawn behavior at this age. In the Waterloo Longitudinal Project we are currently examining this possibility by continuing to study children into the later grades.

The lack of a relation between withdrawal and social-cognitive development can also be explained by reference to Piaget (1926) and Sullivan (1953). These theorists indicated that peer interactions would not prove productive in terms of social-cognitive growth until, at least, the middle years of childhood (although our preschool and kindergarten data *do* suggest an early social-cognitive deficit). Thus, a measurement factor may account for the second-grade findings; possibly the nonsignificant between-group differences were due to a ceiling effect on the social problem-solving instrument. Perhaps the most striking finding in our data set is that despite the proficiency with which withdrawn children suggest relevant and numerous solutions to social dilemmas involving object acquisition, when observed attempting to meet these goals, they are more likely to fail than are their more sociable counterparts (Rubin & Krasnor, 1986). In part, their failures appear to be a function of using indirect, rather than assertive, strategies. From our perspective, the nonrelation between social-cognitive and social-behavioral competence in withdrawn children may be mediated by social anxiety. Anxiety in peer confrontation situations may inhibit the production of relevant and usually successful strategies that are known to be in their repertoire. Not using these strategies may lead to social failure, and these failures, in turn, may lead to negative self-perceptions of social competence.

These speculations fit with our Pathway 2 model and our third set of findings. Continuously withdrawn children do think negatively about their own competencies despite their satisfactory sociometric status and their appropriate social-cognitive functioning. We offer the following findings as supportive of our premise that social anxiety and social failure lead to the negative self-perceptions of continuously withdrawn children. In a recent study, Rubin (1985) found the extremely withdrawn second-grade children were more likely to play submissive/deferent roles while interacting with more sociable dyadic partners. Furthermore, when they did attempt to play the dominant roles, isolate children were less successful in gaining compliance. This combination of deference (perhaps brought on by feelings of anxiety) and social failure may help explain the low perceived self-competency data just described.

In summary, the Waterloo Longitudinal Project has provided new insights concerning the correlates of observed social withdrawal in childhood. Preschool and kindergarten isolates can be portrayed as immature, socially anxious, socially deferent, more likely to experience social failure, and more likely to rely on adults to deal with peer conflict dilemmas. Early elementary school isolates are likewise socially deferent, anxious, and less successful in acting as social control agents during peer interactions. Finally, continued withdrawn status is associated with negative self-perceptions concerning not only social competence but also academic and physical competencies.

Conclusion

We began this chapter by commenting that despite its theoretical and clinical significance in the child development literature, social withdrawal is a surprisingly understudied phenomenon. Two models concerning the possible causes, correlates, and consequences of social withdrawal in childhood were presented. In the first model, we suggested that a number of temperamental, socialization, and setting condition factors, through their interplay in infancy and early childhood, might set the stage for the production of aversive and aggressive behaviors in the peer milieu. These behaviors, in turn, might cause the peer group to reject the child and, eventually, to isolate the child from that group. Finally, we indicated that these *aggressive, rejected,* ultimately isolated children might be at risk for problems of an externalizing nature in later childhood and adolescence.

In the second model, we suggested that the interplay of temperamental, socialization, and setting condition factors in infancy and early childhood might set the stage for the experience of social anxiety and the production of extremely high frequencies of nonsocial activity in the peer milieu. We indicated that these children might be less successful in solving their peer-related interpersonal dilemmas and that the interaction between their insecurities, anxieties, and relative lack of social success might cause later negative self-perceptions of competence. We proposed, further, that when the behavior of the extremely anxious, withdrawn, and socially deferent child became conspicuous to the peer group, he or she would be rejected by that group. Ultimately, all of these factors were predicted to conspire and cause the onset of depression and/or anxiety disorders in later childhood and adolescence.

In our chapter we focused on the second scenario. Drawing from data gleaned from the Waterloo Longitudinal Project, we did find some support for the middle part of this second developmental scenario. For example, withdrawn second-graders were found to be less successful in influencing their peers in interpersonal situations, more deferent in their responses to peers, and more negative in their perceptions of their own abilities. Furthermore, two thirds of these youngsters were identified as extremely withdrawn in kindergarten, a period during which social isolation was associated with initial deficits in hypothetical-reflective social reasoning and suggestions of adult dependency.

Naturally, it rests on researchers to closely examine whether the origins that we have suggested predict the early display of social withdrawal in childhood. Moreover, the validity of our prognosis concerning internalizing problems must be tested. Indeed, *both* developmental pathways await more extensive empirical investigation. In the Waterloo Longitudinal Project we will continue to explore both pathways; however, we began the longitudinal part of our research when the children were in kindergarten. Given the suggestions offered in our conceptual models, it is important to provide an empirical test of the links between familial and biological factors in infancy and early childhood and the quality of peer relations and social skills in the middle and late childhood years.

Finally, it seems appropriate to close this chapter by indicating how one might go about providing intervention experiences for insecure, anxious, withdrawn children. A full-scale review of the extant literature that deals with this topic is beyond the scope of this chapter. Our brief response is drawn liberally from earlier writings by Rubin and his colleagues (Rubin, 1985; Rubin & Borwick, 1984; Rubin & Krasnor, 1986) and from research by Furman, Rahe, and Hartup (1979). If withdrawn children are anxious, deferent, and unsuccessful in managing their milieus, and if they feel negatively about themselves, then one intervention route might be to provide them with confidence-boosting, assertiveness-training experiences. Furman et al. have used the procedure of pairing withdrawn children with younger, dyadic play partners; their results, with preschool-aged isolates, proved highly successful. Ostensibly, by interacting with younger children, withdrawn preschoolers had opportunities to take control, to assert themselves, and to initiate social interactions with a lesser likelihood of rebuff. In future research at Waterloo, we will be examining the efficacy of the peer-pairing procedure with older (second-grade) isolates; we will further explore the processes by which such intervention procedures work. We hope that continued work on the methods used to identify withdrawn children, on the variables that predict and can be predicted from withdrawn behavior, and on intervention procedures will prove informative and clinically useful.

References

Achenbach, T. M., & Edelbrock, C. S. (1981). Behavioral problems and competencies reported by parents of normal and disturbed children aged four through sixteen. *Monographs of the Society for Research in Child Development, 46*(Serial No. 188).

Ainsworth, M. D. S., Bell, S. M., & Stayton, D. J. (1971). Individual differences in stranger-situation behavior of one-year-olds. In H. R. Schaffer (Ed.), *The origins of human social relations* (pp. 17–57). New York: Academic Press.

Ainsworth, M. D. S., Blehar, M., Waters, E., & Wall, S. (1978). *Patterns of attachment.* Hillsdale, NJ: Lawrence Erlbaum.

Alvarez, W. F. (1985). The meaning of maternal employment for mothers and their perceptions of their three-year-old children. *Child Development, 56,* 350–360.

Asarnow, J. R. (1983). Children with peer adjustment problems: Sequential and non-sequential analyses of school behaviors. *Journal of Consulting and Clinical Psychology, 51,* 709–717.

Asher, S. R., Markell, R. A., & Hymel, S. (1981). Identifying children at risk in peer relations: A critique of the rate-of-interaction approach to assessment. *Child Development, 52,* 1239–1245.

Baumrind, D. (1967). Child care practices anteceding three patterns of preschool behavior. *Genetic Psychology Monographs, 75,* 43–88.

Behar, L., & Stringfield, S. (1974). A behavioral rating scale for the preschool child. *Developmental Psychology, 10,* 601–610.

Belsky, J. (1980). Child maltreatment: An ecological perspective. *American Psychologist, 35,* 320–335.

Belsky, J., Robins, E., & Gamble, W. (1984). The determinants of parental competence: Toward a contextual theory. In M. Lewis & L. Rosenblum (Eds.), *Beyond the dyad* (pp. 251–280). New York: Plenum.

Belsky, J., Rovine, M., & Taylor, D. G. (1984). The Pennsylvania Infant and Family Development Project, III: The origins of individual differences in infant–mother attachment: Maternal and infant contributions. *Child Development, 55,* 718–728.

Booth, C. L. (1985, April). *New and old predictors of cognitive and social outcomes in high-social-risk toddlers.* Paper presented at the biennial meeting of the Society for Research in Child Development, Toronto.

Bronfenbrenner, U. (1979). *The ecology of human development: Experiments by nature and design.* Cambridge: Harvard University Press.

Bronfenbrenner, U., & Crouter, A. C. (1983). The evolution of environmental models in developmental research. In W. Kessen (Ed.), *Handbook of child psychology: Vol. 1. History, theory and methods* (pp. 357–414). New York: Wiley.

Buss, A. H., & Plomin, R. A. (1984). *Temperament: Early developing personality traits.* Hillsdale, NJ: Lawrence Erlbaum.

Coie, J. D. (1985). Fitting social skills intervention to the target group. In B. H. Schneider, K. H. Rubin, & J. E. Ledingham (Eds.), *Peer relationships and social skills in childhood: Issues in assessment and training* (pp. 141–150). New York: Springer-Verlag.

Coie, J. D., Dodge, K. A., & Coppotelli, H. (1982). Dimensions and types of social status: A cross-age perspective. *Developmental Psychology, 18,* 557–571.

Coie, J. D., & Kupersmidt, J. B. (1983). A behavioral analysis of emerging social status in boys' groups. *Child Development, 54,* 1400–1416.

Colletta, N. (1979). Support systems after divorce: Incidence and impact. *Journal of Marriage and the Family, 41,* 837–846.

Conger, J. C., & Keane, S. P. (1981). Social skills intervention in the treatment of isolated or withdrawn children. *Psychological Bulletin, 90,* 478–495.

Conners, C. (1969). A teacher rating scale for use in drug studies with children. *American Journal of Psychiatry, 126,* 884–888.

Crockenberg, S. B. (1981). Infant irritability, mother responsiveness, and social support influences on the security of mother–infant attachment. *Child Development, 52,* 857–865.

Dix, T. H., & Grusec, J. E. (1985). Parent attribution processes in the socialization of children. In I. E. Sigel (Ed.), *Parental belief systems* (pp. 201–233). Hillsdale, NJ: Lawrence Erlbaum.

Dodge, K. A. (1983). Behavioral antecedents of peer social status. *Child Development, 54,* 1386–1399.

Dodge, K. A., Coie, J. D., & Brakke, N. P. (1982). Behavior patterns of socially rejected and neglected preadolescents: The roles of social approach and aggression. *Journal of Abnormal Child Psychology, 10,* 389–410.

Dodge, K. A., Murphy, R. R., & Buchsbaum, K. (1984). The assessment of intention-cue detection skills in children: Implications for developmental psychopathology. *Child Development, 55,* 163–173.

East, B. A. (1976). Cross-age tutoring in the elementary school. *Graduate Research in Education and Related Disciplines, 8,* 88–111.

Edelbrock, C., & Achenbach, T. M. (1984). The teacher version of the Child Behavior Profile: I. Boys aged 6–11. *Journal of Consulting and Clinical Psychology, 52,* 207–217.

Egeland, B., & Farber, E. A. (1984). Infant–toddler attachment: Factors related to its development and changes over time. *Child Development, 55,* 753–771.

Elder, G. H. (1974). *Children of the great depression.* Chicago: University of Chicago Press.

Elkind, D., & Flavell, J. H. (1969). *Studies in cognitive development.* New York: Oxford University Press.

Fischer, M., Rolf, J. E., Hasazi, J. E., & Cummings, L. (1984). Follow-up of a preschool epidemiological sample. *Child Development, 55,* 137–150.

Furman, W., Rahe, D. F., & Hartup, W. W. (1979). Rehabilitation of socially withdrawn preschool children through mixed-age and same-age socialization. *Child Development, 50,* 915–922.

Garcia-Coll, C., Kagan, J., & Reznick, J. S. (1984). Behavioral inhibition in young children. *Child Development, 55,* 1005–1019.

Greenwood, C. R., Todd, N. M., Hops, H., & Walker, H. M. (1982). Behavior change targets in the assessment and treatment of socially withdrawn preschool children. *Behavioral Assessment, 4,* 273–297.

Greenwood, C. R., Walker, H. M., Todd, N. M., & Hops, H. (1979). Selecting a cost-effective screening measure for the assessment of preschool social withdrawal. *Journal of Applied Behavior Analysis, 12,* 639–652.

Gronlund, N. E. (1959). *Sociometry in the classroom.* New York: Harper.

Harter, S. (1982). The perceived competence scale for children. *Child Development, 53,* 87–97.

Hartup, W. W. (1983). The peer system. In E. M. Hetherington (Ed.), *Handbook of child psychology: Vol. 4. Socialization, personality, and social development* (pp. 103–196, 4th ed.). New York: Wiley.

Hetherington, E. M. (1979). Divorce: A child's perspective. *American Psychologist, 34,* 851–858.

Hymel, S., & Rubin, K. H. (1985). Children with peer relationships and social skills problems: Conceptual, methodological, and developmental issues. In G. J. Whitehurst (Ed.), *Annals of child development* (Vol. 2, pp. 251–297). Greenwich, CT: JAI Press.

Jacobson, J. L., Tianen, R. L., Wille, D. E., & Aytch, D. M. (1987). Infant–mother attachment and early peer relations: The assessment of behavior in an interactive context. In E. Mueller & C. Cooper (Eds.), *Process and outcome in peer relations.* New York: Academic Press.

Kagan, J., Reznick, S. J., Clarke, C., Snidman, N., & Garcia-Coll, C. (1984). Behavioral inhibition to the unfamiliar. *Child Development, 55,* 2212–2225.

Keller, M. F., & Carlson, P. M. (1974). The use of symbolic modelling to promote social skills in preschool children with low levels of social responsiveness. *Child Development, 45,* 912–919.

Kemper, T., & Reichler, M. (1976). Fathers' work integration and frequencies of rewards and punishments administered by fathers and mothers to adolescent sons and daughters. *Journal of Genetic Psychology, 129,* 207–219.

Kohlberg, L., LaCrosse, J., & Ricks, D. (1972). The predictability of adult mental health from childhood behavior. In B. Wolman (Ed.), *Manual of child psychopathology* (pp. 1217–1284). New York: McGraw-Hill.

Kohn, M. (1977). *Social competence, symptoms, and underachievement in childhood: A longitudinal perspective.* Washington, DC: Winston.

Kupersmidt, J. B. (1983, April). *Predicting delinquency and academic problems from childhood peer status.* Paper presented at the biennial meeting of the Society for Research in Child Development, Detroit.

Ladd, G. W. (1983). Social networks of popular, average, and rejected children in school settings. *Merrill-Palmer Quarterly, 29,* 282–307.

LaFreniere, P. J., & Sroufe, L. A. (1985). Profiles of peer competence in the preschool: Interrelations between measures, influence of social ecology, and relation to attachment history. *Developmental Psychology, 21,* 56–69.

Ledingham, J. E., & Younger, A. J. (1985). The influence of the evaluator on assessments of children's social skills. In B. H. Schneider, K. H. Rubin, & J. E. Ledingham (Eds.), *Children's peer relations: Issues in assessment and intervention* (pp. 111–121). New York: Springer-Verlag.

Main, M. (1981). Avoidance in the service of attachment: A working paper. In K. Tramelmann, G. Barlow, L. Petenovich, & M. Main (Eds.), *Behavioral development: The Bielefeld Interdisciplinary Project* (pp. 651–693). Cambridge: Cambridge University Press.

Masten, A. S., Morison, P., & Pellegrini, D. S. (1985). A Revised Class Play method of peer assessment. *Developmental Psychology, 3,* 523–533.

Michael, C. M., Morris, D. P., & Soroker, E. (1957). Follow-up studies of shy, withdrawn children. 2: Relative incidence of schizophrenia. *American Journal of Orthopsychiatry, 27,* 331–337.

Moore, S. G. (1967). Correlates of peer acceptance in nursery school children. In W. W. Hartup & N. L. Smothergill (Eds.), *The young child* (pp. 229–247). Washington, DC: National Association for the Education of Young Children.

Moreno, J. L. (1953). *Who shall survive?* New York: Beacon House.

O'Connor, R. D. (1972). Relative efficacy of modeling, shaping, and the combined procedures for modification of social withdrawal. *Journal of Abnormal Psychology, 79,* 327–334.

Parten, M. B. (1932). Social participation among preschool children. *Journal of Abnormal Psychology, 27,* 243–269.

Pastor, D. L. (1981). The quality of mother–infant attachment and its relationship to toddlers' initial sociability with peers. *Developmental Psychology, 17,* 326–335.

Patterson, G. R. (1976). The aggressive child: Victim and architect of a coercive system. In L. A. Hamerlynck, L. C. Handy, & E. J. March (Eds.), *Behavior modification and families: Vol. 1. Theory and research.* New York: Brunner-Mazell.

Peery, J. C. (1979). Popular, amiable, isolated, rejected: A reconceptualization of sociometric status in preschool children. *Child Development, 50,* 1231–1234.

Pekarik, E. G., Prinz, R. J., Liebert, D. E., Weintraub, S., & Neale, J. M. (1976). The Pupil Evaluation Inventory: A sociometric technique for assessing children's social behavior. *Journal of Abnormal Child Psychology, 4,* 83–97.

Piaget, J. (1926). *The language and thought of the child.* London: Routledge & Kegan Paul.

Piaget, J. (1932). *The moral judgement of the child.* Glencoe: Free Press.

Reznick, J. S., Kagan, J., & Snidman, N. C. (1985, April). *The stability of behavioral inhibition in children.* Paper presented at the biennial meeting of the Society for Research in Child Development, Toronto.

Robins, L. N. (1966). *Deviant children grow up.* Baltimore: Williams & Wilkins.

Robins, L. N. (1978). Sturdy childhood predictors of adult antisocial behavior: Replications from longitudinal studies. *Psychological Medicine, 8,* 611–622.

Rubin, K. H. (1982a). Non-social play in preschoolers: Necessary evil? *Child Development, 53,* 651–657.

Rubin, K. H. (1982b). Social and social-cognitive developmental characteristics of young isolate, normal, and sociable children. In K. H. Rubin & H. S. Ross (Eds.), *Peer relationships and social skills in childhood* (pp. 353–374). New York: Springer-Verlag.

Rubin, K. H. (1985). Socially withdrawn children: An "at risk" population? In B. H. Schneider, K. H. Rubin, & J. E. Ledingham (Eds.), *Children's peer relations: Issues in assessment and intervention* (pp. 125–139). New York: Springer-Verlag.

Rubin, K. H. (1986). Play, peer interactions, and social development. In A. W. Gottfried (Ed.), *Play interactions: The contribution of play materials and parental involvement to child development.* Lexington, MA: D. C. Heath.

Rubin, K. H., & Borwick, D. (1984). The communication skills of children who vary with regard to sociability. In H. Sypher & J. Applegate (Eds.), *Social cognition and communication.* Hillsdale, NJ: Lawrence Erlbaum.

Rubin, K. H., & Clark, M. L. (1983). Preschool teachers' ratings of behavioral problems: Observational, sociometric, and social-cognitive correlates. *Journal of Abnormal Child Psychology, 11,* 273–286.

Rubin, K. H., & Daniels-Beirness, T. (1983). Concurrent and predictive correlates of sociometric status in kindergarten and grade one children. *Merrill-Palmer Quarterly, 29,* 337–352.

Rubin, K. H., Daniels-Beirness, T., & Bream, L. (1984). Social isolation and social problem solving: A longitudinal study. *Journal of Consulting and Clinical Psychology, 52,* 17–25.

Rubin, K. H., Fein, G. G., & Vandenberg, B. (1983). Play. In E. M. Hetherington (Ed.), *Handbook of child psychology: Vol. 4. Socialization, personality, and social development* (pp. 693–774, 4th ed.). New York: Wiley.

Rubin, K. H., Hymel, S., LeMare, L. J., & Rowden, L. (1989). Children experiencing social difficulties: Sociometric neglect reconsidered. *Canadian Journal of Behavioural Science, 21,* 94–111.

Rubin, K. H., & Krasnor, L. R. (1986). Social cognitive and social behavioral perspectives on problem-solving. In M. Perlmutter (Ed.), *Minnesota symposia on child psychology* (Vol. 18, pp. 1–68). Hillsdale, NJ: Lawrence Erlbaum.

Rubin, K. H., & Lollis, S. (1988). Peer relationships, social skills, and infant attachment: A continuity model. In J. Belsky (Ed.), *Clinical implications of infant attachment* (pp. 219–252). Hillsdale, NJ: Lawrence Erlbaum.

Rubin, K. H., Moller, L., & Emptage, A. (1987). Can the Preschool Behaviour Questionnaire be used with elementary schoolers? *Canadian Journal of Behavioural Science, 19,* 86–100.

Rutter, M. (1967). A children's behavior questionnaire for completion by teachers: Preliminary findings. *Journal of Child Psychology and Psychiatry, 8,* 1–11.

Sameroff, A. J., & Chandler, M. J. (1975). Reproductive risk and the continuum of caretaking casualty. In F. D. Horowitz (Ed.), *Review of child development research* (Vol. 4, pp. 187–244). Chicago: University of Chicago Press.

Serbin, L., Lyons, J., Marchessault, K., & Morin, D. (1983, April). *Naturalistic observations of peer-identified aggressive, withdrawn, aggressive–withdrawn, and comparison children.* Paper presented at the biennial meeting of the Society for Research in Child Development, Detroit.

Shure, M., Newman, S., & Silver, S. (1973). *Problem solving thinking among adjusted, impulsive, and inhibited Head Start children.* Paper presented at the Eastern Psychological Association, Philadelphia.

Sigel, I. (1982). The relationship between parental distancing strategies and the child's cognitive behavior. In L. Laosa & I. Sigel (Eds.), *Families as learning environments for children* (pp. 47–86). New York: Plenum.

Sigel, I., & Hooper, F. (1968). *Logical thinking in children.* New York: Holt, Rinehart & Winston.

Smilansky, S. (1968). *The effects of sociodramatic play on disadvantaged preschool children.* New York: Wiley.

Spivack, G., & Spotts, J. (1966). *Devereaux child behavior rating scale manual.* Devon, PA: Devereaux Foundation.

Sroufe, L. A. (1983). Infant–caregiver attachment and patterns of adaptation in preschool: Roots of maladaption and competence. In M. Perlmutter (Ed.), *Minnesota symposia on child psychology* (Vol. 16, pp. 41–81). Hillsdale, NJ: Lawrence Erlbaum.

Staub, E. (1975). To rear a prosocial child: Reasoning, learning by doing, and learning by teaching others. In D. DePalma & J. Foley (Eds.), *Moral development: Current theory and research* (pp. 113–136). Hillsdale, NJ: Lawrence Erlbaum.

Strain, P. S., & Kerr, M. M. (1981). Modifying children's social withdrawal: Issues in assessment and clinical intervention. In M. Hersen, R. M. Eisler, & P. M. Miller (Eds.), *Progress in behavior modification* (Vol. 11, pp. 203–248). New York: Academic Press.

Strain, P. S., Kerr, M. M., & Raglund, E. (1982). The use of peer initiations in the treatment of social withdrawal. In P. S. Strain (Ed.), *The utilization of classroom peers as behavior change agents* (pp. 101–128). New York: Plenum Press.

Sullivan, H. S. (1953). *The interpersonal theory of psychiatry.* New York: Norton.

Thompson, G. G. (1962). *Child psychology: Growth trends in psychological adjustment* (2nd ed.). Boston: Houghton Mifflin.

Tremblay, R. E., Desmarais-Gervais, L., Gagnon, C., & Charlebois, P. (1985). *The Preschool Behavior Questionnaire: Stability of its factor structure between cultures, sexes, ages, and socioeconomic classes.* Paper presented at the eighth biennial meeting of the International Society for the Study of Behavioral Development, Tours, France.

Vaughn, B. E., Taraldson, B. J., Crichton, L., & Egeland, B. (1981). The assessment of infant temperament: A critique of the Carry Infant Temperament Questionnaire. *Infant Behavior and Development, 4,* 1–17.

Walker, H. (1970). *Walker Problem Behavior Identification Checklist.* Los Angeles: Western Psychological Services.

Wanlass, R. L., & Prinz, R. J. (1982). Methodological issues in conceptualizing and treating social isolation. *Psychological Bulletin, 92,* 39–55.

Waters, E., Vaughn, B. E., & Egeland, B. R. (1980). Individual differences in infant–mother attachment relationships at age one: Antecedents in neonatal behavior in an urban, economically disadvantaged sample. *Child Development, 51,* 208–216.

Younger, A. J., & Boyko, K. A. (1987). Aggression and withdrawal as social schemas underlying children's peer perceptions. *Child Development, 58,* 1094–1100.

Younger, A. J., Schwartzman, A. E., & Ledingham, J. E. (1986). Age-related differences in children's perceptions of social deviance: Changes in behavior or in perspective? *Developmental Psychology, 22,* 531–542.

Zahn-Waxler, C., Cummings, E. M., McKnew, D. H., & Radke-Yarrow, M. (1984). Altruism, aggression, and social interactions in young children with a manic-depressive parent. *Child Development, 55,* 112–122.

Zur-Szprio, S., & Longfellow, C. (1981, April). *Support from fathers: Implications for the well-being of mothers and their children.* Paper presented at the biennial meeting of the Society for Research in Child Development, Boston.

Part IV

Consequences of peer rejection

9   Peer rejection and loneliness in childhood

*Steven R. Asher, Jennifer T. Parkhurst, Shelley Hymel,
and Gladys A. Williams*

> Today everybody's going to Mary Ann's party in the group. I'm sort of the one that gets left behind. I'm not invited to the party so I won't do anything on the weekend. Anywhere the whole group goes, I don't. . . . I'm just the person that gets left back. Maybe they don't realize that I get left, that I'm there, but it happens all the time.
>
> (Sixth-grade female student, from Hayden, Tarulli, & Hymel, 1988)

Other chapters in this volume draw on sociometric, behavioral, and social-cognitive information to describe the dynamics that give rise to and maintain peer rejection. In this chapter, we will focus on the subjective experiences of children who are rejected by their peers. Hymel and Franke (1985) have noted that

> surprisingly little attention has been given to how the children themselves feel about their own relationships with peers. For example, children are typically targeted for social skills intervention programs on the basis of outside or external sources of information, including teachers, peers, or adult observers (see Hymel & Rubin, 1985, for a review). Notably absent within the assessment literature is consideration of the child's own perspective on his or her social situation. Our ultimate aim is to help these children function more effectively or positively within their social worlds, yet we know very little about how they themselves perceive that social world, and how self-perceptions influence subsequent interpersonal behavior and the effectiveness of intervention programs. (pp. 75–76)

The question we will address in this chapter is whether rejected children experience dissatisfaction with their social situation. Based on various kinds of research findings there is good reason to expect that rejected children are dissatisfied with their peer relationships. First, as Asher (Chapter 1, this volume) notes, rejected children are actually disliked by the majority of children in their class. Second, the results of observational studies suggest that the daily social climate of rejected children is rather negative. For example, playground observations reveal that during recess periods rejected children move about from one potential playmate to another, rarely remaining engaged with others for long (Ladd, 1983). Studies of children's attempts to enter existing play groups indicate that when unpopular children attempt to gain entry, they are less favorably received than are popular children (Putallaz & Gottman, 1981), even when they employ similar entry strategies (Dodge, Schlundt, Schocken, & Delugach, 1983). At the same time, unpopular children receive fewer positive initiations and more negative treatment from others (e.g., Dodge, 1983; Gottman, Gonso, & Rasmussen, 1975; Hymel, Tinsley, Asher, & Geraci, 1981; Masters & Furman, 1981). Perhaps as a consequence of all of this, when children who do not know each other are brought together, many of the children who become rejected become more isolated and less interactive over time, even though they were highly interactive early in the life of the group (Coie & Kupersmidt, 1983; Dodge, 1983).

The picture sketched above suggests that rejected children would have reason to be unhappy about their social life at school and would feel lonely. There is evidence that peer relationships matter to rejected children; indeed, they claim to place as much importance on peer relationships as do other children (Taylor & Asher, 1989). Yet, they are not succeeding in their social relationships, and it seems plausible that they experience negative emotional consequences.

Within the past decade, researchers have begun to examine the self-perceptions and affective experiences of rejected children. Unpopular children, relative to their more popular classmates, perceive themselves to be less socially competent (Hymel, 1983; Kurdek & Krile, 1982), have less positive expectations for social success (Hymel et al., 1983), and feel more depressed (Vosk, Forehand, Parker, & Rickard, 1982). Especially among girls, unpopular children also report greater feelings of social anxiety and more social avoidance (Hymel & Franke, 1985; Hymel, Franke, & Freigang, 1985). In the present chapter, we will focus specifically on research concerned with rejected children's feelings of loneliness and dissatisfaction with their peer relationships. Although the broader literature on children's self-perceptions indicates that peer rejection is associated with a variety of negative self-perceptions and affective reactions, we chose in this chapter to focus on studies in which children's responses to their peer relationships are directly assessed.

The experience of loneliness in childhood

The work on children's loneliness we will review in this chapter has been inspired in large part by an extensive body of literature on loneliness in adolescence and adulthood. This literature has developed over the past 15 years, partly as a result of the theoretical writing of Weiss (1973) and the empirical work of scholars such as Peplau, Perlman, Jones, and Russell (Jones, 1985; Peplau & Perlman, 1982; Russell, Cutrona, Rose, & Yurko, 1984). Russell, Peplau, and Ferguson's (1978) UCLA Loneliness Scale is the instrument most widely used to assess loneliness among adolescents and adults, although several other self-report measures have been developed (e.g., Rubenstein & Shaver, 1979, 1982; Schmidt & Sermat, 1983).

Despite extensive research with adults, it is only recently that research has been undertaken on children's loneliness. One reason for this lack of attention to loneliness in children is the not uncommon view that young children are not particularly vulnerable to feelings of loneliness. Weiss (1973), for example, argues from a psychodynamic, developmental perspective that loneliness is a state that probably is not experienced until adolescence, a time when parents are said to be "relinquished as attachment figures" (pp. 89–90). Similarly, Sullivan (1953) has suggested that true loneliness cannot be experienced until preadolescence, when a need for intimacy in a one-to-one relationship is said to emerge.

There is now evidence that these theoretical assumptions are incorrect and that children do experience loneliness. In an attempt to understand children's conceptions of loneliness, Hayden et al. (1988) interviewed third- through eighth-grade children about their definitions of loneliness as well as their own experiences of loneliness. Data obtained from these interviews were qualitatively analyzed (e.g., Strauss, 1987) to develop a descriptive framework of the nature of children's loneliness as understood from the perspective of the children themselves. Results of this qualitative analysis indicated three distinct yet interrelated dimensions in children's descriptions of loneliness: an affective or emotional dimension, a cognitive dimension, and the delineation of specific situational contexts that children associate with the experience of loneliness.

With regard to affect, children's statements reflected their "awareness of the felt or experiential dimension of loneliness or at least their implicit acknowledgement that loneliness is emotional in nature" (Hayden et al., 1988, p. 6). Children's descriptions of loneliness included terms for unpleasant emotions (most notably, sadness and boredom), references to feelings (e.g., "feeling unneeded," "feeling left out," "it feels like no one likes you," "you feel like you're an outsider"), and metaphorical expressions (e.g., "they feel like they're in a corner," "to be left alone, kept in a cage or something," "like you're the only one on the moon," "always in the dark").

With regard to the cognitive dimension of loneliness, children often related loneliness to unfulfilled relationship provisions. The relationship provisions most often mentioned as lacking were companionship (e.g., "not being able to play with or talk to anyone," "having no one around you can do things with"), a sense of acceptance by or belonging to or inclusion in a group (e.g., "feeling left out," "trying to be part of the new group"), emotional support (e.g., "no one to share your private thoughts with," "thinking that you really don't have someone that you can turn to"), and affection (e.g., "without anybody to love you," "like you have no one that really likes you and you're all alone"). Some children also made references to lack of reliable alliances or loyalty, lack of trust and continued availability of contact, lack of enhancement of their sense of worth, and lack of opportunities for nurturance.

Finally, Hayden et al. (1988) found that children commonly associated their experiences of loneliness with several types of traumatic situations or events: loss of an important other, moving to an unfamiliar setting, temporary absence of an important other, conflict, rejection, broken loyalties, exclusion, and being ignored. It is important to note that within each of these categories, loneliness could involve individuals from either the peer or family network.

These reports by children portray loneliness in ways very similar to those obtained from adults. The emotional terms employed by children to describe loneliness are emotions reported by lonely adults (Jones, Cavert, Snider, & Bruce, 1985). The relationship provisions spontaneously offered in children's descriptions of loneliness are also strikingly similar to those identified in previous theorizing and research in the adult literature (e.g., Weiss, 1973; Russell et al., 1984). Furthermore, the situations and events reported by children as leading to loneliness closely parallel the situations and events reported by adults as leading to loneliness (Frieze, Bar-Tal, & Carrol, 1979; Jones et al., 1985).

Moreover, children's references to lack of companionship and sense of belonging and to "feeling left out," on the one hand, and to lack of emotional support and affection and to having "no one to share your private thoughts with," on the other, are reminiscent of Weiss's (1973) theoretical distinction between social loneliness and emotional loneliness. Social loneliness is theorized to stem from the absence of a network of social relationships or from feeling that one is not part of a group. Emotional loneliness is theorized to stem from lack of a close, intimate attachment to another person. The two kinds of loneliness are expressed somewhat differently. Those reporting social loneliness are likely to say they feel left out and that they do not belong. Those reporting emotional loneliness are likely to say that no one really knows them or cares about them. Emotional loneliness is experienced as an aching emptiness. This distinction between social and emotional loneliness is supported by research on loneliness among adults (e.g., Russell et al., 1984). As will be seen, formal assessments of loneliness among children have not examined this distinction, although promising work along these lines is beginning (Hayden-Thomson, 1989).

Research on even younger children's conceptions of loneliness has also been conducted. In a study with kindergarten and first-grade children Cassidy and Asher (1989a) found that young children have an understanding of what loneliness is, how to identify loneliness in others, what kinds of situations give rise to feelings of loneliness, and what kinds of things can be done to overcome feelings of loneliness. For example, when kindergarten and first-grade children were asked what loneliness is, they reported that it is a feeling of being sad and alone. When asked where these feelings come from, they often reported that it is when you have nobody to play with. When asked what one might do about it, the children often said you could try to find a friend or try to find somebody to do something with. The vast majority of subjects in this study, as well as in Hayden et al., reported conceptions of loneliness that were similar to those that would be expected from adults. These findings suggest that the construct of loneliness has meaning to children and can be an object of formal assessment.

Assessing loneliness in children

Several self-report measures have been developed in recent years to assess children's feelings of loneliness. Heinlein and Spinner (1985) developed an 11-item scale that focuses on loneliness in the family context (e.g., "Someone in my family really cares about how I feel inside"). Marcoen and Brumagne (1985) developed a 28-item loneliness measure with 16 of the items focused on peer-related loneliness and 5 of the items focused on parent-related loneliness. Asher, Hymel, and Renshaw (1984) created a loneliness measure in which the items focused primarily on the peer context. Due to its peer focus, this measure or some variation of it has now been used in several studies to examine the relationship between acceptance by the peer group and loneliness. Accordingly, we will discuss this measure in greater detail and then review the research that has made use of it.

Asher et al.'s (1984) questionnaire is a 24-item instrument containing 16 primary items centering on feelings of loneliness and social dissatisfaction and 8 filler items that ask about hobbies, interests, and school subject preferences. The 16 primary items include four different kinds of items. These items assess (a) children's feelings of loneliness (e.g., "I'm lonely"), (b) children's appraisal of their current peer relationships (e.g., "I don't have any friends"), (c) children's perceptions of the degree to which important relationship provisions are being met (e.g., "There's nobody I can go to when I need help"), and (d) children's perceptions of their social competence (e.g., "I'm good at working with other children"). Third- through sixth-grade children responded to each item on a 5-point scale, indicating the degree to which each statement was a true description of themselves (i.e., "that's always true about me; that's true about me most of the time; that's sometimes true about me; that's hardly ever true about me; that's not true at all about me").

Asher and Wheeler (1985), in a subsequent study with third- through sixth-grade children, modified this measure slightly by providing an explicit school focus to each of the 16 primary items (e.g., "I'm lonely at school," "I don't have any friends in class"). Giving an explicit school focus to each item was consistent with an interest in the association between loneliness and peer relationships in school. The items included in this modified version of the measure are listed in Figure 9.1.

Variations of this scale have been developed for use with middle school children (Parkhurst & Asher, 1987) and kindergarten and first-grade children (Cassidy & Asher, 1989b). For older children, relatively minor wording changes were

Item

1. It's easy for me to make new friends at school.
2. I like to read.†
3. I have nobody to talk to in class.
4. I'm good at working with other children in my class.
5. I watch TV a lot.†
6. It's hard for me to make friends at school.*
7. I like school.†
8. I have lots of friends in my class.
9. I feel alone at school.*
10. I can find a friend in my class when I need one.
11. I play sports a lot.†
12. It's hard to get kids in school to like me.*
13. I like science.†
14. I don't have anyone to play with at school.*
15. I like music.†
16. I get along with my classmates.
17. I feel left out of things at school.*
18. There's no other kids I can go to when I need help in school.*
19. I like to paint and draw.†
20. I don't get along with other children in school.*
21. I'm lonely at school.*
22. I am well liked by the kids in my class.
23. I like playing board games a lot.†
24. I don't have any friends in class.*

Figure 9.1. Asher and Wheeler's (1985) Loneliness and Social Dissatisfaction questionnaire. Items with an asterisk are those for which response order is reversed in scoring. Items with a dagger are those classified as hobby or interest items.

made to make items appropriate to the organizational features and types of activities in middle school. These alterations included changing "your class" to "your classes" and rewording filler items such as "I play games a lot" to "I play sports a lot." For kindergarten and first-grade students, item formats were adapted to the cognitive capabilities of younger children, including changing statements to questions (e.g., "I'm lonely at school" was changed to "Are you lonely at school?") and changing the 5-point response scale to a simpler, 3-point scale ("yes; sometimes; no").

There is considerable evidence, from a number of studies, that existing variations of this instrument are psychometrically sound. Children's responses have been factor analyzed, using a Quartimax solution, in several samples of middle to late elementary school students (Asher et al., 1984; Asher & Wheeler, 1985; Crick & Ladd, 1988; Hymel et al., 1983) and more recently in samples of middle school students (Parkhurst & Asher, 1989) and kindergarten and first-grade children (Cassidy & Asher, 1988b). The results of these factor analyses have consistently indicated a single factor composed of the 16 primary items. The internal reliability of the scale (including the 16 primary items) has also been calculated in each study and the alpha coefficients are uniformly high among older children (.90 or above). Among kindergarten and first-grade children the reliability is slightly lower but still satisfactory (.79). The coherence of the items suggests that children's feelings of loneliness, acknowledgment that they lack friends, recognition that certain key relationship provisions are not being met, and feelings of social inadequacy tend to co-occur. The varied content of these items defies easy labeling of the scale, but it is clear that children with high scores are expressing both loneliness and dissatisfaction with the quality of their peer relationships. It is important to note, also, that the highest loading items tend to be items that speak directly to loneliness, such as "I'm lonely at school" and "I feel alone at school."

Another indicator of the psychometric strength of this 16-item self-report measure is its stability over time. In a longitudinal study of children who were in third through fifth grades at initial testing, Hymel et al. (1983) found that children's initial scores correlated .55 with those assessed 1 year later. This finding suggests that children's feelings of loneliness and social dissatisfaction tend to be fairly stable over time.

Before turning to research on the relationship between sociometric status and loneliness, an important validity issue should be addressed. A potential threat to the validity of all self-report measures is the possibility of children providing socially desirable or defensive responses. Such responses would lead to the underreporting of feelings, thoughts, and behaviors that might reflect negatively on the self. In the case of loneliness assessment, a child who is being defensive or responding in a socially desirable direction would deny feeling lonely or having problems in peer relationships. This would lead to a total score that underestimates his or her true feelings. Thus, the validity of low scores may be suspect. However, Kagan, Hans, Markowitz, Lopez, and Sigal (1982) have investigated the validity of children's self-reports in a number of domains, including popularity with peers, and have demonstrated that there is little reason to suspect the scores of children who *do* admit difficulties. In light of Kagan et al.'s results, we can have more confidence in self-report data when children do express feelings of loneliness than when children report that all is well.

Peer status and loneliness

Our main focus in this chapter is on whether children who are poorly accepted by their peers find their social world to be lonely and dissatisfying. Several studies have addressed this issue, examining self-reported loneliness and social dissatisfaction in relation to the average sociometric rating children receive and in relation to status group classification.

In two studies of third- through sixth-grade children, rating-scale sociometric measures were employed to assess overall acceptance by the peer group (Asher et al., 1984; Hymel, 1983). In both studies, children's self-reported loneliness and social dissatisfaction score was negatively and significantly related to acceptance, with correlations of $-.31$ (Asher et al., 1984) and $-.33$ (Hymel, 1983). It appears, therefore, that children who are poorly accepted tend to express greater feelings of loneliness than do their better accepted peers. The magnitude of the correlations obtained in both studies, however, is moderate, reflecting the fact that not all unpopular children report feeling lonely and that some well-accepted children do feel lonely.

Variations in self-reported loneliness have been analyzed in relation to sociometric status in at least five relatively large sample studies (Asher & Wheeler, 1985; Asher & Williams, 1987; Cassidy & Asher, 1988; Crick & Ladd, 1988; Parkhurst & Asher, 1989). In these studies children were classified into sociometric status groups on the basis of positive and negative nomination scores. All studies included popular, average, controversial, neglected, and rejected children except for the Crick and Ladd (1988) study, which did not include a controversial sample. Three of the studies were conducted with middle to late elementary school children. These include one with third- through sixth-grade students (Asher & Wheeler, 1985), another with fourth- through sixth-grade students (Asher & Williams, 1987), and a third with third- and fifth-graders (Crick & Ladd, 1988). In addition, one study was conducted with seventh- and eighth-grade students (Parkhurst & Asher, 1989), and another, with kindergarten and first-grade children (Cassidy & Asher, 1989b). The samples of rejected children ranged in number from 34 (Asher & Wheeler, 1985) to 121 (Asher & Williams, 1987).

Figure 9.2 shows the results from each of the studies of middle to late elementary school students. These studies share a focus on a similar age-group, and all employed the Asher and Wheeler (1985) version of the loneliness questionnaire. Given 16 primary items, each on a 5-point scale, possible loneliness scores ranged from a low of 16 to a high of 80. As can be seen in Figure 9.2, in each study, rejected children expressed significantly more loneliness than nonrejected children. Indeed, the consistency of findings across these three studies is striking. Furthermore, research with middle school (Parkhurst & Asher, 1989) and kindergarten and first-grade children (Cassidy & Asher, 1989b) parallels these findings, despite modifications in the measure and the different ages of the subjects.

Two other smaller sample studies have also been conducted with middle elementary school children (Stein & Hymel, 1986; Rubin, Hymel, LeMare, &

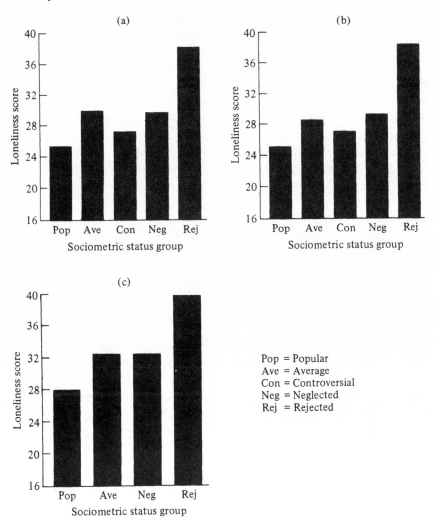

Figure 9.2. Loneliness scores as a function of sociometric status group. (a) From Asher & Wheeler (1985); (b) from Asher & Williams (1987); (c) from Crick & Ladd (1988).

Rowden, 1989). In each study, there were 17 children identified as rejected. In these studies loneliness did not differ significantly as a function of status group classifications. In the study by Stein and Hymel, however, an examination of the mean loneliness scores obtained suggests that rejected children reported greater feelings of loneliness than did children in the other status groups. Our inclination is to attribute these nonsignificant results to smaller sample sizes, because research with larger numbers of subjects consistently reveals significantly more loneliness among rejected children.

It is of interest to note that in all of the preceding studies, neglected children's reports of loneliness were not significantly greater than average-status children's reports. These data concerning neglected children fit well with other emerging evidence that neglected children do not appear to be a group "at risk." Coie and Dodge (1983) and Coie and Kupersmidt (1983) found that children who are neglected by peers at one time or in one context are not commonly neglected at other times or in other contexts. Furthermore, even though neglected children receive few best friend nominations, they are as well liked by peers, on a rating-scale measure, as average-status children (Asher & Wheeler, 1985; French & Waas, 1985; Rubin et al., in press; Stein & Hymel, 1986). Together, the data concerning rejected versus neglected children suggest that it is having few friends in class *and* being widely disliked by the peer group that lead to feelings of loneliness and social dissatisfaction in the school context. Neglected children may not have many friends or be highly visible within the classroom social structure, but they are not typically disliked and do not seem to experience much distress concerning their peer relationships at school.

Variability in loneliness among rejected children

Although rejected children are the most lonely status group, there is considerable variability among rejected students in their expressed feelings about their social world. In all but one of the larger sample studies (Parkhurst & Asher, 1989), the standard deviation in loneliness scores was greater for rejected children than for any other status group. Although many rejected children report extremely high levels of loneliness, a large number of rejected children do not. This degree of variability in loneliness suggests the need to understand more fully the factors that contribute to loneliness among rejected children. Several factors may be hypothesized to influence the likelihood that some rejected children would report greater loneliness than others.

Degree of rejection

One rather basic possibility is that the degree of loneliness that rejected children report corresponds to the degree of rejection they actually experience. Indeed, rejected children are fairly heterogeneous on sociometric measures (see Hymel & Rubin, 1985; Williams & Asher, 1987). It seems plausible that the degree to which rejected children feel lonely or socially dissatisfied may, in part, be a function of the degree to which they are actually disliked or rejected within the classroom peer group. The least lonely rejected children may be those who have some degree of social support. Such a possibility should be considered in future research examining the link between degree of peer rejection and feelings of loneliness.

Chronicity of rejection

Another factor likely to contribute to variability in loneliness among rejected children is the degree to which peer rejection is chronic in nature. The child who experiences difficulties in peer relations from one year to the next might be more likely to report greater loneliness than the child who has experienced only a brief period of peer rejection in school. One general limitation of the literature on sociometric status is that children are classified on the basis of sociometric assessment at a single point in time. It seems plausible that the association between sociometric status and measures such as loneliness would be stronger if status classifications were based on several administrations of sociometric measures. With regard to loneliness in particular, repeated social failure should lead to increasing despondency about one's peer relationships. Certainly the adult literature on loneliness lends support to this idea (Frieze, Bar-Tal, & Carrol, 1979).

Role of friendship

Loneliness may be related not only to the overall severity and longevity of peer rejection in the peer group as a whole but to whether the rejected child has at least one friend at school. It is interesting that some children who are classified as rejected by the Coie and Dodge (1983) system do in fact receive one or more positive nominations from classmates. Having at least one friend in class may provide an important source of emotional support. In this case, the child may still feel left out of the group as a whole but not be experiencing as much emotional loneliness.

The distinction made earlier between social and emotional loneliness suggests that children's feelings of loneliness could arise either from being poorly accepted by the group in general or from lacking a close friend. Within the literature on children's peer relations, there has been increasing recognition that friendship and overall group acceptance may constitute distinct and independent aspects of a child's social world (e.g., Asher & Hymel, 1981; Bukowski & Hoza, 1989; Furman & Robbins, 1985; Oden & Asher, 1977; Parker, 1986). Bukowski and Hoza (1989) recently have argued that having a friend (a close, mutual, dyadic relationship with a peer) and being popular (being liked or accepted by members of one's peer group) have independent effects on a child's feelings of self-worth. This contention receives support from the finding (Bukowski & Newcomb, 1987) that elementary school children's feelings of self-worth were significantly predicted by the experience of having at least one mutual friend within the class, even after the effects of overall popularity on general self-worth were statistically removed through a covariance analysis. It is therefore reasonable to suppose that lack of friendship and lack of acceptance will make independent contributions to children's feelings of loneliness in the peer group.

The effect on children's loneliness of having friends they can talk to intimately is suggested by Cohn, Lohrmann, and Patterson (1985). They found that loneliness based on the Asher et al. (1984) scale correlated −.57 with the number of friends among their peers children said they feel comfortable talking with, a correlation greater than the relation between loneliness and subject-reported friendship network size (−.29). This study, too, suggests the need to examine the separate contributions of friendship and group acceptance to social and emotional loneliness.

Behavioral subgroup differences

Another possible explanation for the variability in loneliness scores observed among rejected children is that the rejected-status group contains several behavioral subtypes that differ in their degree of reported loneliness. Rubin (1985) and Rubin, LeMare, and Lollis (Chapter 8, this volume) have proposed two developmental pathways leading to peer rejection. One of these is an externalizing pattern of behavior that is characterized by aggression and disruption. The other is an internalizing style characterized by apprehensiveness, timidity, social withdrawal, isolation, and submissiveness (e.g., being an "easy mark"). Rubin et al. propose different developmental pathways associated with each pattern and speculate about the types of risks associated with each pathway. Specifically, they suggest that the latter type of rejected child will experience problems such as depression or low self-esteem.

Although researchers have clearly identified an aggressive–rejected subgroup (Bierman, 1986; Chapter 11, this volume), less attention has been given to the internalizing subgroup of rejected children hypothesized by Rubin et al. Certainly, Olweus's (1978) work on bullies and whipping boys in the schools suggests a linkage between apprehensiveness, vulnerability to victimization, low self-esteem, and low status in the peer group. Olweus found that children who had reputations as being frequent victims of bullying reported lower self-esteem and greater apprehensiveness and social anxiety. Although this important research suggests that these victims were not well accepted, in that they received fewer positive nominations than other children, there was no measure of sociometric dislike. Therefore, it cannot be stated with certainty whether these children were rejected. However, a recent study by Perry, Kusel, and Perry (1988) of frequently victimized children did include a negative nomination measure and found that most victims were rejected by peers. Together, these studies support the suggestion that there is a subgroup of rejected students characterized by submissiveness.

Three other recent studies have directly examined the extent to which rejected children could be characterized by a timid, submissive, internalizing style versus an aggressive, externalizing style. All three studies used a variation of the Coie and Dodge (1983) method to identify rejected children and then used specific peer assessment items to identify rejected subgroups.

The first of these studies (Parkhurst & Asher, 1987) was with a middle school sample of seventh- and eighth-grade students. The aggressive subgroup of rejected students was identified with Coie and Dodge's (1983) "starts fights" peer assessment item, and a submissive–rejected subgroup was identified using the item "Who is easy to push around?" The second study (Williams & Asher, 1987), with an elementary school sample of third- through sixth-grade students, again used the "starts fights" peer assessment item to identify aggressive children. The item used to assess timid, submissive tendencies included several of the elements associated with an internalizing style of behavior. Students were asked, "Who is timid and hangs back?" This was defined to include being quiet, not coming over to join in when other children are playing together, and being shy or nervous. In the third study (Boivin, Thomassin, & Alain, 1988) subgroups of third-grade rejected children were identified by using items from the Revised Class Play (Masten, Morison, & Pellegrini, 1985). Specifically, an aggressive, externalizing group was identified using the items "gets into a lot of fights," "too bossy," and "interrupts." A timid, withdrawn, internalizing group was identified using the items "very shy" and "rather play alone than with others."

In support of earlier research on the behavioral correlates of sociometric status (see Chapter 2, this volume), all three studies found that a substantial number of rejected children were characterized by an aggressive, or externalizing, behavioral style. There was, in addition, a second group of children who were characterized by a timid, submissive, internalizing style of interaction. Of particular interest in these studies were differences in loneliness among the subgroups of rejected children. In all three studies the loneliness and social dissatisfaction scores of the submissive–rejected group were significantly higher than those of aggressive–rejected children and average-status children. In one study (Williams & Asher, 1987), aggressive–rejected children were significantly lonelier than average-status children, but in the other two studies there were no significant differences in loneliness between these two groups.

The tendency for aggressive–rejected children to report less extreme feelings of loneliness is consistent with findings from other research concerning the self-conceptions of aggressive children. Aggressive children, especially aggressive boys, tend to overestimate their own competence and to show inflated and inaccurate self-perceptions relative to the evaluations of others (see Gagnon, Dumont, Tremblay, Charlebois, & Larivee, 1988; Olweus, 1978). These overly positive self-perceptions may reflect ego-defensiveness and denial strategies. One form that such defensiveness may take is to discount attachments and deny feelings of sadness or upset with regard to loss. This pattern is illustrated by a recent experience one of us (J. T. P.) had during administration of a questionnaire in which students were asked how upset they would feel about various events, including losing a friend. One eighth-grade student blurted out in class, "What a stupid question! Big deal if you lose a friend. Anybody who gets upset if they lose a friend is really dumb. You just make another one."

Another, quite different, reason why aggressive–rejected children might report less loneliness than do submissive–rejected children is because aggressive–rejected children actually have more friends in their classes. Aggressive children tend to affiliate with one another in school (Cairns, Cairns, Neckerman, Gest, & Gariepy, 1987), and there is evidence that aggressive–rejected children are less extremely rejected on sociometric measures than are submissive–rejected children (Williams & Asher, 1987). It may be, then, that aggressive–rejected children are less likely to feel left out of things.

As research on subgroup differences in loneliness proceeds, we should be alert to possible effects of school and classroom climate on the levels of loneliness among aggressive–rejected versus submissive–rejected children. For example, teachers probably vary in the degree to which they facilitate peer interactions for children who are timid and who take less initiative toward others. As a second example, in schools where bullying is curbed by school policies and close adult supervision, timid, submissive–rejected children will probably report far less loneliness than similar children who attend schools where they are regularly victimized. These children will still be poorly integrated into the group but should suffer less abuse and, as a result, may feel less estranged from group life.

There are additional areas that deserve exploration in future research aimed at understanding differences in the loneliness of internalizing versus externalizing rejected children. These two styles are composed of many cognitive, emotional, and behavioral elements, and the contribution of each of these elements could be assessed. For example, there is evidence from the clinical literature (see Quay, 1979) that the elements of the internalizing style postulated by Rubin (Rubin, 1985; Chapter 8, this volume) to lead to rejection (i.e., submissiveness, timidity, lack of self-confidence, social anxiety, and social avoidance and isolation) are indeed associated with one another. Most of the research cited in our chapter focuses on a submissive, timid behavioral pattern. There is also some evidence that both social anxiety and social avoidance are associated with greater loneliness (Hymel & Franke, 1985; Rubin & Mills, in press). We need to better understand the independent and joint contribution of these and other factors to loneliness.

Attributions for success and failure

Understanding the sources of variability in loneliness among rejected children may also be aided by studying children's attributions for social success and failure. One common bias observed in the way people interpret events is the tendency to accept personal credit for success and to deny personal blame for failure. This tendency has been described as the "self-serving" bias (see Miller & Ross, 1975), "attributional egotism" (Snyder, Stephan, & Rosenfield, 1978), and "benefactance" (Greenwald, 1980). This type of bias is believed to be effective in helping to maintain self-esteem (Heider, 1958). Nonetheless, some individuals do exhibit non-self-serving biases in their attributions.

Within the adult literature on loneliness, Peplau, Russell, and Heim (1979) have proposed that individuals' cognitions and self-evaluations are mediating factors in the relationship between loneliness and social behavior. Consistent with this proposal, lonely adults tend to exhibit a nonadaptive pattern of attributions for their own social successes and failures, attributing success to external and unstable causes and attributing social failure to internal and stable causes (Anderson, Horowitz, & French, 1983; Peplau et al., 1979).

The social attributions of children who differ in sociometric status have been examined in several studies (Ames, Ames, & Garrison, 1977; Goetz & Dweck, 1980; Sobol & Earn, 1985), and a similar pattern of results has emerged despite methodological differences. Children of low sociometric status, whether defined as unpopular, lacking in friends, or rejected, tend to attribute their social successes to unstable and external causes and to attribute their social failures to internal and stable causes. This non-self-serving attributional style is also characteristic of lonely children. Hymel et al. (1983) found that lonelier children were more likely to view social failure as internally caused and stable. More recently, Bukowski and Ferber (1987) have found that it is the combination of low peer acceptance and a non-self-serving attributional bias that is associated with extreme feelings of loneliness. Specifically, they found that poorly accepted children who blamed themselves for social failure were lonelier than poorly accepted children who viewed social failure as externally caused. Thus, consideration of both the child's social experiences with rejection and the child's interpretation of those experiences may help us to understand the phenomenon of loneliness in children.

A focus on attributional biases may also help us to explain differences in loneliness between aggressive–rejected and submissive–rejected children. The work of Dodge and his colleagues (e.g., Dodge, 1980; Dodge & Frame, 1982; Dodge & Somberg, 1987) indicates that aggressive–rejected children tend to be other-blaming in their interpretations of events. Rubin et al.'s (Chapter 8, this volume) portrayal of submissive–rejected children suggests that they are more self-blaming. Thus, differences in attributional style may underlie some of the differences in loneliness between these two subgroups. Further research along these lines is needed.

Summary

The research reviewed here indicates that children's conceptions of loneliness are similar in many ways to adult conceptions and that children's feelings of loneliness can be reliably assessed. As a result, it has become possible to study children's emotional reactions to their peer relationships. Even children as young as 5 and 6 years of age appear to have fairly well developed conceptions of loneliness and give internally consistent responses. Furthermore, it is clear from formal assessments of loneliness that children who are having the greatest difficulty in their peer relationships are indeed reporting the greatest degree of loneliness and social dissatisfaction.

The fact that rejected children are more lonely than other status groups indicates that scholars involved in intervention research are working on behalf of the children themselves. Many rejected children are distressed by their social circumstances in school. Indeed, it is possible that children's reports of loneliness are implicit calls for help. In admitting loneliness, children are telling us that they are unhappy with their social situation and wish it were otherwise.

Although rejected children are more lonely than other status groups, it is also clear that considerable within-group variability exists. We offered several interpretations for this variability in loneliness among rejected children. Heterogeneity could be associated with several factors, including variability in the degree of rejection experienced by unpopular children, variability in the chronicity of rejected status in the peer group, the presence of a friend in the class, differences in behavioral style, and differences in the attributions children make about their social successes and failures. These explanations are not mutually exclusive. Indeed, our view is that these explanations are to a large extent compatible with one another. In fact, there may be a pattern consisting of extreme and chronic low status (including not having friends), timid and submissive behavior, a tendency to attribute failure to internal causes, and extreme loneliness. Further research will be needed to learn the extent to which this pattern exists. It is similar to the pattern hypothesized by Rubin et al. in Chapter 8.

The research reviewed in this chapter is a first step in the direction of understanding the affective experiences of peer-rejected children. One important issue that has been given little attention to date is the role that loneliness plays in children's social lives. Until now, loneliness has been construed as the outcome of negative peer experiences. It is important to ask, however, about the instigational or motivational effects of feeling lonely, as well as the implications of such effects for intervention efforts. Would children who experience loneliness be more likely to take initiative to improve their situation? Would they respond more positively to intervention efforts? Alternatively, might some lonely children, particularly those who have experienced chronic rejection and who have been lonely for a long period of time, have given up on their ability to form satisfying relationships with other children? Research is needed to evaluate these possibilities and to learn about the conditions under which reports of loneliness represent windows of opportunity for facilitating the social adjustment of children in school. We hope that scholars will pursue this issue as research on the important topic of loneliness continues.

References

Ames, R., Ames, C., & Garrison, W. (1977). Children's causal ascriptions for positive and negative interpersonal outcomes. *Psychological Reports, 41*, 595–602.

Anderson, C. A., Horowitz, L. M., & French, R. (1983). Attributional style of lonely and depressed people. *Journal of Personality and Social Psychology, 45*, 127–136.

Asher, S. R., & Hymel, S. (1981). Children's social competence in peer relations: Sociometric and behavioral assessment. In J. D. Wine & M. D. Smye (Eds.), *Social competence* (pp. 125–157). New York: Guilford.

Asher, S. R., Hymel, S., & Renshaw, P. D. (1984). Loneliness in children. *Child Development, 55*, 1456–1464.

Asher, S. R., & Wheeler, V. A. (1985). Children's loneliness: A comparison of rejected and neglected peer status. *Journal of Consulting and Clinical Psychology, 53*, 500–505.

Asher, S. R., & Williams, G. A. (1987, April). New approaches to identifying rejected children at school. In G. W. Ladd (Chair), *Identification and treatment of socially rejected children in school settings*. Symposium conducted at the annual meeting of the American Educational Research Association, Washington, DC.

Bierman, K. L. (1986). Process of change during social skills training with preadolescents and its relation to treatment outcome. *Child Development, 57*, 230–240.

Boivin, M., Thomassin, L., & Alain, M. (1988, July). *Peer rejection and self-perceptions among early elementary school children: Aggressive rejectees vs. withdrawn rejectees*. Paper presented at the NATO Advanced Study Institute: Social Competence in Developmental Perspective, Savoie, France.

Bukowski, W. M., & Ferber, J. S. (1987, April). *A study of peer relations, attributional style, and loneliness during early adolescence*. Paper presented at the biennial meeting of the Society for Research in Child Development, Baltimore.

Bukowski, W. M., & Hoza, B. (1989). Popularity and friendship: Issues in theory, measurement, and outcome. In T. J. Berndt & G. W. Ladd (Eds.), *Peer relationships in child development* (pp. 15–45). New York: Wiley.

Bukowski, W. M., & Newcomb, A. F. (1987, April). *Friendship quality and the "self" during early adolescence*. Paper presented at the biennial meeting of the Society for Research in Child Development, Baltimore.

Cairns, R. B., Cairns, B. D., Neckerman, H. J., Gest, S., & Gariepy, J. L. (1987). *Peer networks and aggressive behavior: Social support or social rejection?* Report from the Carolina Longitudinal Study. Chapel Hill: University of North Carolina at Chapel Hill.

Cassidy, J., & Asher, S. R. (1989a). *Young children's conceptions of loneliness*. Manuscript in preparation.

Cassidy, J., & Asher, S. R. (1989b, April). *Loneliness and peer relations in young children*. Paper presented at the biennial meeting of the Society for Research in Child Development, Kansas City.

Cohn, D. A., Lohrmann, B. C., & Patterson, C. (1985). *Social networks and loneliness in children*. Paper presented at the biennial meeting of the Society for Research in Child Development, Toronto, Ontario.

Coie, J. D., & Dodge, K. A. (1983). Continuities and changes in children's social status: A five-year longitudinal study. *Merrill-Palmer Quarterly, 29*, 261–281.

Coie, J. D., & Kupersmidt, J. B. (1983). A behavioral analysis of emerging social status in boys' groups. *Child Development, 54*, 1400–1416.

Crick, N. R., & Ladd, G. W. (1988, March). *Rejected and neglected children's perceptions of their peer experiences: Loneliness, social anxiety, and social avoidance*. Paper presented at the meeting of the Southeastern Conference on Human Development, Charleston.

Dodge, K. A. (1980). Social cognition and children's aggressive behavior. *Child Development, 51*, 162–170.

Dodge, K. A. (1983). Behavioral antecedents of peer social status. *Child Development, 54*, 1386–1399.

Dodge, K. A., & Frame, C. L. (1982). Social cognitive biases and deficits in aggressive boys. *Child Development, 53*, 620–635.

Dodge, K. A., Schlundt, D. G., Schocken, I., & Delugach, J. D. (1983). Social competence and children's sociometric status: The role of peer group entry strategies. *Merrill-Palmer Quarterly, 29*, 309–336.

Dodge, K. A., & Somberg, D. R. (1987). Hostile attributional biases among aggressive boys are exacerbated under conditions of threats to the self. *Child Development, 58*, 213–224.

French, D. C., & Waas, G. A. (1985). Behavior problems of peer-neglected and peer-rejected elementary-age children: Parent and teacher perspectives. *Child Development, 56*, 246–252.

Frieze, I. H., Bar-Tal, D., & Carrol, J. S. (1979). *New approaches to social problems*. San Francisco: Jossey-Bass.

Furman, W., & Robbins, P. (1985). What's the point? Issues in the selection of treatment objectives. In B. H. Schneider, K. H. Rubin, & J. E. Ledingham (Eds.), *Children's peer relations: Issues in assessment and intervention* (pp. 41–56). New York: Springer-Verlag.

Gagnon, C., Dumont, M., Tremblay, R. E., Charlebois, P., & Larivee, S. (1988, May). *Self-perceptions of aggressive–disruptive boys*. Paper presented at the biennial meeting of the University of Waterloo Conference on Child Development, Waterloo, Ontario.

Goetz, T. E., & Dweck, C. S. (1980). Learned helplessness in social situations. *Journal of Personality and Social Psychology, 39*, 246–255.

Gottman, J. M., Gonso, J., & Rasmussen, R. (1975). Social interaction, social competence, and friendship in children. *Child Development, 46*, 709–718.

Greenwald, A. G. (1980). The totalitarian ego: Fabrication and revision of personal history. *American Psychologist, 35*, 603–618.

Hayden-Thomson, L. (1989). *The development of the Relational Provisions Loneliness Questionnaire for Children*. Unpublished doctoral dissertation, University of Waterloo, Ontario.

Hayden, L., Tarulli, D., & Hymel, S. (1988, May). *Children talk about loneliness*. Paper presented at the biennial meeting of the University of Waterloo Conference on Child Development, Waterloo, Ontario.

Heider, F. (1958). *The psychology of interpersonal relations*. New York: Wiley.

Heinlein, L., & Spinner, B. (1985, April). *Measuring emotional loneliness in children.* Paper presented at the biennial meeting of the Society for Research in Child Development, Toronto.

Hymel, S. (1983, April). *Social isolation and rejection in children: The child's perspective.* Paper presented at the biennial meeting of the Society for Research in Child Development, Detroit.

Hymel, S., & Franke, S. (1985). Children's peer relations: Assessing self-perceptions. In B. H. Schneider, K. H. Rubin, & J. E. Ledingham (Eds.), *Children's peer relations: Issues in assessment and intervention* (pp. 75–92). New York: Springer-Verlag.

Hymel, S., Franke, S., & Freigang, R. (1985). Peer relationships and their dysfunction: Considering the child's perspective. *Journal of Social and Clinical Psychology, 3,* 405–415.

Hymel, S., Freigang, R., Franke, S., Both, L., Bream, L., & Borys, S. (1983, June). *Children's attributions for social situations: Variations as a function of social status and self-perception variables.* Paper presented at the annual meeting of the Canadian Psychological Association, Winnipeg, Manitoba.

Hymel, S., & Rubin, K. H. (1985). Children with peer relationships and social skills problems: Conceptual, methodological, and developmental issues. In G. J. Whitehurst (Ed.), *Annals of child development* (Vol. 2, pp. 251–297). Greenwich, CT: JAI Press.

Hymel, S., Tinsley, B. R., Asher, S. R., & Geraci, R. (1981). *Sociometric status and social skills: The initiating style of preschool children.* Unpublished manuscript, University of Illinois, Urbana-Champaign.

Jones, W. H. (1985). The psychology of loneliness: Some personality issues in the study of social support. In I. G. Sarason & B. R. Sarason (Eds.), *Social support: Theory, research, and applications.* Boston: M. Nijhoff.

Jones, W. H., Cavert, C. W., Snider, R. C., & Bruce, T. (1985). Relational stress: An analysis of situations and events associated with loneliness. In S. Duck & D. Perlman (Eds.), *Understanding personal relationships* (pp. 221–242). London: Sage.

Kagan, J., Hans, S., Markowitz, A., Lopez, D., & Sigal, H. (1982). Validity of children's self-reports of psychological qualities. In B. Maher (Ed.), *Progress in experimental personality research* (Vol. 2, pp. 171–211). New York: Academic Press.

Kurdek, L. A., & Krile, D. (1982). A developmental analysis of the relation between peer acceptance and both interpersonal understanding and perceived social self-competence. *Child Development, 53,* 1485–1491.

Ladd, G. W. (1983). Social networks of popular, average, and rejected children in school settings. *Merrill-Palmer Quarterly, 29,* 283–307.

Marcoen, A., & Brumagne, M. (1985). Loneliness among children and young adolescents. *Developmental Psychology, 21,* 1025–1031.

Masten, A. S., Morison, P., & Pellegrini, D. S. (1985). A Revised Class Play method of peer assessment. *Developmental Psychology, 21,* 523–533.

Masters, J. C., & Furman, W. (1981). Popularity, individual friendship selection, and specific peer interaction among children. *Developmental Psychology, 3,* 344–350.

Miller, D., & Ross, M. (1975). Self-serving bias in the attribution of causality: Fact or fiction? *Psychological Bulletin, 82,* 213–225.

Oden, S., & Asher, S. R. (1977). Coaching children in social skills for friendship making. *Child Development, 48,* 495–506.

Olweus, D. (1978). *Aggression in the schools: Bullies and whipping boys.* New York: Wiley.

Parker, J. G. (1986). Becoming friends: Conversational skills for friendship formation in young children. In J. M. Gottman & J. G. Parker (Eds.), *Conversations of friends: Speculations on affective development* (pp. 103–138). New York: Cambridge University Press.

Parkhurst, J. T., & Asher, S. R. (1987, April). The social concerns of aggressive–rejected children. In J. D. Coie (Chair), *Types of aggression and peer status: The social functions and consequences of children's aggression.* Symposium conducted at the biennial meeting of the Society for Research in Child Development, Baltimore.

Parkhurst, J. T., & Asher, S. R. (1989). *Peer rejection in middle school: Subgroup· differences in behavior, loneliness, and concerns.* Manuscript submitted for publication.

Peplau, L. A., & Perlman, D. (1982). *Loneliness: A sourcebook of current theory, research, and therapy.* New York: Wiley.

Peplau, L. A., Russell, D., & Heim, M. (1979). An attributional analysis of loneliness. In I. Frieze, D. Bar-Tal, & J. S. Carroll (Eds.), *New approaches to social problems* (pp. 53–78). San Francisco: Jossey-Bass.

Perry, D. G., Kusel, S. J., & Perry, L. L. (1988). Victims of peer rejection. *Developmental Psychology, 24,* 807–814.

Putallaz, M., & Gottman, J. M. (1981). An interactional model of children's entry into peer groups. *Child Development, 52,* 986–994.

Quay, H. W. (1979). Classification. In H. C. Quay & J. S. Werry (Eds.), *Psychopathological disorders of childhood* (pp. 1–42). New York: Wiley.

Rubenstein, C., & Shaver, P. (1979, May). *A factor analytic explanation of the experience of adult loneliness.* Paper presented at the UCLA Conference on Loneliness, Los Angeles.

Rubenstein, C., & Shaver, P. (1982). The experience of loneliness. In L. A. Peplau & D. Perlman (Eds.), *Loneliness: A sourcebook of current theory, research, and therapy* (pp. 206–223). New York: Wiley.

Rubin, K. H. (1985). Socially withdrawn children: An "at risk" population? In B. H. Schneider, K. H. Rubin, & J. E. Ledingham (Eds.), *Children's peer relations: Issues in assessment and intervention* (pp. 125–139). New York: Springer-Verlag.

Rubin, K. H., Hymel, S., LeMare, L., & Rowden, L. (1989). Children experiencing social difficulties: Sociometric neglect reconsidered. *Canadian Journal of Behavioural Science, 21,* 94–111.

Rubin, K. H., & Mills, R. (1988). The many faces of isolation. *Journal of Consulting and Clinical Psychology, 6,* 916–924.

Russell, D., Cutrona, C. E., Rose, J., & Yurko, K. (1984). Social and emotional loneliness: An examination of Weiss's typology of loneliness. *Journal of Personality and Social Psychology, 46,* 1313–1321.

Russell, D., Peplau, L. A., & Ferguson, M. (1978). Developing a measure of loneliness. *Journal of Personality Assessment, 42,* 290–294.

Schmidt, N., & Sermat, U. (1983). Measuring loneliness in different relationships. *Journal of Personality and Social Psychology, 44,* 1038–1047.

Snyder, M. L., Stephan, W. G., & Rosenfield, D. (1978). Attributional egotism. In J. Harvey, W. J. Ickes, & R. F. Kidd (Eds.), *New directions in attribution research* (Vol. 2, pp. 91–117). Hillsdale, NJ: Lawrence Erlbaum.

Sobol, M. P., & Earn, B. M. (1985). Assessment of children's attributions for social experiences: Implications for social skills training. In B. H. Schneider, K. H. Rubin, & J. E. Ledingham (Eds.), *Children's peer relations: Issues in assessment and intervention* (pp. 93–110). New York: Springer-Verlag.

Stein, E. L., & Hymel, S. (1986, May). *Neglected versus rejected children: Differences in self and peer perceptions.* Paper presented at the biennial meeting of the University of Waterloo Conference on Child Development, Waterloo, Ontario.

Strauss, A. L. (1987). *Qualitative analysis for social scientists.* New York: Cambridge University Press.

Sullivan, H. S. (1953). *The interpersonal theory of psychiatry.* New York: W. W. Norton.

Taylor, A. R., & Asher, S. R. (1989). *Children's goals in game playing situations.* Unpublished manuscript, University of Maryland, College Park.

Vosk, B., Forehand, R., Parker, J. B., & Rickard, K. (1982). A multimethod comparison of popular and unpopular children. *Developmental Psychology, 18,* 571–575.

Weiss, R. S. (1973). *Loneliness: The experience of emotional and social isolation*. Cambridge: MIT Press.

Williams, G. A., & Asher, S. R. (1987, April). *Peer- and self-perceptions of peer rejected children: Issues in classification and subgrouping*. Paper presented at the biennial meeting of the Society for Research in Child Development, Baltimore.

10 The role of poor peer relationships in the development of disorder

Janis B. Kupersmidt, John D. Coie, and Kenneth A. Dodge

The purpose of this chapter is threefold. First, we will review the research literature linking peer relationship problems in childhood to various disorders in adolescence and in the early-adult years. Second, we will consider the role of early peer rejection in the etiology of these disorders. Third, we wish to contribute to this literature by presenting novel findings concerning the predictive relationships between early peer relations and later adjustment.

A potent stimulus for much of the current interest in children's peer relations has been the presumed power of this variable to predict later outcomes. Indeed, there is a familiar list of studies that is cited in most of the articles published in the area of peer relations research (Cowen, Pederson, Babigian, Izzo, & Trost, 1973; M. Roff, 1960, 1961; M. Roff, Sells, & Golden, 1972). The literature on peer relations as a predictor of risk has been comprehensively reviewed recently by Parker and Asher (1987). They assessed the accuracy of peer acceptance, aggression, and withdrawal as predictors of multiple forms of negative outcome (early withdrawal from school, delinquency and criminality, mental health problems). The results from studies utilizing different sources of information about social adjustment (i.e., peers, teachers, parents) were contrasted. Despite many methodological shortcomings in the longitudinal literature, substantial evidence for the importance of peer relations as a predictor of certain negative outcomes emerged from their analysis.

In the present chapter, we will address several points not covered by the Parker and Asher review. Sex differences in the predictive relation between peer status and disorder will be considered, particularly in connection with the age at which peer status is assessed. Developmental considerations have not been given much attention in previous reviews (Kohlberg, LaCrosse, & Ricks, 1972; Parker & Asher, 1987). Such attention is warranted because the function of social behavior changes with development, and the impact of peer relations on personal adjustment may change from childhood to adolescence. Our review will demonstrate that sex and age do have important effects on the prediction of disorder from earlier peer status. In considering these additional points of emphasis, we will attempt to provide a conceptual outline of several models of the role of peer

274

relations in the development of disorder. We will propose several research strategies for addressing the etiological role of poor peer relations. The chapter will conclude with detailed descriptions of several recent longitudinal studies that offer new findings in this area.

Methodological issues

Three methodological issues need attention when reviewing the prediction literature. The first involves the overall design of the longitudinal studies themselves, namely, whether they were follow-forward or follow-backward designs. A follow-backward design involves the identification of subjects fitting a given criterion for maladjustment against whom a matched group of nonsymptomatic control subjects is compared on childhood data that are usually obtained from institutional records. As Kohlberg, LaCrosse, and Ricks (1972) pointed out, significant follow-backward differences are sometimes quite misleading in terms of their predictive value. Demonstration of good prediction requires the following forward of randomly selected groups of children that have been selected for contrast on a childhood variable suspected to be related to adult maladjustment.

Retrospective interview studies are similar in design to follow-backward studies, but they rely on post hoc recall by the interviewee for information about the predictor variables. Thus, they present considerably more methodological problems, such as distortions in memory, beyond those associated with analysis of archival data in a follow-backward design. In the current review, retrospective and follow-backward studies are described together and follow-forward studies are reviewed separately. Greatest weight in our conclusions about predictive relations will be given to data from follow-forward studies.

A second methodological problem is that the operational definition of poor peer relationships has varied greatly across investigations. Peer, parent, and teacher reports of liking, popularity, friendships, and antisocial behavior have all been used to index social adjustment within the peer group. Parker and Asher (1987) have distinguished between predictor variables that indicate (typically with sociometric measures) how well the child is liked and those that describe what the child is like behaviorally. Most of the existing research has utilized social behaviors as predictor variables rather than sociometric data, so that sociometric status often must be inferred from behavioral measures. The review that follows will cover studies involving predictor variables of three types: sociometric measures based on peer nominations or peer ratings; ratings by adults of children's peer social adjustment; and composite behavioral descriptions of social behaviors with peers that have high correlations with peer rejection.

The third methodological consideration stems from the fact that poor peer relationships in childhood have been associated with a wide range of negative outcomes, from dropping out of school to criminal behavior to psychosis. It is not clear whether specific outcomes can be predicted from specific patterns of early peer relations, or whether difficulty in getting along with one's peers in middle childhood or in preadolescence is a nonspecific predictor of later social or psychological maladjustment. This lack of knowledge about the specificity of peer relations as a predictor variable was addressed by Kohlberg, Ricks, and Snarey (1984), who suggested that "if the particular forms and temporal sequences of peer difficulties are examined, particular kinds of outcomes may be predictable" (p. 148). The current review is thus organized according to four main categories of the outcome variable: schizophrenia, general mental health problems, delinquency and criminal behavior, and school-related problems, particularly early withdrawal from school. Schizophrenia is discussed separately from other mental health problems because of the substantial body of research on the prediction of this specific disorder.

The prediction of schizophrenia

There have been two views of the social character of preschizophrenic children and adolescents. The most prevalent early view has been that the shy, withdrawn behavior of the socially isolated child was quantitatively, but not qualitatively, different from that of the schizophrenic adult (Cadoret, 1973; Kasanin & Veo, 1932; Kohn & Clausen, 1955; Kreisman, 1970; Stephens, Atkinson, Kay, Roth, & Garside, 1975). The social withdrawal of the preschizophrenic individual is continuous over time, suggesting that rejection by peers is merely an indicator, a marker variable, of risk without contributing in any causal way. Interestingly, the less prevalent view was originally articulated by two individuals, Bleuler (1950) and Kraeplin (1919), who were pioneers in the study of schizophrenia. Their view was that the preschizophrenic child is anxious, excitable, irritable, and aggressive in an unsocialized manner and that the seclusive behavior of schizophrenics is a final stage in "a process that began with exclusion or isolation which was not the choice of the patient" (Faris, 1934, p. 159). Note that this view posits a directly causal role of social rejection in the ontogenesis of schizophrenia. It is interesting that this latter characterization of the preschizophrenic child is most congruent with empirical evidence about the behavior of the rejected child.

Follow-backward studies to adolescence

The majority of the evidence linking schizophrenia to earlier social isolation comes from retrospective studies of schizophrenics' high school years as the predictive starting point (Barthell & Holmes, 1968; Bower, Shellhamer, & Daily,

1960; Clausen & Kohn, 1960; Kasanin & Veo, 1932; Kohn & Clausen, 1955). In retrospective interviews teachers who knew the mental illness outcomes of the subjects (Kasanin & Veo, 1932) emphasized the shyness and passivity of the preschizophrenic group, whereas in retrospective interviews teachers and interviewers who were not cognizant of the outcomes did not emphasize such characteristics (Bower et al., 1960). Both kinds of studies showed evidence that more preschizophrenic adolescents had problems relating to peers than control subjects and that many of them exhibited odd or peculiar behavior that may have indicated the onset of schizophrenia.

Two general problems are reflected in these retrospective studies. One is the problem of retrospective recall when the informants are not blind to outcome. As Shweder (1975) and others have noted, when people process social information about others they tend to focus selectively on behaviors that promote the consistency of trait hypotheses they hold about the other persons. In this case, parents or teachers are likely to recall behaviors that best match the current symptomatology of the subjects, and they selectively recall "early signs" of the disorder. Thus, retrospective accounts with nonblinded informants may overstate the evidence for social withdrawal, because this is a behavioral style associated with schizophrenia. Further, even in the Bower et al. study that purports to use blind informants, there is some indication that teachers knew about schizophrenic outcomes in some cases.

The second problem is with the ambiguity of the timing of events to be recounted. Because many schizophrenic episodes first take place in late adolescence, the period of retrospective reporting may overlap with the time during which these adolescents were actually exhibiting initial schizophrenic symptoms. Thus these latter reports may describe the symptoms of adolescent schizophrenia rather than the premorbid antecedents of the disorder.

In a series of projects, Mednick and Schulsinger followed a cohort of 9- to 20-year-olds (mean age of 15) who were designated as at high risk for schizophrenia because each had a mother with a history of chronic schizophrenia. This cohort was matched to a low-risk control group on a variety of demographic variables. An examination of teacher questionnaire data on these two groups revealed that the high-risk group was more easily upset and more disturbing to the class than the low-risk group (Mednick & Schulsinger, 1970). They were also more socially withdrawn. These findings support the notion that deviant peer-directed social behavior is at least a partial function of genetic factors.

John, Mednick, and Schulsinger (1982) continued to follow their high-risk sample to assess which school-related variables were associated with later schizophrenia or borderline schizophrenia. Outcome data were collected when the subjects were approximately 25 years old and consisted of a consensually determined diagnosis of each high-risk subject based upon data collected from a clinical interview and a psychological test battery. Based upon the outcome diagnoses, all of the high-risk subjects were divided into one of three groups: schizophrenic, borderline schizophrenic (consisting of pseudoneurotic and pseudopsychopathic schizophrenic and schizoid and paranoid personality disordered diagnostic groups), and others (including psychopathic, neurotic, other personality disorders, nonspecific conditions, and no mental illness). The premorbidity data from schools were then analyzed for differences between these groups. Unfortunately, although the data were collected longitudinally, the data were analyzed in a follow-backward design, because probability estimates were based on outcome rather than on predictor variables. Adolescents who eventually became schizophrenic and male adolescents who became borderline schizophrenics were rated by their teachers as lonely, isolated, and rejected by peers in comparison to the nonschizophrenic, nonborderline group. Thus, even when genetic variables were controlled as much as possible, early deviant behavior and social rejection were associated with later schizophrenia. These findings neither confirm nor refute the role of rejection as a causal variable, but they are consistent with the popularly held theory that many forms of mental illness follow a diathesis-stress model (Carson, Butcher, & Coleman, 1988), in which social rejection might serve as one stressor.

Premorbid patterns of social behavior among this sample differed somewhat as a function of gender. In adolescence, the preschizophrenic males were more emotional, irritable, and disruptive in class than peers and were expected by teachers to develop later psychotic or emotional problems, whereas the preschizophrenic females were more isolated and nervous.

In general, the findings for adolescent girls are consistent with the notion that preschizophrenic behavior is characterized by social isolation and heightened anxiety, whereas the premorbid behavior of preschizophrenic adolescent boys suggests a more mixed pattern of withdrawn (internalizing) and antisocial (externalizing) behaviors. Despite these differences in behavior, teachers described both boys and girls as rejected by peers; however, the reliability of teacher reports of peer rejection, particularly during adolescence, is somewhat suspect (Gronlund, 1959). Hence, the best data on predicting schizophrenia from adolescent peer behavior are qualified by methodological shortcomings. We found no follow-forward studies from adolescence to adulthood using peer social relations as a predictor variable.

Follow-backward studies to childhood

Three sources of data on the childhood social histories of adult schizophrenics have been utilized in retrospective studies: parental recollections of behavior with siblings, child guidance clinic or hospital records, and school records of subjects who had been evaluated during childhood. Many of these studies have serious methodological problems, such as the lack of control groups and informants' knowledge of the outcome. Some of these studies are worth noting, however, because of the hypotheses that they generated or because of their congruence with other findings. Stabenau and Pollin (1970), for example, conducted interviews with the families of 14 pairs of monozygotic twins discordant for schizophrenia. From age 6 through the early teenage years, the preschizophrenic twin apparently had poorer peer relations and lower school grades than the other twin. In late adolescence, the differences between twins became more pronounced, culminating in the social withdrawal of the preschizophrenic twin. Similar findings have been reported from retrospective parental interviews about schizophrenic and nonschizophrenic siblings. The latter were described as more emotionally independent and physically active, whereas the former were more unsociable, introspective, serious, and less happy (Prout & White, 1956). Even as preschoolers, preschizophrenics have been seen as more irritable, shy, dependent, and nonaffectionate than the "normal" sibling, and subsequently to have poorer peer relations, poorer school performance, and more conduct problems (Pollack, Woerner, Goodman, & Greenberg, 1966).

Watt and his colleagues (Lewine, Watt, Prentky, & Fryer, 1978, 1980; Watt, Stolorow, Lubensky, & McClelland, 1970) assessed the premorbid behavioral patterns of schizophrenics in a series of follow-backward studies based on teacher comments in school records. Although peer status was not directly assessed in these studies, preschizophrenic males were reported to have exhibited a childhood behavioral style that is characteristic of rejected children. They were found to be more antisocial and disagreeable than controls but did not show differences in introversion. Preschizophrenic females, however, exhibited an introverted behavioral style. One problem in interpreting the array of findings from these studies is that school record data were collapsed across school years (in some studies, across kindergarten through twelfth grade), possibly obscuring the hypothesized developmental changes as a function of gender.

Other work by Watt and his colleagues did explore developmental differences. Watt and Lubensky (1976) reported that preschool children who became schizophrenic were characterized by emotional immaturity and social isolation. Preschizophrenic preschool boys exhibited an abrasive and antisocial behavior pattern, and preschizophrenic preschool girls were introverted and socially insecure. In a replication of his original longitudinal study, Watt (1978) confirmed the earlier findings that preschizophrenic girls in kindergarten through sixth grade were also emotionally unstable, introverted, and passive; however, the preschizophrenic boys in those grades were not behaviorally distinguishable from their matched controls. He also confirmed his findings that seventh- to twelfth-grade girls were introverted and boys were characterized as disagreeable compared with matched controls.

There is a series of studies in which data on peer relations are taken from child clinic records to make contrasts between matched adult schizophrenic and non-schizophrenic groups who had been seen in these clinics (Fleming & Ricks, 1970; Frazee, 1953; Ricks & Berry, 1970; M. Roff, 1963; M. Roff, Mink, & Hinrichs, 1966; J. Roff, Knight, & Wertheim, 1976). Because the adult comparison groups were first identified and then background data on each were obtained from clinic files, these studies all constitute follow-backward research and do not provide true incidence rates of disorder for the predictor variable, even taking into account the restricted nature of their samples. The data from each study do support the conclusion that adult schizophrenics have childhood histories of poor peer relationships more than matched nonschizophrenic adult control subjects. For example, M. Roff (1963) reported that 65% of psychotic servicemen (predominantly schizophrenics) had poor peer relations in childhood, whereas this was true for only 25% of the controls.

Several trends in these follow-backward studies can be described. Whenever the quality of peer relationships was assessed, preschizophrenic children were found to show problems in their peer relationships. There is some evidence that a developmental trend may characterize the behavior of preschizophrenic males: from few or no overt behavior problems in childhood to increasingly antisocial behavior in adolescence (Watt, 1978). Preschizophrenic females may be more consistently withdrawn in their behavioral style during childhood and adolescence.

Follow-forward studies of children

A prominent example of a follow-forward study is that by Michael, Morris, and Soroker (1957), in which the prevalence of schizophrenia was investigated on a sample of 606 subjects who had been seen 14 to 29 years earlier at a child guidance clinic for brief evaluation. They coded the child subject pool into three behavior problem categories: extraverts, introverts, and ambiverts (a combination of acting out and withdrawal problems). Of the 10 subjects who had been hospitalized for schizophrenia, one was from the introvert group, three from the extravert group, and six were ambiverts. Because the three groups were of approximately equal size, these figures argue against introversion as a predictor of schizophrenia and have led some investigators (e.g., Ledingham, 1981; Ledingham & Schwartzman, 1984) to consider the ambivert group as being at greatest risk for schizophrenia. Because the behavior characteristics of rejected children most closely match those of the extravert and ambivert groups, it is possible to view these data as congruent with the results of the follow-backward studies.

Conclusions about the prediction of schizophrenia

There are several conclusions that can be drawn about the precursors of schizophrenia. The first is that introversion and social withdrawal in the elementary school years are not general predictors of schizophrenia; rather, they seem to be associated with the disorder among females but not among males. Second, social withdrawal in adolescence has a stronger relation to schizophrenia than does withdrawal in childhood. The childhood predictors all reflect behavioral difficulties of the sort that have been linked to peer rejection in Chapter 2 in this volume. Preschizophrenic children have been described as socially inappropriate, disagreeable, mean, irritable, prone to tantrums or violent behavior, and as having poor peer relations. The developmental course for preschizophrenic boys seems to be one of early antisocial behavior and peer rejection, followed by social isolation in adolescence. Preschizophrenic girls are more consistently socially isolated but also rejected. This developmental pattern suggests that social rejection in childhood precedes rather than follows an increasing tendency toward social withdrawal in the preschizophrenic adolescent. It must be noted, however, that any conclusions about the role of peer rejection in the development of schizophrenia are based on inference from behavioral data or from adult judgment of children's peer group status. No direct sociometric evidence on peer rejection is available within this area of research.

The prediction of nonspecified mental health problems

There is a relatively small group of studies of mental health outcomes in which the type of disorder at outcome is not specified. In most of these studies, contact with a mental health professional constituted evidence for the presence of mental health problems and was utilized as the sole outcome variable. One difficulty in interpreting the findings from these studies is that by using only the presence or absence of a mental health contact as an index of disorder, it is not possible to consider the connections between peer problems and any particular psychiatric diagnosis. Thus, any potential pathway between a particular childhood problem and a specific adult diagnostic entity is obscured in this kind of summary analysis. Literature on this topic is available only on the prediction from childhood; hence conclusions cannot be drawn about prediction from adolescence.

Follow-backward studies to childhood

There have been two childhood follow-backward studies of nonspecific mental health problems. Both of these studies have had a major influence on the study of peer relations in childhood. In the first, M. Roff (1960) utilized data from child guidance clinic records to distinguish between servicemen who were diagnosed as psychoneurotic and those who made an adequate adjustment in the military. Teacher comments on children's social behavior were taken from these records as indices of childhood social adjustment. Roff reported that 34 out of 49 males (69%) who were psychoneurotic while in military service were disliked by their peers as children in comparison to 11 out of 49 males (22%) who had a good outcome during military service who were also disliked by their peers in childhood.

Cowen and colleagues (Cowen et al., 1973) followed up 811 third-graders who were part of an early-detection mental health project in Monroe County, New York. Approximately 11 to 13 years after the initial screening of these children, access was obtained to a psychiatric register of all residents who had received some form of mental health services in this county. The investigators performed t tests on each of 24 childhood predictor variables (taken from child assessments, teacher reports, and school records) in an attempt to discriminate those 60 children (7.4%) who later sought help for psychological problems from those who did not. The children who later appeared in the psychiatric register received significantly more peer nominations for negative roles on the Bower (1969) Class Play measure than their matched, nonregister controls. Given the strong relation between the negative behaviors that make up the Class Play and rejected peer status, many investigators have used these findings to conclude that rejected children may be at heightened risk for psychological difficulties in adolescence or adulthood.

Follow-forward studies of children

Three follow-forward studies of childhood predictors of adult mental health will be discussed. In the first study, 130 nursery school students were followed through school (Westman, Rice, & Berman, 1967). Early peer relations, as noted by coding of nursery school records, were significantly related to the subsequent development of neurotic behaviors in later school years (coded from school and clinical files).

The second project was a 12-year study conducted by Janes and Hesselbrock (1978) and Janes, Hesselbrock, Myers, and Penniman (1979). They followed children who had been seen at a St. Louis child guidance clinic. Individual outcome evaluation interviews were conducted with each subject and his or her mother, and these follow-up interviews were rated in terms of overall adjustment by judges blind to the subject's prior history. Failure to get along with other children, preferring to play with younger children, and selfishness, as reported by teachers on a 31-item behavior checklist, were most predictive of psychiatric hospitalizations. One problem in interpreting the results of this study is that the sample ranged in age from 4 to 15 years of age, so that one cannot readily separate childhood from adolescent predictors of psychological maladjustment.

In the third project, J. Roff and Wirt (1984b) followed 2,453 members of a longitudinal sociometric study originally conducted by M. Roff et al. (1972) and located those who had been treated for psychiatric problems at hospital and outpatient clinics. Peer social status in elementary school (third through sixth grade for this cohort) was determined by the difference between liked most and liked least sociometric nominations. The correlations between childhood peer status and treatment for mental health problems were quite low ($r = .13$ for males and $r = .08$ for females). However, this may be due to the low base rate of disorder for the total population (8%). The prevalence rate of disorder was significantly higher for low-peer-status males (14%) than for middle- (5.1%) or high-status males (4%). The same general pattern held true for females (low = 9%, middle = 6.4%, and high = 3.8%); however, the chi-square for this comparison was only marginally significant.

Conclusions about the prediction of nonspecified mental health problems

In summary, it appears that a consistent prediction picture has emerged from both follow-backward and follow-forward research. Low peer social status in childhood is predictive of nonspecified mental health problems in adolescence or adulthood. The causal role of social rejection in these problems is not at all clear, nor is the strength of this relation.

The prediction of criminality

In this section, we will review evidence for the longitudinal relation between peer social status and criminal activity. No follow-backward studies to adolescence were located that used peer relations as a predictor variable. Several methodological points should be noted with respect to data in this area. First, the term *juvenile delinquency* covers a wide range of acts that are divided into two categories for legal purposes, status and nonstatus offenses. Status offenses are age-specific offenses such as truancy, running away from home, and curfew violations that would not be crimes if they were committed by adults. Nonstatus offenses are crimes regardless of age-group and include more serious offenses such as murder, rape, and robbery. Because such a wide range of offenses often are aggregated in many of the studies reviewed, a heterogeneous array of adolescents often are grouped together under the label of delinquent, and this fact may interfere with the task of finding valid predictors of juvenile delinquency. A

second point concerns the effect on reported crime rates of the selective con-
centration by law enforcement agencies on certain subject populations. Factors
such as age, race, ethnicity, social class, and family structure may contribute
significantly to the official determination of an adolescent's being a delinquent
(Empey, 1978). Status offenders of higher socioeconomic status usually have the
financial resources to defend themselves within the criminal justice system more
successfully than indigent offenders (Nagel, 1966). This bias in the detection and
recording process may lead to a bias in the detection of risk variables.

This last point raises questions about the most appropriate instrument or method for use in identifying cases of juvenile delinquency. The most common
methodology is to match names in a cohort list against juvenile police and court
files in order to identify those youths who have had detected and recorded contact
with the juvenile justice system. A newer methodology involves the use of
confidential self-report questionnaires. There is evidence for the accuracy of the
results from self-report data (Hindelang, Hirschi, & Weis, 1981; Jessor & Jessor,
1977) in that they correspond well to reported cases.

Finally, many of the studies in this section, as in other sections, are based on
populations that are not "normal" in that they are either children who have been
previously apprehended for delinquency or who have had contact with a psychiatric clinic. The processes associated with further criminality among those samples cannot be assumed to apply to unselected samples.

Follow-forward studies of adolescents

Shea (1972; reported in Hafner, Quast, & Shea, 1975) followed up adolescent
psychiatric inpatients and outpatients who were classified according to Achenbach's (1966) Internalizer (I)–Externalizer (E) distinction. Internalizing symptoms included such behaviors as phobias, anxiety, delusions, and hallucinations.
Poor peer relationships and behavior disorders such as lying or vandalism characterized the E subjects. Medical (nonpsychiatric) control patients were matched
with each pair of E and I patients for sex, age, family intactness, socioeconomic
status, intelligence level, and urban versus rural residence. E males were later
found to spend a disproportionate amount of time in correctional institutions in
adolescence and in adulthood relative to other groups. E subjects, in general,
were rated as more disturbed as adults than the I subjects.

Follow-backward studies to childhood

A number of follow-backward studies suggest the presence of a relation between
peer rejection in childhood and subsequent delinquency. The first study involved
a sample of 184 tenth-grade juvenile delinquents and a matched control group

(Conger & Miller, 1966). The groups were compared on teacher ratings of personal and social development and unstructured teacher comments from cumulative school records. In both third and sixth grade, the predelinquents showed greater problems with social acceptability, aggressiveness, and getting along with peers than the nondelinquents.

M. Roff (1961) located the military records of 164 men who had been seen at child guidance clinics in their youth. The clinic records were evaluated for evidence of good, neutral, or bad peer relations. Men who had bad-conduct discharges or disciplinary records of bad conduct were compared with men matched for IQ who had no bad-conduct problems. Fifty-six percent of the bad-conduct group had poor peer relationships as children, whereas only 26% of the good-conduct men had poor peer adjustment.

Follow-forward studies of children

There is one study of teacher reports of peer problems as a predictor of subsequent criminality. In a child guidance clinic sample of 4- to 15-year-old boys followed forward for 12 to 14 years, Janes et al. (1979) found that failure to get along with other children was significantly related to more trouble with the law and more arrests.

There are three follow-up studies in which peers were the primary source of data on childhood peer status in unselected populations of children. Skaberne, Blejec, Skalar, and Vodopivec (1965) had elementary school children in Yugoslavia rate their peers on popularity, aggression, untruthfulness, and withdrawn behavior. They conducted a 7-year follow-up of this sample and reported that a high peer rating on untruthfulness was the best predictor of future delinquency. Aggression was the next best predictor of delinquent behavior. These findings provide cross-cultural validation of the notion that there is continuity in antisocial behavior from childhood to adolescence. Peer ratings of popularity were not significant predictors of delinquency.

West (1969; West & Farrington, 1973, 1977) followed 411 schoolboys who had resided originally in a working-class urban area in England, selected for its relatively high rate of delinquency. When the boys were 8 years old, ratings were obtained from their teachers as well as from social workers who individually interviewed each subject's family. Positive peer nomination data were also collected. Records of juvenile court contacts over the next 11 years indicated that a quarter of the entire sample had committed an offense between the ages of 10 and 18. Most of these offenses were committed in the company of one or more peers. The delinquents and nondelinquents were not distinguishable by their number of positive peer nominations. Teacher and peer assessment ratings were combined to form a "troublesomeness" score for each subject. Those subjects with a subsequent record of delinquency were significantly more troublesome as children than nondelinquents. In fact, troublesomeness alone was a better predictor of delinquency than a combination of five background variables consisting of low family income, large family size, poor parental behavior, parental criminality, and low intelligence. Each of these background variables was significantly correlated with the troublesomeness index. Delinquents scored higher than nondelinquents on troublesomeness even when matched on each of these background variables. The composite troublesomeness index may reflect more general social qualities that are highly correlated with negative nominations and with peer rejection.

M. Roff et al. (1972) followed a sample of 18,000 children in Minnesota and Texas to study the relation between peer social status and later social deviance. A peer nomination sociometric technique involving "like most" and "like least" items was used to acquire information about childhood social adjustment. Liked most and liked least scores were standardized within a classroom, and then standardized liked least scores were subtracted from standardized liked most scores to obtain a social preference measure. Children were classified into one of eight socioeconomic status groups based on 1960 census tract data for the school in which they were enrolled. For this reason, the socioeconomic status assignments for individuals may be less accurate than is appropriate for individual-difference analyses. Male juvenile delinquency was assessed by consulting police or juvenile court records. One of the most important findings from this project was that delinquency was significantly predicted by peer rejection among lower middle, middle, and upper class subjects. In fact, there were very few upper class, *popular* boys who became delinquent, whereas there were upper class, unpopular boys who became delinquent. On the other hand, delinquency occurred with about equal frequency among most rejected and best liked boys in the very lowest socioeconomic octile. Thus, peer status was an important predictor variable for all classes of boys except for the most poverty-stricken.

The focus of most longitudinal research on the prediction of juvenile delinquency has been on boys. Males commit proportionately more reported crimes than females, and the crimes committed by males were reported to be much more aggressive and dangerous than those committed by females. Historically, the crimes committed by females primarily have been those (e.g., alcohol use, truancy) that were more destructive to themselves than to others. Because female delinquent behavior has been less salient and less destructive, female delinquency may have been underreported. Thus, many investigators have stated that the prevalence of delinquency among females was too low to be included in statistical analyses. In most cases, either females have been excluded from the data collection or data have been collapsed across males and females.

However, M. Roff (1975) reanalyzed the data collected by Roff et al. (1972) for the females in this sample. Despite the fact that the females had primarily committed status offenses such as running away from home, he found a positive relation between low peer social status and delinquency at all four of the lowest socioeconomic octiles. The utility of this information is limited by the fact that only about 7% of the total number of female subjects were delinquent. It is interesting to note that unlike the findings for males, low peer status in childhood was an important predictor of delinquency across all levels of family income among females.

As noted earlier, J. Roff and Wirt (1984a) reported a second follow-up analysis on the subsample of 2,453 of the predominantly white and lower class children from the Roff, Sells, and Golden sample. Delinquency was assessed from juvenile court records. Peer social status and socioeconomic status proved to be significant additive predictors of delinquency for both males and females at all levels of socioeconomic status. For example, of the low peer status, low social class males, 46.3% became delinquent, compared with only 26.3% of the entire male sample and 23.4% of the high peer status, lowest social class male group. J. Roff and Wirt also had teachers provide behavioral descriptions of the children and found that aggression was the best predictor of male and female delinquency and of male adult criminality. In a comparison of the pattern of correlations for delinquency, mental health treatment contact, and welfare status, childhood aggression was related to the specific outcome of delinquency among males and to both delinquency and welfare status among females.

Conclusions about the prediction of criminality

The results of the studies just reviewed suggest that delinquency and adult criminality are predicted by a pattern of childhood behavior that can be characterized as aggressive, troublesome, antisocial, and marked by violations of peer group and school norms. These characteristics are highly correlated with social rejection in childhood, and not surprisingly, in studies in which negative sociometric nominations were employed to assess peer status, unpopularity was predictive of future delinquency. The relative predictive value of aggressive and antisocial behavior and peer rejection was not addressed in these studies, however. One plausible interpretation of the relation between aggressive behavior, poor peer relationships, and delinquency is that children who break rules and are aggressive will be disliked by peers because of that behavior, and that delinquency is the continuation of this constellation of antisocial behaviors on a more serious level. Such a pattern would implicate rejection as a marker but not a causal variable. Some evidence that seems to support this conclusion will be described at the end of this chapter in a study that utilized both peer rejection and aggressiveness indices as predictors of both delinquency and early school withdrawal.

The prediction of school adjustment and early school withdrawal

In 1985, 14.1% of 18- to 21-year-olds were high school dropouts (U.S. Bureau of Census, Current Population Reports, 1988). Thus, in a society where education is presumably valued highly, we find many youth who are truant and who withdraw from school even though the social consequences of these acts may include ostracism, future unemployment, and being perceived by others as deviant (Zeller, 1966). There is some retrospective evidence to suggest that other negative outcomes are associated with dropping out of school. For example, in a follow-backward study of adult sociopaths, all of whom were chronic offenders, Robins (1966) found that 98% were school dropouts.

Follow-backward studies to adolescence

Two follow-backward studies suggest a relation between peer rejection and early school withdrawal. Ninth-grade teachers were asked to describe retrospectively members of a group of school dropouts and a matched group of high school graduates on seven different rating scales (Amble, 1967). The teachers described 46% of the male dropouts as being socially rejected or not tolerated by their peers, whereas only 7% of the male graduates were so described. The difference for females was somewhat less: 14% of the female dropouts were socially rejected, compared with only 4% of the female graduates.

Kuhlen and Collister (1952) compared high school graduates and dropouts on peer nomination data collected when the cohort was in the ninth grade. Positive sociometric nomination scores did not differentiate future dropouts from future graduates; however, the two groups did differ on nominations for being unpopular with peers. In addition, the groups differed on other questions when the data were analyzed separately by gender. In addition to being unpopular with peers, male dropouts were distinct from male graduates on nominations for enjoying fighting, being unkempt in their appearance, unfriendly, depressed, and physically unattractive. Thus, it is possible that negative sociometric items would have distinguished male graduates from dropouts. The female dropouts were not viewed by their ninth-grade peers in behavioral terms that were as antisocial as those of the male dropout group; however, what is common to both the male and the female predropouts is the tendency to be unpopular with peers. In this case, then, peer unpopularity may be a general indicator of dropout risk even though specific accompanying behaviors may vary by gender. Thus, there is some basis for hypothesizing that social rejection plays a causal role in early school withdrawal.

Follow-forward studies of adolescents

Ullmann (1957) conducted a follow-forward study of all of the ninth-graders in three Maryland junior high schools using teacher ratings and peer ratings and self-descriptive personality test scores to predict dropping out of school. Sociometric and teacher ratings significantly predicted school dropout for the males, whereas the self-descriptive personality test predicted females' school adjustment. Unfortunately, the type of sociometric test used was not described, making it difficult to interpret or to replicate these results.

Both of the adolescent follow-backward studies, as well as the one follow-forward study reviewed, suggest the possibility that there are sex differences in the behavioral precursors of early school withdrawal. Lack of friends in adolescence is predictive for females, whereas active peer rejection and behavior problems are most predictive for male adolescents. There are data indicating that the reasons given by adolescents for dropping out of school vary according to gender as well. For example, girls have been reported to leave school early because of a desire to marry or because of pregnancy, but a desire for marriage has not been cited by boys as a reason for early withdrawal (Bowman & Matthews, 1960; Snepp, 1953).

Follow-backward studies to childhood

Although there are several studies examining the concurrent relationship between childhood acceptance and academic achievement (e.g., Green, Forehand, Beck, & Vosk, 1980; Muma, 1965), there are relatively few long-term longitudinal studies that address the relation between dropping out of school and either of these two early indices.

Kuhlen and Collister (1952) contrasted dropouts and graduates on earlier sixth-grade sociometric and peer assessment data. Male dropouts had received significantly fewer positive sociometric nominations from same-sex peers than male graduates. Both male and female dropouts had been described by peers as being less attractive, more listless, appearing sad, and more unpopular in the sixth grade than those who eventually graduated. The male dropouts also had been described as unfriendly and unable to enjoy jokes about themselves, whereas the female dropouts had been seen as acting overly mature for their age and being quieter and more unkempt than female graduates.

Lambert (1972) investigated the relation between peer relationships and a composite measure of academic adjustment by administering the Bower (1969)

Class Play questionnaire to two cohorts of second- and fifth-graders. Each cohort was followed for 7 years, and at that point, subjects were categorized as being either high, average, or low on two adjustment variables. One was high school scholarship as determined by weighted scores for grade point average and achievement test scores for mathematics and reading. The other was a "lack of success in school" score based on disciplinary reports, remedial instruction status, probationary academic standing, or having dropped out of school. In both cohorts, those nominated significantly more often for negative Class Play roles were low on scholarship and showed less success in high school than those not nominated for negative roles.

Follow-forward studies of children

Gronlund and Holmlund (1958) determined the sociometric status of 1,073 sixth-grade pupils from positive nomination sociometric measures and followed 53 high-status and 49 low-status students. The high-status children had a relatively low dropout rate of 13%, whereas 45% of the low-status children dropped out of high school. Even though males had a higher dropout rate than females, the peer status difference held true for both males and females.

In a 4-year follow-up of fifth- through ninth-graders, sociometrically low-, medium-, and high-accepted children were compared for later dropout rates (Barclay, 1966). The dropout rate for low-accepted boys was 14% but was only 3% for high-accepted boys. The dropout rate for low-accepted girls was 15.5% and 6% for high-accepted girls.

Conclusions about the prediction of early school withdrawal

Peer rejection, as assessed by sociometric measures or by behavior descriptions that are congruent with the characteristics of rejected children, is consistently predictive of early school withdrawal. The effects may be more potent for boys than for girls, but the pattern is consistent regardless of sex. The behavior descriptions of boys at risk for dropping out seem to be associated with externalizing behaviors, whereas the behavior descriptions of girls at risk for dropping out are less clear. It is not surprising, therefore, that early patterns of aggression also have been linked strongly to early school withdrawal. What is left unanswered by these findings is the relative importance of aggression and social rejection as independent predictors of early school withdrawal. Available evidence suggests that social rejection might play a unique incremental role in this prediction. One reason for this may be that being rejected by the peer group may make coming to school an aversive experience for adolescents and thus motivate them to think of leaving school.

The role of rejection in the development of negative outcomes

Much of the research that supports a predictive connection between peer group rejection and negative personal adjustment is based on archival information that was not originally designed to explore this relation. Not surprisingly, therefore, there are few empirical data to address the important question of whether the experience of being rejected by one's peer group contributes causally to the negative outcomes discussed in this chapter. The developmental process by which various and multiple forms of disorder take shape has not yet been explored beyond the establishment of simple correlational findings. As Parker and Asher (1987) have suggested, there is a need to move beyond these rudimentary epidemiological models toward inquiry that will enhance our understanding of developmental process.

Several plausible hypotheses can be posited regarding the role of peer rejection in the development of psychopathology. The first hypothesis is that peer rejection is merely a marker variable indicating that risk has accrued from some more basic factor. A genetic interpretation, for example, would posit that the early peer group might be able to detect the "defective" aspect of a child headed for psychopathology, even though the experience of rejection plays no role in this development. A similar argument might be made from a social learning theory perspective. For example, social skill deficits (such as poor problem-solving skills and poor intention cue reading skills) might lead a child to be rejected by the peer group in early life, and these same deficits might account for maladjusted behavior in later life, without there being any direct causal relation between early peer rejection and later maladjustment.

A second hypothesis is that the experience of being accepted by peers, although lacking a direct causal link with the onset of psychopathology, may play a moderating role in the development of psychopathology. Thus, on the one hand, social support might buffer a vulnerable child from the emergence of psychopathology by enhancing self-esteem and providing opportunities for adaptive development (Garmezy, Masten, & Tellegen, 1984). On the other hand, the vulnerable child who is socially rejected might experience the additional stress of peer rejection and isolation.

A third hypothesis is that the experience of social rejection is directly causally related to psychopathological outcomes. There are at least two developmental trajectories that plausibly illustrate this hypothesis. One possibility is that acceptance into the peer group provides the child with an opportunity to interact with same-age equal partners in a manner that promotes social and cognitive development (Berndt & Ladd, in press; Piaget, 1965; Youniss, 1980). Piaget (1965) speculated that a child develops socially and intellectually through interactions with peers, particularly in settings involving play. The socially rejected child may be deprived of these early beneficial experiences and fail to develop adaptive capacities. Thus, social rejection, or social exclusion, might be a causal determinant of later maladaptive outcomes.

A second possible developmental trajectory is that being actively rejected by one's peer group induces internal reactions in the child that then lead to psychopathological or antisocial outcomes. Feelings of personal inadequacy or loneliness (Asher & Wheeler, 1985) or anger and resentment (Coie, Dodge, & Coppotelli, 1982) may lead to social orientations that give rise to more extremely maladaptive behavior. Children who internalize negative messages from peers may be at heightened risk for affective disorders, whereas those who turn against the peer group may be at risk for antisocial disorders.

The existing literature on risk prediction has not been designed to examine these hypotheses; thus it is difficult to discuss the relative support for each of these hypotheses without becoming highly speculative. Nonetheless, there is considerable support for the simplest contention, namely, that peer rejection is, at least, a marker of developmental risk. The hypothesis that peer rejection is *only* a marker requires the support of data on the parallel paths from early social behavior to later disorder and early peer status to later disorder. The studies reviewed thus far do not provide this evidence, although we will review several studies that begin to yield this kind of information in the next section.

There is, as yet, no empirical basis on which to evaluate the second of our hypothetical linkages between peer rejection and disorder, namely, that peer acceptance moderates the developmental process for children who are vulnerable to psychopathology on nonsocial grounds. In fact, vulnerability has not been established independently of peer status, but if this were done, it might be possible to evaluate this hypothesis by examining the effects of intervention on children identified as both rejected by peers and vulnerable for psychopathology due to nonsocial factors. One way to do this would be to consider the effects of interventions designed to make the peer group more accepting of rejected children and then to follow the impact of increased group acceptance. This paradigm might provide a strong test of the hypothesis that acceptance has a buffering role against other risk factors.

How might the causal role of social rejection in developmental outcomes be examined? Ultimately, support for both aspects of the third hypothesis will have to come from longitudinal or intervention designs in which changes in the behavior, feelings, and self-concepts of rejected children are tracked in relation to changes in peer status and psychological adjustment. We can suggest several research designs that could be employed in this effort, as well as a data analytic strategy. One type of design, of course, involves experimental manipulation of social acceptance or rejection. Even though we favor this approach, there are at least two problems with it. First, most interventions address the problem of peer rejection by attempting to enhance the social skills or behavior of individual children. This leaves the issue of changed peer status confounded with changes in the social repertoire of formerly rejected children. Second, one cannot be sure that by helping children improve their peer status, one has undone all of the negative consequences of peer rejection on future development. It is possible that exposure to the experience of social rejection can have enduring causal implications for future risk, even if that rejection is subsequently relieved. Thus, one can anticipate certain logical limitations to what can be learned about the development of psychopathology from intervention designs.

A different sort of design would be to look for "natural experiments" and to assess the developmental courses of children in these experiments. Different groups of rejected children who are considered at low risk on other grounds (e.g., lack of behavior problems and family risk factors) would need to be compared longitudinally with groups of rejected children who are considered at high risk (e.g., due to behavior problems or problematic family backgrounds). In addition, these groups would need to be systematically compared with control groups of unrejected children matched on the behavioral and family risk factors. These groups of children would then be followed longitudinally to assess the relative importance of rejection in causing subsequent psychological disorder. Another approach might be to examine the developmental course of children who are arbitrarily rejected by virtue of their race or ethnic group (or some other reason not related to the child's skills or behavior). It would be important in such studies to determine that the rejection was, in fact, arbitrary and not related to the social behavior of the children. If these children are ultimately proved to be at greater risk for disorder than children who are not in an environment that is rejecting of them, one might conclude that the experience of rejection contributes to future risk.

The developmental process can be examined in descriptive studies as well, at least to a greater extent than has been attempted thus far. A process-oriented longitudinal study would include assessments taken in at least four distinct developmental periods. The focus would be on children who become rejected but do not remain rejected. The four phases of assessment would be (a) prerejection (or preacceptance) by the peer group, (b) concurrent with rejection (or acceptance), (c) immediately postrejection (or postacceptance), and (d) long-term outcomes. In such a design, the problem of deciphering the causal role of rejection is similar to the problem of selection bias that has been described by psychometricians. That is, the question is whether one can mathematically model the development of rejection to the point that the rejection variable no longer plays a statistically significant role in the prediction of later outcomes. If variables collected prior to rejection (Time 1) can account for the variance in outcomes that is attributable to rejection, then rejection would be mathematically determined to play no incremental (causal) role. To the extent that rejection continues to contribute incrementally to this prediction, it cannot be ruled out as a causal variable. On the other hand, if rejection is determined to lead to a change in the child's behavior (or affect) from Time 1 to Time 3 and this change in behavior can be determined to be predictive of the maladaptive outcome, then one might conclude that rejection does play a causal role. In this way, one process model of the development of psychopathology would be articulated. Causal modeling and structural equations analysis are well suited as the statistical analyses required to test these hypotheses.

In summary, the role of social rejection as a causal variable in the development of maladaptive outcomes has rarely been examined in longitudinal research. Research designs and statistical analytic methods do exist that can be employed to address this problem. One minimal requirement of some of these designs is the concurrent assessment of peer status and variables that are related to social rejection (such as aggressive behavior and loneliness). The predictive increment accounted for by rejection could then be examined in relation to the increments provided by these other variables. A study involving this type of design will be described in the next section.

Peer rejection as a predictor of multiple forms of maladjustment

Peer rejection has been inconsistently defined across the range of studies reviewed in this chapter and in many cases was not the primary focus of the longitudinal research. The following study was designed to address several shortcomings in the research on the prediction of disorder and has several features that have not appeared previously in the literature. First, the predictive validity of peer rejection was directly assessed using current methods for defining sociometric status. Second, the study utilized a follow-forward design with an unselected school-aged sample. Finally, multiple adjustment outcome measures were used to determine whether rejection served as either a specific or a general predictor of disorder.

Kupersmidt (1983) followed 112 fifth-grade children from a nonselected semi-rural school sample for 5 years until the conclusion of tenth grade. Data on adolescent delinquency and school problems, including early withdrawal, were analyzed in relation to fifth-grade peer social status, using status as defined by Coie et al. (1982). The sample was racially mixed, with about 80% of the children being white and the remainder black. The results of the prediction analyses were more coherent when only the white subsample was considered.

During the 5 years subsequent to the initial assessment of peer status, the white children in this sample who were rejected in the fifth grade had more problems, in general, than did white children of other social status groups; however, the relationship between sociometric status and the outcomes of early school withdrawal and delinquency was only marginally significant, with the rejected children being more likely to develop either problem than children in other status groups. The rate of delinquency among rejected children was twice (35%) the base rate for the entire sample (17%), and their rate for dropping out of school was almost twice (38%) that of the total sample (21%); however, the small size of the sample made it difficult to obtain significant results, despite these differences in rates. Because of the small number of black children in the sample, it was not possible to explore the relationship between sociometric status type and outcome for the black children.

A recently completed investigation by Kupersmidt and Coie (1985) involved a follow-up ($n = 112$) 7 years later, when the majority of the Kupersmidt (1983) sample had graduated from high school. Information about the adjustment of the children in the sample was re-collected at that time, thus updating the data from the Kupersmidt (1983) study. The data were analyzed in a way that made it possible to assess the relative importance of aggression and peer rejection for each type of negative outcome. As in Kupersmidt's (1983) study, sociometric status was determined from positive and negative nominations. Preadolescent aggressive behavior was assessed by the use of peer nominations for starting fights. Information about academic adjustment (i.e., course grades and attendance) was also collected to evaluate the relative strength of sociometric, behavioral, and academic predictors of negative outcomes. The negative outcomes consisted of early school withdrawal, contact with the police or juvenile courts, and suspension from high school due to disciplinary problems.

A series of stepwise logistic multiple regression equations was used to assess the relative strength of each of the predictor variables in the prediction of negative outcomes. The five predictor variables included dichotomous coding of rejection, peer-perceived aggression, low class grades, gender, race, and excessive absences from school. The only significant predictor of juvenile delinquency was peer-perceived aggressiveness in the fifth grade. Both aggressiveness and excessive absences were predictive of dropping out of school. Thus, when rejection and aggression were used simultaneously as predictors of negative outcome in a mixed racial sample, rejection did not emerge as a significant predictor.

Because racial bias factors may have led to distortions in the sociometric status of the black children, these analyses were recalculated for only the white members of the cohort. As in Kupersmidt (1983), the small number of black children precluded separate analyses for the black subjects. Aggression in fifth grade best predicted delinquency and school dropout for the white children. In an analysis focused on predicting negative outcomes of any type (i.e., delinquency, dropping out of school, or being suspended from school), both peer rejection and aggression were significant predictors. Thus, peer rejection is additively related to the prediction of maladjustment of some type; however, these results also demonstrate that more specific behavioral predictors (i.e., aggressive behavior) are stronger predictors of specific negative outcomes. Furthermore, peer rejection may prove to be less useful as a predictor variable in cases where intergroup dynamics between minority and majority racial or ethnic groups affect sociometric patterns. In these cases, behavioral measures, such as aggression, may be more useful in predicting negative outcomes for the minority group members.

Peer rejection and aggressive behavior were jointly considered as predictors of disorder in a recent longitudinal study of a sample of 361 black children followed from the third through the sixth grades (Coie, Lochman, Terry, & Lee, 1987). In this sample, where racial bias could not confound sociometric choices, the prediction of early-adolescent negative outcomes from data on third-grade peer rejection could be adequately tested among black children. Maladjustment was assessed somewhat differently in this study than in the work discussed previously in that it consisted of teacher ratings of general adjustment to middle school. Evidence from other research suggests that the transition from elementary school to middle school is a difficult one for children (Berndt, 1987; Eccles, Midgley, & Adler, 1984) and may be particularly problematic for black and other minority students (Felner, Primavera, & Cauce, 1981). Children with a history of peer rejection in the third grade, especially males, had a difficult time adjusting to middle school, according to the teacher ratings. In fact, rejected children were almost three times more likely to have made a poor adjustment to middle school than nonrejected children. Aggression was not a significant predictor of middle school adjustment once rejection was controlled for in the model. By fourth grade, however, both rejection and aggression were significant and additive predictors of adjustment outcome.

One caveat in applying these findings to the identification of individuals for the purposes of preventive interventions is that although both variables are predictive of negative adjustment, the practical utility of this assessment procedure has not yet been established. For example, in the Coie et al. (1987) study the practical utility of both predictors was evaluated in three ways: as individual predictors, in a multiple gating procedure (aggression and rejection), and in a disjunctive procedure (aggression or rejection). Using individual predictors, false positives and false negatives outnumbered true positive estimates by a ratio of 2 to 1. The multiple gating procedure reduced the false positive rate dramatically, but by maintaining the same cutoff points as were used in the individual-predictor-variable analyses, the false negative rate was increased dramatically. Accuracy of identification was improved with the use of the disjunctive selection procedure; however, even this procedure yielded a false positive rate twice that of the true positives. These results highlight the problems associated with using a single predictor variable for predicting a single specific negative outcome and give some indication of the difficulty of applying basic research findings to the assessment of individual clinical cases.

The difficulty of applying basic research findings to individual clinical research applications merits some discussion in light of most of the conclusions reached in this chapter. There does appear to be evidence that childhood peer rejection is related predictively to multiple forms of maladjustment in adolescence. This fact has and will continue to serve as a stimulus for preventive intervention programs with rejected elementary-school-age children. Intervention programs require specifiable selection criteria and cutoff points for including subjects in the risk population. The preceding results suggest that the fact of a predictive relation does not guarantee good selection efficiency. For efficiency to be of an acceptable level, the general population from which risk subjects are to be selected should have a reasonably high level of risk in order to avoid the problems inherent in predicting low base rate phenomena. Peer rejection has the promise of being a good selection criterion because it seems to be related to multiple forms of maladjustment and hence is likely to be associated with higher base rates of disorder. Much of this argument is based on speculation, because few studies have included multiple negative outcome measures. In the case of the preceding study, for example, the base rate for disorder might be increased if nonschool indices of maladjustment such as delinquency, mental health problems, or drug and alcohol abuse were added to the teacher data and found to be related to earlier peer rejection.

The last study to be discussed was designed to address several shortcomings in the longitudinal literature in that it was a short-term, longitudinal study of a randomized sample stratified by peer social status (Coie, Christopoulos, Terry, Dodge, & Lochman, 1989). The outcome measures provided an index of psychological adjustment in early adolescence and included the assessment of both internalizing and externalizing behavior problems as reported by mothers and the children themselves. A representative subsample of 171 children from the Coie et al. (1987) study were interviewed using the Hodges (1986) Child Assessment Schedule and the National Youth Survey (Elliott & Huizinga, 1983), and their mothers completed the Achenbach Child Behavior Checklist. The Achenbach Child Behavior Checklist (Achenbach & Edelbrock, 1981) yielded a total externalizing and total internalizing problem score. The Child Assessment Schedule resulted in a total score for self-reported internalizing disorders, and the National Youth Survey provided an index of self-reported conduct disorder problems. Peer rejection, aggression, and gender were used as predictors of each of the outcome variables.

Results from the children and their mothers indicated that peer rejection in fourth grade was significantly predictive of both internalizing and externalizing problems at the end of sixth grade. The prediction from third grade was less straightforward, in that only aggression was predictive of self-reported conduct disorder for males. Mothers' reports on early-adolescent adjustment were significantly predicted by peer rejection in both the third and the fourth grade. This was true for both internalizing and externalizing problems. Aggressiveness was not a significant predictor of either type of problem as assessed by mothers.

The prediction of self-reported early-adolescent maladjustment was more complicated and involved different combinations of variables for male and female subjects. Third-grade data were predictive only of adolescent conduct disorder among males, which was predicted by third-grade aggressiveness. Rejection in fourth grade was a more consistent predictor of disorder among male and female adolescents than was aggression. Rejection predicted more internalizing problems and more total disorder among males. Rejection and aggression both predicted more conduct disorder among females, as well as more total disorders. Thus, data from two sources, parents and the adolescents themselves, provide convergent evidence on the prediction of adolescent disorder from childhood peer rejection. Contrary to many findings cited earlier in this chapter, peer rejection was as good as or better than aggression as a predictor of problems. Rejection in childhood is, therefore, a consistent predictor of multiple forms of disorder according to parent and teacher reports.

Conclusions about predictors of maladjustment

The purpose of this chapter was to provide an extensive analysis of the longitudinal research on the prediction of four different types of negative outcomes from childhood peer relations and to present recent findings on childhood peer rejection as a predictor of disorder. The quality of a child's peer relations was assessed by a variety of different methods, including teacher, parent, clinician, and peer reports. Peer rejection consistently emerged as a general predictor of subsequent maladjustment. The data supporting this conclusion were particularly impressive for the predictions made from childhood predictor variables. If, in fact, risk status can be most accurately assessed from peer rejection during childhood, then general screening programs for the selection of intervention targets may be most effective when conducted with this age-group. It should also be noted that the prediction ratios are more consistently impressive for males than for females, but this may be a consequence of the attention given to externalizing behavior patterns and negative outcomes such as delinquency, both of which are associated more with males.

Although peer rejection may be useful in the identification of a general risk group, this review also suggests that other variables may be more powerful predictors of specific forms of negative outcome, particularly when age and gender are taken into account. The remainder of this section will focus upon conclusions concerning *specific* negative outcomes.

Adults who seek out help for mental health problems tend to have a childhood behavioral profile that is quite similar to that of people with the more specific outcome of schizophrenia. The follow-forward studies from childhood suggest that active rejection by the peer group (based upon either clinic records, teacher reports, or peer assessments) is a predictor of schizophrenia and of unspecified mental health problems (Cowen et al., 1973; Janes & Hesselbrock, 1978; Janes et al., 1979; J. Roff & Wirt, 1984b; M. Roff, 1960, 1963; M. Roff et al., 1966; Westman et al., 1967). The only follow-forward study in which a general population of children was screened by sociometric procedures and used to predict mental health problems was that of J. Roff and Wirt (1984b), and they found significant but low positive relations between peer rejection and psychological disorder. The recent data by Coie et al. establishes a predictive link only from childhood to early adolescence but provides strong support for concluding that rejection is predictive of internalizing forms of psychological disorder. Clearly, then, although the general trends in this area support the idea that rejection is a predictor of mental health problems, there is still the need for well-designed, long-range prediction studies to confirm this thesis.

The form of social behavior that accompanies peer rejection in predicting schizophrenia is quite different for males and females, and this point is worth highlighting because there is an absence of data on this point for other forms of disorder. In general, social withdrawal was linked to risk for schizophrenia among females. Disruptive behavior and irritableness were the childhood behaviors most characteristic of preschizophrenic boys (John et al., 1982). Preschizophrenic adolescent males and females were described as lonely, isolated, and socially inept in addition to being rejected by their peers (John et al., 1982; Mednick & Schulsinger, 1970). Thus, knowledge of social isolation or extreme shyness may help to refine the prediction of schizophrenia based on rejected status alone for female children and adolescents, whereas disruptive behavior and emotional lability may improve the identification of at-risk male children. This sex difference may be useful in the prediction of general mental health problems as well; however, gender effects have not been carefully assessed in this area.

The preceding review indicates that delinquency can be better predicted by aggressive or antisocial behavior than by peer rejection. This relationship holds for predictions either from childhood or from adolescence and is consistent with the conclusions of Kohlberg, LaCrosse, and Ricks (1972) and Parker and Asher (1987). It should be noted that in the most recent large-sample study in which both aggression and rejection were used to predict conduct disorder in a racially homogeneous sample, rejection was the more powerful early predictor (Coie et al., 1987). Thus, the ultimate resolution of this question awaits further research involving the simultaneous use of both types of measures employed systematically with specific age-groups.

A different set of conclusions can be reached about the relation between peer rejection and school adjustment. Peer rejection was predictive of middle school adjustment and early school withdrawal, particularly in a racially homogeneous sample. However, in the most recent study of the prediction of school dropout, aggression and excessive absence were stronger predictors (Kupersmidt & Coie, 1985).

Future directions

The findings from this chapter suggest several possible avenues for future longitudinal research on risk prediction based upon childhood peer relations. Some of these possibilities relate to developmental differences, some to types of outcome that might be explored, and some to more innovative forms of analysis such as causal modeling.

Developmental differences

Different predictors associated with childhood and adolescence for certain outcome variables are suggested by this review. Rejection and aggression during childhood were associated with all four of the negative outcomes reviewed. By adolescence, however, the overall importance of aggression decreased and other predictor variables such as isolation and emotionality predominated. Several important questions are prompted by these differences. First, are the same children at risk at these two different periods? If so, does this mean that their behavior has changed and that those who are aggressive and violate peer and classroom rules during childhood become more isolated and emotionally labile in adolescence? Obviously these are questions that need to be addressed by longitudinal investigations in which prediction measures are assessed at repeated intervals, as discussed earlier in the chapter.

A second developmental issue that needs to be addressed pertains to the relative intensity and duration of rejection and aggression. No distinctions have been made in the literature between children whose social rejection is limited in duration or to certain peer contexts and those for whom rejection has been a persistent social experience. For some children rejection is limited to certain years of their school life, whereas for others rejection continues even into new peer situations. The latter group might be expected to be at greater long-term risk than the former. This same point could be made regarding aggression in childhood.

Outcome variables

Many of the follow-forward studies have focused upon externalizing behaviors and serious psychopathology as outcome variables; however, there are many other types of outcomes that were not considered here and are not well studied in the literature. Adolescents may compromise their own standards of behavior in compensation for a lack of friends and social support, so that phenomena such as teenage pregnancy and drug or alcohol abuse may be related to peer rejection. It is quite possible that different types of outcomes that are more similar in form to childhood peer rejection can be significantly predicted given prior knowledge of a child's peer status. For example, peer rejection may be associated with difficulties in the types of future adjustment that require at least adequate social skills. Loneliness and the inability to make friends as an adult may be predicted by earlier peer rejection. Marital adjustment and the ability to sustain intimate friendship are forms of behavior that should be most affected by social skill deficits. The workplace might emerge as another setting in which social deficiencies prove to be a serious handicap. Work attendance, job satisfaction, and productivity may be negatively associated with prior social rejection. For example, in the Janes et al. (1979) study, children who failed to get along well with their peers had more job dismissals due to behavior problems than children who did not have peer relationship problems.

The major focus of longitudinal research to date has been upon a single measure of negative adjustment. Often this is because limited data on outcomes are available in archival sources. As prediction studies come to be the result of prior planning, we hope that they will incorporate multiple outcome variables as well as outcome variables that reflect both externalizing and internalizing problems. One consequence of looking at internalizing problem outcomes might be that childhood aggression will take on less importance as a predictor variable and other features of peer relations will assume greater predictive significance (see Chapter 8, this volume).

There is exciting and important work to be done in the detection of children who are at risk for subsequent life adjustment problems. The general hypothesis that rejected peer status is the best predictor of a *nonspecific* negative outcome, consisting of both internalizing and externalizing problems, has yet to be addressed in a single comprehensive project or in multiple projects involving comparable measurement strategies. As these studies emerge, they will provide both a framework for thinking about the developmental implications of children's social relationships and a clearer definition of the groups at risk for the problems of interest to educators and clinicians.

References

Achenbach, T. M. (1966). The classification of children's psychiatric symptoms: A factor analytic study. *Psychological Monographs, 80*(7, Whole No. 615).

Achenbach, T. M., & Edelbrock, C. S. (1981). Behavioral problems and competencies reported by parents of normal and disturbed children aged 4 through 16. *Monographs of the Society for Research in Child Development, 46*(Serial No. 188).

Amble, B. R. (1967). Teacher evaluations of student behavior and school dropouts. *Journal of Educational Research, 60,* 53–58.

Asher, S. R., & Wheeler, V. A. (1985). Children's loneliness: A comparison of rejected and neglected peer status. *Journal of Consulting and Clinical Psychology, 53,* 500–505.

Barclay, J. R. (1966). Sociometric choices and teacher ratings as predictors of school dropout. *Journal of Social Psychology, 4,* 40–45.

Barthell, C., & Holmes, D. (1968). High school yearbooks: A nonreactive measure of social isolation in graduates who later became schizophrenic. *Journal of Abnormal Psychology, 73,* 313–316.

Berndt, T. J. (1987, April). *Changes in friendship and school adjustment after the transition to junior high school.* Paper presented at the biennial meeting of the Society for Research in Child Development, Baltimore.

Berndt, T. J., & Ladd, G. W. (Eds.) (1989). *Peer relationships in child development.* New York: Wiley.

Bleuler, E. (1950). *Dementia praecox or the group of schizophrenias.* New York: International Universities Press.

Bower, E. M. (1969). *Early identification of emotionally handicapped children in the school* (2nd ed.). Springfield, IL: Charles C. Thomas.

Bower, E. M., Shellhamer, T. A., & Dailey, J. M. (1960). School characteristics of male adolescents who later became schizophrenic. *American Journal of Orthopsychiatry, 30,* 712–729.

Bowman, D. H., & Matthews, C. V. (1960). *Motivations of youth for leaving school.* U.S. Office of Education Cooperative Research Program (Project 200).

Cadoret, R. J. (1973). Toward a definition of the schizoid state: Evidence from studies of twins and their families. *British Journal of Psychiatry, 122,* 679–685.

Carson, R. C., Butcher, J. N., & Coleman, J. C. (1988). *Abnormal psychology and modern life* (5th ed.). Glenview, IL: Scott Foresman & Co.

Clausen, J. A., & Kohn, M. L. (1960). Social relations and schizophrenia: A research report and a perspective. In D. D. Jackson (Ed.), *The etiology of schizophrenia* (pp. 295–320). New York: Basic Books.

Coie, J. D., Christopoulos, C., Terry, R., Dodge, K. A., & Lochman, J. E. (1989). Types of aggressive relationships, peer rejection, and developmental consequences. In B. H. Schneider, G. Attili, J. Nadel, & R. P. Weissberg (Eds.), *Social competence in developmental perspective.* Dordrecht: Kluwer Press.

Coie, J. D., Dodge, K. A., & Coppotelli, H. A. (1982). Dimensions and types of social status: A cross-age perspective. *Developmental Psychology, 18,* 557–569.

Coie, J. D., Lochman, J., Terry, R., & Lee, C. (1987, November). *Aggression and peer rejection as predictors of school adjustment during a transition to middle school.* Paper presented at the annual meeting of the Association for Advancement of Behavior Therapy, Boston.

Conger, J. J., & Miller, W. C. (1966). *Personality, social class, and delinquency.* New York: Wiley.

Cowen, E. L., Pederson, A., Babigian, H., Izzo, L. D., & Trost, M. A. (1973). Long-term follow-up of early detected vulnerable children. *Journal of Consulting and Clinical Psychology, 41,* 438–446.

Eccles, J. E., Midgley, C. M., & Adler, T. F. (1984). Age-related changes in the school environment: Effects on achievement motivation. In J. H. Nichols (Ed.), *The development of motivation* (pp. 283–331). Greenwich, CT: JAI Press.

Elliott, D. S., & Huizinga, D. (1983). Social class and delinquent behavior in a national youth panel. *Criminology: An Interdisciplinary Journal, 21,* 149–177.

Empey, L. T. (1978). *American delinquency: Its meaning and construction.* Homewood, IL: Dorsey.

Faris, R. (1934). Cultural isolation and the schizophrenic personality. *American Journal of Sociology, 40,* 155–164.

Felner, R. D., Primavera, J., & Cauce, A. M. (1981). The impact of school transitions: A focus for preventive efforts. *American Journal of Community Psychology, 9,* 449–459.

Fleming, P., & Ricks, D. F. (1970). Emotions of children before schizophrenia and character disorder. In M. Roff & D. F. Ricks (Eds.), *Life history research in psychopathology*. Minneapolis: University of Minnesota Press.

Frazee, H. E. (1953). Children who later became schizophrenic. *Smith College Studies on Social Work, 23*, 125–149.

Garmezy, N., Masten, A. S., & Tellegen, A. (1984). The study of stress and competence in children: A building block for developmental psychology. *Child Development, 55*, 97–111.

Green, K. D., Forehand, R., Beck, S. J., & Vosk, B. (1980). An assessment of the relationship among measures of children's social competence and children's academic achievement. *Child Development, 51*, 1149–1156.

Gronlund, N. E. (1959). *Sociometry in the classroom*. New York: Harper.

Gronlund, N. E., & Holmlund, W. S. (1958). The value of elementary school sociometric status scores for predicting pupils' adjustment in high school. *Educational Administration Supervision, 44*, 225–260.

Hafner, A. J., Quast, W., & Shea, M. J. (1975). The adult adjustment of one thousand psychiatric and pediatric patients: Initial findings from a twenty-five year follow-up. In R. D. Wirt, G. Winokur, & M. Roff (Eds.), *Life history research in psychopathology* (Vol. 4). Minneapolis: University of Minnesota Press.

Hindelang, M. J., Hirschi, T., & Weis, J. G. (1981). *Measuring delinquency*. Beverly Hills, CA: Sage Publications.

Hodges, K. (1986). *Manual for the child assessment schedule*. Unpublished manuscript, Duke University Medical Center, Durham, NC.

Janes, C. L., & Hesselbrock, V. M. (1978). Problem children's adult adjustment predicted from teachers' ratings. *American Journal of Orthopsychiatry, 48*, 300–309.

Janes, C. L., Hesselbrock, V. M., Myers, D. G., & Penniman, J. H. (1979). Problem boys in young adulthood: Teachers' ratings and twelve-year follow-up. *Journal of Youth and Adolescence, 8*, 453–472.

Jessor, R., & Jessor, S. L. (1977). *Problem behavior and psychosocial development: A longitudinal study of youth*. New York: Academic Press.

John, R., Mednick, S., & Schulsinger, F. (1982). Teacher reports as a predictor of schizophrenia and borderline schizophrenia: A Bayesian decision analysis. *Journal of Abnormal Psychology, 91*, 399–413.

Kasanin, J., & Veo, L. A. (1932). A study of the school adjustment of children who later became psychotic. *American Journal of Orthopsychiatry, 2*, 212–230.

Kohlberg, L., LaCrosse, J., & Ricks, D. (1972). The predictability of adult mental health from childhood behavior. In B. Wolman (Ed.), *Manual of child psychopathology* (pp. 1217–1284). New York: McGraw-Hill.

Kohlberg, L., Ricks, D., & Snarey, J. (1984). Childhood development as a predictor of adaptation in adulthood. *Genetic Psychology Monographs, 110*, 91–172.

Kohn, M., & Clausen, J. (1955). Social isolation and schizophrenia. *American Sociological Review, 20*, 265–273.

Kraeplin, E. (1919). *Dementia praecox and paraphrenia*. New York: Robert E. Krieger Publishing Co.

Kreisman, D. (1970). Social interaction and intimacy in preschizophrenic adolescents. In J. Zubin & A. M. Freedman (Eds.), *The psychopathology of adolescence* (pp. 299–318). New York: Grune & Stratton.

Kuhlen, R., & Collister, E. G. (1952). Sociometric status of sixth- and ninth-graders who fail to finish high school. *Educational and Psychological Measurement, 12*, 632–637.

Kupersmidt, J. B. (1983, April). *Predicting delinquency and academic problems from childhood peer status*. Paper presented at the biennial meeting of the Society for Research in Child Development, Detroit.

Kupersmidt, J. B., & Coie J. D. (1985). *The prediction of delinquency and school-related problems from childhood peer status.* Unpublished manuscript, Duke University, Durham, NC.

Lambert, N. A. (1972). Intellectual and nonintellectual predictors of high school status. *Journal of Scholastic Psychology, 6,* 247–259.

Ledingham, J. E. (1981). Developmental patterns of aggressive and withdrawn behavior in childhood: A possible method for identifying preschizophrenics. *Journal of Abnormal Child Psychology, 9,* 1–22.

Ledingham, J. E., & Schwartzman, A. E. (1984). A 3-year follow-up of aggressive and withdrawn behavior in childhood: Preliminary findings. *Journal of Abnormal Child Psychology, 12,* 157–168.

Lewine, R. R., Watt, N. F., Prentky, R. A., & Fryer, J. H. (1978). Childhood behaviour in schizophrenia, personality disorder, depression, and neurosis. *British Journal of Psychiatry, 132,* 347–357.

Lewine, R. R., Watt, N. F., Prentky, R. A., & Fryer, J. H. (1980). Childhood social competence in functionally disordered psychiatric patients and in normals. *Journal of Abnormal Psychology, 89,* 132–138.

Mednick, S. A., & Schulsinger, F. (1970). Factors related to breakdown in children at high risk for schizophrenia. In M. Roff & D. F. Ricks (Eds.), *Life history research in psychopathology* (pp. 51–93). Minneapolis: University of Minnesota Press.

Michael, C. M., Morris, D. P., & Soroker, E. (1957). Follow-up studies of shy, withdrawn children, II. Relative incidence of schizophrenia. *American Journal of Orthopsychiatry, 27,* 331–337.

Muma, J. R. (1965). Peer evaluation and academic performance. *Personnel and Guidance Journal, 44,* 405–409.

Nagel, S. S. (1966). The tipped scales of American justice. *Trans-action, 3,* 3–9.

Parker, J. G., & Asher, S. R. (1987). Peer relations and later personal adjustment: Are low-accepted children at risk? *Psychological Bulletin, 102,* 357–389.

Piaget, J. (1965). *The moral judgment of the child.* New York: Free Press. (Original publication in English in 1932 by Routledge & Kegan Paul, London)

Pollack, M., Woerner, M., Goodman, W., & Greenberg, I. W. (1966). Childhood development patterns of hospitalized adult schizophrenic and nonschizophrenic patients and their siblings. *American Journal of Orthopsychiatry, 36,* 510–517.

Prout, C. T., & White, M. A. (1956). The schizophrenic's sibling. *Journal of Nervous Mental Disease, 123,* 162–170.

Ricks, D. F., & Berry, J. C. (1970). Family and symptom patterns that precede schizophrenia. In M. Roff & D. F. Ricks (Eds.), *Life history research in psychopathology.* Minneapolis: University of Minnesota Press.

Robins, L. N. (1966). *Deviant children grown up: A sociological and psychiatric study of sociopathic personality.* Baltimore, MD: Williams & Wilkins.

Roff, J., Knight, R., & Wertheim, E. (1976). Disturbed preschizophrenics: Childhood symptoms in relation to adult outcome. *Journal of Nervous and Mental Disease, 162,* 274–281.

Roff, J. D., & Wirt, R. D. (1984a). Childhood aggression and social adjustment as antecedents of delinquency. *Journal of Abnormal Child Psychology, 12,* 111–126.

Roff, J. D., & Wirt, R. D. (1984b). Childhood social adjustment, adolescent status, and young adult mental health. *American Journal of Orthopsychiatry, 54,* 595–602.

Roff, M. (1960). Relations between certain preservice factors and psychoneurosis during military duty. *Armed Forces Medical Journal, 11,* 152–160.

Roff, M. (1961). Childhood social interactions and young adult bad conduct. *Journal of Abnormal and Social Psychology, 63,* 333–337.

Roff, M. (1963). Childhood social interactions and young adult psychosis. *Journal of Clinical Psychology, 19,* 152–157.

Roff, M. (1975). Juvenile delinquency in girls: A study of a recent sample. In M. Roff & D. F. Ricks (Eds.), *Life history research in psychopathology* (Vol. 4, pp. 135–151). Minneapolis: University of Minnesota Press.

Roff, M., Mink, W., & Hinrichs, G. (1966). *Developmental abnormal psychology.* New York: Holt.

Roff, M., Sells, S. B., & Golden, M. M. (1972). *Social adjustment and personality development in children.* Minneapolis: University of Minnesota Press.

Shea, M. J. (1972). *A follow-up study into adulthood of adolescent psychiatric patients in relation to internalizing and externalizing symptoms: MMPI configurations, social competence, and life history variables.* Unpublished doctoral dissertation, University of Minnesota, Minneapolis.

Shweder, R. A. (1975). How relevant is an individual difference theory of personality? *Journal of Personality, 43,* 455–484.

Skaberne, B., Blejec, M., Skalar, V., & Vodopivec, K. (1965). Criminal prevention and elementary school children. *Revue de Criminologie, 16,* 8–14.

Snepp, D. W. (1953). Why they drop out: Eight clues to greater holding power. *Clearing House, 27,* 492–497.

Stabenau, J., & Pollin, R. (1970). Experiential differences for schizophrenics as compared with their nonschizophrenic siblings: Twin and family studies. In M. Roff & D. F. Ricks (Eds.), *Life history research in psychopathology* (pp. 94–126). Minneapolis: University of Minnesota Press.

Stephens, D. A., Atkinson, M. W., Kay, D. W. K., Roth, M., & Garside, R. F. (1975). Psychiatric morbidity in parents and sibs of schizophrenics and non-schizophrenics. *British Journal of Psychiatry, 127,* 97–108.

Ullmann, C. A. (1957). Teachers, peers, and tests as predictors of adjustment. *Journal of Educational Psychology, 48,* 257–267.

U.S. Bureau of Census, Current Population Reports. (1988). *School enrollment: Social and economic characteristics of students, October 1985 and 1984* (Series P-20, No. 426). Washington, DC: U.S. Government Printing Office.

Wadsworth, M. (1979). *Roots of delinquency.* Oxford: Martin Robertson.

Watt, N. F. (1978). Patterns of childhood social development in adult schizophrenics. *Archives of General Psychiatry, 35,* 160–165.

Watt, N. F., & Lubensky, A. (1976). Childhood roots of schizophrenia. *Journal of Abnormal Psychology, 85,* 363–375.

Watt, N. F., Stolorow, R. D., Lubensky, A. W., & McClelland, D. C. (1970). School adjustment and the behavior of children hospitalized for schizophrenia as adults. *American Journal of Orthopsychiatry, 40,* 637–657.

West, D. (1969). *Present conduct and future delinquency: First report of the Cambridge study in delinquent development.* London: Heinemann.

West, D. J., & Farrington, D. P. (1973). *Who becomes delinquent?* London: Heinemann.

West, D. J., & Farrington, D. P. (1977). *The delinquent way of life.* London: Heinemann.

Westman, J. C., Rice, D. L., & Berman, E. (1967). Nursery school behavior and later school adjustment. *American Journal of Orthopsychiatry, 37,* 725–731.

Youniss, J. (1980). *Parents and peers in social development: A Sullivan–Piaget perspective.* Chicago: University of Chicago Press.

Zeller, R. H. (1966). *Lowering the odds on student dropouts.* New York: Prentice-Hall.

Part V

Issues in intervention research

11 Adapting intervention to the problems of aggressive and disruptive rejected children

John D. Coie and Gina Krehbiel Koeppl

The case for providing rejected children with help in their relations with peers is established in other chapters in the volume: These children are at risk for a variety of problems in adolescence and adulthood, and they feel the pain of loneliness and lowered self-esteem more so than other children. Without intervention, rejected children often continue being rejected in their ongoing school peer groups. The thesis of our chapter is that detailed knowledge about the characteristics of socially rejected children can be used to devise more effective programs of intervention than have been used thus far. Our hypothesis is that successful intervention depends upon a close match between the maladaptive behavioral characteristics of the sample and the specific goals of the intervention program. In particular, we are concerned that with respect to intervention thinking, insufficient attention has been given to the role of aggressive and disruptive behavior in peer rejection. Social skills training procedures for rejected children have thus far focused on positive play skills, and although it can be argued that the acquisition of these skills attenuates the frequency of aversive social behavior, we will examine the methods for reducing aversive behavior directly, including those that could be integrated into an expanded conception of social skills training.

Over the past decade a solid base of information about children's relationships with peers has been amassed. Much of this literature has focused on individual differences that account for children having problematic peer relations. Differences relating to peer social adjustment have been found in children's social cognitive processes (see Chapter 5 in this volume). Differences in coping with particular social situations have been analyzed (see Chapter 3). The largest body of research has involved studies of social behavior in naturally occurring or quasi-naturalistic children's groups (see Chapter 2). The framework for the present chapter is based on results from this last set of findings.

Preparation of this chapter and the collection of data reported herein were supported, in part, by grants from the National Institute of Mental Health.

What are the particular behavior characteristics of peer rejection that deserve our closest attention? Our view is that aggressiveness and disruptiveness have proved to be especially strong correlates of peer rejection. However, efforts to decrease aggressiveness or disruptiveness have been indirect and have not figured prominently in the design of most intervention programs for rejected children. Our contention is that more explicit attention to aggression and disruptiveness will result in improved intervention effectiveness. We will first review previous intervention attempts with rejected children. Particular attention will be given to the behavior change goals of each program and the relation between social status and improvements in behavior. We will then consider the implications of more recent information about the bases of peer rejection for future intervention programs. Finally, the adaptation of intervention strategies for use with specific types of rejected children will be discussed, drawing heavily from the child-clinical literature.

Social skills training

A number of intervention studies have been attempted with low-accepted children, but the modes of intervention have differed in their focus for change. One group of early studies is based on the assumption that low-accepted children interact infrequently with peers and are deprived of opportunities to learn new skills or to make friends. From this perspective, the goal of intervention has been to increase the children's frequency of interactions with peers through the use of reinforcement procedures (e.g., see Allen, Hart, Buell, Harris, & Wolf, 1964). The operationalization of poor peer adjustment in terms of low rates of interaction poses obvious problems, which have been discussed by Asher, Markell, and Hymel (1981), and most investigators now recognize that peer rejection is a phenomenon with more at issue than low frequency of interaction. The more recent premise upon which intervention has been based is that low-accepted children lack critical skills for positive social interaction. Referred to as the "deficit hypothesis" (Asher & Renshaw, 1981), this premise suggests that children who lack certain skills of social interaction will experience less in the way of successful interaction and will acquire a poorer social status.

The goal of most deficit hypothesis intervention studies is to teach low-accepted children skills that may promote positive interactions with peers. These studies vary widely with regard to which children are targeted, what skills are taught, and whether or not behavior and social status changes are demonstrated. In the first of these studies, Gottman, Gonso, and Schuler (1976) studied the short-term effects of a social skills training program on two socially isolated third-grade girls. Gottman et al. emphasized initiating interactions with other children, making friends, and practicing referential communication skills; these were skills in which low-accepted children had been found to be deficient (Gott-man, Gonso, & Rasmussen, 1975). Although the subjects were identified on the basis of sociometric nomination scores, change as a result of skills training intervention was assessed by comparing peer sociometric ratings before and after intervention. Significant improvement was demonstrated for one intervention subject and marginally significant improvement for the other, whereas no significant change was found for the two control subjects. Behavior observations revealed no increases in the total frequency of interaction with peers. As the authors noted, frequency of interaction was not likely to have been a very sensitive measure of social change. Unfortunately, improvements in the three targeted social skills were not assessed.

The study by Gottman et al. (1976) and the one by Oden and Asher (1977) to be described below represent an important transition in the planning of social skills research with children. Prior to these studies the focus of skill training was on increasing social interaction. Although increasing social interaction was one of the goals of the Gottman et al. project, the results of earlier research (Gottman et al., 1975) led them to develop a special focus on skills for making friends. In contrast to earlier studies, Gottman et al. did not look for increased peer interaction as the primary criterion for change but instead aimed for increases in skilled behavior and improvements in sociometric standing. Although Oden and Asher continued the tradition of labeling the target group for intervention as "socially isolated" children, they expanded the social skills coaching agenda and used sociometric change and increases in skilled behavior as the primary criteria for intervention success. One of the skills that was taught was increased participation; however, the focus of this training for increased social participation was qualitative (e.g., "pay attention to what other children are doing") rather than quantitative. For most purposes, then, the emphasis on increasing the frequency of social interaction was discontinued in these two studies.

Oden and Asher (1977) developed a program to teach the skills of cooperation, participation, communication, and supportiveness (skills thought to promote acceptance) to poorly accepted third- and fourth-graders. A total of 33 lowest rated children from 11 classrooms were selected as subjects. The specific selection measures included same-sex peer ratings on three sociometric measures: "play with" ratings; "work with" ratings, included as a measure of the generalization of acceptance to other settings; and "best friend" nominations to assess the extent to which coaching might affect specific friendship status.

Children assigned to the coaching group received verbal instruction, rehearsed the skills during 12-min play interactions with an average-accepted peer (peer pairing), and discussed the play interactions with the coach. Compared with children in a peer-pairing-only group (with no coaching) and those in a control group who came out of the classroom to play solitary games, coached children received significantly higher ratings as preferred playmates. There were no significant improvements in "work with" ratings or friendship nominations. Follow-up analyses conducted 1 year later on 22 of the original 33 subjects showed that the improvements in mean "play with" ratings of the coached children were maintained or increased. Of the 8 coached children, 4 had mean "play with" ratings above the group mean, whereas only 1 of 7 peer-pairing-only children and 1 of 7 control children received mean "play with" ratings that fell above the group mean.

Oden and Asher also observed the behavior of the children during their dyadic play sessions with average-status partners. Surprisingly, no improvements in the amount of positive social behavior were observed during these dyadic play sessions. The fact that the children did not display the coached skills with greater frequency after six sessions of instruction poses a dilemma. The coached subjects may not have acquired the skills that were taught, or if they did acquire them, they did not display them in this limited circumstance, in which case the real impact of coaching upon social status and behavior could not be assessed in this study. Still another explanation is that the low- and high-accepted groups may not have differed initially in terms of their possession of the targeted skills. Before intervention began, Oden and Asher assessed the behavior of low-accepted and high-accepted classmates in dyadic play sessions. No significant differences were found between these groups on any of the behavioral measures.

Why, then, were there improvements in peer ratings for these low-accepted children when they did not show improvements in the skills for which they had been trained? Two possibilities come to mind, both relating to issues of behavior observation. The assessments of social interaction did not take place in the natural peer setting of the classroom or playground but in dyadic interactions between subjects and average-status children. Oden and Asher suggest that their observation methodology was insensitive to real group differences. First, the observation scheme or coding system may have been inadequate to capture meaningful behaviors. This is not an uncommon problem in observation studies. Second, it seems quite possible that the use of such a brief dyadic interaction in which presumably one partner is socially skilled (or at least socially average) facilitates competent interaction. In that case, coached and uncoached pairs may appear equally skilled because the brief session nearly precludes the chance that relationship difficulties will occur. For example, the development or escalation of aroused play is less likely to occur during a brief play session. Indeed, Oden and Asher designed and piloted the play paradigm to minimize the possibility of "out-of-control" play.

The success of the Oden and Asher positive play skills training paradigm, particularly the maintenance and improvement of peer status at follow-up a year later, stimulated a series of investigations designed to test modifications of this approach. These have met with varying degrees of success. Gresham and Nagle (1980) compared coaching, modeling, a combined coaching–modeling procedure, and an attention-control condition with 40 low-accepted third- and fourth-grade children. The children assigned to the modeling group viewed videotapes of same-age youngsters engaged in positive and negative interactions. Adult commentators instructed the viewers in participation, cooperation, communication, and support. The children assigned to the coaching group received instruction and an opportunity to rehearse skills according to the procedure described by Oden and Asher. Those assigned to the combination coaching–modeling group participated in abbreviated sequences of the coaching and modeling procedures. The difference between coaching and modeling conditions seems to have been in the opportunity to rehearse skills in the coaching condition; both conditions involved adult instruction. Those children in the attention-control group viewed films about animals and received no instruction. An analysis of changes immediately after training indicated no significant effects of training upon peer ratings. However, follow-up data obtained 3 weeks after training revealed significant increases in peer "play with" ratings for all treatment groups. As in the Oden and Asher study, there were no improvements in "work with" ratings or best friend nominations.

Improvements in observed behavior were connected with treatment, but the pattern of changes was complicated. All observations were conducted in classroom settings, including group discussions, individual work, and small-group activities. All three treatment groups received more frequent positive interactions from other children after training, whereas the control group showed no change on this variable. No significant differences were reported for initiating positive interactions, the ostensible goal of the training procedure. Differences between the treatment groups and the control group in both receiving and initiating negative interactions were largely a consequence of the increases in negative interactions involving the control group. Only the coached group showed marked decreases in negative interactions from pretest to posttest. (The other two intervention groups showed very little negative behavior on any occasion.) All three treatment groups showed less negative behavior than the control group at follow-up. In sum, although the goal of the training program was for children to initiate more prosocial interactions as a consequence of social skills training, this did not occur. Nonetheless, Gresham and Nagle were able to document some group differences in negative interaction as well as improvements in peer ratings following their intervention.

Ladd (1981) altered the Oden and Asher paradigm and demonstrated positive effects on both behavior changes and peer ratings with a particular subset of low-accepted third-grade children. The subjects were white, middle-class boys and girls selected because of low peer ratings. Ladd, however, selected from among this low-accepted group those children observed to be the most deficient in the three verbal social skills targeted for training (asking questions, making suggestions, and offering support). One third of the 36 subjects were assigned to a coaching condition. The coaching curriculum included training in question asking, suggestion making, and supportive verbal behavior. Emphasis was placed on skill rehearsal and self-evaluation of performance. Children in the attention-control group were only instructed in the basic game rules before the play interaction, and nontreatment control subjects received neither coaching nor attention.

The results indicated that children in the coaching condition had significantly increased the frequency of their question-asking and suggestion-making behavior at posttest and at the follow-up assessment 4 weeks after posttest, which were conducted in specially arranged free-play settings in the classroom. Almost no supportive behavior was observed in the sample on either occasion, suggesting that supportive behavior is infrequent in group settings at this age. In addition to behavioral change on two of the three criteria, the coached children evidenced significant gains in overall classroom acceptance as demonstrated by increases in peer ratings that were maintained at follow-up. No improvements in peer ratings were noted for either control group. Thus, Ladd was able to produce significant improvements in two of the three targeted social skills, and these changes were accompanied by changes in social status.

Several explanations for the symmetry of Ladd's findings are plausible. One is that they are the result of the greater specificity and linkage between the training procedures, the targeted behaviors, and the observational codes. Furthermore, Ladd seems to have observed behavior in a revealing context. Unlike Oden and Asher (1977), who used brief dyadic interaction as the basis for their observations, Ladd used group free play within the classroom. This setting is more likely to allow behavior differences to emerge. It is also important to note that Ladd's program was especially well suited to the subset of low-accepted children selected for intervention, because each child had demonstrated deficiency in the behaviors coached in the social skills program. It is possible that by restricting his sample to children with low frequencies of certain kinds of prosocial behavior, Ladd may have eliminated many socially active rejected children and thus selected a particular subsample of rejected children. Many aggressive children may have been eliminated, because aggression is related to highly interactive play, particularly rough-and-tumble play (Dodge, 1983; Ladd, 1983).

In another coaching study, La Greca and Santogrossi (1980) used videotapes to train 30 low-accepted third-, fourth-, and fifth-grade children in groups. The targeted social skills (good grooming, smiling, greeting, joining, conversing, sharing, and complimenting) were taught as discrete behaviors rather than as actions that could be tried to make play more enjoyable, as was the case in the

Ladd and the Oden and Asher studies. Children in the training group viewed narrated videotapes of positive social interactions, discussed the tapes, and role-played the skills emphasized in the tapes. Each child was given feedback and was encouraged to practice the skills throughout the week. The attention-control group viewed television show excerpts and played charades, whereas the control group participated only in the pretest and posttest assessments.

Posttest data revealed that relative to the children in the control groups, the children trained in social skills demonstrated superior knowledge of the targeted social skills on a verbal test of these skills and increased knowledge of the process of making friends in a posttraining role-play task. In classroom observations they initiated more interactions with other children. However, group differences were not found on changes in peer status as assessed by peer ratings, nor were there significant differences in increased positive social interaction. Although the intervention subjects appeared to have learned the skills they were taught, there was no evidence that they increased their utilization of these skills in actual peer interactions or that possession of these skills had much impact upon social status.

Bierman and Furman (1984) examined the effectiveness of a procedure designed to enhance peer attitudes toward low-accepted fifth- and sixth-grade children by implementing that procedure both with and without coaching procedures similar to those described above. Reasoning that hostility and negative social stereotypes could be reduced by having children work together toward a common superordinate goal (Sherif, Harvey, White, Hood, & Sherif, 1961), Bierman and Furman had low-accepted children work with classmates on a group task (peer involvement) of producing videotape films illustrating friendly interactions. As with the Ladd (1981) study, subjects were first screened for low peer acceptance on peer ratings, and those low-accepted children who were deficient in certain conversational skills were selected for intervention. Male and female subjects ($n = 56$) were randomly assigned to one of four groups: a peer involvement condition, an individual-coaching condition, a combined peer involvement and individual-coaching condition, and a no-treatment control condition. The coaching program was similar to that of the Ladd version of the Oden and Asher (1977) program. Training in asking questions, in some aspects of leadership, and in self-expression was emphasized.

The results of this study are more complicated than those of most of the preceding studies. Significant positive effects were obtained for the general measure of intervention success (peer acceptance ratings) for only the peer involvement and the combined individual-coaching and peer involvement conditions. However, these effects, while significant at posttesting, were not present at follow-up testing. Significant improvements in peer acceptance at both posttesting and follow-up were found for children in the combined coaching and peer involvement condition when the analysis of peer acceptance ratings was restricted to the ratings of fellow participants in the peer involvement task.

As far as changes in behavior are concerned, behavioral observations during the lunch period revealed significant increases in frequency of positive peer interaction for the coached children at follow-up. Increases in peer interaction were observed for peer involvement subjects at posttreatment but were not sustained at follow-up. Thus, it appears that coaching in conversational skills had observable effects on the social behavior of children, but these improvements did not translate into improved sociometric status, at least not within the limited time frame of the 6-week follow-up. The only sustained improvements in peer acceptance came about between children who worked together at the group task, regardless of whether or not they received coaching.

Bierman (1986) subsequently analyzed videotapes made of children in the peer involvement conditions during their 6th and 10th sessions in order to learn whether or not increases occurred in the use of the trained skills. Another major purpose was to learn whether children who gained the most in social skills and positive peer response also gained the most in acceptance measured sociometrically. Videotapes of the groups at work were coded for the occurrence of the three types of conversational skill that were the focus of coaching. The responses (positive, negative, and neutral) of fellow group members to each behavioral initiation were also coded. Children who received either individual coaching or individual coaching plus peer involvement increased their use of these conversational skills in the taped interactions from the 6th to the 10th sessions. Coached children also received more positive responses than did noncoached children, and the frequency of these positive responses increased from the 6th to the 10th sessions. Most important, the frequency of conversation and number of positive peer responses were positively correlated with peer interaction and peer acceptance at posttreatment and follow-up (r ranging from .25 to .68) when the effects of pretreatment sociometric rating scores or behavior data were statistically controlled. The strongest relations found were those between positive peer responses and outcome measures at follow-up. At follow-up, positive peer responses had a .41 partial correlation to classroom sociometric ratings and a .37 partial correlation to group partner ratings. These analyses suggest that social skills coaching had some positive effects on social relations when coaching was translated into actual improvements in conversational behavior in the peer involvement condition. Bierman was the first to test the process–outcome relationship by linking gains in social skill to gains in sociometric peer data.

Most investigators employing skills training have identified intervention subjects using a rating-scale sociometric that requires children to indicate how much they like playing with each classmate. In contrast to selection procedures based solely on positive nomination sociometrics, the peer-rating measures make it possible to identify a sample of children about two thirds of whom are actively rejected (Hymel & Asher, 1977). However, some children who are categorized as low-accepted on the basis of rating scales may be neglected or controversial rather than rejected. Because the behavior of those two groups is different from the behavior of rejected children, one might expect that the same intervention procedures would not be equally effective for all children who receive low ratings from peers.

The recent shifts in emphasis

The preceding review of social skills training research with rejected children was intended to provide an appraisal of the current state of the field. It might be useful to attempt a brief historical analysis of the changes in emphasis that have taken place in peer relations intervention over the last 20 years. The major preoccupation of peer relations training in the 1960s was with peer isolation. As noted earlier, the thrust of several studies, using reinforcement by adults (Allen et al., 1964; Buell, Stoddard, Harris, & Baer, 1968) or modeling (Evers & Schwartz, 1973; Keller & Carlson, 1974; O'Connor, 1969, 1972), was to increase the social interaction of isolate children, primarily preschoolers. Later intervention strategies in this direction involved the combined use of adult reinforcement and modeling (Walker & Hops, 1973) or the use of peers as "therapists" through mixed-age socializing procedures (Furman, Rahe, & Hartup, 1979). The primary criterion for social progress in these studies was social contact rather than sociometric status. The comparative work of Harlow and his colleagues (e.g., Harlow, 1969) with young monkeys who suffered from the negative effects of early isolation from peers provided some of the rationale for this line of study.

An emphasis on social competence (Goldfried & D'Zurilla, 1969) entered into the thinking about children's peer relations in the 1970s (e.g., Gottman et al., 1975); however, as we noted earlier, the target population continued to be labeled as isolates even though they were identified by sociometric measures (Gottman, 1977; Gottman et al., 1976; Oden & Asher, 1977). The primary intervention criterion for the social competency–oriented studies was sociometrically defined peer status rather than frequency of social interaction. There was a clear recognition of the importance of having the skills to relate effectively, in addition to whatever motivational factors also might be operative (Asher & Renshaw, 1981).

The shift in intervention goals from promoting increased peer interaction to enhancing positive play skills paralleled a shift upward in the age of the target groups for intervention. Whereas almost all of the research directed at increasing social interaction frequency was conducted with preschool and kindergarten children, most of the social skills training research was implemented with elementary school children from the middle grades. This parallel may be significant for understanding the focus that social skills training took, if one considers the relationship between the results of observational studies of peer status and the goals of peer relations intervention. It was not unreasonable for intervention work with preschoolers to have been focused on frequency of interaction, because as has been noted in Chapter 2 of this volume, the only variable investigated consistently across preschool and primary grade school observational studies was rate of social participation. Most of these studies documented some relationship between low acceptance (as indexed by low scores on positive nomination sociometrics) and solitary behavior. Not surprisingly then, much of the preschool intervention research was aimed at increasing social participation. (It should be noted, however, that solitary behavior has not been related consistently to the measures of peer status currently in use, such as rating-scale sociometrics or combinations of positive and negative nominations. Thus, the importance of increasing frequency of interaction would now be questioned, even with preschool populations.) When social skills training was introduced to older children, there was very little in the way of an observational research literature on which to base these new interventions. A pivotal observation study by Hartup, Glazer, and Charlesworth (1967), albeit with preschool subjects, provided two different clues that could be followed by interventionists. On the one hand, Hartup et al. found that positive social behavior was related to positive sociometric nominations but was unrelated to negative sociometric nominations. On the other hand, aversive behavior was related to negative nominations by peers but not to positive nominations. To some extent the decision to train low-accepted children in positive play skills followed the first lead rather than the second.

As observational data have become increasingly available on older children (Asarnow, 1983; Coie & Kupersmidt, 1983; Dodge, 1983; Dodge, Coie, & Brakke, 1982; Ladd, 1983; Vosk, Forehand, Parker, & Rickard, 1982), three variables have emerged as reliable discriminators between the behavior of rejected and nonrejected children. Rejected children are reported to be more aggressive, more disruptive, and more often off task in the classroom. Less consistently, rejected children have also been reported to be solitary in inappropriate ways and less often engaged in prosocial activity. They are not usually described as low interactors with their peers overall, however.

If research on the behavioral bases for peer rejection were to be used to form the agenda for social skills training, then it would seem that a first priority would be placed on reducing these negative behaviors. However, as the previous literature review indicates, there is evidence for the success of social skills training directed at the enhancement of positive social behavior among rejected children. One explanation for this apparent contradiction is that the enhancement of prosocial skills serves to reduce the occurrence of negative behavior. This might happen in several ways. Children learn to substitute positive social strategies for maladaptive ones that in the past have led to conflict and a deterioration of relationships. Thus, the acquisition of prosocial skills may reduce the number of interactions in which aggressive behavior otherwise might be set off. In addition, previously rejected children who learn to provide positive reinforcement to their peers may come to receive preferential treatment by peers (Dodge, 1983), such as not being teased as often and being sought out for play more often. This, in turn, would make it easier for them to stay engaged socially and avoid disruptive and argumentative interactions.

There is also some indication in the preceding review of social skills training research that social skills training is most effective with those children who are demonstrably deficient in the skills that the training is designed to promote. Ladd, and to some extent Bierman and Furman, obtained improvements in social status that could be traced to the acquisition of positive social skills in a subset of rejected children who seemed to be most lacking in those skills. It can be argued then that by fitting the intervention program to the observed deficits of this subgroup, these researchers have advanced the general social skills training paradigm (Asher, 1985; Ladd & Asher, 1985) and that further advances might follow from a closer scrutiny of the basis for peer rejection within samples selected for intervention (Coie, 1985). Not all rejected children are deficient in the social skills of conversation or positive play; for some there may be other reasons for their rejection. Intervention, if it is to be successful, must address these reasons. In the following section we will examine data that speak to the heterogeneity of rejected children. In particular, we will present evidence on the relative frequency of serious aggression and disruptive off-task behavior among rejected children as a background for discussing several approaches to dealing with these problems in intervention programs.

Incidence of aggressiveness and disruptiveness among rejected children

Rejected children have been described repeatedly as more aggressive than nonrejected children (see Chapter 2). Data from studies of rejected children in new peer situations (Coie & Kupersmidt, 1983; Dodge, 1983) suggest that these behaviors contribute to rejected status and are not simply a consequence of being disliked. Aggression seems to be a special problem among rejected boys, in particular. Much of the aversive or hostile behavior of rejected children is verbal; however, some of the aggression is physical. This may come about, in part, because of the greater involvement of rejected boys in rough play, an activity that often shifts into physical fighting.

Because aggression has been the most consistently reported and salient characteristic of children who are rejected by their peers, it is important to learn what proportion of rejected children actually are described by peers as aggressive. Peer assessment information relevant to this question was available on four large-sample cohorts of third- and fourth-graders ($n > 500$ in each case). One of these fourth-grade groups was a 1-year follow-up sample of one of the third-grade cohorts. All the samples were primarily composed of low to middle socioeconomic status black children from a southern urban school population. A convention was adopted by which aggressive children were defined as those 1 standard deviation or more above the group mean in "starts fights" nominations. The findings for all four samples were strikingly similar, with the percentage of rejected children who were nominated by their peers as significantly aggressive ranging from 30% to 33%. By contrast, the percentage of aggressive children among nonrejected samples ranged from 8% to 11%.

A second behavioral factor strongly linked to peer rejection is disruptiveness. Rejected children are reported to be less often engaged in academic tasks and are more often off task, either in solitary, inappropriate behavior or in disruptive behavior. In our project, the percentage of rejected children who are described by peers as disruptive (by a similar criterion as with aggression) ranged from 36% to 38%. For rejected children who are either extremely aggressive or disruptive, the proportions ranged from 47% to 49%, compared with a range of 12% to 18.5% for the nonrejected classmates. It appears that roughly half of all rejected children can be characterized as behaving in ways that would interfere with the social order of the peer group. This conclusion is supported by data on white, middle-class males reported by French (1988). French cluster analyzed behavioral information on two samples of rejected 8- to 10-year-old boys. He found that 50% of these rejected boys formed a cluster that was marked by antisocial behavior such as aggression and loss of control.

Some of this disruptive behavior has been reported to involve social approaches to peers during class time, an activity not likely to endear rejected children to their teachers. In fact, negative teacher–student interactions in the classroom may influence a child's social standing among classmates (Sutherland, Algozzine, Ysseldyke, & Freeman, 1983). The tendency of rejected children to be frequently off task in the classroom has been linked to the fact that many rejected children have academic difficulties (Coie & Krehbiel, 1984). The causal pathways between social rejection, off-task behavior, and low academic achievement have not been made clear, and in all likelihood, more than one causal pathway occurs. Certainly it is plausible that failure to stay on task in the classroom would lead to poorer academic performance, leaving a child ill-prepared to complete assignments. In that case, the child may have unoccupied time, which then becomes filled with behavior that is disruptive to the rest of the class. There is research documenting the fact that the amount of time students spend on task during academic instruction is related to academic achievement (Berliner & Rosenshine, 1977; Good & Beckerman, 1978).

The relationship between academic performance and peer status has been well described in the literature. Correlations between academic achievement and sociometric status have ranged from .2 to .4 (Coie & Krehbiel, 1984; Glick, 1972; Green, Forehand, Beck, & Vosk, 1980; Muma, 1965; Yellott, Liem, & Cowen, 1969). Although these are relatively modest correlations, the proportion of black rejected children we have found to have serious problems with academic work, based on standardized achievement test scores, is twice that found among average-status children.

Krehbiel (1984) designed a study to explore the relations between academic achievement, rejected status, off-task behavior in the classroom, and disruptive behavior through the observations of socially rejected males who were either low or high achievers. These observations were compared with those of average-status males who were either low or high achievers. Black, fourth-grade males who met selection criteria based on sociometric and academic achievement scores participated in this study. The decision to compare rejected children with socially average children rather than with high-status (popular) children was based on previous observational findings (Coie & Kupersmidt, 1983; Dodge, 1983) indicating that the behavior patterns of high social status are not simply the inverse of those of low-status children and that popular children differ from average-status children.

Children's behavior was observed both in the classroom (in order to assess the implications of schoolwork-related behavior for social adjustment) and on the playground (to assess the relationship of academic status to social behavior in the play setting). Significant status group differences were observed for some classroom and playground behavior variables. As in previous studies (Coie, Dodge, and Coppotelli, 1982; Dodge et al., 1982), rejected children were found to be more disruptive, more aggressive (without provocation), and generally less effective with their peers. This characterization applied to both classroom and playground observations. In the play setting, rejected males spent a significantly greater proportion of the time alone or initiating aversive contact with peers. In the classroom, rejected males spent proportionately less time on task, and their episodes of on-task behavior were of shorter duration. These rejected-status males spent more time off task and were more often disruptive when off task. They initiated more aversive interactions, and they were more often ignored by their peers when they initiated social interaction. Interestingly, the rejected males initiated proportionately more peer contacts during structured classroom time than they did during nonclassroom time. This is a confirmation of the data discussed by Dodge et al. (1982), who found that rejected children initiated more interactions in the classroom than on the playground. The finding suggests again that rejected boys are more likely to make ill-timed approaches without regard for the environmental context, which, for other children, offers cues for appropriate behavior.

Of particular interest is the fact that the rejected low achievers spent significantly more time off task than socially average low achievers. Whereas average-status low achievers spent equivalent amounts of time on and off task, the rejected low achievers spent nearly twice as much time off task as on task. Thus, the extensive off-task activities of the rejected low achievers cannot be attributed solely to poor achievement. Furthermore, rejected low achievers spent more than twice as much time off task as rejected high achievers and spent three times as much time engaged in disruptive off-task behavior as the socially rejected high achievers or the socially average low achievers. More than 17% of the rejected low achievers' off-task behavior was disruptive, compared with 9% for the rejected high achievers and 4.5% for the average low achievers. As a result of these exaggerations in their off-task, disruptive behavior, the rejected low-achieving boys must have been highly visible in the classroom, visible in such a negative manner as to contribute greatly to their unfavorable image with their teachers and peers. An important inference from these data is that it may be socially acceptable for boys to do poorly at school as long as this poor academic performance does not lead to behavior that interferes with others doing their work.

In this section, we estimated the proportions of rejected children who seem to have serious problems with aggression and disruption, two major determinants of peer rejection. Thus far the intervention approaches to reducing aggression and disruption among rejected children have been indirect, encouraging the acquisition of positive play skills as a means to better peer relations. Whether aggression and disruptive behavior are reduced by this strategy cannot be determined from the observational data in these studies, because the observations have centered on positive play behavior. In some of these successful studies the link between behavior change and improved peer status was not established. In others where the connection has been demonstrated, intervention was conducted with subsamples of rejected children who exhibited low frequencies of peer interaction. We have argued that these subsamples may underrepresent the aggressive population of rejected children. There is good reason, then, to give greater attention to interventions that directly deal with the aversive behavior of rejected children. The next section provides a review of two of the more promising directions found in the child-clinical literature.

Intervention strategies for aggressive behavior

There are at least two lines of thought that can be followed in developing intervention programs for the highly aggressive subset of rejected children. One we already discussed is inherent to the prosocial skills training model. The logic of this model is one of substituting positive behavior for negative behavior without explicitly attempting to reduce the use of aggressive behavior. The reasoning behind this perspective is that skillful prosocial behavior pays off in positive social consequences (e.g., more acceptance, more social influence) and eliminates the need for aggressive strategies, which have mixed or negative consequences. An alternative to this conceptualization is that aggressive behaviors do not merely substitute for prosocial skills that are missing from a rejected child's behavioral repertoire but are determined by other factors, which must be dealt with directly. According to one variant of this alternative conceptualization, aggressive behaviors have been reinforced for the child and thus constitute an important element in the child's interpersonal repertoire. Another variant would suggest that aggression occurs as a consequence of deficits in the child's coping skills, especially the inability to control anger. Whether by altering the system of social reinforcers for the child or by training the child in more effective anger-coping patterns, these formulations directly focus on the sources of aggressive behavior.

There are two major strategies that have been followed in attempting to reduce aggressive behavior among children. The first strategy involves altering the reinforcement contingencies that support the aggressive behavior of children. In this case, intervention time and activity are directed primarily at the aggressive child's caretakers, typically the parents but often teachers. The logic of this approach is that the child has been trained to be aggressive and therefore needs to be trained not to be aggressive. Because the persons who were most involved in providing the initial training to be aggressive presumably continue to reward aggressive behavior inadvertently, these same socialization agents need to learn to reward and shape nonaggressive behavior and punish and extinguish inappropriate aggressive behavior. The obvious underlying premise of this approach is that most undesirable aggression has had instrumental value for the child, and the focus of change is therefore on that instrumentality.

The most impressive and well-documented example of this first approach is found in the work of Patterson and his colleagues (Patterson, 1974; Patterson, 1982). Their approach emphasizes the primary influence of aggressive interaction processes in the home. The heart of this process is the coercive cycle. Coercive behavior is reinforced and learned by the child whenever that child achieves desirable consequences by means of aversive behavior. This can happen in several ways. Some parents are inconsistent and careless in their reactions to behaviors such as hitting, insulting, and the making of threats. As Patterson, Littman, and Bricker (1967) have documented, the probable frequency of these behaviors tends to increase when not countered by some resistance or punishing response. A more complex acquisition process often involves much of the family system. This coercive cycle typically begins when one family member confronts another with an aversive demand that is countered with an aversive response. Each member, with other family members often joining in, escalates the level of aversive behavior, and the tension and anger in the group rise until one person withdraws. By breaking the chain of aversive responses, the individual who withdraws reinforces the aversive behavior of the other and demonstrates the value of such behavior to other family members. Because the withdrawal of aversive participation usually leads to a cessation of aversive behavior by all participants, the withdrawing party has been negatively reinforced for withdrawing, as well. This person, typically the mother, then learns to reinforce the aversive behavior of her children because of the relief it provides her.

In the system of intervention employed by Patterson and his colleagues, the unit to which change is addressed is the family. Parents are presented with a comprehensive training program on the principles of social learning theory (Patterson, 1971). They then learn to identify both aversive and prosocial behaviors in their children and are trained to spot the antecedent conditions that may evoke these behaviors or the consequent events that may serve to reinforce them. Parents are carefully trained to record these sequences in the home. Next, parents are taught to reinforce prosocial behavior and to extinguish aversive and unacceptable behavior. Trainers model these activities for the parents with the children, and the parents are required to identify the steps that have been taken. Parents are helped to recognize prosocial responses and encouraged to reward them rather than take them for granted. Parents are taught to use time out – removing the child from potential reinforcers and placing the child in isolation for a brief, specified period – as a method for extinguishing aversive behavior. Role playing by the parents is often carried out in parent-training groups. Staff members sometimes talk to the parents by phone to monitor the progress of family contracts. The term *contract* refers to agreements among family members regarding rewards and benefits for the fulfillment of targeted behavioral goals.

The success of this program has been documented in reduced levels of aggression observed in the home of treatment families (e.g., Fleischman, 1981; Patterson, 1974). The success of the Patterson group's parent-training model has been compared favorably with more conventional eclectic therapy procedures with samples of antisocial children (Patterson, Chamberlain, & Reid, 1982). For the former sample there was a 63% reduction in aversive behavior from preintervention figures, as opposed to 17% reductions for the latter samples. Parent ratings of improvement showed parallel effects. Thus far there have been no published reports of the long-term maintenance effects of this approach. Because parent participation is essential, the ultimate value of this approach depends on parental involvement. McAuley (1982), in a review of parent-training research, suggests that aggressive children from stable, well-adjusted families tend to respond rapidly to behaviorally oriented procedures, whereas children with antisocial or delinquent patterns who are from multiproblem families respond less rapidly. Other investigators have struggled to encourage better generalization and maintenance of positive effects that are often short lived (Eyberg & Johnson, 1974; Kent & O'Leary, 1976). Patterson and his colleagues have found it important to recontact families during postintervention follow-up periods to provide "booster shot" training. All of these considerations suggest that an important contributor to the effectiveness of this approach is the skillfulness and sensitivity with which the intervention staff engages the family.

The rationale for this first approach is to resocialize aggressive children by removing the positive consequences of aggressive behavior. A useful distinction has been made by Hartup (1974) between hostile and instrumental types of aggression. The former is directed toward persons in reaction to frustrating or threatening behavior of the other, at least as perceived by the aggressor. The latter is directed toward the acquisition of objects or advantages in the social milieu. The Patterson approach can be characterized as oriented mostly toward the alteration of instrumental aggression. The second major approach can be said to be directed toward reducing hostile aggression. The first approach entails altering the social environment so that aggression no longer works, whereas the second approach is an attempt to alter the child so that frustrating and provocative events no longer elicit the same level and intensity of aggressive response. Essentially, this second strategy is to train aggressive children to acquire greater self-control.

Self-control training procedures for aggression developed out of a procedure for reducing impulsive behavior in hyperactive children (Meichenbaum, 1985; Meichenbaum & Goodman, 1971). Children are taught to interrupt their impulsive behavior by being trained to say things to themselves, first aloud and then silently, that would serve to keep them on task and remind them of the steps they were to take in carrying out their tasks. Such self-instructional methods have been translated into techniques for the control of anger among aggressive children (Camp, 1977; Camp, Blom, Herbert, & VanDoorninck, 1977). Variants of this "think aloud" technique have been employed with mixed but generally promising short-term effects (e.g., Forman, 1980; Kettlewell & Kausch, 1983; Lochman, 1985; Lochman, Burch, Curry, & Lampron, 1984).

Lochman has developed an 18-session program to be used with aggressive children in school settings. The program combines a number of techniques fitting within the general framework of cognitive-behavioral treatment methods. Children are trained to recognize their body cues to anger arousal and to utilize self-statements to inhibit reflexive aggressive responses (e.g., "I'm getting angry," "don't let him make me lose it now"). This is combined with training in social-problem-solving skills (Spivak, Platt, & Shure, 1976) to help children generate more adaptive solutions to anger-arousing situations. Trainers discuss frustrating situations with the children as problems to be solved and use examples to take them through a series of steps in which they identify what the problem is and what they would like to see happen in the situation. Children are helped to learn to generate different solutions and to evaluate the consequences of each so that they can choose the most effective solution. When the two procedures are combined, children are taught to react to their bodily anger-arousal cues by telling themselves to "stop and think about what I want to do." Although it is unrealistic to expect children to go stepwise through problem-solving steps in actual stressful situations, this procedure teaches them to interrupt an anger arousal–aggressive behavior chain by stopping to think. The goal is to get children to remember well-rehearsed "best solutions" as substitutes for aversive, but maladaptive, solutions. A third step in the anger control procedure is training in what Meichenbaum (1985) and Novaco (1978) have called stress inoculation. Here, children practice these procedures of arousal recognition, self-statements to inhibit aggression, and selection of best solutions under role-playing conditions. Members of the child's peer group enact situations in which the target child would normally be provoked to anger. These give the child an opportunity to practice anger control skills, beginning with mildly provocative situations and moving successively to more arousing examples as the child experiences success in controlling angry responses. Children are then encouraged to set goals for themselves in actual peer situations, including goals to reduce the frequency of aggressive outbursts in the school setting, where these outbursts can be monitored.

Boys who were trained in this program decreased significantly in observed aggressive and disruptive behavior in the classroom and in parents' ratings of aggression (Lochman et al., 1984). The addition of the goal-setting procedure tended to produce stronger effects than the anger control technique alone (Lochman, 1985). Although generalization effects have been demonstrated, no long-term follow-up results have been reported.

Each of these two approaches to children's aggression has advantages and disadvantages. In dealing with the family system, the parent-training strategy is aimed directly at the origin of the problem, and if it is successful, it is likely to have more consistent influence on the child. On the other hand, by focusing directly on the child as the locus for change, the self-control approach may have more long-term potential for generalized change. Having the parents cooperating in the effort represents the addition of major resources, and yet the parents are more likely to be firmly entrenched in old behavior patterns than their child. In some ways the question of relative advantage may reduce to an issue of motivation. Parent training requires motivation on the part of parents and self-control training requires that the child become motivated to change. As an addition to social skills training efforts in school settings, self-control procedures have obvious advantages, because like the positive play version of social skills training, they can be implemented in the school setting without an investment of time being required of caretakers. In fact, it makes sense to think of procedures like anger control training as social skills training procedures that could be added to the positive play skills training programs already in use. This would have the advantage of providing aggressive, rejected children with skills for managing angry reactions and with positive play skills to reduce the occurrence of frustrating circumstances.

Another way of comparing the two approaches for dealing with aggression is to consider each of them as coming to terms with a different aspect of aggression. Parent training addresses the reward value of aggression; one reason why aggression is more resistant to clinical intervention than most problems (Levitt, 1963) is that aggression does pay off in some ways. The self-control approaches, on the other hand, address the hostile side of aggression, the desire to mete out punishment in response to frustration or perceived provocation. Thus one approach may be better suited to some aggressive children than to others, and the two approaches may be complementary for many other aggressive children. It should be kept in mind that these are not the only available strategies for reducing aggressiveness (see Parke and Slaby, 1983); however, other methods have not been as well developed or researched as these two.

Intervention strategies for disruptive and off-task behavior

A number of methods for reducing disruptive behavior in the school classroom have been successfully employed. They fall into two major categories: those incorporating reinforcements or response-cost methods for increasing appropriate classroom behavior (cf. Pace & Forman, 1982) and those involving incentives for improved academic performance as a competing response to problematic classroom behavior. There is good evidence that the use of tokens as reinforcers is effective in reducing disruptive behavior and increasing on-task behavior in the classroom (Kazdin, 1977). Response-cost procedures are equally effective (Kaufman & O'Leary, 1972). Ayllon and Rosenbaum (1977) note that these methods do not always result in improved academic performance unless reinforcement is provided specifically for this performance. Ayllon and Roberts (1974) provide an example of this approach in a study involving 5 boys who exhibited high levels of disruptive behavior in the classroom. Rather than rewarding boys for periods of nondisruptive behavior, Ayllon and Roberts provided positive reinforcement for the accurate completion of their academic work. A return-to-baseline experimental design was implemented in which baseline observation data were collected and a token system was initiated, then discontinued, and then reinstated. The percentages of disruptive behavior and accurate academic work were compared across these phases. The reinforcement of accurate work resulted in both improved academic performance and dramatically reduced disruptive behavior. Increased attention to academic tasks served effectively as a competing response to disruptive and other off-task behavior.

One assumption implicit in the Ayllon and Roberts program is that children who are not attending to their schoolwork do possess the requisite academic ability to perform the tasks. For those children who have fallen a grade level or more behind their classmates in academic achievement, simply reinforcing academic accuracy may not be as effective as Ayllon and Roberts found it to be. We wonder about the long-term effectiveness of reinforcement for attending to academic work with a population of children who are lacking in some of the basic skills in reading or mathematics.

There is evidence, then, for the effectiveness of an approach to reducing disruptive behavior that substitutes adaptive behavior – namely, task-focused, achievement-oriented activity – for disruptive behavior. This substitution is achieved by altering the classroom reinforcement contingencies rather than by training children in more socially acceptable behavior. Although there are no data to speak to the maintenance of these effects, the long-term success of this strategy may depend on the continued control of classroom reinforcements for the child.

A second problem, as noted above, is that some children are simply unable to perform some of their classroom tasks. An alternative strategy for these children would be to coach them in academic skills. Coie and Krehbiel (1984) tested the effects of academic skills training and social skills training on a subset of 40 socially rejected children who were all poor academic achievers. The subjects were randomly assigned to one of four groups: academic skills tutoring, social skills coaching, a combination of academic tutoring and social skills coaching, and a no-attention control. Achievement and sociometric data were obtained at the end of third grade (pretest), fourth grade (posttest), and fifth grade (follow-up). Classroom observations were made at pretest and at posttest. The results revealed that academic training produced significant improvement in achievement and social preference scores. These gains were maintained at the time of the follow-up. The social skills training (modeled after the Oden and Asher coaching procedure) was associated with reading comprehension progress that was not maintained across time and improvement in peer ratings immediately after intervention. The tutoring and combination tutoring-plus-coaching groups showed significantly reduced off-task behavior and increased on-task behavior. These groups also received increased amounts of positive teacher attention by the end of the intervention period.

It is easy to understand why improvements in ability to remain on task would result in corollary improvements in social standing with classmates. Once the low-achieving child has acquired skills relevant to the classroom task, that child can begin to stay on task and has less occasion to disrupt nearby peers. As these behavioral changes become noticeable to classmates, the low-achieving child is likely to receive better social treatment.

Implications for social skills training with rejected children

In this chapter we have attempted to take stock of the current efforts to help rejected children achieve better social relations with their peers. Although social skills training research with children began over 40 years ago (e.g., Chittenden, 1942), the focus on peer-rejected children is more recent, extending back only 10 years. During this time there has been documented success for the positive play skills training model; however, we have suggested that this model works best with those rejected children who are observably deficient in those prosocial skills. The population of rejected children is heterogeneous, and we have argued that more dramatic success in helping rejected children may take place when intervention efforts take better account of that heterogeneity. In particular, interventions are needed for the most visible subsets of the rejected child population, namely, those who are aggressive or disruptive. Many of these children also may be deficient in prosocial skills, but the hypothesis we are raising in this chapter is that they require help beyond that contained in positive play skills training in order to become less aversive to their peers.

In thinking about methods for intervening with aggressive and disruptive rejected children, we have entertained a debate between the benefits of a prosocial skills training model and models directed specifically at reducing the frequency of aggressive or disruptive behavior. On the one hand, it can be argued that children who acquire the skills to relate to their peers more effectively will find themselves less often needing to resort to aggressive solutions to interpersonal crises or will find that they are given access to valued objects or social advantages because they are better liked by their peers. On the other hand, it can be argued that this positive status with peers will take time to achieve and that it will be hard for peers to change their opinion of a child if the child still employs aggressive behavior. Furthermore, aggression usually leads to reinforcement, at least in the short run, and disruptive behavior can generate social attention and provide the bored child with some stimulation. Accordingly, the argument goes, it is necessary to eliminate these aversive behaviors or reduce them in frequency so that a child's prosocial behavioral repertoire, either newly acquired or preexisting, can be employed to socially successful ends.

Interestingly enough, when we examined methods for eliminating aversive behavior, another version of this debate emerged. The focus for reducing aversive behavior could be placed either on reducing aversive behavior by changing the reinforcement contingencies associated with aversive behavior or on building up skillful behavior that would substitute effectively for the aversive behavior and thus eliminate it. These latter methods differ from prosocial skills strategies in that they are more specific to the situations that aggressive or disruptive children have difficulty in handling. Instead of being taught participation or communication skills, these children can be taught anger control skills or academic skills.

Bierman, Miller, and Stabb (1987) compared the effects of positive social skills instruction and a prohibition designed to reduce aversive behavior by managing reinforcers. Their sample was composed of rejected boys who were aggressive or disruptive. In the skill-coaching condition, children were coached in the positive social skills of questioning others, helping and cooperating in play, and sharing and taking turns. In the prohibition/reinforcement condition, children were presented with rules for the session, rules involving no fighting, yelling, being mean, whining, or showing a bad temper. A response-cost technique was employed for rule violations. That is, the coach provided nonspecific praise and tokens on a random schedule as long as children were engaged in positive activities and not breaking any rules. When a child broke a rule, he continued to play but lost the opportunity to earn tokens for 1 minute. Children in the skill-coaching condition also received tokens for skillful behaviors as they occurred, but the response-cost technique was not employed. Boys from first, second, and third grades were selected for participation on the basis of negative sociometric nominations and high levels of observed negative peer interaction. Boys were randomly assigned to either the skill-coaching condition, the prohibition condition, a combined coaching and prohibition condition, or a no-treatment control condition.

Boys in both of the prohibition conditions showed reductions in negative behavior immediately after treatment and received more positive responses from other boys. Observations at 6 weeks after treatment revealed that subjects in all three treatment groups initiated fewer negative behaviors. Boys in the two skill instruction conditions received more positive behavior from others and tended to initiate more positive behaviors. Changes in sociometric status with peers were less promising, however. No treatment effects were obtained for status changes at posttreatment or follow-up, based on nominations from the total peer group. However, at follow-up, boys who were in the combined treatment condition (instructions plus prohibitions) had fewer negative sociometric nominations from treatment partners (nonrejected boys who served as play partners in the treatment play sessions) than did boys in the other conditions. No improvements in peer assessments of aggression were found, and no significant sociometric changes were found 1 year after treatment when the boys were in new classrooms. Bierman et al.'s findings suggest that prohibition and reinforcement contingencies lead to the most immediate reductions in negative behavior but that both prohibition/reinforcement and coaching approaches resulted in the same improvement assessed 6 weeks later. Skills coaching seemed to lead to somewhat more positive behavior, although positive reinforcement also accompanied the skills training. The combination of approaches was found to be necessary in order to effect any social status improvements, and the fact that these did not generalize to the classroom underscores the point that it is difficult to intervene successfully with children who are rejected because of aggressive or disruptive behavior. The fact that children changed their behavior in the eyes of neutral observers but not in the eyes of their classmates probably means that they have reputations that are quite resistant to change. Six weeks was obviously not sufficient time for peer judgments to catch up with behavior change. Still, the use of a combination of techniques has promise and suggests one resolution to the debate we have carried forward in the chapter.

Engaging the child in social skills training

Our focus on techniques for reducing aversive behavior has tended to mask the role of other factors of great importance to successful intervention work with rejected children. Some of these fit within the broad category of motivational factors. Motivational issues were mentioned earlier in connection with parents' and children's commitment to participate in social skills training. Unlike most forms of reinforcement methods, social skills procedures require that the child agree to participate in the training with some degree of activity and commitment. This means that participation must make sense to the child and appear to be worthwhile and not a waste of time; also, the child must not be offended that he or she has been asked to participate. In the case of positive skills training procedures, Oden and Asher found an inoffensive and engaging way of getting past these potential sticking points by suggesting to children that the investigators had some ideas about ways to make play go better and that they would like the subject to try these out for them to see how they work. The child is thus enlisted as a research collaborator. This strategy does not fit so nicely with the agenda of self-control programs or even academic skills training programs. Although self-control skills can be introduced as ideas to be tested in difficult situations, the child must agree that he or she faces difficult situations and that better ideas are needed. At some level the child must recognize the need for better anger control skills. The response of many aggressive children to the suggestion that sometimes there are things that make everyone irritated is to agree that this is true and that the thing to do is to "bust 'em good" and let the others know they cannot get away with those things.

Getting children to try out these self-control skills often leads the trainer into a dilemma – namely, the aggressive child's intense commitment to the peer code that says if someone does something to you, you are justified (even compelled) in retaliating, providing the offense was intentional (Dodge, 1980). The dilemma is that the child's view of the best solution to a frustrating situation is to hurt the source of frustration. These situations are construed by aggressive children as ones in which they are forced to maintain their integrity and self-esteem through aggressive actions. In fact, children are often correct in this appraisal, particularly so for those living in low-income urban neighborhoods, where aggression is quite prevalent. However, from our observations of some of these boys in play groups (Coie & Kupersmidt, 1983), we have concluded that one distinguishing feature of popular boys from this same peer culture is that they tend not to construe the marginally provocative situations as challenges but are able to interpret them for themselves and for others as occasions for humor or for a demonstration of self-control. As one boy put it, when urged to fight another, "I'll hit him if he hits me, but if he doesn't hit me, then I won't hit him." The code is maintained, but the other is forced to declare himself as the aggressor.

One way to understand this adaptive behavior on the part of popular children is to see them as reframing the event (Watzlawick, Weakland, & Fisch, 1974). In our recent intervention efforts (Coie, Underwood, & Lochman, in press) we have begun to offer a reframing idea to aggressive children and find that it provides them with an acceptable alternative to the "fight or flight" choice with which they otherwise feel themselves confronted. We suggest to them that sometimes other children may attempt to provoke them into losing their temper and doing something that will get them into trouble. We reframe this situation not as one in which the subject is being asked to defend his or her honor, but one in which his or her self-control is being tested. The other child is reframed as attempting to control them by making them respond in aggressive ways. This seems to address the larger principle of the peer code, namely to be in control and not to let others control you. With the last of three successive intervention cohorts composed of aggressive, rejected fourth-grade children, we were able to obtain significant improvements in peer social status and ratings of prosocial behavior and marginally significant improvement in teacher ratings of aggression (Coie, Underwood, & Lochman, in press). Greater emphasis was placed on the reframing principle with this last cohort than with the first two. Although we have not evaluated the effects of this strategy systematically, it does seem to provide a breakthrough with some of the resistance to learning anger control.

The fact that aggressive children have a reputation for aggressiveness is a major impediment to behavior change. As Dodge (1980) first noted, aggressive children are expected by peers to have hostile intentions, and behaviors that might be given a benign interpretation for nonaggressive children are met with hostility and confrontation when aggressive children are involved. Thus by middle childhood, aggressive children face a different social situation than most other children, and it is very difficult for them to take the first few steps in practicing self-control because they face so many more tests of self-control than other children. The school setting is often a difficult place for children to begin this retraining because there is not very much environmental support for their efforts. We have found that some teachers find it difficult to give recognition to the first faint efforts at self-control. Because these children have made their jobs more difficult for so long, teachers often have built up the same resentment and tendency to anticipate aggressive intention as the peer group. This makes it difficult for teachers to perceive change or the intention to change on the part of aggressive children.

Motivational problems also arise in the process of intervention with children whose predominant form of aggressive behavior is instrumental. Children who bully or dominate or take things from other children find these acts to have immediate, reinforcing value. Adult efforts to talk them out of this behavior are not very successful, and often, adults provide them with role models of this style of behavior. As one boy in our project discussed with his trainer, "My uncle does this stuff (i.e., intimidation, stealing) all the time and he's never caught, and he never goes to jail." For these children it appears we must reverse the payoff matrix in their environment.

In this chapter we have concentrated our attention on the behavioral determinants of peer rejection that we consider to be the most significant and intractable. Although we have presented different strategies for intervening with the problems of aggression and disruption and have compared the logic by which they are thought to work, we have not meant to put them into competition with each other. By seeing each alternative clearly we hope it may be easier to see how each can play a role in developing approaches that will be most effective with different rejected children. For many aggressive, rejected children it may be necessary to systematically employ a combination of methods. Intervention with peer-rejected children is a new endeavor. This is a time for generating new solutions, solutions tailored to our best assessments of the problem, and not a time for foreclosing on ideas.

References

Allen, E., Hart, B., Buell, J., Harris, F., & Wolf, M. (1964). Effects of social reinforcement on isolate behavior of a nursery school child. *Child Development, 35*, 511–518.

Asarnow, J. R. (1983). Children with peer adjustment problems: Sequential and nonsequential analysis of school behaviors. *Journal of Consulting and Clinical Psychology, 51*, 709–717.

Asher, S. R. (1985). An evolving paradigm in social skill training research with children. In B. H. Schneider, K. H. Rubin, & J. E. Ledingham (Eds.), *Children's peer relations: Issues in assessment and intervention* (pp. 157–171). New York: Springer-Verlag.

Asher, S. R., Markell, R. A., & Hymel, S. (1981). Identifying children at risk in peer relations: A critique of the rate of interaction approach to assessment. *Child Development, 52*, 1239–1245.

Asher, S. R., & Renshaw, P. D. (1981). Children without friends: Social knowledge and social skills. In S. R. Asher & J. M. Gottman (Eds.), *The development of children's friendships* (pp. 273–296). New York: Cambridge University Press.

Ayllon, T., & Roberts, M. D. (1974). Eliminating discipline problems by strengthening academic performance. *Journal of Applied Behavior Analysis, 7*, 71–76.

Ayllon, T., & Rosenbaum, M. S. (1977). The behavioral treatment of disruption and hyperactivity in school settings. In B. B. Lahey & A. E. Kazdin (Eds.), *Advances in clinical child psychology* (Vol. 1, pp. 83–118). New York: Plenum.

Berliner, D. C., & Rosenshine, B. V. (1977). The acquisition of knowledge in the classroom. In R. Spiro & W. Montague (Eds.), *Schooling and the acquisition of knowledge* (pp. 375–396). Hillsdale, NJ: Lawrence Erlbaum.

Bierman, K. L. (1986). Process of change during social skills training with preadolescents and its relation to treatment outcome. *Child Development, 57*, 230–240.

Bierman, K. L., & Furman, W. (1984). The effect of social skills training and peer involvement on the social adjustment of preadolescents. *Child Development, 55*, 151–162.

Bierman, K. L., Miller, C. L., & Stabb, S. D. (1987). Improving the social behavior and peer acceptance of rejected boys: Effects of social skill training with instructions and prohibitions. *Journal of Consulting and Clinical Psychology, 55*, 194–200.

Buell, J., Stoddard, P., Harris, F. R., & Baer, D. M. (1968). Collateral social development accompanying reinforcement of outdoor play in a preschool child. *Journal of Applied Behavior Analysis, 1*, 167–175.

Camp, B. W. (1977). Verbal mediation in young aggressive boys. *Journal of Abnormal Psychology, 86*, 145–153.

Camp, B. W., Blom, G. E., Herbert, F., & VanDoorninck, W. J. (1977). "Think Aloud": A program for developing self-control in young aggressive boys. *Journal of Abnormal Child Psychology, 5*, 157–169.

Chittenden, C. E. (1942). An experimental study in measuring and modifying assertive behavior in young children. *Monographs of the Society for Research in Child Development, 7* (1, Serial No. 31).

Coie, J. D. (1985). Fitting social skills intervention to the target group. In B. H. Schneider, K. H. Rubin, & J. E. Ledingham (Eds.), *Children's peer relations: Issues in assessment and intervention* (pp. 141–156). New York: Springer-Verlag.

Coie, J. D., Dodge, K. A., & Coppotelli, H. (1982). Dimensions and types of social status: A cross-age perspective. *Developmental Psychology, 18*, 557–570.

Coie, J. D., & Krehbiel, G. (1984). Effects of academic tutoring on the social status of low-achieving, socially rejected children. *Child Development, 55*, 1465–1478.

Coie, J. D., & Kupersmidt, J. B. (1983). A behavioral analysis of emerging social status in boys' groups. *Child Development, 54*, 1400–1416.

Coie, J. D., Underwood, M., & Lochman, J. E. (in press). Programmatic intervention with aggressive children in the school setting. In D. J. Pepler & K. H. Rubin (Eds.), *Development and treatment of childhood aggression*. Toronto: Lawrence Erlbaum.

Dodge, K. A. (1980). Social cognition and children's aggressive behavior. *Child Development, 51*, 162–170.

Dodge, K. A. (1983). Behavioral antecedents of peer social status. *Child Development, 54*, 1386–1399.

Dodge, K. A., Coie, J. D., & Brakke, N. P. (1982). Behavior patterns of socially rejected and neglected preadolescents: The roles of social approach and aggression. *Journal of Abnormal Child Psychology, 10*, 389–410.

Evers, W. L., & Schwartz, J. C. (1973). Modifying social withdrawal in preschoolers: The effect of filmed modeling and teacher praise. *Journal of Abnormal Child Psychology, 1*, 248–256.

Eyberg, S. M., & Johnson, S. M. (1974). Multiple assessment of behavior modification with families: Effects on contingency contracting and order of treated problems. *Journal of Consulting and Clinical Psychology, 42*, 594–606.

Fleischman, M. J. (1981). A replication of Patterson's "Intervention for boys with conduct problems." *Journal of Consulting and Clinical Psychology, 49*, 342–351.

Forman, S. G. (1980). A comparison of cognitive training and response cost procedures in modifying aggressive behavior of elementary school children. *Behavior Therapy, 11*, 594–600.

French, D. C. (1988). Heterogeneity of peer rejected boys: Aggressive and non-aggressive subtypes. *Child Development, 59*, 976–985.

Furman, W., Rahe, D. F., & Hartup, W. W. (1979). Rehabilitation of socially withdrawn preschool children through mixed-age and same-age socialization. *Child Development, 50*, 915–922.

Glick, O. (1972). Some social-emotional consequences of early inadequate acquisition of reading skills. *Journal of Educational Psychology, 63*, 253–257.

Goldfried, M. P., & D'Zurilla, T. J. (1969). A behavioral-analytic model for assessing competence. In C. D. Spielberger (Ed.), *Current topics in clinical and community psychology* (Vol. 1, pp. 151–196). New York: Academic Press.

Good, T. L., & Beckerman, T. N. (1978). Time-on-task: A naturalistic study in sixth grade classrooms. *Elementary School Journal, 78*, 193–201.

Gottman, J. M. (1977). Toward a definition of social isolation in children. *Child Development, 48*, 513–517.

Gottman, J. M., Gonso, J., & Rasmussen, B. (1975). Social interaction, social competence, and friendship in children. *Child Development, 46*, 709–718.

Gottman, J. M., Gonso, J., & Schuler, P. (1976). Teaching social skills to isolated children. *Journal of Abnormal Child Psychology, 4*, 179–197.

Green, K. D., Forehand, R., Beck, J., & Vosk, B. (1980). An assessment of the relationship among measures of children's social competence and children's academic achievement. *Child Development, 51*, 1149–1156.

Gresham, F. M., & Nagle, R. J. (1980). Social skills training with children: Responsiveness to modeling and coaching as a function of peer orientation. *Journal of Consulting and Clinical Psychology, 48*, 718–729.

Harlow, H. F. (1969). Age-mate or peer affectional system. In D. S. Lehrman, R. A. Hinde, & E. Shaw (Eds.), *Advances in the study of behavior* (Vol. 2, pp. 333–383). New York: Academic Press.

Hartup, W. W. (1974). Aggression in childhood: Developmental perspectives. *American Psychologist, 29*, 336–341.

Hartup, W. W., Glazer, J. A., & Charlesworth, R. (1967). Peer reinforcement and sociometric status. *Child Development, 38*, 1017–1024.

Hymel, S., & Asher, S. R. (1977, April). *Assessment and training of isolated children's social skills.* Paper presented at the biennial meeting of the Society for Research in Child Development, New Orleans (ERIC Document Reproduction Service No. ED 136 930).

Kaufman, K. F., & O'Leary, K. D. (1972). Reward, cost, and self-evaluation procedures for disruptive adolescents in a psychiatric hospital school. *Journal of Applied Behavior Analysis, 5*, 293–309.

Kazdin, A. E. (1977). *The token economy: A review and evaluation.* New York: Plenum.

Keller, M. F., & Carlson, P. M. (1974). The use of symbolic modeling to promote social skills in preschool children with low levels of social responsiveness. *Child Development, 45*, 912–919.

Kent, R. N., & O'Leary, K. D. (1976). A controlled evaluation of behavior modification with conduct problem children. *Journal of Consulting and Clinical Psychology, 44*, 586–596.

Kettlewell, P. W., & Kausch, D. F. (1983). The generalization of the effects of a cognitive–behavioral treatment program for aggressive children. *Journal of Abnormal Child Psychology, 11*, 101–114.

Krehbiel, G. G. (1984). *Sociometric status- and achievement-based differences in behavior and peer-assessed reputation.* Unpublished doctoral dissertation, Duke University, Durham, NC.

Ladd, G. W. (1981). Effectiveness of a social learning method for enhancing children's social interaction and peer acceptance. *Child Development, 52*, 171–178.

Ladd, G. W. (1983). Social networks of popular, average, and rejected children in school settings. *Merrill-Palmer Quarterly, 29*, 283–307.

Ladd, G. W., & Asher, S. R. (1985). Social skill training and children's peer relations. In L. L'Abate & M. A. Milan (Eds.), *Handbook of social skills training and research* (pp. 219–244). New York: Wiley.

La Greca, A. M., & Santogrossi, D. (1980). Social skills training with elementary school students: A behavioral group approach. *Journal of Consulting and Clinical Psychology, 48,* 220–227.

Levitt, E. E. (1963). Psychotherapy with children: A further evaluation. *Behavior Research and Therapy, 60,* 326–329.

Lochman, J. E. (1985). Effects of different treatment lengths in cognitive behavioral interventions with aggressive boys. *Child Psychiatry and Human Development, 16,* 45–56.

Lochman, J. E., Burch, P. R., Curry, J. F., & Lampron, L. B. (1984). Treatment and generalization effects of cognitive-behavioral and goal-setting interventions with aggressive boys. *Journal of Consulting and Clinical Psychology, 52,* 915–916.

McAuley, R. (1982). Training parents to modify conduct problems in their children. *Journal of Child Psychology and Psychiatry, 23,* 335–342.

Meichenbaum, D. H. (1985). *Stress inoculation training.* New York: Pergamon Press.

Meichenbaum, D. H., & Goodman, J. (1971). Training impulsive children to talk to themselves: A means of developing self-control. *Journal of Abnormal Psychology, 77,* 115–126.

Muma, J. R. (1965). Peer evaluation and academic performance. *Personnel and Guidance Journal, 44,* 405–409.

Novaco, R. W. (1978). Anger and coping with stress. In J. P. Foreyt & D. P. Rathjen (Eds.), *Cognitive behavior therapy: Research and application* (pp. 135–173). New York: Plenum.

O'Connor, R. D. (1969). Modification of social withdrawal through symbolic modeling. *Journal of Applied Behavior Analysis, 2,* 15–22.

O'Connor, R. D. (1972). Relative efficacy of modeling, shaping, and the combined procedures for modification of social withdrawal. *Journal of Abnormal Psychology, 79,* 327–334.

Oden, S., & Asher, S. R. (1977). Coaching children in social skills for friendship making. *Child Development, 48,* 495–506.

Pace, D. M., & Forman, S. G. (1982). Variables related to the effectiveness of response cost. *Psychology in the Schools, 19,* 365–370.

Parke, R. D., & Slaby, R. G. (1983). The development of aggression. In E. M. Hetherington (Ed.), *Handbook of child psychology: Vol. 4. Socialization, personality, and social development* (pp. 547–641, 4th ed.). New York: Wiley.

Patterson, G. R. (1971). *Living with children.* Champaign, IL: Research Press.

Patterson, G. R. (1974). Interventions for boys with conduct problems: Multiple settings, treatments, and criteria. *Journal of Consulting and Clinical Psychology, 42,* 471–481.

Patterson, G. R. (1982). *Coercive family processes.* Eugene, OR: Castilia Press.

Patterson, G. R., Chamberlain, P., & Reid, J. B. (1982). A comparative evaluation of a parent-training program. *Behavior Therapy, 13,* 638–650.

Patterson, G. R., Littman, R. A., & Bricker, W. (1967). Assertive behavior in children: A step toward a theory of aggression. *Monographs of the Society for Research in Child Development, 32,* (5, Serial No. 113).

Sherif, M., Harvey, O. J., White, B. J., Hood, W. R., & Sherif, C. W. (1961). *Intergroup conflict and cooperation.* Norman: University of Oklahoma.

Spivak, G., Platt, J. J., & Shure, M. B. (1976). *The problem-solving approach to adjustment.* San Francisco: Jossey-Bass.

Sutherland, J. H., Algozzine, B., Ysseldyke, J. E., & Freeman, S. (1983). Changing peer perceptions: Effects of labels and assigned attributes. *Journal of Learning Disabilities, 16,* 217–220.

Vosk, B., Forehand, R., Parker, J. B., & Rickard, K. (1982). A multimethod comparison of popular and unpopular children. *Developmental Psychology, 18,* 571–575.

Walker, H. M., & Hops, H. (1973). The use of group and individual reinforcement contingencies in the modification of social withdrawal. In L. A. Hamerlynck, L. C. Hancy, & E. J. Mash (Eds.),

Behavior change: Methodology, concepts, and practice (pp. 269-307). Champaign, IL: Research Press.

Watzlawick, P., Weakland, J., & Fisch, R. (1974). *Change: Principles of problem formulation and problem resolution.* New York: Norton.

Yellott, A., Liem, G., & Cowen, E. L. (1969). Relationships among measures of adjustment, sociometric status, and achievement in third graders. *Psychology in the Schools, 6,* 315–321.

12 Toward the development of successful social skills training for preschool children

Jacquelyn Mize and Gary W. Ladd

In response to evidence concerning the potential concurrent and long-term consequences of peer rejection in childhood (see Chapter 10, this volume), researchers have worked to develop interventions capable of improving children's social skills and peer acceptance. To date, most of these programs have been geared to children in the middle to late elementary school years. In this chapter, we will consider the possible benefits of planning interventions for preschool children. Along with potential rationales for social skills training with preschool children, we will consider a model of social skills training and discuss the means by which this model can be used to design and implement effective interventions.

Rationales for developing social skills training for preschool children

Peers play an important role in children's development well before children reach elementary school (Hartup, 1983; Mize, Ladd, & Price, 1985). Moreover, differences in preschoolers' social competence and peer acceptance remain somewhat stable well into the early elementary years (Ladd & Price, 1987; Waldrop & Halverson, 1975). As a result, early social rejection may be difficult for children to overcome and, in the long run, may interfere with their ability to develop important social skills.

Additional reasons for considering social skills training during preschool lie in the changing dynamics of children's peer groups. By the middle school years, forces such as reputational biases and the tendency for children to establish cliques (Chapter 6, this volume; Ladd, 1983) appear to make it increasingly difficult for marginal group members to participate and gain acceptance from peers, even if they succeed in learning more appropriate and effective social

The research reported in this chapter was supported, in part, by a grant to the authors from the Agricultural Experiment Station at Purdue University.

skills (see Bierman & Furman, 1984). These constraints are not as evident in preschool peer groups, and thus, efforts to change children's group status may be more successful with younger, as opposed to older, children.

Finally, the nature of the preschool experience makes it amenable to social skills interventions. Preschool is a time when parents and teachers generally place greater emphasis on social development than on academic achievement. Further, the objectives of social skills training, such as increasing cooperative interactions and reducing aggression, are likely to be compatible with the goals of most preschool curricula. The instructional design of most social skills interventions is also consistent with the teaching and behavior management styles of many preschool educators. Typically, a coach or a skilled teacher interacts intensively with one or more children to teach selected social skills.

Given that peer relations are important during the preschool years and that children may benefit from skill-based interventions, it is important to develop effective methods for this purpose. One place to begin is with skills-training programs that have been shown to be effective with elementary school children. However, it is unlikely that the procedures found to be effective with older schoolchildren will also succeed with preschoolers. For instance, a training procedure used by Ladd (1981) requires that children not only interpret and understand concepts that are verbally presented by the coach but also respond to the coach's questions with verbal descriptions of behaviors and translate verbal descriptions into actions (see Ladd, 1981, p. 174). As such, this procedure requires cognitive and linguistic skills that are, for the most part, beyond the abilities of preschool children. Compared with their older counterparts, preschool children may have considerable difficulty with tasks such as inferring specific behaviors from general concepts, responding to requests for exemplary behaviors, or using information from discussions to formulate behavioral strategies for subsequent play sessions with a peer. Thus, in developing social skills interventions for young children, we must design instructional methods that are commensurate with their learning styles and abilities.

We sought to create a skills-training curriculum for preschoolers by drawing upon a previously developed model of social skills learning and instruction (Ladd & Mize, 1983). Although not developed for a particular age-group, we saw this model as a useful blueprint for designing interventions because it specifies skill-learning principles that can be translated into curricula for different ages. The model specifies both (1) the social-cognitive and behavioral skills likely to facilitate competent social interaction and (2) instructional principles that may be used to teach children these skills. Following our description of this model, we shall turn our attention to issues such as the development of training curricula and our efforts to empirically evaluate a specific training program that we developed for preschool children.

A cognitive-social learning model of social skills training

In an earlier paper (Ladd & Mize, 1983), we proposed that in order for children to act in situationally appropriate and socially skilled ways they must (a) possess knowledge or concepts of appropriate social goals, contexts in which those goals can be pursued, and strategies for achieving those goals; (b) be able to translate these cognitive representations into skillful behavior; and (c) continuously monitor and interpret the social environment and the effects of their behavior on that environment. Children who lack skills in one or more of these three areas are seen as likely to behave in ways that lead to peer rejection or neglect. Thus, this model serves as a guide for (a) assessing social-cognitive and behavioral deficits that may lead to children's relationship difficulties and (b) for designing interventions to ameliorate these problems.

In the following discussion we will highlight certain skill deficits and the potential consequences of such deficiencies for preschool children's peer relations. Because research on preschool samples is limited, studies on elementary-age children will be cited where relevant.

Components of social competence and children's peer relations

Social situations are complex, and children's success in them depends on factors such as how they process social information, what they know about social interactions, and whether or not they can act appropriately on their knowledge and perceptions. In the following sections we shall use frequently encountered interactional contexts, such as group entry (see Chapter 3, this volume), to illustrate the cognitive and behavioral abilities that children must possess and orchestrate in order to operate in socially skilled ways.

Component 1: The role of social knowledge. The knowledge children derive from social experience may serve as a blueprint for social action by allowing them to construct goals or reasons for social action, generate possible courses of action, and adapt their responses to situational norms or expectations. Children who lack an awareness of goals, strategies, and normative expectations for specific contexts may be at risk for behaving maladaptively and engendering peer censure. The importance of social knowledge may be illustrated in the context of peer group entry situations. For many children, successful entry attempts appear to reflect a goal of being accepted into the group, whereas less successful attempts frequently appear to be based on the entering child's desire to control the group or to save face (see Chapter 3, this volume; Renshaw & Asher, 1982). Context may play an important role in goal construal and strategy execution. Selecting an appropriate time for group entry may mean waiting until there is room in an activity for an additional person or attempting entry during a transition in group activities, rather than risking disruption by entering during peers' ongoing activities. Successful strategies for group entry may include acting in concert with group members (i.e., performing "relevant" behavior) and delaying attempts to direct the group until one is an established group member (Garvey, 1984; Chapter 3, this volume).

Differences in goal orientation apparently have an impact on the social interactions of young children and may even affect their sensitivity to social skills interventions. Evers-Pasquale and Sherman (1975) found that preschoolers who expressed a preference for peer-oriented activities, as opposed to solitary or teacher-oriented activities, made greater gains in peer interaction after viewing a film of young children modeling interaction (see Taylor & Asher, 1984, for a discussion of goal orientations and their effects on children's social interaction). Preschoolers' knowledge of social strategies may also affect their relationships with peers. In one study (Mize & Ladd, 1984) aggressive preschoolers were found to suggest solutions to hypothetical dilemmas that were less friendly than those proposed by nonaggressive peers. Similarly, when compared with popular peers, unpopular kindergarten children tend to suggest more vague or negative strategies for hypothetical dilemmas (Asher & Renshaw, 1981).

Component 2: The role of performance proficiency. Children who can construct appropriate goals for social interaction and can identify an appropriate strategy for pursuing that goal may still act in inappropriate ways because they are unable or unwilling to use their knowledge to guide performance. This "translation" problem, or the inability to implement "skillful" or appropriate behavioral strategies to achieve a social goal, may occur either because children choose not to act (i.e., to withdraw or remain isolated) or because they act in an inappropriate way. Children may observe, for example, how a skillful child enters a group and wish to adopt the same strategy, but due to inexperience, they employ it ineptly.

Unfortunately, most of the studies that document behavioral differences between well-liked and unaccepted children do not provide data on children's social knowledge versus performance proficiency. Evidence indicating that some children do apparently have difficulty translating social knowledge into useful behavioral sequences can be found, however, in recent anecdotal observations. One 4-year-old boy in a preschool in which the authors were working seemed to want to play with others (i.e., an appropriate social goal) and usually appeared to have appropriate ideas for participation (i.e., social strategies). However, his execution of these ideas lacked finesse. He often spoke too rapidly and with so much exuberance that he was difficult to understand. Thus, although his purpose and strategies were appropriate, his inept performance often resulted in exclusion by peers. (For examples of work with adults and adolescents emphasizing verbal and nonverbal stylistic differences in social skills, see Argyle, 1985).

Component 3: The role of monitoring and self-evaluation. Of the three types of underlying skill processes and deficits, monitoring and self-evaluation may be the most complex. Monitoring social interaction involves, among other things, paying attention to others' behavior so that one can act in ways that are relevant to their actions or interests. In a recent study by Putallaz (1983), kindergarten children's ability to accurately interpret peers' behavior and contribute to conversation in relevant ways was found to be predictive of their peer acceptance 4 months later in first grade (Putallaz, 1983).

Other important monitoring skills include the ability to observe one's own behavior and accurately interpret social cues for evidence of others' reactions and the ability to make attributions about self and others that are conducive to continued interaction and skill adaptation (cf. Dodge & Somberg, 1985; Goetz & Dweck, 1980). Even if a child learns appropriate social concepts and can perform corresponding behaviors, these new skills may not generalize and be maintained in the peer group if the child cannot assess their impact across persons and contexts. Thus, children learn to be sensitive to cues from peers that carry important information, such as the peer's current interest or focus, a desire to be left alone, or censure of the subject's actions. Further, children must learn to interpret these cues in constructive, nondefeating ways. A sensitivity to social cues may help children to construct situation-specific strategies and to recognize that some actions are more effective in some situations than others.

Attributional bias is one type of monitoring problem that has received research attention. Based on a two-process model of the development of social attributions (Costanzo & Dix, 1983), Dodge (1985) proposes two pathways by which attributional biases in children may occur. Problems occurring during the first process, termed *formal informational analysis,* involve deficits or biases in encoding or representing social cues. For example, Dodge reported that low-status kindergarten, second-, and fourth-grade children were less accurate than their accepted peers in discriminating cues indicative of peers' intention in videotaped vignettes. Specifically, neglected and rejected children tended to mistakenly label peers' prosocial intentions as hostile (Dodge, Murphy, & Buchsbaum, 1984). Aggressive preschoolers attend more to aggressive portions of puppet shows and recall more aggressive cartoon episodes than do their less aggressive peers (Gouze, Gordon, & Rayias, 1983). In each of these examples, although children may have applied logical rules of inference during social information processing, they did so on the basis of biased or inaccurate readings of social cues. Dodge (1985) suggests that prevention programs include training in the accurate encoding and interpretation of others' social cues.

The second social information process proposed by Costanzo and Dix (1983) to account for attributional biases is termed *preemptive processing.* Preemptive processing refers to the automatic application of norms or beliefs about persons or social situations (Costanzo & Dix, 1983). That is, attributions arising from preemptive processing occur automatically when specific cues are presented (Dodge, 1985). For instance, the tendency to attribute failure to lack of ability rather than to consider other possible causes for failure may be the result of preemptive processing (Costanzo & Dix, 1983). The implications of this type of attributional bias for social competence are apparent in a study by Goetz and Dweck (1980) that indicated that children who attributed social rejection to lack of personal competence, appeal, or attractiveness were less likely to persist at efforts to gain acceptance following social failure than were their peers. Moreover, susceptibility to preemptive processing may be greater when children are under stress. Dodge and Somberg (1985) found that when presented with a peer's ambiguous but potentially negative act, aggressive boys are likely to assume hostile intent only when they feel threatened.

Thus, problems in social monitoring may occur as a result of Process 1 errors (inaccurate or biased encoding or representing of social cues) or Process 2 errors (automatic, illogical application of rules). In either case, however, monitoring deficits are likely to lead to recurring difficulties and discomfort in peer situations and probably require specific intervention techniques to help children learn to read and interpret the social environment accurately.

Using a cognitive-social learning model to develop social skills training procedures

In developing social skills interventions for preschoolers we draw upon Ladd and Mize's (1983) cognitive-social learning model to identify (a) areas of potential social-cognitive and behavioral deficits (i.e., knowledge, performance, and monitoring) that may impede constructive peer relations and (b) instructional principles for remedying these deficits (i.e., a training paradigm). Of paramount importance is the question of how these instructional principles can be adapted to preschool children.

A review of skill-based training studies with elementary school children suggests that many of the interventions employed are implicitly based on a cognitive-social learning model of social skills training (see Ladd & Mize, 1983). For instance, in a study by Ladd (1981), the coach taught third- and fourth-grade children concepts about offering support to peers, leading peers, and asking questions of peers. Children were encouraged to try out (i.e., perform) these new ideas in a game with peers. Finally, the children were asked to evaluate their own performance in terms of whether they had actually performed the behaviors, how peers had reacted, and how they might improve performance. If the peer did not react positively, the coach encouraged the child to attribute the failure to inappropriate skill use (rather than personal characteristics) and to adjust skill performance. Children were also asked to try to use the skills in classroom interaction between coaching sessions and to report to the coach the results of their efforts. Thus, children were taught new ideas about social interaction and were encouraged to perform the corresponding behaviors, evaluate their performance, read social cues accurately, and make constructive interpretations about the results of their efforts.

Although the basic goals of social skills training for preschoolers may be essentially the same as those identified for elementary school children, examination of the training protocol used with older children indicates that these instructional procedures may not be readily adaptable to 4- and 5-year-olds. The individual's developing cognitive, behavioral, and emotional characteristics determine in part which intervention procedures will be effective, inefficient, or ineffective (Kendall, Lerner, & Craighead, 1984). Accordingly, it is important to consider how the previously employed cognitive-social learning principles can be adapted to yield effective skills training procedures for preschool children (Mize, 1984).

Adapting social skills training for preschool children

Target skills. Perhaps the first step in planning a developmentally appropriate intervention for preschool children is to identify skills that are likely to promote peer acceptance. Our own efforts to create a developmentally appropriate curriculum were guided by a review of the empirical literature and by our own informal classroom observations, which led us to select four target skills for the training curriculum: leading peers, asking questions, commenting, and supporting peers.

Prosocial leading, or making positive suggestions in an attempt to influence peers, is associated with peer competence (Scarlett, 1980). Leading seems to be a key way for young children to initiate, direct, elaborate, and maintain joint play themes. This skill is significant because the development of joint play themes seems to be especially important in fostering early peer relations (Olson, Johnson, Belleau, Parks, & Barrett, 1983; Scarlett, 1980). Socially skilled preschoolers often use a style that is somewhat directive (Scarlett, 1980), yet not bossy, and that is apparently quite effective in their peer group. For instance, the command given by one 4-year-old boy to another in the dramatic play corner of a preschool, "Hey, I be the cashier, and you come, you pretend you have to buy all these for your wife," changed a "kitchen" into a "store" and eventually attracted several other children to a group in which the "cashier" was, for a time, the central player.

A second skill, asking questions of peers in a friendly or neutral tone, was included because it has been associated with social competence in preschool children (White & Watt, 1973). Turning to peers for help and using questions as a means of initiating and maintaining social interaction or obtaining attention and social support may be another mark of social competence in preschoolers.

Commenting was included as a third skill because our informal observations revealed that well-liked children frequently made descriptive remarks about their ongoing play. It seemed to us that commenting in preschoolers' play situations served to keep peers apprised of the play theme and created dyadic or group solidarity and cohesion. For instance, while donning fire-fighter hats and aiming a hose at a block structure, children announced to each other, "We're putting out the fire! We're putting out the fire!" Such comments are made frequently during play, and although they may often seem unsophisticated to adults, they may well help preschoolers define common social goals and maintain group interest. For instance, as some children identified the play theme in the example cited above, other children picked up on the theme and began to offer additional suggestions and comments.

Supporting (making explicitly positive statements to peers, giving peers help, or showing affection to peers) was included as a target skill because although it seems to occur infrequently among preschool children, it is associated with some markers of social competence (Eisenberg, Cameron, Tryon, & Dodez, 1981). For instance, preschoolers who perform spontaneous prosocial behavior, including supportive behavior, relatively frequently tend to have many social contacts with peers and to be positively responsive to peers' prosocial acts (Eisenberg et al., 1981).

The training context. The selection of an appropriate context for training may be an important variable for fostering skill acquisition (Kendall, 1984). We therefore chose to conduct skill training against a background of thematic or fantasy play, because for preschool children, pretend play is an extremely important occupation. The frequency with which children engage in social fantasy increases until about kindergarten, when it drops somewhat (Rubin, Fein, & Vandenberg, 1983). A high level of sociodramatic play in preschool children is associated with sustained and reciprocal verbal interaction and high levels of affective role taking (Connolly & Doyle, 1984). Fantasy play seems to be a context that affords young friends an opportunity to develop intimacy (Gottman & Parkhurst, 1980) and work out emotional issues such as fears (Gottman, 1986).

Thus, for children of preschool age, not only is sociodramatic play an important context in which perspective taking, social participation, group cooperation, and intimacy skills develop, but it can actually be viewed as a skill to be fostered. As we developed our intervention program, we selected materials that facilitate sociodramatic play, including blocks; stuffed animals and medical equipment (for a pretend veterinary hospital); a toy pickup truck with trailer, boat, driver, and passenger; Legos; a Sesame Street railroad set; and small animals, people, and vehicles.

Subject selection and design of the intervention program. Consistent with previous skill-based training research, we selected children who were experiencing peer acceptance problems in the classroom. In elementary school, rejected children appear to be at a higher risk than neglected children and, therefore, perhaps in greater need of social skills training. However, less is known about the behavioral differences between neglected and rejected children in preschool or the long-term outcomes for these two groups of children. Because so little is known about the stability and consequences of neglected status in preschool we believed that it was useful to include neglected as well as rejected children in this study. Rejected and neglected children were identified based on peers' sociometric ratings and positive and negative play nominations. Rejected children were defined as those who fell at least 0.5 standard deviation below their classroom mean on sociometric ratings, were below their class mean on positive sociometric nominations, and were above their class mean on negative nominations. Neglected children fell at least 0.5 standard deviation below their class mean on the sum of their positive and negative nominations.[1]

In addition to these sociometric criteria, children were observed in classroom play with peers to ensure that those who were selected for intervention did in fact exhibit behavior that differentiated them from their more popular peers. This gave us confidence that our subjects' low sociometric status was more likely the result of their social-cognitive or behavioral deficits rather than other factors such as their racial or cultural backgrounds, newness to the school, or physical appearance. Specifically, children who were observed to be more aggressive toward peers relative to their class average or who were below their class average in their use of the targeted social skills, or both, qualified for inclusion. Thus, there were both unskilled, nonaggressive children and aggressive children who were targeted for training. However, it is interesting to note that in contrast to numerous studies documenting the tendency for rejected children to be more aggressive than their peers (see Chapters 2 and 11, this volume), the rejected children in our sample were not, on the average, more aggressive than children in other status groups. (There was, however, a slight trend for them to be so, and teachers rated the rejected group as being more aggressive.) Failure to find significant differences in observed aggression between rejected and other status groups may have been a function of the relatively lenient sociometric criteria we used to select rejected children (see note 1). Of 19 rejected and 25 neglected children identified sociometrically, 14 rejected and 17 neglected children qualified for intervention on behavioral criteria. In addition, 2 children who almost met the sociometric criteria were included in the control group in order to provide all children with a partner. Of these neglected and rejected children, 29 actually completed the training.

Children who qualified for participation were randomly assigned to either a skill-training or an attention-control condition. Children in the skill-training condition were trained in dyads (both partners were low-status children) during eight sessions lasting approximately 30 min each. Sessions were conducted in a room near the children's classrooms, and teachers were unaware of which children were assigned to training or control conditions. In each of the eight sessions, training focused on how to achieve the broad social goal of all children having fun together in one social context (such as joining a peer) by using the target social skills (leading peers, etc.). At the end of each training session, two children who had not qualified for intervention were selected to join the subjects for a brief play period. Children in the control condition were treated in a similar manner except that the focus of attention during their interactions with the coach was on learning to play with the toys that were used in the study, rather than on specific social skills.

Thus, subject selection procedures and the design of this intervention closely resembled features of social skills interventions developed for older children (e.g., Ladd, 1981; Oden & Asher, 1977). The specific instructional procedures were explicitly based on the previously described model (Ladd & Mize, 1983) but were adapted for young children. Early studies (Chittenden, 1942; see Renshaw, 1981, for a review) in which preschoolers' "ascendant" behavior was modified (sociometric selection criteria were not employed) provided useful ideas about instructional techniques that might be effective with young children. For instance, Chittenden (1942) used dolls to teach children alternative ways to solve conflicts, a technique that we adapted by using puppets. In the following sections, we provide a brief description of the procedures used to teach children social concepts, to encourage them to perform the trained skills, and to teach them to monitor interaction and maintain and generalize skill use. We will also consider characteristics of preschool children that may affect the efficacy of specific instructional procedures.

Teaching social concepts to preschool children. Basic cognitive processes, such as selective attention, coding and storage, and inferential reasoning (Rosenthal & Zimmerman, 1978; Shantz, 1983; Siegler, 1983), determine in part how much children can learn from any training procedure. Younger children are less efficient processors than older children because they are more vulnerable to perceptual distraction and possess less developed mnemonic and conceptual organizing skills. Their cognitive capabilities and performance can often be improved, however, with procedures aimed at correcting flaws in their processing strategies

(Rosenthal & Zimmerman, 1978). Data from cognitive skill training indicate that with appropriate task structure and experimenter assistance, even young children's memories can be dramatically improved by teaching them to rehearse or to organize material to be remembered (Brown, Bransford, Ferrara, & Campione, 1983).

Based on studies of early learning and the instructional guidelines proposed by Ladd and Mize (1983), we sought to develop a method that would facilitate the acquisition of social skill concepts by preschool children. Our basic instructional procedures for teaching social concepts (i.e., inducing social goals and corresponding strategies) included (a) establishing an intent to learn the concept – for instance, by stressing the functional relevance of the skill; (b) defining the concept in terms of attributes; (c) providing exemplars, both positive and negative; (d) encouraging rehearsal and recall of the skill concept; and (e) helping the child refine and generalize the concept by correcting erroneous ideas and identifying other situations in which the concept could be applied (Ladd & Mize, 1983, p. 134).

Consistent with research indicating that "active" and "interactive" images are more easily recalled by young children (Siegler, 1983), we chose to present both didactic and modeled concept information to children through the medium of two active human hand-puppets (who were called Sandy and Mandy, after Chittenden, 1942) and an active and enthusiastic dog hand-puppet (Fluffy). Additional human puppets were used in some training sessions – for instance, when Mandy wanted to play with Sandy and another puppet, who were already playing together. The following is a description of how these puppets were used to accomplish the training objectives identified by Ladd and Mize (1983).

In order to establish an *intent to learn*, Fluffy greeted the children at the beginning of each session and explained that (a) seeing children playing together and having fun made him feel happy but that (b) seeing children playing alone or fighting made him sad, because the children were not having fun.[2] The instructor used Fluffy to encourage the children to attend to the ensuing interactions between Sandy and Mandy; the children were told that Sandy and Mandy might need the children's help in finding a way to play so that both (or all) puppets had fun together. A "scene" was then enacted in which one puppet expressed a desire to achieve a prosocial goal, that is, to play with the other puppet without conflict. A negative exemplar[3] of the skill concept was initially provided; that is, Mandy first attempted an ineffective strategy, such as hovering near Sandy, who was involved with attractive toys, trying to grab a toy, or intruding in an inappropriate way. The children were then asked whether or not this strategy was working (i.e., Fluffy asked whether Sandy and Mandy were playing and having fun together). At Mandy's insistence that he/she wanted to play with Sandy, Fluffy suggested a strategy to achieve the goal and in so doing defined the concept (e.g., "Well, maybe you could have a 'fun idea'; that means. . . .").

In attempting to *define* concepts for children, we tried to frame them at multiple levels of abstraction. Although older children and adults may be able to benefit when concepts are presented at higher levels of abstraction (e.g., "positive self-presentation," "other-enhancement") (Scott & Edelstein, 1981), concepts framed at a more behavioral and situational level (e.g., "asking someone to play," "saying something nice") may be easier for preschool children to grasp (Meyers & Cohen, 1984). However, higher order or general concepts may be needed to allow children to recognize applications beyond the original learning context. Thus, in order to ensure success in the original context and allow transfer of the concept to new situations (Brown et al., 1983), we included concepts defined at three levels of abstraction: (a) general strategies applicable in most social situations ("ways for everybody to have fun playing together"), (b) fairly concrete strategies that would have meaning for preschool children (e.g., "having a fun idea") but still be applicable in many settings, and (c) examples of strategies that were useful in specific situations but were unlikely to be useful outside that context (for instance, a "fun idea" might be suggesting playing *The Empire Strikes Back* when appropriate props are available). At the midlevel of abstraction, the skill of leading was called "having a fun idea" and was defined as "having a fun idea about something that both kids could do so that both can have fun playing together." Supporting was presented to children as "'doing something really nice' that makes the other kid happy." Questioning was defined as "'asking the other kid a question' so they can tell you something." Commenting was defined as "'just talking' about what you and the other kid are doing."

Sandy and Mandy and Fluffy were used to provide *positive and negative exemplars* of skill concepts. For example, in one vignette, Fluffy suggested that a "fun idea" (i.e., one that would allow both puppets to have more fun together) would be for Mandy's horse to race the train with which Sandy was playing. Fluffy continued to prompt Mandy with other suggestions, such as to "ask a question" about where the race should start. In their interactions, Sandy and Mandy modeled examples of all the skills. Because young children are less proficient than older children at inferring causes of behavior (Shantz, 1983), both Fluffy and the other puppets made explicit the connections between a character's reaction and another character's social behavior. For instance, in one vignette, Mandy took a truck from Sandy; when Sandy reacted negatively, Fluffy explained that taking a toy to play with alone was not a way to have fun together. Subsequently, when Mandy suggested a way to play together with the truck and Sandy reacted positively, Fluffy explained that this was a way for two children to have more fun than they could have alone.

During each session, children were asked to *recall* and verbally *rehearse* the skill concepts. Rehearsal was emphasized because young children's recall of conceptual material may be enhanced by having them enact relevant events. Research conducted by Silvern and his colleagues (Silvern, Taylor, Williamson, Surbeck, & Kelley, 1986) indicates that young children's story recall can be enhanced through reenactments of stories they have heard but that the recall of children over $6\frac{1}{2}$ years old does not appear to be improved by thematic enactment. The process of enacting vignettes probably not only helps children recall the specifics of the actions but provides an opportunity to construct generalized schemes about stories (Silvern et al., 1986) or, possibly, in the case of social skills interventions, about social interaction. Thus, we encouraged our preschool learners to use the puppets to reenact the vignettes originally presented by the instructor.

Preschool children seem better able to remember the content of instruction when they are asked to generate verbal responses to questions about the lesson (Price, 1984). Therefore, to reinforce our recall and rehearsal procedures, we also posed additional dilemmas for Sandy and Mandy to negotiate during which Fluffy turned to the children for advice. In one vignette, both puppets wanted to play with a large truck and Fluffy asked the children to suggest a solution. Prompts were used to aid rehearsals in the first few training sessions, but eventually, Fluffy began each session by asking the children to recall what things made Fluffy happy (playing together, having fun ideas, etc.) and what things made Fluffy sad (playing alone, not talking to other children, etc.).

Fluffy was also used to help children *refine* and *generalize* skill concepts. This was accomplished by showing children photographs of typical preschool toys and asking them to identify ways to use the skills when playing with those toys. For instance, children were shown a picture of toy housekeeping materials (pots, a broom) and asked how two children could "get to play with these together, so that both children have fun." By the final training sessions, most children could enthusiastically report what things made Fluffy happy and what things made Fluffy sad, and suggest key concepts for dealing with many social situations (e.g., "have a fun idea").

Promoting preschool children's skill performance. The second goal of social skills training was to enhance children's skill proficiency, that is, to help children achieve a match between the instructed skill concepts and their corresponding performance. To develop a procedure to promote preschoolers' skill performance, we adapted the instructional objectives outlined in our cognitive-social learning model (Ladd & Mize, 1983). These included (a) providing opportunities for guided rehearsal, beginning in a sheltered context; (b) evaluating children's performance through informative feedback; and (c) helping children refine their skill performance. As in the concept enhancement phase of each training session, Fluffy was used to instigate *performance* (i.e., to get children to try the skill) and provide *feedback* (i.e., to inform children whether or not their performance was adequate and to give positive reinforcement). Children were first encouraged to try out the skills in a brief play session with their training partner as Fluffy observed and prompted skill use. For instance, if the two children were playing separately, Fluffy would suggest that one child think of a "fun idea" or a "question to ask." At the beginning of training it was often necessary for Fluffy to model an appropriate behavior and ask the child to repeat it. During these sessions, Fluffy was again the source of specific feedback and praise.

Following the practice sessions with Fluffy, the children were told that the instructor and Fluffy wanted to make movies (i.e., videotapes) of them to show how children have fun playing together; they were told to use the skills that they had been practicing. A key purpose for this procedure was to create a context in which children could feel competent and develop feelings of self-efficacy. Prior to videotaping, Fluffy reminded the children of the skills and said that he would be watching for skill use and that after the children played for a few minutes they would have a chance to watch the movie they had made. In this way, children practiced first in a sheltered context (i.e., with Fluffy providing ideas and encouragement) and subsequently in a less sheltered context (i.e., without direct support from an adult). By the final training sessions, many children were using the skills in these practice sessions routinely, and they often prefaced a play suggestion with the words, "Hey, I have a fun idea!"

Fostering skill maintenance and generalization. Encouraging a learner to generalize and use a new skill beyond the training context can be difficult. The problem is especially formidable with preschoolers, because immature learners suffer to a greater extent from context "welding," that is, the inability to generalize a skill beyond the setting in which it is learned (Brown et al., 1983). Thus, preschool children probably require more elaborate efforts than do older children to help them see the connection between skills learned in a training context and their use in other settings, such as the classroom.

Skill maintenance and generalization appear to be enhanced by phasing out instructor support as the learner moves into more lifelike contexts (Bandura, Jeffrey, & Gajdos, 1975; Bronfenbrenner, 1979), helping the learner develop feelings of self-efficacy (Bandura, 1977), and fostering the learner's ability to accurately interpret social cues and adjust behavior in light of new information (Bandura, 1982). Toward this end, we adapted the following instructional procedures for use with preschool children (cf. Ladd & Mize, 1983): (a) extending skill rehearsals from the sheltered milieu to contexts that approximate real-life settings; (b) encouraging performance while withdrawing adult support and cues;

and (c) fostering self-evaluation and skill adjustment by helping children learn to evaluate their own performance, monitor the consequences of skill use, adopt constructive attributions for skill outcomes, and use information from monitoring to adjust behavior.

Following children's participation in guided rehearsals, the process of encouraging *self-directed rehearsals* in lifelike contexts was begun by bringing two additional peers into the training room immediately following each skill instruction session and encouraging the children to use the trained skills in a short, videotaped play session (referred to here as out-of-classroom generalization sessions). Control group children were also videotaped as they played with two other peers immediately following each attention-control session.

Children in the skill-training condition were also prompted to use the skills in their classrooms during two short visits from the social skills instructor (termed in-class generalization sessions), which occurred between the sixth and eighth out-of-class sessions. During the in-class generalization sessions, the instructor remained near the child for approximately 20 min and suggested ways to use the skills with peers. For instance, during one of these visits when the instructor observed that the subject was playing near other children in a sand table, she whispered to the subject that a "fun idea" would be for the subject and a peer to fill a large container together. The subject then turned to the peer and said, "I have a fun idea; let's fill up this bucket"; and the two children began to play together. Control group children received the same type of visits from the instructor, but suggestions were focused on uses for the toys with which children were playing (e.g., how to use a large scoop to fill a bucket with sand rapidly, or how to build a bridge with blocks). Children were prompted only when teachers were out of earshot, so that teachers could not overhear the instructor's conversations with children. Because the instructor routinely spent some time in the classroom at each visit to the school (e.g., sitting with children at story or snack times), neither children nor teachers seemed to take special notice of these brief in-class generalization sessions. Although teachers were aware that an intervention was in progress, they did not know how many or which children were specific targets. In fact, probably because all children who had parental permission to participate in the study left the classroom with the instructor on several occasions (either as a skill-training or control child or to act as a peer partner in the generalization sessions), most of the teachers and classmates did not seem to be aware that the skill-training and control children were receiving somewhat more attention than the others.

Children's *self-evaluation* and *monitoring skills* were encouraged in very specific and concrete ways. First, after each practice session, children were asked to recall whether or not they had "asked a question," "had a fun idea," and so on, and to report the peer's reaction to skill use. By the end of training most children could report at least one instance of their own or a peer's skill use when asked. Then, following each "self-review," children watched the videotape of the practice session and were asked to identify instances of skill use. Each time a skill was observed on the videotape monitor, the tape was stopped and the children were asked to describe what had occurred and to try to recall the peer's reaction. Fluffy showed excitement at each instance of skill use and said that he was happy because children were playing together and having fun. If children had not played together or had played aggressively or fought, Fluffy said that he felt sad.

Although some theoretical positions portray the preschool child as incapable of taking another's perspective, work by Shatz and Gelman (1973) and others (see Gelman, 1979) shows that 4-year-olds do adjust communication to a listener's developmental level, which, in turn, reflects an awareness of their impact on another. Thus, during observations of videotapes, children were encouraged to make accurate *attributions* for social outcomes and to modify their performance based on *monitoring* of others' reactions. Monitoring and assignment of attributions occurred at a very basic level, but growth in children's abilities could be observed during the training sessions. The experience of one 4-year-old boy, whom we will call Biff, and who was noted for his aggressive, rough-and-tumble play, is illuminating. During the second training session, while practicing the skills with his training partner, Biff repeatedly pushed the Sesame Street railroad track off the table and took the track apart and swung it in the air, laughing all the while. Biff's partner asked again and again that Biff "stop it" and appeared quite frustrated, but this only seemed to encourage Biff to wilder play; Biff, rather than trying to harm the other child, apparently interpreted her pleas to "stop" as part of a game that she, too, enjoyed. As Biff watched the videotape he was encouraged to listen to what his playmate said (i.e., "stop it") and to watch the face of his playmate and try to determine whether or not "both kids are having fun." Biff's response was that both children were not having fun; after this session, he did not engage in one-sided rough-and-tumble play during skill training.

Results of the intervention. To evaluate the impact of this intervention, behavioral observations, sociometric interviews, and assessments of children's social knowledge were conducted by persons who were unaware of the children's status or assignment to condition. The strongest evidence for the effectiveness of our skill-training program came from classroom observations. The subjects who participated in the skill-training condition more than doubled the percentage of intervals they spent using the target skills in classroom interaction with peers, whereas children in the control group evidenced a slight decline in these same skills. However, there were no significant changes in aggression for either group. The overall and significant increase in skill use was attributable primarily to the trained children's gains in their use of the skills Comments and Leads, although nonsignificant increases also occurred in Questions and Supports. Although we had suspected that rejected and neglected children might be differentially affected by the intervention, we found no evidence of a status by condition interaction.

These gains in the use of trained skills were accompanied by changes in strategies children suggested for dealing with hypothetical dilemmas during social knowledge interviews. Compared with pretraining levels, children in the skill-training condition suggested friendlier but less assertive strategies after the intervention, whereas control group children suggested less friendly but more assertive strategies. This finding suggested that gains in social knowledge might be partially responsible for the changes that were observed in children's peer behavior. Further analyses were conducted to examine this hypothesis. Scores representing changes from pretraining to posttraining in the friendliness of children's social strategies were correlated with changes in their skill use with peers. The result ($r = .34$) indicated that, indeed, those children who suggested friendlier strategies during social knowledge interviews tended to show gains in their social skill use with peers.

Sociometric interviews conducted immediately following training indicated that children in both the control and skill-training conditions improved slightly but nonsignificantly on ratings and positive sociometric nominations and did not change with respect to the number of negative nominations received from peers. Although children who received skill training did not make significant improvements in peer acceptance immediately following the intervention, gains in skill usage were found to be associated with improvement in sociometric ratings from peers ($r = .28$). This relationship suggests that the acquisition of new social skills may have been responsible for children's improved social acceptance, where it occurred.

About a month after the intervention, a follow-up sociometric interview was conducted. Findings indicated that children who had participated in the skill-training condition evidenced continued gains in peer acceptance, as measured by positive nominations, and a trend toward higher group status, as measured by sociometric ratings. Findings for the control group children revealed nonsignificant declines in peer ratings and positive nominations at the 1-month follow-up and a trend toward a higher number of negative nominations from posttest to follow-up. Multivariate analyses indicated a significant condition by time effect for the three sociometric measures across the three testing times, but only the univariate test for positive nominations was significant. Unfortunately, conclusions drawn from these data must remain tentative, because the follow-up assessment was conducted in June, when many children had withdrawn from school for the summer, leaving fewer children, especially in the control group.[4] However, our results indicating that children in the control condition experienced temporary gains in peer acceptance and that children who received skill training displayed more lasting gains are consistent with previously observed patterns in the skill-training literature (e.g., Ladd, 1981). The temporary gains in peer status made by control group children may be attributable to pairing control subjects with peers or to experimenter attention.

Conclusions and future directions

We have argued that there is a need for effective social skills training interventions for preschool children. Our efforts to develop an effective methodology were based on a previously articulated model of skill learning and on corresponding instructional principles (Ladd & Mize, 1983). Much of this chapter has described how we adapted and translated these principles into training procedures suitable for preschool children. Based on observed changes in children's use of the targeted skills in classroom interaction and on improvements in social knowledge and sociometric scores, we can claim some success in devising a useful skill-training method for preschool children. However, in planning and carrying out this program, it became clear that many important issues remain to be resolved. Consideration of these issues may provide additional directions for future intervention research conducted with young children.

One issue in need of further research attention is the timing of interventions aimed at children with problems in their peer relations. We have argued that the preschool years may be a strategic time to intervene and may, in fact, be the optimal time in a child's school career to facilitate social competence. Counter to these points, however, are problems such as the instability of young children's friendships, the difficulties involved in teaching young children complex social concepts, and the uncertainty involved in reliably eliciting a preschool child's cooperation and participation. These concerns can be seen as arguments in favor of delaying social skills training until children reach elementary school. Further, although social skills training during preschool may prevent problems for many children, it is possible that peer relationship problems for other children may emerge only in later years. Thus, it may be that social skills training is beneficial at several points in time within differing school environments. Determining when children will most likely reap lasting benefits from skill-based interventions will no doubt require further research. Also, the search for optimal times for intervention should not obscure the fact that social relationship learning is an ongoing, lifelong process.

A second issue involving the timing of social skills training concerns the limits of the procedures described in this chapter. At what age, for instance, are children likely to be most responsive to the procedures described here, as opposed to procedures that rely heavily on the verbal exchange of ideas between the instructor and child (e.g., those used by Oden & Asher, 1977, and Ladd, 1981)? It seems unlikely that the puppets used in our procedure would sustain much interest among third- and fourth-grade children, but these props may remain attractive to first-graders or to developmentally delayed children of grade-school age.

Other concerns include the selection of appropriate candidates for early intervention and the adaptation of intervention to subgroups of children. Emerging evidence suggests that in elementary school, rejected children may be most at risk for later difficulties and, therefore, in greatest need of help. More information is needed, however, on the consequences of peer neglect as well as rejection in preschool and the effects of social skills intervention, or lack thereof, on later peer relations and school adjustment for these groups of children. Moreover, it was our impression that further subdivision of our group of rejected children would be necessary in order to provide training suited to individual needs (see Chapter 11, this volume). For instance, there appeared to be a subgroup of children included in training who, although capable of behaving in skilled ways, strategically used aggression in peer situations. These children appeared to be fairly unimpressed with the suggestions we offered on how to get along better with peers. It may be that a different type of intervention is necessary to decrease the aggression of this type of child. On the other hand, other aggressive children appeared to lack an awareness of alternative strategies for achieving goals, and these children seemed to benefit more from training.

Another critical issue in developing social skills training for young children is the selection of training content. Until recently, we have not been able to delineate the specific behaviors that distinguish higher from lower status children beyond offering global descriptions of them as friendlier and more prosocial. In recent years, researchers have made remarkable strides in identifying the complex and often subtle skills children employ as they become acquainted, form relationships, and establish reputations in the peer group. Recent studies evidence more sophisticated designs and data analytic procedures than were common during earlier eras (Asher, 1983), but most of this work has been conducted with elementary-age children (e.g., Coie & Kupersmidt, 1983; Dodge, 1983) and less has been done with younger children (e.g., Gottman, 1983; Putallaz, 1983). To design more sophisticated and effective social skills training programs for preschoolers, we need more information on the social skills of young children in important peer contexts.

Further research is also needed on the processes underlying social skillfulness (knowledge, performance, and monitoring) and the development of techniques for their measurement. As noted elsewhere (e.g., Ladd, 1985; Ladd & Mize, 1983), it is important not only to know that behavioral change occurs as a result of social skills training but also to understand why changes occur. The fact that we found that improvements in children's social knowledge were related to increased skill use with peers underscores the value of teaching skill concepts and suggests that social knowledge deficits may have been the source of peer difficulties for some of the children. The availability of better assessment instruments would not only allow researchers to document the effects of the intervention on underlying processes but would allow researchers to develop interventions that are more sensitive to the deficits and needs of individual children.

Finally, further work is needed on the development of appropriate methods for teaching social skills to young children. The intervention we devised represents one attempt to translate an existing model of skill learning and instruction into specific training procedures. We believe that the field of social skills training could benefit from an examination of the principles and practices that characterize intervention research in other domains, such as cognitive skills training. To illustrate, we found that the "zone of proximal development" concept, as it has been used in reading comprehension training (Palinscar & Brown, 1984), was useful for thinking about the process of adapting training to the needs and abilities of our subjects. In teaching to the child's zone of proximal development, the instructor first attempts to teach the child at a level only slightly higher than his or her current level of competence, and then fosters performance at somewhat more advanced levels. That is, the child is asked to perform with adult help at a level slightly above his or her current independent ability but is not asked to perform well beyond the level that he or she is capable of attaining (Campione, Brown, Ferrara, & Bryant, 1984). In this type of learning process, the adult functions as a leader and the child participates in small ways at first, but eventually takes over more mature roles (Palinscar & Brown, 1984). The child's skill level helps determine the pace of instruction; the adult's role is to break the task down into manageable units and help the child attain a definition of the task that is more compatible with expert performance or that approaches the adult's definition (Wood, Bruner, & Ross, 1976).

Operating in the child's zone of proximal development involves an adult and a child collaborating on solving a problem (Campione et al., 1984). Prior social skills interventions may have succeeded partly because the child was involved in a joint venture with an adult who began at his or her developmental level and nurtured more advanced conceptions of social interaction, more proficient performance, and more mature monitoring of the social environment.

Notes

1. These definitions differ in several ways from those developed by Coie, Dodge, and Coppotelli (1982) for elementary school children. Coie et al. based status categories on positive and negative nominations, with cutoff criteria of 1 standard deviation. We used sociometric ratings instead of nominations whenever possible, because sociometric ratings are more reliable than nomination data with preschoolers (Asher, Singleton, Tinsley, & Hymel, 1979). It was necessary to use 0.5

standard deviation rather than 1 standard deviation as the criterion to obtain enough subjects for the intervention. The more lenient cutoffs for the criteria used to create our definitions resulted in some children who were not severely rejected or neglected being included in the study.

2. We are aware that this phrasing could give the impression that playing alone is not a valuable activity for preschool children, which of course is untrue. However, given the age of our subjects, we felt it necessary to avoid subtle distinctions and elected, instead, to try to make a strong impression about the pleasures of playing with friends.

3. The difficulty with providing negative exemplars of some behaviors, especially in modeling aggression as a negative exemplar of "doing something really nice," is that children are often attracted to these very active behaviors and imitate them gleefully. We were careful, therefore, to make all negative exemplars very brief and low-key. Rather than modeling an extended fight between two puppets, an aggressive act would consist, for instance, of one puppet gently taking a toy from the peer puppet. This was followed by a quiet explanation by the peer puppet or by Fluffy that this action made the peer unhappy and would not result in the taker having fun. Our subjects did not laugh at our negative exemplars nor did they attempt to imitate them.

4. Cell sizes for the experimental and control groups were, respectively, 18 and 15 (pretest), 17 and 14 (posttest), and 12 and 4 (follow-up).

References

Argyle, M. (1985). Social behavior problems and social skills training. In B. H. Schneider, K. H. Rubin, & J. E. Ledingham (Eds.), *Children's peer relations: Issues in assessment and intervention* (pp. 207–224). New York: Springer-Verlag.

Asher, S. R. (1983). Social competence and peer status: Recent advances and future directions. *Child Development, 54,* 1427–1434.

Asher, S. R., & Renshaw, P. D. (1981). Children without friends: Social knowledge and social skill training. In S. R. Asher & J. M. Gottman (Eds.), *The development of children's friendships* (pp. 273–296). New York: Cambridge University Press.

Asher, S. R., Singleton, L. C., Tinsley, B. R., & Hymel, S. (1979). A reliable sociometric measure for preschool children. *Developmental Psychology, 15,* 443–444.

Bandura, A. (1977). Self-efficacy: Toward a unifying theory of behavior change. *Psychological Review, 84,* 191–215.

Bandura, A. (1982). Self-efficacy mechanisms in human agency. *American Psychologist, 37,* 122–147.

Bandura, A., Jeffrey, R. W., & Gajdos, E. (1975). Generalizing change through participant modeling with self-directed mastery. *Behavior Research and Therapy, 13,* 141–152.

Bierman, K. L., & Furman, W. (1984). The effects of social skills training and peer involvement on the social adjustment of preadolescents. *Child Development, 55,* 151–162.

Bronfenbrenner, U. (1979). Contexts of child rearing: Problems and prospects. *American Psychologist, 34,* 844–850.

Brown, A. L., Bransford, J. D., Ferrara, R. A., & Campione, J. C. (1983). Learning, remembering, and understanding. In J. H. Flavell & E. M. Markman (Eds.), *Handbook of child psychology: Vol. 3. Cognitive development* (pp. 77–166). New York: John Wiley.

Campione, J. C., Brown, A. L., Ferrara, R. A., & Bryant, N. R. (1984). The zone of proximal development: Implications for individual differences and learning. In B. Rogoff & J. V. Wertsch (Eds.), *Children's learning in the zone of proximal development* (pp. 77–91). San Francisco: Jossey-Bass.

Chittenden, G. F. (1942). An experimental study in measuring and modifying assertive behavior in young children. *Monographs of the Society for Research in Child Development, 7*(1, Serial No. 31).

Coie, J. D., Dodge, K. A., & Coppotelli, H. (1982). Dimensions and types of social status: A cross-age perspective. *Developmental Psychology, 18,* 557–570.

Coie, J. D., & Kupersmidt, J. B. (1983). A behavioral analysis of emerging social status in boys' groups. *Child Development, 54,* 1400–1416.

Connolly, J. A., & Doyle, A. B. (1984). Relation of social fantasy play to social competence in preschoolers. *Developmental Psychology, 20,* 797–806.

Costanzo, P. R., & Dix, T. H. (1983). Beyond the information processed: Socialization in the development of attributional processes. In E. T. Higgins, D. N. Ruble, & W. W. Hartup (Eds.), *Social cognition and social development: A sociocultural perspective* (pp. 63–81). New York: Cambridge University Press.

Dodge, K. A. (1983). Behavioral antecedents of peer social status. *Child Development, 54,* 1386–1389.

Dodge, K. A. (1985). Attributional biases in aggressive children. In P. C. Kendall (Ed.), *Advances in cognitive-behavioral research and therapy* (Vol. 4, pp. 73–110). Orlando, FL: Academic Press.

Dodge, K. A., Murphy, R. R., & Buchsbaum, K. (1984). The assessment of intention-cue detection skills in children: Implications for developmental psychopathology. *Child Development, 55,* 163–173.

Dodge, K. A., & Somberg, D. R. (1985, April). The affective bases of hostile attributional biases among aggressive children. In K. A. Dodge (Chair), *The role of affect and goals in the development of social cognition.* Symposium conducted at the biennial meeting of the Society for Research in Child Development, Toronto.

Eisenberg, N., Cameron, E., Tryon, K., Dodez, R. (1981). Socialization of prosocial behavior in the preschool classroom. *Developmental Psychology, 17,* 773–782.

Evers-Pasquale, W., & Sherman, M. (1975). The reward value of peers: A variable influencing the efficacy of filmed modeling in modifying social isolation in preschoolers. *Journal of Abnormal Child Psychology, 3,* 170–180.

Garvey, K. (1984). *Children's talk.* Cambridge: Harvard University Press.

Gelman, R. (1979). Preschool thought. *American Psychologist, 34,* 900–905.

Goetz, T. E., & Dweck, C. S. (1980). Learned helplessness in social situations. *Journal of Personality and Social Psychology, 39,* 246–255.

Gottman, J. M. (1983). How children become friends. *Monographs of the Society for Research in Child Development, 48*(2, Serial No. 201).

Gottman, J. M. (1986). The world of coordinated play: Same- and cross-sex friendship in young children. In J. M. Gottman and J. G. Parker (Eds.), *The conversations of friends: Speculations on affective development* (pp. 139–191). New York: Cambridge University Press.

Gottman, J. M., & Parkhurst, J. T. (1980). A developmental theory of friendship and acquaintanceship processes. In W. A. Collins (Ed.), *Minnesota symposia on child psychology* (Vol. 13, pp. 197–253). Hillsdale, NJ: Lawrence Erlbaum.

Gouze, K., Gordon, L., & Rayias, M. (1983, April). *Information processing correlates of aggression: A look at attention and memory.* Paper presented at the biennial meeting of the Society for Research in Child Development, Detroit.

Hartup, W. W. (1983). The peer system. In E. M. Hetherington (Ed.), *Handbook of child psychology: Vol. 4. Socialization, personality, and social development* (pp. 103–196, 4th ed.). New York: John Wiley.

Kendall, P. C. (1984). Social cognition and problem solving: A developmental and child-clinical interface. In B. Gholson & T. L. Rosenthal (Eds.), *Applications of cognitive-developmental theory* (pp. 115–148). New York: Academic Press.

Kendall, P. C., Lerner, R. M., & Craighead, W. E. (1984). Human development and intervention in childhood psychopathology. *Child Development, 55,* 71–82.

Ladd, G. W. (1981). Effectiveness of a social learning method for enhancing children's social interaction and peer acceptance. *Child Development, 52,* 171–178.

Ladd, G. W. (1983). Social networks of popular, average, and rejected children in school settings. *Merrill-Palmer Quarterly, 29,* 283–308.

Ladd, G. W. (1985). Documenting the effects of social skill training with children: Process and outcome assessment. In B. H. Schneider, K. H. Rubin, & J. E. Ledingham (Eds.), *Children's peer relations: Issues in assessment and intervention* (pp. 243–269). New York: Springer-Verlag.

Ladd, G. W., & Mize, J. (1983). A cognitive-social learning model of social skill training. *Psychological Review, 90*, 127–157.

Ladd, G. W., & Price, J. M. (1987). Predicting children's social and school adjustment following the transition from preschool to kindergarten. *Child Development, 58*, 1168–1189.

Meyers, A. W., & Cohen, R. (1984). Cognitive-behavioral interventions in educational settings. In P. C. Kendall (Ed.), *Advances in cognitive-behavioral research and therapy* (Vol. 3, pp. 131–166). Orlando, FL: Academic Press.

Mize, J. (1984). *Enhancing children's peer relations: A cognitive-social learning procedure for social skills training with preschool children.* Unpublished doctoral dissertation, Purdue University, West Lafayette, IN.

Mize, J., & Ladd, G. W. (1984, April). Preschool children's goal and strategy knowledge: A comparison of picture-story and an enactive assessment. In G. W. Ladd (Chair), *From preschool to high school: Are children's interpersonal goals and strategies predictive of their social competence?* Symposium conducted at the meeting of the American Educational Research Association, New Orleans.

Mize, J., Ladd, G. W., & Price, J. M. (1985). Promoting positive peer relations with young children: Rationales and strategies. *Child Care Quarterly, 14*, 221–237.

Oden, S., & Asher, S. R. (1977). Coaching children in social skills for friendship making. *Child Development, 48*, 495–506.

Olson, S. L., Johnson, J., Belleau, K., Parks, J., & Barrett, E. (1983, April). *Social competence in preschool children: Interrelations with sociometric status, social problem-solving, and impulsivity.* Paper presented at the biennial meeting of the Society for Research in Child Development, Detroit.

Palinscar, A. S., & Brown, A. L. (1984). Reciprocal teaching of comprehension-fostering and comprehension-monitoring activities. *Cognition and Instruction, 1*, 117–175.

Price, G. G. (1984). Mnemonic support and curriculum selection in teaching by mothers: A conjoint effect. *Child Development, 55*, 659–668.

Putallaz, M. (1983). Predicting children's sociometric status from their behavior. *Child Development, 54*, 1417–1426.

Renshaw, P. D. (1981). The roots of current peer interaction research: A historical analysis of the 1930s. In S. R. Asher & J. M. Gottman (Eds.), *The development of children's friendships* (pp. 1–20). New York: Cambridge University Press.

Renshaw, P. D., & Asher, S. R. (1982). Social competence and peer status: The distinction between goals and strategies. In K. H. Rubin & H. S. Ross (Eds.), *Peer relationships and social skills in childhood* (pp. 375–395). New York: Springer-Verlag.

Rosenthal, T. L., & Zimmerman, B. J. (1978). *Social learning and cognition.* New York: Academic Press.

Rubin, K. H., Fein, G. G., & Vandenberg, B. (1983). Play. In E. M. Hetherington (Ed.), *Handbook of child psychology: Vol. 4. Socialization, personality, and social development* (pp. 693–774). New York: John Wiley.

Scarlett, W. G. (1980). Social isolation from agemates among nursery school children. *Journal of Child Psychology and Psychiatry, 21*, 231–240.

Scott, W. O. N., & Edelstein, B. A. (1981). The social competence of two interaction strategies: An analogue evaluation. *Behavior Therapy, 12*, 482–492.

Shantz, C. U. (1983). Social cognition. In J. H. Flavell & E. M. Markman (Eds.), *Handbook of child psychology: Vol. 3. Cognitive development* (pp. 495–555). New York: John Wiley.

Shatz, M., & Gelman, R. (1973). The development of communication skills: Modifications in the speech of young children as a function of listener. *Monographs of the Society for Research in Child Development, 38*(5, Serial No. 152).

Siegler, R. S. (1983). Information processing approaches to development. In W. Kessen (Ed.), *Handbook of child psychology: Vol. 1. History, theory, and methods* (pp. 129–212). New York: John Wiley.

Silvern, S. B., Taylor, J. B., Williamson, P. A., Surbeck, E., & Kelley, M. F. (1986). Young children's story recall as a product of play, story familiarity, and adult intervention. *Merrill-Palmer Quarterly, 32,* 73–86.

Taylor, A. R., & Asher, S. R. (1984). Children's goals and social competence: Individual differences in a game-playing context. In T. Field, J. L. Roopnarine, & M. Segal (Eds.), *Friendships in normal and handicapped children* (pp. 53–78). Norwood, NJ: Ablex.

Waldrop, M. F., & Halverson, C. F. (1975). Intensive and extensive peer behavior: Longitudinal and cross-sectional analyses. *Child Development, 46,* 19–26.

White, B. L., & Watt, J. C. (1973). *Experience and environment.* Englewood Cliffs, NJ: Prentice-Hall.

Wood, D., Bruner, J. S., & Ross, G. (1976). The role of tutoring in problem solving. *Journal of Child Psychology and Psychiatry, 17,* 89–100.

Conclusion

13   Toward a theory of peer rejection

John D. Coie

Each of the chapters in this book records a portion of the unfolding story of children who experience social rejection by their peers. In this chapter I am going to try to summarize this story by discussing it in terms of four phases of development: a precursor phase, in which the behavior patterns, attitudes, social expectations, affective response patterns, social goal priorities, and competencies that relate to eventual peer status take shape; an emergent status phase, in which the child's interactions with a significant peer group result in the child being rejected by that group; a maintenance phase, during which time rejection by the group becomes a stable and enduring reality for some rejected children; and, finally, a consequence phase, in which other aspects of the individual's life adjustment have deteriorated to the point of identifiable disorders. The phases, as they are described here, represent large time periods. Within these large time periods the developmental processes involved can be described at a finer level of analysis. For example, there are microprocesses reflecting recursive sequences of behavior by the child, reactions by the group, affective and cognitive processes, and even patterns of parental influence that determine a course of social development that sometimes results in persistent peer rejection. Some of these microprocesses will be discussed, but the chapter is directed more toward understanding peer rejection within a larger time frame than these microprocesses involve.

This story of peer rejection is part of a larger scientific undertaking that is now referred to as developmental psychopathology (Sroufe & Rutter, 1984). Developmental psychopathologists are concerned with understanding the evolution of patterns of adaptation and maladjustment throughout the life span. They are interested in the etiology of conditions that are predictive of disorder and in the development of coping skills that buffer individuals against disorder. The recent emergence of developmental psychopathology as an identifiable area of research closely parallels the revival of interest in children's peer relations over the past 10 to 15 years. Thus far, both enterprises have been guided largely by an orientation that is pragmatic and empirical. Although the implicit assumptions of various theoretical frameworks – psychoanalytic, social learning, organismic, ethological, or psychobiological – can be seen in some of this work, for the most part the research has been descriptive and not guided by a single overarching theoretical perspective (Rutter & Garmezy, 1983). Nevertheless, in examining the research on peer rejection described in the preceding chapters, it is possible to trace the outlines of a theory, or at least a model, of the development of disorder as this relates to childhood peer rejection. I will attempt to explicate this model using the data base provided by the chapters in this volume, but sometimes taking time to suggest alternative explanations for various aspects of the phenomenon of peer rejection that have not yet been evaluated empirically but merit future investigation.

The model outlined here is based on several assumptions. One of these assumptions is that social behavior is primarily responsible for rejection by peers. Although nonbehavioral factors such as appearance, academic achievement, or athletic ability have an undeniably important impact on the evaluation of peers, I maintain that children dislike individual peers not simply because they are deficient in these areas but because of the way they handle themselves with the peer group over issues related to these and other aspects of social interaction. I would argue, for example, that while overweight children may receive more than their share of teasing, it is the way they react to teasing that influences peers' evaluations of them. Similarly, children who are inept at games will be chosen last on teams and may be ridiculed for their awkwardness by some of their peers. Those who respond with tears or anger will have a difficult time socially, as will those who attempt to compensate by cheating or bragging about other accomplishments. Children who react good-naturedly or are generous in their positive comments about the skill of others do not have the same problem with peers. The difficulties of rejected children result from the way they interpret specific social situations, the way they react affectively, and their acquired strategies for dealing with them.

The second major assumption is that these situation-specific cognitive processes, affective reactions, and behavioral patterns emerge out of the child's socialization history. Individual differences in biologically linked attributes such as temperament, physique, and cognitive abilities are significant determinants of subsequent social functioning, but the character of a child's reactions to specific social circumstances is largely shaped by the history of that child's interactions with parent-figures, siblings, and nonsibling acquaintances. Some young children may be temperamentally disposed to handle some social circumstances in a manner that would trigger an exaggerated and uncharacteristic reaction from any parent, and thus they would be more at risk for adverse responses than other children. A child who is highly reactive to social stimuli will generate a different reaction from parents than one with a placid temperament, for example. However, some parents will handle an irritable infant more effectively and with less long-term disruption to their relationship than other parents. A highly punitive but inconsistent parent will have a deleterious effect on most children. It is in this early crucible of family interaction that the young child's social dispositions are influenced. It is this social history that leads a child to have difficulty in handling particular types of interpersonal events and these difficulties become the basis for future social problems. Here, for example, young children learn to avoid certain social situations or they develop a guardedness and suspicion about the intentions of others or they fail to learn the value of humor for deflecting insults. This early social training ground is an interactive one, involving not just parents and children but other family members and frequent associates. Parents reinforce both negative and positive interactions between a child and that child's siblings. The child observes parental interactions and these observations serve as models for future behavior. The search for the origins of rejected children's maladaptive behavior is necessarily complex and, as will be seen in this chapter, has only begun.

A third assumption of the model is that the process of acquiring social status in the child peer group has different dynamics than those by which a stable identity as a rejected person is maintained. I believe that during the emergence of rejected status the behavior of the child is primary and the behavior of the peer group is secondary, except in extreme circumstances. My assumption is that most child peer groups have similar standards for behavior and are reasonably empirical in their evaluation of children who are new to them. Although they will have expectations based on appearances, children usually are fair-minded in their appraisals of peers' actual behavior. However, if a child is disliked by a significant number of peers, the balance shifts and group dynamics become more important. Now the child does not have as much control over peer evaluations and must work harder to overcome a negative reputation. Group opinion has influence in two ways. It sets in motion dynamics that can perpetuate social roles in the group, such as the tendency to keep certain individuals in a deviant role by scapegoating. Group opinion also influences the thoughts, feelings, and responses of the rejected child. As that child experiences rejection, feelings about the self change. The child becomes less socially secure and confident. Anticipations of future reactions by peers lead the child to make adjustments in social behavior and may cause the child to overreact to some events or to refrain from responding to others. However, it would be a mistake to assume that all of these adjustments to peer reaction are maladaptive and make things worse for rejected children. Some of them may be quite adaptive. We know very little about the naturally occurring processes of change in social behavior among children and this is a very important area of inquiry still to be investigated.

The final assumption is that sustained peer rejection has indirect causal effects on the long-term adjustment of the rejected child. Although it is possible that peer rejection may serve merely as a marker of early adjustment problems that simply continue into adolescence and adulthood, another hypothesis is that there are several consequences of sustained peer rejection that contribute significantly to the incidence of future disorder. One contributing effect that has already been mentioned is the way the experience of rejection alters the child's cognitive processes, affective reactions, and behaviors. Sustained rejection also translates, by means of altered cognitive, affective, and behavioral reactions, into inadequate skills for coping with stressful events in later life. A third indirect effect is that the child who has been consistently rejected becomes an adolescent who does not have an adequate network of social support to serve as a buffer against the effects of unusual stress. Each of these effects contributes to a greater risk for future maladjustment among rejected children.

Implicit to this entire formulation is an underlying assumption of a fundamental shift in the socialization influences on the growing child. Initially, parent and family values, beliefs, and social interaction patterns have the major influence on the social orientation of the young child (Costanzo & Fraenkel, 1987). This early socialization experience prepares, or fails to prepare, the young child for social interactions in the larger social world of nonfamilial adults and peers. The world of peers takes on increasing significance for the child, and the failure to establish adequately a place in this social world is both a reflection and a precursor of individual maladjustment.

Because this is a model of peer rejection covering a large time frame of development, there are aspects of the model that may seem oversimplified. This is a danger with all such models. For example, the model seems to imply that there is a period of early life in which the child has no meaningful relations with peers, so that nothing akin to peer rejection occurs prior to the child's encounter with school peers. Such a social discontinuity may be true of some children's development, but most children have nonsibling relationships prior to elementary school, and many may be part of a small play group or day-care center, in which nascent peer groups exist. In these early social contexts, it may be argued that some children already establish a pattern of social difficulty that continues for them or becomes more generalizable during the school years. For these children it may be difficult to draw the line of separation between a precursor phase and an emergent status phase. The point of the model with respect to status emergence is that at some point in time, for some children, the experience of profound rejection takes place within a meaningful peer group.

A second point made by the model is that it is important to distinguish between children who continue to be rejected in their school peer groups and those who are able to move toward more acceptable peer status. This distinction is captured by the discussion of the maintenance phase and the contrasts between it and the emergent status phase. Although our discussion of peer rejection sometimes may suggest that rejection is an enduring condition, not all children who are rejected at one point in time are rejected at later points in time. Coie and Dodge (1983) documented a level of continuous rejected status across a 5-year period of no more than 50% for children followed longitudinally from the fifth grade on. For a younger cohort, rejection was less stable across a similar time span. Although few children seem to move from rejected status to popular status, there is some instability to being identified as rejected, and thus it is important to consider what factors distinguish continued rejection from temporary rejection.

Among researchers of peer relations, there has been a debate as to whether peer rejection is a determinant of subsequent disorder or whether it serves as a marker variable for the psychological antecedents of disorder. The model, as it is outlined, seems to suggest that rejection causes disorder or sets up conditions that give rise to disorder. Yet it is equally plausible to argue that peer rejection is an index of social disapproval for the kinds of behavior that, if continued or intensified, will be labeled as disordered in later life. If the latter argument is true for some children, then it is specious to talk about a disorder phase following a phase of well-entrenched peer rejection. For the purpose of debate, I will maintain that for most children the prolonged experience of peer rejection is a major contributor to subsequent disorder in several ways. This point can be explicated in terms of George Albee's equation for the incidence of disorder. Albee (1984) proposes that the incidence of disorder increases as a result of stress, organic variables, and exploitation factors and that coping skills, self-esteem, and social support serve to reduce disorder.

In the Albee equation, peer rejection can be interpreted as contributing to disorder in four ways. First, it is, itself, an element of stress operating on the child. Rejected children tend to receive worse treatment by peers than nonrejected children. There is evidence that rejected children are the objects of aggression more often and are less likely to have their social approaches received positively (Dodge, 1983) than other children. Over time, their lack of social success leaves them on the outskirts of social activity, struggling to hook up with other less socially acceptable peers (Chapter 4, this volume). Indeed, rejected children do report themselves to be more lonely than other children (Chapter 9). Once on the outskirts of the peer group, rejected children continue to serve a role for the group, but it is the role of group deviant and carries with it the potential for stigmatization that may engender still more deviant behavior. Each of these circumstances can be stressful for children.

In addition to producing greater stress, rejection can contribute to having fewer resources for countering the various factors leading to disorder. Rejected children have less in the way of support groups, they are hindered in their development of coping skills, and increasingly they are likely to have lower self-esteem. Children who are rejected are likely to become adolescents who are rejected or neglected (Coie & Dodge, 1983), and thus it is plausible that they are less likely to have access to social support from their peers. Observational evidence (Coie &

Dodge, 1988; Dodge, Coie, & Brakke, 1982) suggests that rejected children are less likely to receive social support from their teachers. Because of their relative isolation from peers as they move into adolescence, rejected children are likely to be deprived of opportunities to develop the social competencies that might enable them to cope more effectively. Finally, there is some evidence (e.g., Finn, 1985) that rejected children have lower self-esteem than other children. Thus, it can be argued that children who are already predisposed toward disorder in later life by biological or other factors and who are rejected because of behavioral abnormalities that can be linked to later disorder are at even greater risk because of the contributing effects of peer rejection.

The organization of this chapter is as follows: Factors influencing the emergence of peer rejection will be discussed first, followed by a discussion of factors related to the maintenance of rejected status, and, next, an evaluation of the consequences of rejection. Only then will I return to a consideration of the precursors of peer rejection. The emergent status phase is the point of departure for the discussion of the model because of its centrality to most discussions of peer rejection. The central focus of most analyses of the basis for peer rejection is on the social behavior of the children who become rejected. The largest body of research on rejected children deals with the behavioral correlates of rejection (see Chapter 2). The methodology of most of this research is concurrent and correlational in nature and thus has questionable validity for determining causal relations between social behavior and peer evaluations; however, it is clear that the intent of most investigators is to establish the causal basis of peer rejection in the social behavior of the rejected child. Implicit to all this work is the assumption that children who are rejected by their peers do something to become rejected by peers. The causal sequence being postulated, implicitly or explicitly, is that certain types of social behavior create a negative impact on the child's peer group and relevant adults, such as teachers. As these children come to be identified as consistently behaving in these negative ways, they receive increasingly negative evaluations by many of their peers and thus acquire the status of rejected children. This much of the sequence is referred to as the emergent status phase.

The emergent status phase

Evidence for the first step in the sequence by which some children become rejected is reviewed in Chapter 2. The clearest documentation of the behavior patterns that lead to peer rejection indicates that children who are more aggressive and disruptive than others are most likely to be rejected by their peers. Evidence for this conclusion comes not just from concurrent studies of behavior and status but from predictive studies as well. It is not hard to understand why such behavior would have a negative impact on both peers and adult caretakers.

Children are apt to dislike those who have hurt them or have interrupted their activities. In addition to this direct effect on peers, aggression and disruption may lead to peer rejection because of their impact on adults. Because caretakers, such as teachers, have the responsibility for maintaining order and seeing to the safety of their charges, they are likely to resent the behavior of overly aggressive and disruptive children and to spend more time and effort restraining and punishing these children than others. Teachers may have an indirect influence on the rejection of aggressive and disruptive children by calling attention to their misbehavior.

Not all aggressive behavior has equally deleterious implications for peer status, as Coie, Dodge, and Kupersmidt note in their review in Chapter 2. For example, there appear to be age differences in the social role that proactive aggressive behavior plays, such that in younger children some of this behavior seems to be related to establishing oneself in the peer dominance hierarchy and is thus unrelated to peer rejection. In older children, by third grade for example, this same behavior is much more characteristic of boys who become rejected. Defending oneself by physical aggression, however, is viewed by children of all ages as acceptable, even admirable, behavior. Conversely, some qualitative aspects of aggression, such as the tendency to escalate the level of aggression once it starts or the refusal to stop fighting until the other submits, are associated with peer rejection (Coie, 1987). In unusual group circumstances, such as groups in which aggressive interaction is the norm (Wright, Giammarino, & Parad, 1986), aggressive children may not be rejected at all. Thus we see that the behavioral determinants of rejection are not a simple matter even in the case of obviously aversive behaviors such as aggression. The conclusion we can draw from this is that children's groups have norms for what is acceptable and appropriate, and these norms may involve distinctions that, at first glance, seem subtle and complex to adult observers. The key to understanding rejection in children's groups is to understand what constitutes unacceptable deviance from their norms. This requires an understanding of both the definition of group norms and the limits of acceptable deviance from these norms.

Although the aversive quality of the behavior of highly aggressive or disruptive children makes it easy to understand why they are disliked by peers, not all rejected children have these characteristics. By several estimates (see Chapter 11), aggressive and disruptive children constitute only one half of the rejected-status category. It is harder to account for the basis of rejection for the other half. Aggression and disruption are each highly visible behaviors and can be observed more readily than other forms of behavior. As a result, these are the categories of negative behavior that are most often included in the research designs by which rejected and nonrejected children are compared. Most studies of the behavioral correlates of status involve group comparisons of rejected and nonrejected children, and if it is true that the largest subgroups of rejected children are either aggressive or disruptive, then differences on these two dimensions of behavior are more likely to emerge as statistically significant in group comparisons. Given that other bases for rejection account for smaller proportions of rejected children, then the search for these bases will have to proceed with slightly different methods. Rather than comparing rejected and nonrejected groups on a battery of behavioral measures, it may be more useful to see whether children who have extreme scores on one or more of a number of potential determinants of peer rejection do in fact become rejected more often than children who do not have these characteristics. This difference in method is analogous to the difference between follow-back and follow-forward designs in longitudinal studies of risk. What is proposed here is that the incidence rates of peer rejection be compared on groups of children who are identified as aggressive or withdrawn or bossy, or whatever behavioral pattern is hypothesized to be causally related to peer rejection. In this way the contribution of behavior characteristics to peer rejection can be contrasted as main effects or in interaction with each other.

There are a number of other causes for peer rejection that have received some empirical support. Rubin, LeMare, and Lollis (Chapter 8) have proposed a second major pathway to peer rejection, one involving excessive social withdrawal in later childhood. Evidence for a connection between isolate behavior and social rejection in the early school years is mixed at best, but by preadolescence there are more data supporting this relation. Two lines of thought have been proposed regarding the relation between isolate behavior and peer rejection in later childhood. Both may be correct. In their chapter, Coie et al. have argued that the best observational evidence for a relation between isolate behavior and peer rejection suggests that children withdraw inappropriately from group interaction once it is clear they are not liked by members of the group. They argue that there is clear support for rejection leading to withdrawal but not so much evidence for withdrawal leading to rejection. In fact, Coie and Dodge (1988) report observational data collected in school play settings that show neglected boys, but not rejected boys, being more isolated in their play than other boys. These data were collected on both first- and third-grade boys. On the other hand, Rubin et al. report stronger correlations between the Sensitive–Withdrawal factor of the Revised Class Play and negative peer ratings than between the Aggression factor and negative ratings. This pattern is particularly strong for fourth-, fifth-, and sixth-grade boys and girls. On the basis of these data they propose that children who are stably withdrawn in early grade school are likely to become rejected in later elementary school years. It should be noted that the definition of withdrawn behavior utilized by Rubin et al. includes anxiety and negative self-concept, elements not included in the observation category of isolate behavior used by Coie and Dodge. Thus Rubin et al. are not arguing that withdrawal per se leads to rejection but withdrawal in combination with other characteristics. The truth of the matter, in all probability, is that some children withdraw from peer contact in the face of consistent peer rejection and other children become rejected by peers across time as they are observed to be consistently self-isolating because of anxiety and personal insecurity.

Rubin et al. argue that withdrawal is increasingly a cause of rejection as children grow older because self-isolating behavior is a rarer phenomenon with increasing age. Unlike aggression, social withdrawal does not have directly aversive consequences for peers, but rather it stands out as unusual and odd behavior. Being unusual is not, in itself, a sufficient criterion for rejection, however, because many well-liked children appear to be unusual in ways that are enviable. They are unusually good at sports, for example, or they possess unusual social skills and sensitivities. More than likely, it is not simply unusual levels of solitary behavior that lead to rejection but solitary behavior associated with social anxiety, self-consciousness, and ineptness that is met with peer dislike. Children who are socially anxious are less predictable to peers and are likely to do things that embarrass themselves and others. As a result, they make other children anxious and their presence has an aversive impact. Thus the type of solitary behavior that may lead to rejection is one that is characterized by social insecurity and ineptness, and it may be that it is these qualities that are the true cause of peer rejection for these children.

Although there is empirical support for both hypotheses regarding the link between social withdrawal and peer rejection, and the two hypotheses are not mutually exclusive, both hypotheses still lack the confirming support of longitudinal data. The hypothesis that rejection leads to withdrawal is based on short-term longitudinal data for boys in new peer group situations. It may be true that longer term developmental sequences mirror these short-term sequences; however, the short-term data suggest that the tendency to withdraw in the face of rejection may be situation specific, because the boys who withdrew once they were rejected by peers were socially active during the initial stages of the newly formed play groups. Thus we do not have strong evidence here for rejection leading to stable, cross-situational social withdrawal. Rubin and his colleagues, on the other hand, are interested in those children who are more consistently self-isolating in a variety of social situations. The question remains as to whether longitudinal data will reveal that such children come to be rejected by peers as they enter later childhood and early adolescence.

Most of what is known about behavior leading to rejection is quantitative and is framed in terms of frequency of types of behaviors, observed in general play situations. On the other hand, most of what we know about strategies of interaction related to evolving peer status comes from the work on peer group entry behavior. Putallaz and Wasserman (Chapter 3) conclude that the most salient qualitative difference between those children who become popular and those who become unpopular is that the former take the time to find out what is going on in a new group situation and attempt to match their behavior to that of the group. Less popular children are more likely to disrupt the group, partly as a result of not attending to what is going on in it.

This last point is very instructive regarding the part of the problem of peer rejection that has not been well researched and remains unarticulated. The preceding discussion of the primary bases for the emergence of peer rejection deals with behaviors that are well researched because ways to observe them have been firmly established. Aggression, disruption, and withdrawal are behavior patterns that can be observed readily. Yet these variables account for no more than two thirds of the population of rejected children, at best (Chapter 11). Furthermore, we know that there are children who are equally aggressive and disruptive who are not rejected by their peers. What, then, is missing from this picture? The answer, we think, is something that was noted in connection with the withdrawal issue. There are ways that children fail to behave or social ineptnesses that they display that make a difference in peers' reactions to them.

Asher and Williams (1987) have captured the essence of this other dimension of peer rejection in their enumeration of the characteristics associated with peer acceptance and rejection. They suggest six core questions that are implicitly answered when children make determinations of social acceptance: Is the other child fun to be with? Trustworthy? Similar to me? Does this child facilitate and not undermine my goals? Make me feel good about myself? Do we influence each other in ways I like? Affirmative answers to one or more of these questions may be an adequate basis for friendship; obviously someone who fits all six criteria would be an excellent friend. Conversely, the questions tell us something about the basis for social rejection. As we have noted, children who are aggressive or disruptive or apprehensive and withdrawn come up short on several of these criteria. Perhaps whether or not these children are rejected depends on their other characteristics. For example, some aggressive children may be unpleasant to be with and not very trustworthy, but other aggressive children may have positive social attributes that compensate for their occasionally aversive behavior. They may influence other children in acceptable ways or may facilitate the goals of others by being helpful and cooperative at times. Thus, they may not be rejected even though they are highly aggressive. There are data that identify such children as being controversial in status (Coie, Finn, & Krehbiel, 1985).

Not only do Asher and Williams's questions help us understand why some children who are aggressive are not necessarily socially rejected, they also help us think about other reasons for some children to be rejected. Children who are bossy and domineering will not be fun to be with or will not influence others in acceptable ways. Children who are dishonest or betray confidences will not be trustworthy. Children who are resistant or rigid will tend to influence others in undesirable ways. Children who are insulting, nonresponsive, or self-centered will not make other children feel good about themselves.

One of the conclusions of Chapter 3 was that a key dimension to social success was the ability to consider the concerns and goals of others (and, I suspect, even the personal dignity of others) and make one's own behavior relevant to these issues. Not doing this, because of a lack of social ability or because of an unpleasant personal disposition, places a child on the negative side of many of Asher and Williams's questions. There are many ways a child can fail other than the more obvious and easily observable patterns of aggression and disruption. Not too much is known about children who are rejected for these other reasons. Only by examining the behavior of children in significant types of social encounters, as was done by Putallaz and others in the peer entry situation, may we discover more about this other side of peer rejection.

There is a darker side to the Asher and Williams set of core questions that helps explain some aspects of both friendship selection and peer rejection that have not been examined much in the peer relations literature. One of their core questions was, "Does this child make me feel good about myself?" There is a positive side to this that is usually found in programs for teaching children about making friends. Ladd (1981), for example, taught rejected children to validate others. Children (and adults) tend to seek out those who focus on their good qualities and highlight their competencies for them. However, sometimes children seek out peers for friends because they wish to bask in the reflected glory of the other. Thus, some children seek out good athletes or attractive classmates not because of their likable behavior but because they wish to be identified with them. Conversely, some children also snub or avoid children with handicaps or other socially embarrassing attributes because they want to avoid being associated with them. As observers of children, those of us who conduct research on peer relations have encountered this phenomenon and know it to be an important dynamic in peer rejection. The next section, on physical appearance and rejection, discusses one area of research that comes close to dealing with this point.

Physical appearance and rejection

Although the central thrust of most of the research on peer rejection has been directed at understanding the behavioral basis for rejection, evidence for nonbehavioral contributors to rejection has been available for some time. The most important and well studied of these factors is physical appearance. Physical attractiveness, as assessed by judgments of facial or full-body photographs, usually has been associated with positive sociometric status. However, in reviewing the literature on this topic, Langlois and Stephan (1981) cite evidence from two studies (Langlois & Styczynski, 1979; Styczynski & Langlois, 1977) that indicates that attractive boys are viewed negatively by familiar peers, suggesting that in the initial stages of peer acquaintance physical attractiveness may be a social advantage but with increasing contact attractive boys may be viewed less positively.

Methodological factors may play a part in these seemingly contradictory findings. In the two studies by Langlois and Styczynski, only photographs of faces were shown to judges, whereas in many of the studies in which positive correlations between attractiveness and peer liking were found (Dion & Berscheid, 1974; Kleck, Richardson, & Ronald, 1974; Lerner & Lerner, 1977) photographs revealing body build were employed. Thus the issue of male attractiveness may not be one of level of acquaintance but the relative importance of male "prettiness" versus athletic body type. For preadolescent males, body type may connote socially desirable characteristics other than attractiveness. Body type may provide clues to athletic ability and physical dominance, both of which are linked to positive peer status among males. The data on attractiveness among girls are less controversial. With girls there is consistent evidence for at least a moderately positive correlation between physical attractiveness and peer status, regardless of the method for determining attractiveness.

Usually only moderate levels of correlation have been found between physical appearance and peer liking. Cavior and Dokecki (1973) found that this relation holds only at the extreme ends of the appearance continuum: Very attractive children are liked and very unattractive children are disliked. Across the broad midrange of the attractiveness span there is no relation between relative attractiveness and peer liking.

Other authors have found empirical support for the connection between physical attractiveness and peer status but suggest that the connection between appearance and peer evaluation may be mediated by differences in social behavior. Coie, Dodge, and Coppotelli (1982) found that physical attractiveness was a significant predictor of peer social preference scores but that behavioral factors could be substituted for attractiveness in the same multiple regression analyses and largely account for the same variance. More convincing evidence was produced by Dodge (1983) in his study of unfamiliar boys in a new play group situation. Boys who were ultimately rejected in these groups were rated by unbiased adult judges as less physically attractive than boys in other peer status categories. (Dodge's photos provided some indications of body type). However, multivariate analyses of covariance revealed that behavior differences predicted 71% of the variance in status, controlling for physical attractiveness, but attractiveness did not significantly predict status when behavior was controlled statistically. The implication of these findings is that unattractive children behave in ways that are socially unacceptable, and it is their behavior that leads to peer rejection rather than unattractiveness per se.

Langlois and Stephan (1981) have proposed a model of development linking differences in physical appearance to differences in social behavior. They argue that adults and peers have differential expectations of attractive and unattractive children that lead to different treatment of these children. Because of this differential treatment, unattractive children come to behave in ways that are consistent with the expectations of others. These differences in behavior, in turn, reinforce the prejudices of significant others and enhance the power of this vicious cycle of expectations and behavior. One could argue that this model serves to explain Dodge's data in two ways: Within the framework of the eight play sessions with new peers, rejected boys may have played out this expectations–behavior sequence with their new peer acquaintances; but more importantly, perhaps they may have come to this new peer situation with behavioral propensities borne of prior experiences with adults and children in their normal life circumstances.

The role of the group in emerging peer rejection

Hymel, Wagner, and Butler (Chapter 6) have made a strong case for considering the role of group dynamics in peer social status distinctions, both in maintaining existing status assignments and in accounting for the emergence of status in new peer situations. Peer status, in the research covered in this volume, is operationalized by summing up the individual judgments of school peers and treating these summary scores as the index of peer group status. This means that all individual judgments are treated as having equal value in the peer group. It also suggests that status is the cumulative reflection of individual values and judgments rather than the outcome of a dynamic group process in which some group members have more influence than others, in which pressures on the group or tensions within it create a need for scapegoats and outcasts, or lead to cliques and subgroups with strong and, sometimes, arbitrary rules for inclusion and exclusion. Hymel and her colleagues have reminded us of the potential importance of these dimensions of the peer rejection process.

Hymel et al. suggest two principal ways in which group dynamics may relate to peer rejection. The one given the most attention by them and having the strongest empirical support concerns the way group processes serve to maintain the status of rejected children. The evidence indicates both that children have different expectations for the behavior of popular and rejected children and that they interpret their behavior differently. Peers also treat rejected and popular children differently, being more inclined to initiate social contact with popular children and less likely to be aggressive against them or behave aversively toward them. Although there is less evidence for the group's negative behavior toward rejected children, aggressive, rejected children are presumed by peers to have hostile intentions more often and are more likely to receive hostile reactions from peers in circumstances where popular children would be treated more benignly.

The second way in which group dynamics may relate to social rejection is by actually creating rejection. Arguing that because few behavioral differences are sometimes found between rejected and nonrejected children, status differences, in these cases, must be a creation of the group rather than a reaction of the group. Hymel et al. outline two slightly different ways in which social perception biases may lead members of a group to reject a newcomer. Following Darley and Fazio (1980), they propose that prior to actual interaction with a newcomer, negative expectations may be generated indirectly by observations of interactions with other people or by stereotypes based on nonbehavioral characteristics. The example of physical appearance discussed earlier illustrates one such newcomer route to rejection. A second route is through gossip. Members of a group may have negative expectations because of the newcomer's reputation.

There are few empirical tests of the newcomer reputation hypothesis with children; however, Coie, Dodge, McClaskey, and Belding (1987) have examined the relative impact of newcomer reputation, on the one hand, and direct observation of the behavior of the newcomer with peers, on the other. In this study, judges (8- to 11-year-old males) were presented with short video excerpts showing boys (targets) from another community engaged in conflictual interactions. In four of these episodes, one boy could be distinguished reliably as provoking the conflict (high-fault targets) and the other boy as much less culpable (low-fault targets); in the other four episodes the boys could be judged as having roughly comparable responsibility for the conflict. Before viewing these video episodes, subjects were given information about the way classmates of the two boys felt about each of them. The target figures in each episode were identified either as being rejected in their peer group or of average social status, with these reputation inductions being given just prior to a showing of each episode and counterbalanced across all other design conditions. The subjects in this study were asked to pretend they were going to be moving to this new community and to have the boys in the videotapes as classmates. They were asked to choose which member of each pair they would prefer to have as friends.

The results of this study reflect the significant impact of both reputation and behavior differences in the social evaluation of newcomers. Average-status targets were preferred over rejected targets, and low-fault targets were preferred over high-fault targets. These results provide some support for the hypothesis that gossip (reputation) can influence the initial peer status of newcomers, but they also demonstrate that children are empiricists in their making of social judgments.

One thought that is prompted by the Hymel et al. chapter, although not raised explicitly, is that the dynamics of group life require that someone be rejected. This idea is akin to a much older idea in sociology, stated by Durkheim (1938), that society requires deviants so that the boundary conditions of acceptable behavior can be defined. On a smaller social scale Bowen (1966) has theorized that triangles are the basic units of family life because they permit pairs of individuals to stabilize their relationship by means of shared negative feelings and involvements toward a third family member. One way that Bowen illustrates his point is by pointing out the extent to which two family members sustain their interactions by talking about other family members. Similar observations can be made of the conversations of adolescent friendship pairs. Indeed, many friendships may be sustained as much by shared animosities toward others as by genuine intimacy and affection. These ideas all suggest that, sometimes, individuals may serve as scapegoats for the benefit of group cohesiveness and that, whatever their inadequacies, they may be rejected less because of their own behavior than for the peer group's need of a target for negative affect. The importance of this dynamic for the phenomenon of peer rejection requires further investigation, as does the question of how enduring these group-generated effects might be. Although there is some evidence for the continuity of peer status in general (Coie & Dodge, 1983; Newcomb & Bukowski, 1984), it is less likely that children who are rejected for these more arbitrary and less behavioral reasons will continue to be rejected across time as the composition and interaction contexts of the peer group change. For this reason, children who are unfortunate enough to be rejected by peers for reasons owing to group dynamics may experience an unpleasant period of social life, but they should experience some relief when they join new groups in which they are not cast in this same deviant role, and thus they should be less at risk for future problems than those children whose peer rejection is caused by their own behavior. We do not know very much about the enduring effects of short-term or temporary rejection on children, however, and we can only speculate that the affective aftermath is less harmful than the consequences of sustained peer rejection.

The maintenance phase of rejection

In the preceding sections the conditions under which some children are consensually viewed as disliked by their peers have been described. Once this consensus has been reached, even though it may never be explicitly discussed by the peer group, the dynamics of group life change for these children. This hypothesized change has been designated in the model as the transition from the emergent status phase to the maintenance phase of rejected status. Changes occur on the part of the peer group and the rejected child. The peer group changes their behavior toward rejected children, and rejected children change in their behavior toward peers, in their feelings about themselves and their peers, and in the thoughts and expectations they have about themselves and others.

In reality it would be hard to draw a temporal line in the social lives of rejected children and designate events on one side of this line as part of the emergent status phase and events on the other side as parts of the maintenance phase. Empirically, investigators sample the social order of a school-aged peer group at a point in the school year when they think children have had sufficient time to become acquainted that they can make valid social judgments about their classmates. Scores on these sociometric samplings are then submitted to statistical procedures and some children are designated as having negative scores so extreme that they are labeled as rejected. At that point we say their status has emerged and we can look at subsequent interactions between them and their peers as part of the status maintenance phase. Not all children will be at the same point of development in their negative relationships with peers. For some, their negative relationships may be temporary and circumstantial; for others, they may be stable and generalized. Just when this shift from emergent to enduring status comes about may be hard to document, even if we were to follow these children on a day-to-day basis.

It is useful to speak of the distinction between these two phases, emergence and maintenance, because it seems to make a difference for both the child and the group. In terms of social role society (Sarbin & Scheibe, 1983), being rejected becomes part of a child's social identity, determining a number of new social expectations held by the group for that child, and by the child for himself or herself.

First of all, Putallaz and Wasserman's chapter on entry behavior suggests that rejected children recognize their status problems by the way they enter familiar peer group situations. In unfamiliar peer group entry contexts (the "newcomer" situation), it is adaptive to take some time to size up the situation (to "hover") so that one can take the most appropriate entry steps and avoid being too conspicuous. Most child newcomers seem to recognize that they may be intruding and hence need to move cautiously. Yet they also know that it is incumbent on them to make the initiating moves, because group members are less likely to take the initiative to include them. Thus in unfamiliar entry contexts (Putallaz, 1983), hovering was not related to peer status. Popular boys were equally as likely to hover as were unpopular boys. Yet in familiar peer group entry contexts (Putallaz & Gottman, 1981) unpopular boys are more likely to wait longer to attempt entry than popular boys. This suggests that when entering groups where their status has already been established, unpopular boys recognize the need for caution more than popular boys, who, in unfamiliar groups, would ordinarily be quite attentive to such considerations. It is as though unpopular boys anticipate they will have difficulty joining the familiar peer group and alter their behavior because of these fears. Further evidence for this hypothesis comes from Putallaz and Gottman's analysis of the correlation between the cost–benefit ratios associated with different types of entry strategies and the probability that a child will employ a certain strategy in the entry situation. For popular boys these correlations were highly positive, whereas for unpopular boys the two variables were uncorrelated. Such apparently maladaptive behavior patterns on the part of unpopular boys seem to be related to an awareness of their standing with familiar boys, and their behavior may be highly influenced by face-saving concerns and the need to compensate for their low status. As Putallaz and Wasserman note, there are several ways to do this, all of which fit with existing data. They may hold back from attempting to enter and hover around the group instead. They may attempt to elevate their status in the eyes of the group by means of self-referent and self-aggrandizing statements, or they may be directly intrusive and assaultive. Overall, Dodge (1983) found that across the short history of newly formed peer groups, children who are rejected in these groups tend to approach peers less as the group sessions increase. Coie and Kupersmidt (1983) found the same temporal trend, in that solitary, inappropriate activity increased for boys just after the point in time when they became named by peers as disliked.

There is also evidence that the group alters its behavior toward peers as a consequence of their peer status. Some of this evidence indicates that popular children have an easier time of it than other children, rather than that rejected children have a harder time. For example, Coie and Kupersmidt report that popular boys are the targets of less aversive activity than other boys in familiar groups but there were no status differences in unfamiliar groups. Likewise, Dodge (1983) found that popular boys are positively approached by other boys more often than all other status groups. Dodge also found some support for the idea that rejected boys are treated less well by the group than other boys. Across time, in these newly formed groups, the responses to social initiatives were increasingly positive for all but the rejected groups. Of course, this finding may simply reflect the fact that the group was coming to identify these boys as rejected, but it does indicate that there is a behavioral reality that corresponds to patterns of sociometric choice. Early in this chapter I have alluded to evidence that children have negative expectations of other children who are known to be rejected, and Hymel and her colleagues have documented the fact that children make less favorable inferences about even the intentions of rejected peers.

Ladd, Price, and Hart (Chapter 4) have reported interesting within-year longitudinal data on social contact patterns, and these data indicate that once children become rejected, they are more likely to be on the outside of well-established, coherent play groups. Thus their social choices seem to be restricted to other children who, like themselves, have less skills for sustaining effective relationships. Not surprisingly, these social outliers do not seem to get along well, even with each other. Apparently, rejected children have as much, or more, trouble getting along with each other as they do with nonrejected children, even though some of them will name each other as best friends.

I have just summarized reasons for believing that both the rejected child and the rejecting peer group recognize the fact of rejection and respond to it in measurable ways. The data also suggest that there is some diversity in the reactions of rejected children. I will outline evidence that suggests that not all rejected children react to rejection in the same way. This fact makes the task of tracking the reactions of rejected children more difficult when one simply examines group differences between rejected and nonrejected children.

On the affective level, rejected children repeatedly have been found to describe themselves as more lonely than nonrejected children (Chapter 9). When one takes a closer look at rejected children, it turns out that the nonaggressive rejected children consistently report this greater loneliness, whereas aggressive rejected children are less consistently lonely across studies. Indeed, in one middle school study (Parkhurst & Asher, 1987), aggressive rejected children reported no greater loneliness than average-status children.

Most assessments of the self-esteem of rejected children indicate that they have lower self-esteem than nonrejected children (e.g., Finn, 1985; Horowitz, 1962; Kurdek & Krile, 1982; Putallaz, White, & Shipman, 1985). However, sometimes the differences in self-esteem are quite small or nonexistent (Guardo, 1969). A central problem for all of this research is the dependence on self-report measures. Some rejected children do not appear to recognize that they are rejected by peers, and others may overinflate their reported sense of self out of defensiveness. There is reason to believe that males are less disclosing about negative feelings than females, and this may be true for rejected boys' descriptions of their internal reactions to peer rejection. Asarnow and Carlson (1985) report that boys who have been diagnosed as depressed are less likely to report feelings of depression and low self-worth than are girls.

Evidence for the impact of peer rejection at the cognitive level is less available from direct assessments, and it is hard to distinguish between cognitive patterns that were instrumental in causing rejection and those that arose from the experience of being rejected. This is true for studies of social-problem-solving strategies, social information processing, and children's goals. The data we have reviewed on peer entry behavior do indicate, indirectly, changes in the social expectations of children who have been rejected. Rejected children seem to anticipate being excluded from peer group activity and react either with hesitancy or intrusiveness. These two very different reactions to the expectation of social rebuff call to mind the importance of separating aggressive and nonaggressive rejected children when evaluating the effects of rejection on the child. Parkhurst and Asher (1987) found these two subgroups to have quite different social concerns. When young adolescents were interviewed about their social concerns, aggressive rejected children were more concerned about prevailing against others, whereas nonaggressive rejected children were more concerned about being scorned and attacked by others. This would suggest, although there are no data yet on this point, that aggressive rejected children would be the ones to handle their concerns about being excluded from peer activities by intruding with self-referent remarks or hostile comments. Nonaggressive children would be more likely to hold back from attempting to enter lest they be ridiculed or attacked and thus would tend to hover about the group. Both reactions seem destined to have the unfortunate effects of self-fulfilling prophecy.

An important question, one not yet fully addressed in the literature, is why, in the face of much negative reaction from peers, many rejected children continue to behave in maladaptive ways and even acquire more maladaptive reactions. The latter part of this question has been addressed, to some extent, in the discussion of the role the group plays in consolidating rejected children in their roles as social deviants. However, it must be emphasized that the group's reaction does provide rejected children with incentives for changing, because peers do respond much more positively to positive than negative social behavior.

There are a number of reasons that can be put forward in answer to this question of why rejected children do not readily change. Each explanation reflects an approach to intervention. The first answer is that some rejected children lack the requisite social skills to behave more effectively and, more importantly, do not know how to acquire them on their own. This answer provides the rationale for the predominant intervention strategy taken with rejected children thus far, as can be seen in Chapters 11 and 12. This skill-training approach has met with some success, and Chapter 12 provides a close look at the methodology for implementing skill training, particularly with very young children. Coie and Koeppl (Chapter 11) argue that positive social skills, such as those promoted by the Mize and Ladd program (Chapter 12), will not solve the skill deficits of all rejected children, especially those of aggressive rejected children, the largest rejected subgroup. For this group, they propose that training in self-control of reactive aggression and reeducation in the social consequences of proactive aggression may be necessary.

One impediment to the efficacy of skill training may be the possibility that many rejected children do not recognize that it would be useful to them to acquire new social skills. This motivational issue is implied by a second answer to the question of why rejected children do not change. Rejected children may not change because they do not realize fully that they are in trouble with their peers. Ruble (1982) and her colleagues have demonstrated that many children fail to recognize their academic problems until the third or fourth grade (9 or 10 years of age), because they do not process the social comparison information that would enable them to judge their performance relative to that of their classmates. Because clues to social standing are likely to be more difficult to read than those of academic standing, it should not be surprising that many rejected children do not know where they stand with classmates. Furthermore, even if they do know they are not liked by peers, they may not know why they are disliked, because it is rare for children or adults to be given specific feedback about their social behavior. Thus they have no clear way to identify what it is they do to get themselves into trouble with peers.

A third reason that rejected children may fail to change their behavior is that when small changes are effected, their peers fail to perceive these changes or respond to them. Hymel et al. have reported on data suggesting that once a child is categorized as disliked, positive acts by that child are more likely to be attributed to external causes and peers may reinterpret the child's motives in less positive terms than if that child was not rejected. Thus, rejected children who attempt to alter their negative impact on peers have an uphill climb ahead of them and may be inclined to give up and revert to old social solutions when their efforts are not initially successful.

A fourth reason for rejected children not to change their behavior, or to change it to more maladaptive reactions, is rooted in their expectations for social success. As noted earlier, the group entry literature strongly suggests that some rejected children anticipate peer group rebuff and that their compensations for these expected rejections are almost guaranteed to keep them excluded. The social role theory formulations of Sarbin and Scheibe (1983) suggest that rejected children begin to perform socially in a manner consistent with the shared expectations both they and their peers have for them, by virtue of their rejected status. Similarly, self-consistency theorists (Lecky, 1945; Swann, 1983) have proposed that people are sufficiently motivated to maintain their views of themselves that they will behave in ways that are consistent with those views, even when it means further damage to their self-esteem. On the other hand, self-enhancement theory, a perspective consistent with our "Why don't they change?" question, suggests that people with negative self-views would be motivated to enhance their self-views more than would those with positive self-concepts. In a recent test of these competing propositions, Swann, Griffin, Predmore, and Gains (1987) exposed college students having either positive or negative social self-concepts to either positive or negative feedback about their apparent social confidence. At a cognitive level, the self-consistency hypothesis was supported. Negative self-concept subjects endorsed the correctness of negative feedback more than positive feedback, and the opposite trend held true for the positive self-concept subjects. Data on the impact of feedback on the subjects' moods were congruent with the predictions of self-enhancement theory. Both positive and negative self-concept subjects felt better after the positive feedback. These results suggest that although rejected children with low social self-esteem might feel better after receiving positive social feedback, they will be more likely to remember and internalize negative feedback.

Although direct attempts to improve the social expectations of rejected children have not been incorporated into intervention programs thus far, Rabiner and Coie (1989) did conduct a brief experimental test of the effects of a positive social expectancy induction on rejected children. Each experimental subject was led to believe that two boys whom he had just met in a brief play group held several days earlier were looking forward to playing with him again and that they seemed to like him. Shortly after this induction the subject was taken to a room in which the two boys were at play in a situation similar to Putallaz and Gottman's peer entry paradigm. When host pairs were interviewed individually about their reactions to the experimental subject and a control subject (also rejected), who had not been given the induction, the hosts rated the experimental subjects favorably significantly more often than the control subjects. No differences in social preferences were expressed between experimental and control popular-status subjects, suggesting that the induction had little effect on popular boys because they already anticipated social success. This test of the effects of altering the negative social expectations of rejected children provides support for including a focus on self-expectations in future intervention programs. Because of the limited duration of social contact between subjects and host pairs, we do not know whether this positive social experience will have any enduring impact on the experimental subjects' thoughts about themselves in more extended social situations.

Although each of these four reasons for the stability of rejection have been posed as alternatives, it is highly probable that they all hold true in interactive combinations. Systems theories of social behavior (e.g., Watzlawick, Beavin, & Jackson, 1967) suggest that there is reciprocal feedback between the expectations and behaviors of all the individuals in a group. Thus rejected boys who come to a social encounter with low expectations give clues to the group of their low self-confidence at the same time they are reading the negative expectations of the group. Furthermore, children who do not have the requisite skills for handling particular social situations will experience some negative feedback in those situations even though they may not know just what they have done wrong. Across time they will develop pessimistic expectations regarding these same social situations, and in this way a downward spiraling cycle of maladaptive behavior can easily be set in motion for rejected children. Such cycles may account for the maintenance of rejected peer status.

Consequences of peer rejection

In an earlier section of the chapter, Albee's equation for explaining disorder was used to outline the different ways peer rejection could contribute to the incidence of disorder. All of these hypotheses were based on the premise of sustained rejection. Children who are presumed to be most at risk for future disorder are those who have experienced more than temporary peer rejection. The effects of rejection on self-esteem depend on there being some prolonged experience of rejection, otherwise, for example, the child will not be likely to internalize the judgments of peers. Transitory experiences of peer rejection are not assumed to have the same serious, long-term implications as sustained rejection. This use of the Albee equation implicitly recognizes the difference between being rejected socially and experiencing disorder. Although some children may be rejected because of disordered behavior, being rejected is not necessarily a sign of disorder. Disorder, according to Albee, is a set of reactions that are persistently maladaptive and harmful to self and others. Disorder is a response to stressful circumstances, circumstances that may be exacerbated by peer rejection. As was noted earlier, rejection can occur because of factors other than the behavior of the person who is rejected.

When the connection between peer rejection and disorder is posited, it is peer rejection during middle childhood and preadolescence that is presumed to lead to disorder that occurs in adolescence and early adulthood. This view of the development of disorder is consistent with Sullivan's (1953) theory of childhood as a time in which preparations are made for being able to develop the intimate relationships of adolescence and adulthood. Early-adolescent relationships, according to Sullivan, serve as an important resource and buffer against the stresses of adolescent life transitions that sometimes trigger disordered reactions. Sullivan's emphasis on the importance of best friends in early adolescence can be put into current context by data on junior high school friendship patterns. In contrast to elementary school sociometric data, in which it is relatively rare for a child to be named by no one as either liked most or liked least, this is a very frequent phenomenon in junior high school (Coie, Dodge, & Coppotelli, 1982). Thus, in junior high school it is not unusual for many young adolescents to go unnoticed, virtually, by their classmates. Berndt and Hoyle (1985) found that eighth-graders made fewer new friends than fourth-graders did, even though the stability of established friendships was generally equivalent. Thus one developmental stressor that increases predictably in adolescence is that of an increased social alienation and isolation. To a large extent this phenomenon may be a result of the structure of the school system in our country rather than a necessary developmental phenomenon. Junior high schools consist of a merger of several large groups of early adolescents who are assigned to classes with constantly shifting composition. This structure limits the opportunity for old friends to stay in touch and for new friendships to develop. Berndt (1987) has reported that friendships generally are disrupted by the transition to junior high school and that adolescents with close friendships adjust more successfully to junior high school. Similarly, the design of secondary schools reduces the possibility for these adolescents to develop a supportive relationship with teachers. One reason, therefore, for looking to the period of adolescence as the beginning of an outcome phase for disorders related to peer rejection is that cultural and developmental changes result in greater social stresses on adolescents.

Kupersmidt, Coie, and Dodge (Chapter 10) have limited their review just to the predictive implications of peer rejection and have not tried to examine systematically the developmental implications of specific types of social behavior, such as aggression and withdrawal, that often are correlated with peer rejection. For an excellent treatment of the latter issues, the reader is referred to a recent review by Parker and Asher (1987). Both of these reviews are in agreement on several important points. First of all, the strongest case for the predictive relation between peer rejection in childhood and disorder in adolescence can be made with respect to school adjustment during adolescence. Rejected children are rated as having more academic problems in school, and they are truant more often, have more discipline problems, and drop out of school more often than nonrejected children.

Because peer rejection is a phenomenon that is assessed within the school setting, it is not surprising that rejection is most consistently predictive of the incidences of future problems within the school setting. Peer problems in elementary school have two negative consequences for social adjustment in junior and senior high school. First, the carryover of negative status leads to less social support being available when these children face the transitional stresses of junior and senior high school. Second, the lack of friendship or inclusion in early peer groups robs the rejected child of important social learning experiences compared with other children. This leaves rejected children with fewer skills for coping with the social demands of the adolescent period.

Early adolescence seems to be a time of intense social self-consciousness. Concerns for fitting in with the peer group are greatest, and the peer group's influence on the judgments of young teenagers is stronger than at any other point in development (Berndt, 1979; Costanzo, Coie, Dorval, & Young, 1977; Costanzo & Shaw, 1966). The structure of junior high school is such that individual teachers have much less contact with pupils than in elementary school and therefore are less available for support and guidance. Eccles, Midgley, and Adler (1984) have described junior high schools as less supportive emotionally and more competitive academically than elementary school and attribute this to the environment of junior high schools. The rejected adolescent is likely to find junior high school to be a very unrewarding place to spend most of a day unless there are strong compensating factors such as the rewards that come from doing well academically, athletically, or in extracurricular activities such as music or drama. Rejected adolescents who do not have these compensations are likely to become truant or to drop out of school. Those who stay in school may act out in class and become subject to disciplinary actions. This is the pattern of events suggested by the Kupersmidt et al. review (Chapter 10).

A second point made in both the Parker and Asher review and Chapter 10 is that although there is good evidence that peer rejection is a predictor of delinquency, aggression is consistently found to be the better predictor. In light of our earlier thesis that disorder takes on the form and substance of earlier premorbid behavior, it makes sense that aggression is a potent predictor of delinquency. Aggression, by late childhood and early adolescence, is a violation of formal and informal rules for children's conduct. Thus it is not surprising that children who flagrantly violate rules of such high visibility are likely to go on to violate other rules. Likewise it is reasonable to expect children who are both aggressive and rejected to be especially delinquency prone, because peers describe the aggressive behavior of this subgroup of aggressive children as being more sneaky and indirect than that of nonrejected aggressive children (Bierman, Smoot, & Aumiller, 1987). That is, it is aggression that violates the peer norms for legitimate, or tolerable, aggression. Rejection may contribute to increased risk for delinquency in several other ways. Adolescents who feel socially alienated from peer society may be motivated to strike out in reaction to their feelings of anger and frustration. Quay (1964) has described one major form of delinquency, unsocialized delinquency, in terms that would fit these children. Another factor that may lead rejected adolescents to become delinquent is their increased risk for truancy and dropping out of school. Robins and Wish (1977) have proposed a cumulative risk sequence that begins with truancy and is followed by early school withdrawal and then later forms of antisocial disorder. One obvious explanation for this sequence is that adolescents who are not in school have more idle, unsupervised time in which to get into trouble. Furthermore, social role theory suggests that being a truant or a drop-out is a type of miscreant status that could easily lead a young person to take on more of the role-related characteristics of the social outlaw. In this way developmental factors that increase the likelihood of truancy and early school withdrawal also set the child at risk for even more serious problems.

The third type of disorder connected to earlier peer rejection is mental health problems. Two types of prediction data link peer rejection to psychological disorder. The Cowen, Pederson, Babigian, Izzo, and Trost (1973) study, reviewed in Chapter 10, best illustrates the connection between early peer rejection in a nonselected childhood sample and subsequent treatment for psychological problems. This study contains the strongest evidence for the mental illness implications of childhood peer rejection. It is unfortunate that the Cowen et al. data were never analyzed in a follow-forward design to calculate the subsequent incidence of disorder among children with differing degrees of social adjustment, because then we would know more about the relative degree of risk introduced by peer rejection. The second type of data linking early childhood rejection to psychological disorder in later life comes from studies of children who were seen in child guidance clinics. Adult adjustment data on these selected samples reveal greater risk for adult mental health problems, ranging from psychoneurosis to psychosis (Roff, 1960, 1961, 1963). One problem with such data is that it may not be valid to generalize these findings to the general population of non-clinic-referred children. A second problem is whether or not the two groups of clinic-referred children, those with peer problems and those without peer problems, had comparable levels of psychological disorder at the time they were referred for treatment. In other words, should having peer problems be taken as a sign of more serious disorder? If so, then the Roff data mean that children with more serious psychological problems are at greater risk for disorder in early adulthood. If not, then the data can be seen as supporting the model presented in this chapter, namely, that rejection contributes more to the incidence of disorder than do other vulnerability factors.

In Chapter 8, Rubin, LeMare, and Lollis proposed that the type of disorder would be related to the basis for peer rejection. Externalizing forms of disorder, such as delinquency, would be predicted best by rejection based on aggression and disruptive behavior. Internalizing forms of disorder, such as depression, would be predicted best by rejection based on anxious, withdrawn behavior. Data on the prediction of delinquency are consistent with this hypothesis. Neither the school adjustment nor the mental health outcome data have been analyzed in a way that would address this distinction, because it is possible to conceive of both externalizing and internalizing reactions falling within both of these domains of disorder. Truancy could be considered a type of social withdrawal, for example; on the other hand, it is a flagrant violation of school administration rules. Conversely, although it may seem appropriate to view mental health problems generally as evidence of internalizing disorders, many of the children referred for psychological treatment in the Cowen et al. study may have been referred for externalizing problems, because a high proportion of referrals in middle childhood and beyond are for externalizing disorders (Rutter, Cox, Tupling, Berger, & Yule, 1975). Ultimately, it may be possible to trace the predictive pathways between the different bases for peer rejection and the types of disorder displayed in later life, as Rubin et al. suggest. However, it is likely that one will need to know more than just the initial behavioral basis for peer rejection. In our view, the way the experience of peer rejection translates into subsequent social behavior will tell us most about the form disorder may take. It is also important to recall that peer rejection is viewed as just one of many factors in the overall equation for predicting disorder. In following cohorts of children longitudinally from childhood to early adulthood, my colleagues and I have encountered several instances where dramatic life events caused surprising shifts in the life adjustment of children in our samples and resulted in forms of disorder one would not have predicted from knowledge of earlier social behavior.

It should be noted that the Albee equation can be used to understand the factors contributing to psychological well-being as well as disorder. When peer status is considered in this light, the question can be raised whether popularity among peers could serve as a buffer against disorder and as a predictor of future well-being. In support of this idea is the evidence that popular children have an easier time of it than other children once their status is established. However, not as much attention has been given to the long-term consequences of popularity as has been given to rejection. We do know that popularity is associated with social skill and is not just a consequence of superficial characteristics, so it seems reasonable to suppose that positive peer status may be a predictor of future well-being.

Before moving to a discussion of the precursors to peer rejection, I would like to elaborate briefly on one premise of this chapter that has not been given much treatment. Some years back Brown (1973) wrote an essay on schizophrenia in which he pointed out an important difference between the way psychosis is often portrayed in texts on abnormal behavior and what one encounters when one actually interacts with a diagnosed psychotic individual. Brown noted that although psychosis is described in terms that would lead one to anticipate constant irrationality, one usually finds normal behavior interspersed only occasionally with moments of irrationality. Brown's point is that disordered individuals express their disorder only in response to specific themes and in particular circumstances. Brown's point is instructive for us here in several ways. We should expect disorder only in response to circumscribed events and settings, rather than across a wide range of conditions. This fact makes it difficult for us to assess the phenomenon of disorder, particularly when following up on groups of individuals who can be expected to express disorder in different ways and under different circumstances. The second implication of Brown's observation concerns the behavior patterns that mark a child's vulnerability to rejection and the connection between those patterns and subsequent disordered behavior. We should not expect, as we have stated earlier, that aggressive children will be constantly aggressive in their interactions with peers. Some types of interactions may provoke them to immediate uncontrolled anger, whereas others will be managed without loss of control. Our ability to assess these situational parameters will enhance our ability to provide instructive assistance to specific children, but we may further expect that in the long run, children who fail to learn to handle these difficult situations may be expected to manifest disorder in response to analogous, age-relevant circumstances in later life. This speculation is consistent with an approach to analyzing consistency in human functioning across the life span that has yielded interesting results (Caspi, 1987).

Precursors to peer rejection

The discussion of peer rejection began with an analysis of the behavioral antecedents of peer rejection, acknowledging that there are other causal factors for rejection but contending that to understand why some children are rejected consistently by peers one has to know how they behave with peers. If we now take a step further back and ask how it is that they come to behave in these maladaptive ways, then two kinds of answers can be suggested, involving either proximal or distal causes. Proximal causes have to do with the immediate competencies, thoughts, and feelings these children bring to the social situation. Distal causes are those that describe the socialization processes by which children acquire the behavioral, cognitive, or affective orientations that are the proximal causes of peer rejection.

Distal causes

On the distal side of the causal equation we place such factors as early socialization and temperament. There is less systematic research in these domains, at least as it relates directly to peer rejection. Rubin, LeMare, and Lollis (Chapter 8) offer some interesting speculations about the role of differences in temperament in the evolution of peer status. They note the early linkages of temperament to parental attachment and, later, the continuing impact of temperament on the behavior of children in the peer contexts of toddler play and preschool activity. Rubin et al. and Putallaz and Heflin (Chapter 7) each address the role of parental socialization influences on the behaviors that lead to peer rejection. For the most part, they do so in slightly different ways.

Dishion (1988) makes a useful distinction between two models of the influence of the parent–child relationship on a child's peer relations. In one model, the parent–child relationship is construed to be the prototype of all future relationships. Attachment theory, as described in Chapter 8, is a prime example of this model. The degree to which parent and child have a strong attachment bond is predictive of the extent to which the child can experience intimacy in future relationships. Rubin and his colleagues take this premise further and speculate that the type of attachment bond will be predictive of the type of peer relationship. Babies who have an insecure and hostile attachment with their mothers (overactive, difficult-to-soothe babies) will have aggressive and hostile relationships with peers. Babies who have an insecure and anxious or inhibited attachment with their mothers will be anxious and withdrawn in their relationships with their peers. Although Rubin et al. regard the temperamental orientations of infants as having a continuing influence on future relationships, one can see in their model the importance of the mother–child bond as a prototype for later relationships.

The second model in Dishion's dichotomy is one that relates parental training practices and parent–child relationships to the evolution of specific forms of social behavior. These forms of social behavior, in turn, determine the character of future relationships, including the future of that same parent–child relationship. Dishion cites the coercion model of Patterson and Reid (1973, 1984) as a good example of this more indirect influence model. The coercion model describes families in which interactions are marked by high levels of negative affect. The children of these families learn that they can resist parental demands by behaving aversively. This behavior then carries over into other social situations such as the school. However much immediate, instrumental payoff this coercive behavior receives, the additional social consequences for the child are quite negative and likely include rejection by peers. Most of the research described by Putallaz and Heflin in Chapter 7 fits this second type of model of parental influence. They describe parent–child interactions in which the parent either models or reinforces social behaviors that also characterize the child's interactions with peers. Thus, through mechanisms of modeling, coaching, and operant conditioning, parents influence the acquisition of social behaviors and social skills that their children then display in peer social encounters. Putallaz and Heflin also describe ways that parents can influence their children's social development by the environment they establish in their home and the types of social situations toward which they direct their children. Putallaz and Heflin do not discuss parental influence on the types of relationships their children have, except for their analysis of the impact of parental affective tone on a child's social orientation. They speculate that by a mechanism similar to classical conditioning, warm, positive parents foster a positive orientation toward social interaction, whereas negative parents foster a negative and avoidant orientation.

When the parental influence on a child's peer relations is cast in terms of these two contrasting models, the formulations of Rubin et al., on the one hand, and of Putallaz and Heflin, on the other hand, represent quite different explanations of the early antecedents of peer rejection. Most of the existing research on peer rejection fits with the more indirect model of Putallaz and Heflin. To this point, almost all research directed at understanding the basis for peer rejection has been focused on an articulation of social behavior and social skill deficits on the part of the rejected child, and this research is more compatible with the model of influence articulated by Putallaz and Heflin. Likewise, most intervention projects have been based on the assumptions of their more indirect model. The focus of most intervention has been on coaching social skills and reinforcing acceptable social behavior. The model described by Rubin et al. leads to different conclusions. One conclusion is that there is great consistency among the many social relationships of the child. A second is that this consistency is a consequence of early parent–child interaction, because the young child acquires a modal pattern for relating socially to others from that first interaction. Thus, although particular behavioral patterns of the child may be viewed as important to future peer relations, of greatest importance is that the child learns a particular way of relating to other people that is more comprehensive than behavioral acts or skills. The full implications of this model have not yet been explored. Assessment, according to this view, would be conducted in relational terms rather than in terms of individual social behavior categories. Similarly, the focus of intervention should be on giving the rejected child a restorative relationship rather than attempting to alter the child's skill repertoire or behavioral tendencies. It will be interesting to see whether this alternative perspective will come to have greater impact on the future of research on peer relations. Clearly, the field is at a point where multiple theories of development will serve a useful role in broadening the conceptual framework of peer relations research.

Proximal causes

In the earlier section on the emergence of rejected status, social behavior was cited as the primary reason for being rejected by peers. Thinking about the causes of these behaviors can take two directions. One, which has just been described, is to consider the child-rearing antecedents of behavior. The second is to consider the processes internal to the child that are responsible for that child's social actions. The chapter by Dodge and Feldman (Chapter 5) provides us with an analysis of the social-information-processing biases or deficits that determine behaviors leading to peer rejection. Their review encompasses most of the research on the cognitive processes underlying maladaptive social behavior among children. Although less is known about the affective processes that contribute to peer rejection, there are some promising initiatives in this direction, which will be mentioned briefly in this section.

Dodge and Feldman provide us with an analysis of the antecedents of the behavior leading to peer rejection that is conducted at a different level than has been discussed elsewhere in this chapter. Their perspective is that socially maladaptive behavior can be explained in terms of the patterns of social information processing carried out by rejected children. Their analysis does not substitute for the analysis of socialization factors. In fact it seems to call for a new approach to socialization research that would explain the development of social thinking.

As Dodge and Feldman recall in Chapter 5, there have been many attempts to link social behavior to social cognition, including those designed to explain peer social status in terms of general cognitive processes, such as the Piagetian concept of egocentrism. These earlier efforts failed, as we can now see in light of the success that Dodge, Pettit, McClaskey, and Brown (1986) have recorded, because too much was attempted with a single general cognitive construct. Dodge and his colleagues have been more successful because they have been more specific about both the process of social thinking and the context of social behavior to which that social thinking is relevant. Dodge and his colleagues seem to suggest that the process of thought that is completed in the moments of actual social interaction mirrors all the steps of their five-step information-processing model. Even if one does not accept this aspect of their model, one must acknowledge that it provides a powerful heuristic for examining the influence of thought on social behavior. For the interventionist it also provides a schematic for assessing deficits in social thinking.

The general model for looking at relations between social cognition, social behavior, and peer status provided by Dodge and Feldman seems obvious, as well as correct, in hindsight. Children are rejected because they have trouble managing specific social situations, not all situations. There are many factors that determine which specific situations will be critical to a child's social acceptance. The general principle is that a child's social role will determine the importance of adequately handling a given situation in order to pass muster with one's peers. Such factors as gender, age, social milieu, and culture make certain situations more salient and more problematic for some children and not others. Our knowledge of these factors and their importance to a child's social identity can help us better predict the relation between aspects of social cognition and social interaction.

The premise of the Dodge and Feldman chapter is that social-cognitive processes determine social behavior, which, in turn, is a major determinant of peer status. In this sense, then, deficient or deviant social cognitions are a precursor of peer rejection. Dodge and Feldman do not deny the importance of socialization antecedents of the social-cognitive processes they describe, but neither do they speculate about them. To speculate about one aspect of Dodge's social cognition model, it is relatively easy to see how children might internalize a parent's ways of thinking about social phenomena. Children who regularly hear of parental suspicions about the hostile intentions of others might soon come to have these suspicions themselves in their dealings with peers. This example would fit the indirect model of explanation described earlier. The same phenomenon might be explained in terms of the direct model: Certain patterns of parent–child interaction could lead children to attribute hostile intent to their parents in negative-outcome situations and then carry this thinking into their peer interactions.

Very little has been written about the role of affect as a proximal antecedent factor in the social behavior of rejected children. Explicitly, the social-information-processing model appears to describe "affectless" cognitions directed toward a goal of rational problem solving. Implicitly, however, it is clear that social cognitions are not affectively neutral. The attribution of hostile intent, for example, occurs in a context of negative consequence and triggers angry feelings toward the other. The model does imply that attributions temporally precede affect, because it is the way ambiguous cues are read that determines whether one tends to overattribute hostile intent. So to this extent there is an implicit priority of cognition over affect. However, for much of the model it might be said that all cognitions are affectively loaded and that the distinction between cognition and affect is specious and misleading. Certainly the evaluation of alternative strategies is a process that heavily involves the affective dimension, because these decisions reflect the individual values and goals of the child. One primary reason for helping rejected children rehearse their social behavior in a problem-solving framework (see Chapters 11 and 12) is so that planning for future social interaction can be carried out in a more controlled affective state. Thus, the role of affective arousal in retraining social-thinking processes is implicitly recognized in these intervention paradigms.

We know very little about the distal antecedents of self-control and this is a major area in need of future research. Gottman and Mettetal (1986) have provided a conceptual framework for thinking about the relationship between emotional development and major developmental changes in the social processes children are involved with from early childhood through adolescence. Their basic thesis is that "developmental change occurs because of changes in the affective competence demands of the ecological niches children are forced by our culture to occupy and to maneuver within" (p. 193). Gottman and Mettetal's conceptual outline does not tell us how emotional control develops; however, it does suggest the way that child peer interactions may shape the emergence of individual emotional control. Young children who learn to respond to the feedback of play partners and adjust their behavior to the emotional requirements of social play will be prepared to cope with the emotional learning tasks of later forms of social interaction.

In the coordinated play of early childhood, children learn to control strong negative emotions that arise out of conflict with the play partner. They also learn to control and modulate their excitement during dramatic play. Although most preschoolers have difficulty with these situations, those who fail to acquire control mechanisms run the risk of alienating peers during the early school years. Thus the most common bases for peer rejection in this period are aggressive and disruptive behavior. This would suggest that parents and other caretakers might do well to give greater attention to this aspect of their preschooler's play with peers. Patterson's (1982) research suggests that some parents actually train their children *not* to regulate negative emotion by reinforcing increasingly intense displays of coercive behavior in the home. Such children are at a marked disadvantage for their future interactions with peers, because they have failed to acquire critical social skills in the control of their emotions. It is tempting to speculate about children at the opposite end of the emotional control continuum, those who are so controlled that they fail to generate sufficient emotional excitement to maintain the interest of play partners. We know so little about the actual mechanisms of early self-control and the role that socialization agents play in their development. This is one of the areas of children's social development begging for the attention of researchers. Other compelling targets of future research are discussed in the following section.

Looking ahead

Although sociometric research with children has a history of more than 50 years, the study of peer rejection in childhood has been given concerted attention only in the last 10 years. The achievements of this short period of inquiry have been quite impressive on several fronts, as the chapters in this volume illustrate. There is now a solid foundation of research on children's peer relations in general and on the phenomenon of social rejection in particular. There is much more to be understood, and the general framework introduced in this chapter is intended to provide some direction for those who wish to join this exploration.

Some aspects of peer rejection have received more attention from investigators than others, and so the quantity of research is not the same in all areas. Nonetheless, some general comments can be made about progress thus far and the kind of work that still needs to be done. We know more about the behavioral correlates of peer rejection than most other areas, for example, yet the level of analysis of behavior is still at a fairly global level, and the focus has been on the central tendencies of rejected children as a group. This state of affairs is beginning to change, as several chapters make evident. In future research, the competence of children is going to be examined more often in specific social contexts in order to learn more about particular deficits that lead to disorder. The peer group entry literature illustrates this trend, as does recent research on conflict resolution behavior (e.g., Hartup, 1987; Shantz, 1986). Perhaps, investigators will begin to track multiple pathways to rejection as Rubin et al. have urged in Chapter 8, even when examining maladaptive patterns of response to specific social situations. This will be necessary if we are to get beyond the current emphasis on aggressiveness and socially disruptive behavior. We need to know more about socially awkward and ineffective behaviors as determinants of rejection.

Asher, Parkhurst, Hymel, and Williams (Chapter 9) reviewed data on the internal experiences of rejected children, and as one might expect, there is evidence that rejection by peers is a source of pain and loneliness to these children. Their chapter also demonstrates how little is known about the feelings and concerns of rejected children and the role these internal states play in the process of rejection. Hymel and Franke (1985) discuss some of the problems in measuring internal experience and affect. The solution of these problems is a major task for future peer relations research. This is particularly true if we are to understand more of the nonaggressive side of peer rejection, in which anxiety and social insecurity are almost certainly implicated. Similar problems of assessment are faced in trying to determine just how children's motives and goals for social interaction affect their behavior (see Parkhurst & Asher, 1985; Dodge, Asher, & Parkhurst, 1989). One inference that can be drawn from much that has been written in this volume is that the maladaptive behavior of some rejected children can be explained by the goals they set for themselves in certain situations. Thus far it has been necessary to infer these goals and concerns from behavioral data, because either children are not sufficiently self-conscious about their goals or they are influenced by social desirability considerations in their responses. Thus, there are aspects of the problem of peer rejection that still are hidden.

Rejection is a social process, yet the focus of most of our research, both in terms of causes, consequences, and intervention paradigms, has been on the individual rejected child. There is some indication that the composition of the peer group and the norms of the group determine the criteria for rejection in the group. Some social theories presuppose the necessity of there being group deviants as a focus for group animus and tension. In the model of peer rejection outlined, the importance of group dynamics for the maintenance of peer rejection has been emphasized. We should explore these and other group-related issues in the next wave of research on children's social behavior.

The question of change in status has been dealt with primarily in terms of formal intervention, usually involving social skills training. The data on the stability of peer status suggest that much change occurs naturally, even though the Coie and Dodge (1983) longitudinal data indicate that rejected children rarely attain popular status. It is important to know what factors, other than adult-initiated intervention, bring about changes in peer status. What role, for example, does self-monitoring have in producing positive shifts in social behavior and peer regard? In general, what transpires between a child and peers to make the peers change their minds about him or her? How do parents and other caretakers respond to signs of social maladjustment in their children, and what steps do they take that effect positive change? These "natural" forms of intervention may prove instructive to those who are intent on developing more effective approaches to systematic intervention.

Finally, we need more detailed investigations of the two end points of the peer rejection cycle, the origins and consequences of rejection. The literature on consequences is strongly suggestive of the influence of peer rejection on disorder, yet there is a clear need for more definitive research, particularly research that will clarify the relation between rejection and other causal factors. Similarly, there is a growing research literature on the socialization processes that contribute to social adjustment or rejection. Both of these lines of inquiry require carefully constructed longitudinal designs. Such research is expensive and time-consuming and may require the coordination of effort among multiple teams of investigators.

The authors of this volume have summarized an impressive body of research on peer rejection, a highly significant psychological event in the lives of some children. Social rejection is a painful experience for children. To recall such childhood experiences is unpleasant, because it implicates us all, on one side of the event or the other. We must recall experiences of personal rejection and experiences of rejecting others. These recollections certainly violate the image of childhood as a time of innocence and joy. Yet rejection and its associated pain are real. Recognizing the reality of rejection is an important first step toward doing something about it, and understanding its origins and consequences will help us to avoid or modify its negative effects. It is gratifying that so much increasingly sophisticated research activity is being devoted to this important problem.

References

Albee, G. W. (1984). Prologue: A model for classifying prevention programs. In J. M. Joffe, G. W. Albee, & L. D. Kelly (Eds.), *Readings in primary prevention of psychopathology: Basic concepts* (pp. 228–245). Hanover, NH: University Press of New England.

Asarnow, J. R., & Carlson, G. A. (1985). Depression self-rating scale: Utility with child psychiatric inpatients. *Journal of Consulting and Clinical Psychology, 53,* 491–499.

Asher, S. R., & Williams, G. A. (1987). Helping children without friends in home and school. In *Children's social development: Information for teachers and parents.* Urbana, IL: ERIC, Clearing House on Elementary and Early Childhood Education.

Berndt, T. J. (1979). Developmental changes in conformity to peers and parents. *Developmental Psychology, 15,* 608–616.

Berndt, T. J. (1987, April). *Changes in friendship and school adjustment after the transition to junior high school.* Paper presented at the biennial meeting of the Society for Research in Child Development, Baltimore.

Berndt, T. J., & Hoyle, S. G. (1985). Stability and change in childhood and adolescent friendships. *Developmental Psychology, 21,* 1007–1015.

Bierman, K. L., Smoot, D. L., & Aumiller, K. (1987, April). *Distinguishing characteristics of aggressive–rejected, aggressive–nonrejected, and rejected–nonaggressive boys.* Paper presented at the biennial meeting of the Society for Research in Child Development, Baltimore.

Bowen, M. (1966). The use of family theory in clinical practice. *Comprehensive Psychiatry, 7,* 345–374.

Brown, R. (1973). Schizophrenia, language, and reality. *American Psychologist, 28,* 395–403.

Caspi, A. (1987). Personality in the life course. *Journal of Personality and Social Psychology, 53,* 1203–1213.

Cavior, N., & Dokecki, P. R. (1973). Physical attractiveness, perceived attitude similarity, and academic achievement as contributors to interpersonal attraction among adolescents. *Developmental Psychology, 9,* 44–54.

Coie, J. D. (1987, April). *An analysis of aggression episodes: Age and peer status differences.* Paper presented at the biennial meeting of the Society for Research in Child Development, Baltimore.

Coie, J. D., & Dodge, K. A. (1983). Continuities and changes in children's sociometric status: A five-year longitudinal study. *Merrill-Palmer Quarterly, 29,* 261–282.

Coie, J. D., & Dodge, K. A. (1988). Multiple sources of data on social behavior and social status. *Child Development, 59,* 815–829.

Coie, J. D., Dodge, K. A., & Coppotelli, H. A. (1982). Dimensions and types of social status: A cross-age perspective. *Developmental Psychology, 18,* 557–569.

Coie, J. D., Dodge, K. A., McClaskey, C., & Belding, M. (1987, April). *The impact of peer reputation and behavior factors on new friendship choices.* Paper presented at the biennial meeting of the Society for Research in Child Development, Baltimore.

Coie, J. D., Finn, M., & Krehbiel, G. (1985, August). *Controversial children: Peer assessment evidence for status category distinctiveness.* Paper presented at the annual meeting of the American Psychological Association, Toronto.

Coie, J. D., & Kupersmidt, J. B. (1983). A behavioral analysis of emerging social status in boys' groups. *Child Development, 54,* 1400–1416.

Costanzo, P. R., Coie, J. D., Dorval, B. R., & Young, J. (1977, August). *Changes in conformity to peer and adult opinion pressures.* Paper presented at annual meeting of the American Psychological Association, San Francisco.

Costanzo, P. R., & Fraenkel, P. (1987). Social influence, socialization, and the development of social cognition: The heart of the matter. In N. Eisenberg (Ed.), *Advances in developmental psychology* (pp. 190–215). New York: Wiley.

Costanzo, P. R., & Shaw, M. E. (1966). Conformity as a function of age level. *Child Development, 37,* 967–975.

Cowen, E. L., Pederson, A., Babigian, H., Izzo, L. D., & Trost, M. A. (1973). Long-term follow-up of early detected vulnerable children. *Journal of Consulting and Clinical Psychology, 41,* 438–446.

Darley, J. M., & Fazio, R. H. (1980). Expectancy confirmation processes arising in the social interaction sequence. *American Psychologist, 35,* 867–881.

Dion, K. K., & Berscheid, E. (1974). Physical attractiveness and peer perception among children. *Sociometry, 37,* 1–12.

Dishion, T. J. (1988). *A developmental model for peer relations: Middle childhood correlates and one-year sequelae.* Unpublished doctoral dissertation, University of Oregon.

Dodge, K. A. (1983). Behavioral antecedents of peer social status. *Child Development, 54,* 1386–1399.

Dodge, K. A., Asher, S. R., & Parkhurst, J. T. (1989). Social life as a goal-coordination task. In C. Ames and R. Ames (Eds.), *Research on motivation in education* (Vol. 3, pp. 107–135). New York: Academic Press.

Dodge, K. A., Coie, J. D., & Brakke, N. P. (1982). Behavior patterns of socially rejected and neglected preadolescents: The roles of social approach and aggression. *Journal of Abnormal Child Psychology, 10,* 389–410.

Dodge, K. A., Pettit, G. S., McClaskey, C. L., & Brown, M. M. (1986). Social competence in children. *Monographs of the Society for Research in Child Development, 51*(2, Serial No. 213).

Durkheim, E. (1938). *The rules of sociological method.* Glencoe, IL: Free Press.

Eccles, J. E., Midgley, C. M., & Adler, T. F. (1984). Age-related changes in the school environment: Effects on achievement motivation. In J. P. Nicholls (Ed.), *The development of achievement motivation* (pp. 283–331). Greenwich, CT: JAI Press.

Finn, M. G. (1985). *Being disliked: Self-report and social status.* Unpublished doctoral dissertation, Duke University, Durham, NC.

Gottman, J. M., & Mettetal, G. (1986). Speculations about social and affective development: Friendship and acquaintanceship through adolescence. In J. M. Gottman & J. G. Parker (Eds.), *Conversations of friends: Speculations on affective development* (pp. 192–240). New York: Cambridge University Press.

Guardo, C. J. (1969). Sociometric status and self-concept in sixth graders. *Journal of Educational Research, 62,* 320–322.

Hartup, W. W. (1987, April). *Friendship and conflict: Synergies in child development.* Paper presented at the biennial meeting of the Society for Research in Child Development, Baltimore.

Horowitz, F. D. (1962). The relationship of anxiety, self-concept, and sociometric status among fourth, fifth, and sixth grade children. *Journal of Abnormal and Social Psychology, 65,* 212–214.

Hymel, S., & Franke, S. (1985). Children's peer relations: Assessing self-perceptions. In B. H. Schneider, K. H. Rubin, & J. E. Ledingham (Eds.), *Children's peer relations: Issues in assessment and intervention* (pp. 75–91). New York: Springer-Verlag.

Kleck, R. E., Richardson, S. A., & Ronald, L. (1974). Physical appearance cues and interpersonal attraction to children. *Child Development, 45,* 305–310.

Kurdek, L. A., & Krile, D. (1982). A developmental analysis of the relation between peer acceptance and both interpersonal understanding and perceived social self-competence. *Child Development, 53,* 1485–1491.

Ladd, G. W. (1981). Effectiveness of a social learning method for enhancing children's social interaction and peer acceptance. *Child Development, 52,* 171–178.

Langlois, J. H., & Stephan, C. W. (1981). Beauty and the beast: The role of physical attractiveness in the development of peer relations and social behavior. In S. S. Brehm, S. M. Kassin, & F. X. Gibbons (Eds.), *Developmental social psychology* (pp. 152–168). New York: Oxford University Press.

Langlois, J. H., & Styczynski, L. E. (1979). The effects of physical attractiveness on the behavioral attributions and peer preferences of acquainted children. *International Journal of Behavioral Development, 2,* 325–342.

Lecky, P. (1945). *Self-consistency: A theory of personality.* New York: Island Press.

Lerner, R. M., & Lerner, J. V. (1977). Effects of age, sex, and physical attractiveness on child-peer relations, academic performance, and elementary school adjustment. *Developmental Psychology, 13,* 585–590.

Newcomb, A. F., & Bukowski, W. M. (1984). A longitudinal study of the utility of social preference and social inpact sociometric classification schemes. *Child Development, 55,* 1434–1447.

Parker, J. G., & Asher, S. R. (1987). Peer relations and later personal adjustment: Are low-accepted children at risk? *Psychological Bulletin, 102,* 357–389.

Parkhurst, J. T., & Asher, S. R. (1985). Goals and concerns: Implications for the study of children's social competence. In B. B. Lahey & A. E. Kazdin (Eds.), *Advances in clinical child psychology* (Vol. 8, pp. 199–228). New York: Plenum.

Parkhurst, J. T., & Asher, S. R. (1987, April). *The social concerns of aggressive–rejected children.* Paper presented at the biennial meeting of the Society for Research in Child Development, Baltimore.

Patterson, G. R. (1982). *Coercive family processes.* Eugene, OR: Castilia Press.

Patterson, G. R., & Reid, J. B. (1973). Intervention for families of aggressive boys: A replication study. *Behavior Research and Therapy, 11,* 383–394.

Patterson, G. R., & Reid, J. B. (1984). Social interactional processes within the family: The study of moment-by-moment family transactions in which human social development is embedded. *Journal of Applied Developmental Psychology, 5*, 237–262.

Putallaz, M. (1983). Predicting children's sociometric status from their behavior. *Child Development, 54*, 1417–1426.

Putallaz, M., & Gottman, J. M. (1981). An interactional model of children's entry into peer groups. *Child Development, 52*, 986–994.

Putallaz, M., White, A. S., & Shipman, R. (1985, April). *Sociometric status and adjustment: A developmental perspective.* Paper presented at the biennial meeting of the Society for Research in Child Development, Toronto.

Quay, H. C. (1964). Personality dimensions in delinquent males as inferred from the factor analysis of behavior ratings. *Journal of Research in Crime and Delinquency, 1*, 33–36.

Rabiner, D. L., & Coie, J. D. (1989). Effect of expectancy inductions on rejected children's acceptance by unfamiliar peers. *Developmental Psychology, 25*, 450–457.

Robins, L. N., & Wish, E. (1977). Childhood deviance as a developmental process: A study of 223 urban black men from birth to 18. *Social Forces, 56*, 448–471.

Roff, M. (1960). Relations between certain preservice factors and psychoneurosis during military duty. *Armed Forces Medical Journal, 11*, 152–160.

Roff, M. (1961). Childhood social interactions and young adult bad conduct. *Journal of Abnormal and Social Psychology, 63*, 333–337.

Roff, M. (1963). Childhood social interactions and young adult psychosis. *Journal of Clinical Psychology, 19*, 152–157.

Ruble, D. N. (1982). The development of social comparison processes and their role in achievement-related self-socialization. In E. T. Higgins, D. Ruble, & W. W. Hartup (Eds.), *Social cognition and social behavior: Developmental perspectives* (pp. 134–157). New York: Cambridge University Press.

Rutter, M., Cox, A., Tupling, C., Berger, M., & Yule, W. (1975). Attainment and adjustment in two geographical areas: I. The prevalence of psychiatric disorder. *British Journal of Psychiatry, 126*, 493–509.

Rutter, M., & Garmezy, N. (1983). Developmental psychopathology. In E. M. Hetherington (Ed.), *Handbook of child psychology: Vol. 4. Socialization, personality, and social development* (pp. 775–911, 4th ed.). New York: Wiley.

Sarbin, T. R., & Scheibe, K. (1983). *Studies in social identity.* New York: Praeger.

Shantz, D. W. (1986). Conflict, aggression, and peer status: An observational study. *Child Development, 57*, 1333–1348.

Sroufe, L. A., & Rutter, M. (1984). The domain of developmental psychopathology. *Child Development, 55*, 17–29.

Styczynski, L. E., & Langlois, J. H. (1977). The effects of familiarity on behavioral stereotypes associated with physical attractiveness in young children. *Child Development, 48*, 1137–1141.

Sullivan, H. S. (1953). *The interpersonal theory of psychiatry.* New York: Norton.

Swann, W. B., Jr. (1983). Self-verification: Bringing social reality into harmony with the self. In J. Suls & A. G. Greenwald (Eds.), *Social psychological perspectives on the self* (Vol. 2, pp. 33–66). Hillsdale, NJ: Lawrence Erlbaum.

Swann, W. B., Jr., Griffin, J. J., Jr., Predmore, S. C., & Gains, B. (1987). The cognitive-affective crossfire: When self-consistency confronts self-enhancement. *Journal of Personality and Social Psychology, 52*, 881–889.

Watzlawick, P., Beavin, J. H., & Jackson, D. D. (1967). *Pragmatics of human communication: A study of interactional patterns, pathologies, and paradoxes.* New York: Norton.

Wright, J. C., Giammarino, M., & Parad, H. W. (1986). Social status in small groups: Individual-group similarity and the social "misfit." *Journal of Personality and Social Psychology, 50*, 523–536.

Author index

403

Subject index

academic competence, 366
  and peer status, 43, 50, 320–2
aggressive behavior, 17, 32, 145
  biased perceptions of rejected children, 45
  cycle of family coercion, 226
  and delinquency, 285, 287, 295–6, 299,
    388, 389
  developmental differences, 30, 43, 50–1,
    371
  and empathy, 137
  intervention, 310, 322–7
  parent–child similarities in, 191
  and peer rejection, 50, 226, 310, 319–20,
    371–2
  by popular children, 47
  and power-assertive discipline, 195
  reputation for and effects on attributions of
    hostility, 167
  and school withdrawal, 300
  and sociometric status, 21, 22–3, 26, 29,
    33–4, 36, 106, 107, 136
  and status in high vs. low aggressive peer
    groups, 48–9, 371
altruistic behavior
  parent–child similarities in, 191
assimilation into a peer group, 65–8
attachment
  and caretaking practices, 196, 221
  and social competence, 196–7, 226, 227–8
  and social support, 226, 227
  and sociometric status, 391–2
  types of, 196
attributions
  of aggression, 121
  for behaviors of liked vs. disliked peers,
    167–70
  for behaviors of popular vs. unpopular
    peers, 170–4
  and biases in social perception, 161–3,
    342–3, 384
  of hostile intent, 45, 125–6, 146–7, 167,
    342, 395

of parents, 228
for social failure, 126–7, 142, 267–8, 343
in social interactions, 342

balance theory, 158, 161
behavioral correlates of sociometric status, 8,
  61, 90–1, 396
  in adolescents, 28
  as shown in new peer groups, 44–9
  context effects, 91
  developmental differences, 17, 20, 52
  in elementary school children, 21–8, 32–4,
    39–42
  group context effects, 49
  in preschool children, 20–1, 35–9
  vs. reputation effects, 106–10
  sex differences, 20, 23, 32, 136
  situational influences on, 390–1
  see also controversial children, entry behav-
    ior, neglected children, popular children,
    rejected children, unpopular children

conflict resolution, 142, 396
controversial children, 23, 24–5, 27, 33–4,
  43, 48, 52, 374
cooperative behavior, 17
  sex differences, 137
  and sociometric status, 21, 23, 106, 107,
    136
criminality
  and aggression, 285, 287, 295–6, 299
  methods of studying, 283–4
  and peer rejection, 284–8, 295–6, 299, 388
critical age for relating social-cognitive skills
  to status, 138

delinquency, *see* criminality
developmental lag hypothesis, 139

emotional control, 395–6
empathy, 138
  and aggression, 137

413